A HOUSE DIVIDED

Consolidating one of the most complex and multi-faceted eras in American history, this new edition of Jonathan Wells's *A House Divided* unifies the broad and varied scholarship on the American Civil War. Amassing a variety of research, this accessible and readable text introduces readers to both the war and the Reconstruction period, and how Americans lived during this time of great upheaval in the country's history. Designed for a variety of subjects and teaching styles, this text not only looks at the Civil War from a historical perspective, but also analyzes its ramifications on the United States and American identities through the present day. This second edition has been updated throughout, incorporating new scholarship from recent studies on the Civil War era, and includes additional photographs and maps (now incorporated throughout the text), updated bibliographies, and a supplementary companion website.

Jonathan Daniel Wells is Professor of Afroamerican and African Studies at the University of Michigan.

A HOUSE DIVIDED

The Civil War and Nineteenth-Century America

Jonathan Daniel Wells

Routledge
Taylor & Francis Group
NEW YORK AND LONDON

Please visit the companion website at www.routledge.com/cw/wells

Second edition published 2017
by Routledge
711 Third Avenue, New York, NY 10017

and by Routledge
2 Park Square, Milton Park, Abingdon, Oxon, OX14 4RN

Routledge is an imprint of the Taylor & Francis Group, an informa business

First edition published by Routledge 2012

Library of Congress Cataloging in Publication Data
Names: Wells, Jonathan Daniel, 1969– author.
Title: A house divided: the Civil War and nineteenth-century America / Jonathan Daniel Wells.
Description: Second edition. | New York : Routledge, 2016. | Includes index. | Includes bibliographical references and index.
Identifiers: LCCN 2015045911 | ISBN 9781138956841 (hardback) | ISBN 9781138956858 (pbk.) | ISBN 9781315665511 (e-book)
Subjects: LCSH: United States—History—Civil War, 1861–1865. | United States—History—19th century.
Classification: LCC E468. W45 2016 | DDC 973.7—dc23
LC record available at http://lccn.loc.gov/2015045911

ISBN: 978-1-138-95684-1 (hbk)
ISBN: 978-1-138-95685-8 (pbk)
ISBN: 978-1-315-66551-1 (ebk)

Typeset in Optima
by Keystroke, Neville Lodge, Tettenhall, Wolverhampton

Printed and bound in the United States of America by
Edwards Brothers Malloy on sustainably sourced paper

Brief Table of Contents

FULL TABLE OF CONTENTS

INTRODUCTION

War: The Red Animal

The mere mentioning of the American Civil War conjures images of bravery in the face of adversity, a fight for deeply held principles, the end of American slavery, and the glory of wise statesmanship and bold leadership. At the same time we know that Americans in the 1860s also witnessed unimaginable death and destruction on the battlefields and in towns and villages, especially in Virginia, Maryland, Tennessee, and the Carolinas. Although the Civil War (1861–1865) ended more than a century and a half ago, Americans from schoolchildren to scholars still show passionate interest in the war. Almost as consuming has been the struggle to understand what caused the catastrophic breakdown of the Union over the course of the first half of the 1800s (known as the "antebellum" or "pre-Civil War era") as well as the consequences of the war for black and white Americans during the period known as Reconstruction (1865–1877). Only by examining the decades preceding and following the war can we understand the meaning and significance of this crucial period of the nation's history.

And only by looking at American life and culture in all its complexity and nuance can we appreciate the magnitude of the suffering, the battle of ideas, and the anxiety experienced by Americans on and off the battlefield. The course-altering consequences of the war included the emancipation of nearly four million African American slaves, a new political system that revised the meaning of citizenship, the subjugation of the South, new roles for women, the triumph of the free labor economy, and a new realism in American literature. To grasp the significance of all these changes, students must examine not only battles and soldiers, but also poetry, politics, and culture as well. This volume seeks to understand and appreciate the significance of the Civil War era from a number of perspectives, from battlefield maneuvers to literature.

In Stephen Crane's *The Red Badge of Courage*, one of the greatest novels about the American Civil War, young men must reconcile what they imagine to be the glorious triumphs of battle with the bloody authenticity of real war. One band of uneasy soldiers, lurking in a broken line through dense forests, know not what lies ahead as they march. As Crane describes them, "one or two stepped with overvaliant airs as if they were already plunged into war. Others walked as upon thin ice. The greater part of the untested men appeared quiet and absorbed. They were going to look at war, the red animal – war, the blood-swollen god."[1] Although Crane himself was born in 1871 and so never experienced the Civil War firsthand, he employed his literary talents to help us comprehend the trauma of a young soldier heading into battle.

So while this textbook covers key battles in detail, offers insight into military strategy and the actions of generals and armies, and traces the evolution of battlefield technology, it also helps the reader appreciate the era's political, cultural, social, and intellectual shifts. After all, Americans experienced war and its aftermath in countless ways, from communities that lost whole families, to fugitive slaves who escaped bondage both before and after civil authority in the South broke down, to businessmen who sought profit in the wartime economy, to women who nursed soldiers in hospitals behind the lines, and many, many other kinds of lived experience. To comprehend the importance of the Civil War era, and indeed to do justice to the memory of Americans who witnessed the triumph and suffering of the war, we will examine the period in its totality.

One of the remarkable aspects of the war's legacy is how the battles, leaders, and soldiers of the era still capture our attention. Although it began more than a century and a half ago, the war still conjures strongly held opinions. The recent passionate debates over the Confederate flag, entrenched racism, and the meaning of the war and its legacy for the South and the nation demonstrate that the war remains at the heart of our politics and culture.

Like other Americans, modern historians continue to debate the causes, meaning, and consequences of the war. Scholars have long argued over whether or not the Civil War was inevitable. For some scholars the differences between the North and South were so vast as to be insurmountable, rendering the nation that emerged from the ratification of the Constitution mortally weak. After all, the economic differences between the sections were real and substantial. The North was far more urbanized and industrialized than the South, although both regions remained largely dependent upon agriculture through the 1850s. The existence of slavery in the South and free labor in the North would seem to render a clash of cultures and economies unavoidable. For many historians, too significant a gulf separated the North and South, and the collapse of cross-sectional institutions in the 1840s and 1850s made war more likely. For example, the major national Baptist and Methodist associations split over slavery beginning in the 1830s and more formally in the 1840s. In addition, the collapse of a Whig Party that had helped stitch the northern and southern wings of the country together further weakened the Union. Perhaps war was not inevitable by 1861, according to these historians, but the nation was truly a house divided well before the fighting broke out at Fort Sumter.

Other historians point to the inability of American politicians to compromise to avoid war. In this assessment, the nation in the late 1850s lacked the sort of skilled compromiser, such as Henry Clay (who died in 1852), to find the path to peaceful resolution. Of course, any peaceful settling of the sectional crisis in 1861 would likely have left slavery intact and might therefore be unwelcome anyway. And there were attempts at compromise even in 1861 as war was erupting. In reality any compromise would seem to have been doomed, for by 1860 and 1861 there was little room to negotiate between the hardened positions of northern and southern politicians.

Despite the broad disagreements over the causes and legacy of the war, historians generally agree on a few key points. First, they agree that the causes of the war are complex and varied and that slavery and states' rights ideology were intertwined. It is hard to imagine the Civil War breaking out without slavery. While there were cultural, religious, economic, and political differences separating the sections, slavery was the single most divisive issue within the nation. This is not to say that most northerners opposed slavery or cared deeply what happened to southern African Americans. In fact, considerable evidence shows that most northerners considered slavery to be primarily a southern problem. Where many northerners drew the line was in keeping slavery out of the territories and states of the West, especially the new states that would enter the Union as a result of the war with Mexico. Another area of agreement among historians is the level of death and devastation the war caused. Recent research suggests that perhaps more than 700,000 died during the four years of the war;

many succumbed to disease if they were not killed on the battlefield.[2] Scholars agree that wartime suffering was profound, and continued to shape the nation long after the fighting ended in 1865, which brings us to a final point of consensus. There is no doubt that the war had lasting and profound effects on America's economy, society, and politics. In fact, though Reconstruction (the period immediately following the war) has been traditionally dated from 1865 to 1877, many historians now argue for using a much broader definition of Reconstruction. For the war shaped conflicts over race, political authority, emancipation, and many other issues into the twentieth century.

Notes

1 Stephen Crane, *The Red Badge of Courage* (1896; Norton Critical Edition, 1962), 23.

2 J. David Hacker, "A Census-Based Count of the Civil War Dead," *Civil War History* 57 (December 2011), 307–348.

SLAVERY AND THE LONG-TERM ROOTS OF THE CIVIL WAR

Topics Covered in this Chapter:

- Slavery Takes Root in Early America
- Rise of the Slave Trade
- Slavery and the Constitution
- The Cotton Boom
- The Plantation South
- Divisions Within the South
- Northern Industrialization
- Slavery and Sectionalism in the Early Republic

1

Introduction

It might seem surprising to begin a study of the Civil War, which erupted in 1861 and lasted four long and bloody years, with a discussion of the history of American slavery from its inception in the seventeenth century. What could events in the 1600s have to do with a war that would break out two hundred years later? The answer is simple: when historians trace the causes and origins of the Civil War, the continuance of slavery as America evolved from a collection of colonies to an independent nation was a central factor in the evolution of the sectional conflict between the North and South. This is not to say that war was inevitable or that slavery was the only cause of the hostilities. As we will see, the road to civil war was complex and multi-faceted, and its causes are still hotly debated among historians. Yet, if we had to point to a single issue that rose above all others in importance in causing the Civil War, it would be the entrenchment of slavery in the South, and the equally powerful movement among some northerners to keep the institution from spreading outside the South.

Slavery Takes Root in Early America

Imagine the thoughts of English colonists who undertook the treacherous journey across the Atlantic to settle in the New World. They had risked their lives to venture to a mysterious land only dimly understood. Maps only vaguely represented the New World, and vast stretches of the North American continent remained *terra incognita*, shrouded in obscurity. Along the Atlantic Coast of North America hundreds of Native American tribes, vast acres of virgin forests, and innumerable species of native birds and other game filled the landscape. It was a land at once promising and scary.

When English colonists set foot in the Americas in the early 1600s, they found an abundance of land available for growing cash crops. Though it took them a few years to realize it, tobacco in particular would become vital to the economy of colonial America. The first permanent English colony, Jamestown, was founded in 1607 but from the beginning there were relatively few white colonists to exploit the tens of thousands of acres of potentially cultivatable land. Even a significant increase of British immigrants to the New World in the seventeenth and eighteenth centuries failed to provide sufficient numbers of colonists for agricultural labor.

Almost as soon as the Jamestown colony was settled, large farms called plantations began to emerge along the rivers of Virginia and Maryland, known together as the Chesapeake region.

FIGURE 1.1 *The settlement of Jamestown in 1607. Courtesy of the New York Public Library, 808025*

The crops grown in the colonial South, especially rice, cotton, tobacco, and indigo (a plant used for making dye), were very labor-intensive, meaning that they required hours of daily toil in harsh conditions. Despite the widespread use of the indenture system, labor in the colonial South remained scarce; there were simply not enough people to do all of the necessary agricultural work.

In the search for more laborers, Native Americans were among the first to be enslaved. In Jamestown's early years, relationships between the English colonists and Native Americans like the Powhatan tribe alternated between peace and warfare. By the 1630s the Chesapeake colonists maintained a consistently brutal policy toward the Native Americans in their midst, including capturing men, women, and children and forcing them to work as slaves. According to historian Alan Gallay, between 30,000 and 50,000 Indians had been enslaved by the early 1700s in North America. But because of a high death rate and susceptibility to disease, Native American slaves could not fill the labor needs of the colonies. In addition, Indian men often refused to do agricultural labor, which they considered to be "women's work," and because the Indians knew the land much better, and knew how to survive in the wilderness, they could escape easily and make their way back to their villages. In the end, although the Indian slave trade persisted in the English colonies into the eighteenth century, Indian slave labor proved impractical.

Colonial leaders and planters turned to indentured servitude to help solve the initial labor shortage. Under this system, poor whites in England (usually men but sometimes women) would enter into a contract with an employer in the colonies who offered transatlantic passage in exchange for a predetermined number of years in labor. Contracts varied from four to seven years but, whatever the length of the contract, the servant was bound to the employer. Indentured servants were more than slaves; there were laws that protected them from bodily harm, although colonial authorities were not always very responsive to abuses. But they were similar to slaves in that they were not free; they needed passes, or legal documents, when traveling, and essentially were the property of their masters for the length of the contract. Finally, masters could sell their servants for the remaining terms of their contracts whenever they pleased. In general all these changes moved the institution of colonial servitude closer to a system of slave labor in which workers were considered property and their labor traded and sold. Indentured servitude, then, was something of a halfway point between free and slave labor.

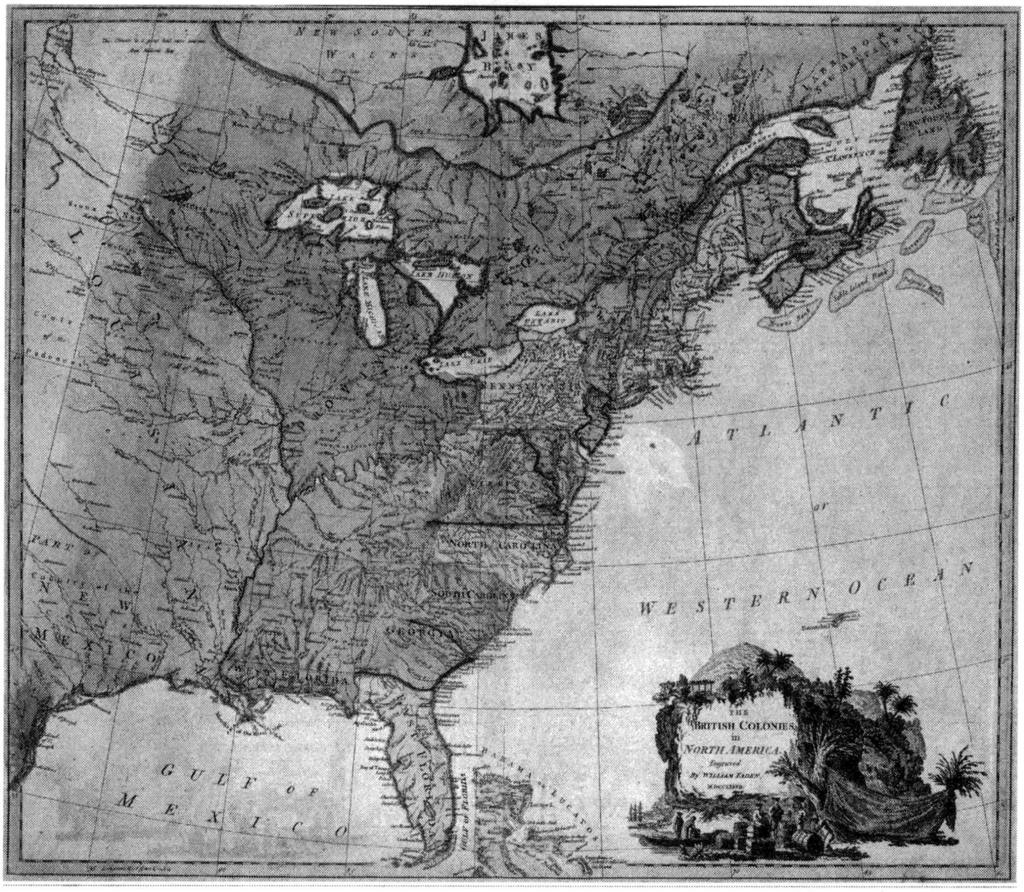

MAP 1.1 *The British colonies in North America. Courtesy of the New York Public Library, 484202*

At the same time, colonial farmers and planters turned to the African slave trade to fill their labor needs. Beginning in the 1670s, slaves imported from Africa became a dominant feature of the colonial American economy, especially in the South. The English colonists who came to settle in the southern colonies found that land was abundant and relatively easy to obtain. The first Africans arrived in Virginia in 1619, but the black population was slow to rise until the 1660s and 1670s. Only 300 to 400 Africans lived in the Chesapeake colonies in 1650, a mere 2% of the population. Even in 1670, the black population was only 5%. But by 1700, Africans or those of African descent comprised 35% of the total number of those living in the Chesapeake colonies.

Between 1675 and 1700, there were many reasons why the colonists saw black slavery as a more attractive labor system than white servitude. First, indentured servitude was only temporary; this practice meant that each year a new group of servants who had completed their contracts became a burden on colonial society. As Edmund S. Morgan argued in his important book *American Slavery, American Freedom*, Bacon's Rebellion, which saw blacks and poor whites banding together to fight authority, demonstrated to colonial leaders the dangers of importing more indentured servants. Usually servants ended their contracts with no money, no shelter, few skills, and only the clothes on their backs. Colonial elites in the South became concerned about the potential political hazard posed by the abundance of former servants. Second, changes in immigration meant that by the mid- to late 1600s, as economic conditions slowly improved in England, fewer white servants wanted to migrate. In addition, as life expectancy for all races rose in the Chesapeake in the 1600s, slaves became a better investment. Slaves were more expensive than indentured servants, but as the likelihood of slaves living longer increased, their high cost was more justified. Colonial laws, such as a Maryland statute explicitly stating that the children of slave mothers would also be slaves, ensured that bondage would pass from one generation to the next; this doctrine was never applied to white indentured servants, only to black slaves. Finally, racial prejudice, especially long-held beliefs about African inferiority, spurred the growth of the slave trade. Winthrop D. Jordan and other historians have underscored long-standing white European beliefs that God destined Africans and other dark-skinned peoples for hard, physically demanding labor.

Only about 5% of all Africans that were brought to the New World went to the English colonies along the Atlantic Coast of North America; the vast majority went to Brazil, the Caribbean, and other Latin American colonies. Slavery took root as well in the northern colonies, and New York City would remain an important center of slavery throughout much of the colonial era. Slaves in the northern colonies not only worked on farms, but also helped load ships in port towns, worked as artisan laborers in carpentry, iron-forging, masonry, and other skilled crafts, and worked in physically demanding jobs such as digging trenches.

Those slaves who did come to the English colonies were sold mostly in the South. The rocky soil in New England was not as useful for growing crops like tobacco. Tobacco required much work, as did other crops that dominated the South, such as indigo, rice, sugar, and later cotton. These crops required many hours in the sun, sometimes in swampy conditions infested with mosquitoes and other pests. The English believed that Africans were better

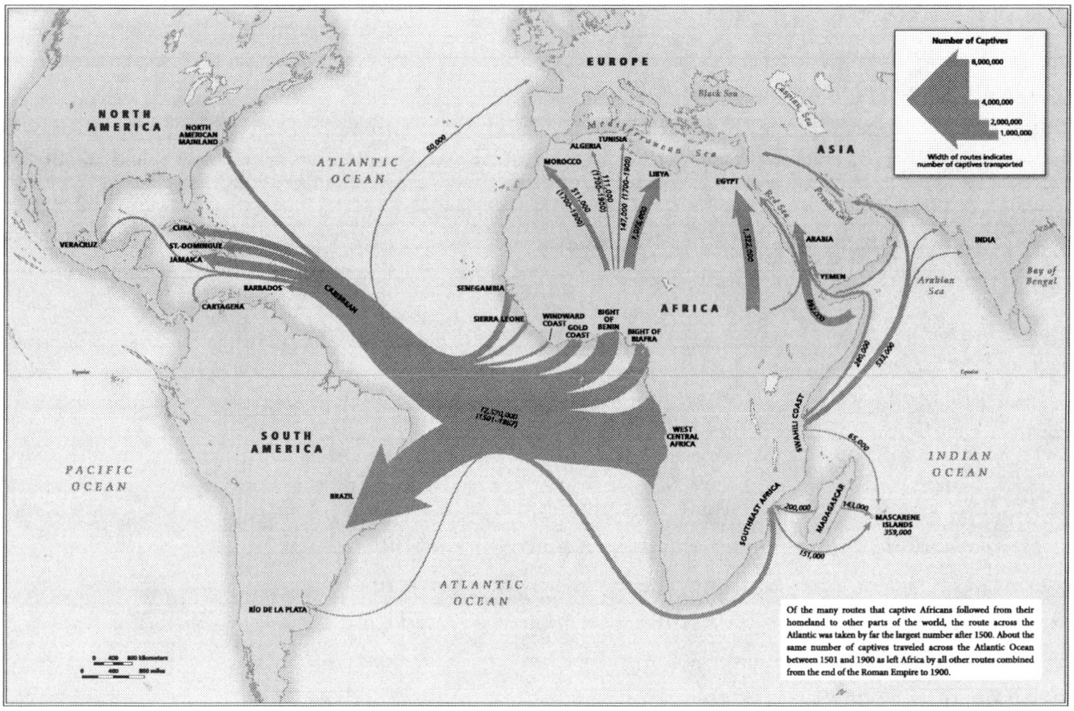

MAP 1.2 *Overview of the slave trade out of Africa, 1500–1900. David Eltis and David Richardson, Atlas of the Transatlantic Slave Trade (New Haven, CT: Yale University Press), 2010*

suited to these kinds of working conditions. As one white woman, Louisa McCord of South Carolina, put it: "The white man will never raise, *can* never raise, a cotton or a sugar crop in the United States. In our swamps and under our suns the negro thrives, but the white man dies." Employing such rationalizations, colonial racism made the expansion of African slavery possible and ensured that slavery would play a central role in the nation's founding. However, some religious groups in the northern colonies thought slavery was immoral. Quakers in Pennsylvania, for example, remained largely opposed to bondage before and after American won independence from Britain.

Rise of the Slave Trade

The African slave trade is one of the darkest stories in human history. The ruthlessness with which men and women of all ages were forcibly transported to the New World is stunning. Yet the slave trade did not begin with the opening of the Americas in the 1600s. Europeans had owned slaves (both white and black) long before the beginning of American colonization. In ancient civilizations in Egypt, Greece, and Rome, slavery was an important part of the economy and society. Africans themselves had been active for hundreds of years in capturing other Africans and selling them into slavery. But slavery meant different things at different times, and scholars have discovered that the concept of slavery is a complicated one. If you are used to thinking of slaves as agricultural laborers, you might be surprised to find that in world history, slaves were often soldiers, government officials, wives, concubines, and tutors, and that some societies even allowed their slaves to participate in politics.

Despite the long and sad history of human slavery, bondage seemed particularly brutal in the New World. The first colonists and traders to bring Africans to the Americas were the Spanish and Portuguese, who used them to replace or supplement the dwindling numbers of Indian slaves toiling in Caribbean colonies. Large plantations, some with thousands of slaves, grew sugar and other crops. Jamaica, Haiti, Cuba, Bermuda, and other islands were the centers of the slave trade in the New World. Slavery in the Caribbean was brutal, with punishments swift and harsh on large sugar plantations or in mining operations. Tens of thousands of slaves also went to South America, particularly Brazil, which in the 1880s became the last country in the western Hemisphere to outlaw slavery. In fact, after the South lost the Civil War many southerners moved to Brazil, carrying their slaves with them, and reestablished their plantations where a community of descendants from the American South lives to this day. Slavery, therefore, was not confined to the colonial South; it was a worldwide practice that had involved many of the world's leading nations, and had spread to the New World particularly rapidly.

How did Africans get to the New World? With the permission of local African rulers, Europeans built forts and trading posts on the West African Coast and bought slaves from African traders. African rulers also occasionally enslaved and sold their own people as punishment for crimes or for being in debt; others enslaved fellow Africans as prisoners of war. Attracted by European cloth, iron, liquor, guns, and other goods, West Africans fought increasingly among themselves to secure captives and began sending raiding parties to kidnap individuals from the interior. This trade created a snowball effect whereby one tribe would receive metal products, food, and weapons in exchange for slaves. The tribe would then become stronger, enabling it to push into the interior of Africa, conquering even more tribes in a vicious cycle.

FIGURE 1.2 *Enslaved Africans on board a slave ship. Library of Congress, Images of African-American Slavery and Freedom, LC-USZ62-41678*

Slaves who survived the ordeal of transportation to the trading forts on the coast faced an almost unimaginable ordeal on the ships to the colonies, a six- to eight-week-long forced migration that has come to be called the "Middle Passage." Captains wedged men below the decks into spaces about six feet long, sixteen inches wide, and thirty inches high. Slaves were often packed so tightly that they could barely move. Women and children were packed even tighter than men. Slaves were sometimes allowed on deck for fresh air, but most of the time they remained below the decks, where the hot and humid air grew foul from the vomit, blood, and excrement in which they were forced to lie. Some slaves nearly went insane; others tried to commit suicide by starving themselves or jumping overboard to drown. On many voyages, scores of enslaved people died from disease, but captains figured this into their calculations for profit and packed enough slaves in the ship to make money.

Those enslaved men and women who survived the kidnapping from their homelands then had to endure the fear and humiliation of being sold. Historian Walter Johnson has found that in slave markets, such as those in New Orleans, slaves were subjected to close and demeaning inspection by speculators who often abused female slaves. For abolitionists who wanted to end slavery, the slave trade was the worst feature of bondage. In fact, many northerners were abolitionists based solely on their opposition to the buying and selling of human beings. Southern port towns such as Wilmington, Savannah, Charleston, and New Orleans boasted active slave markets, and traders and speculators often purchased slaves in the older states like Virginia and South Carolina only to sell them in the booming southwestern states like Alabama, Louisiana, and Texas. Sometimes slaves were purchased right off the ships, and sometimes a public auction was held. In the "scrambles," potential buyers rushed on board to peruse slaves at a fixed price. Others were put up for auction, where those who had been husband and wife in Africa could find themselves sold to masters who lived far apart. There was also no guarantee that children would be sold with their mothers. Some masters were mindful of these attachments and tried not to break up families, but few legal barriers prevented the breaking up of enslaved families.

FIGURE 1.3 *Plantation—cotton picking. Courtesy of the New York Public Library, 427779*

PLANTATION—COTTON PICKING.

In fact, laws called "slave codes" passed in every southern state governed a wide range of rules, from declaring the children of enslaved mothers to be property also, even if they had a white father, to whether or not slaves could learn to read or write, to what documents free African Americans needed to demonstrate that they were not slaves. Bondspeople were not permitted to travel freely and documentation was required to leave the plantation. As a result, for most slaves, the plantation was their entire world.

Slavery and the Constitution

Though many bondspeople had hoped that the American Revolution might lead to the end of slavery, the opposite proved to be true. By the Constitutional Convention in 1787, slavery was well entrenched in the young country. Several delegates to the convention, particularly those in the North who had already begun to outlaw slavery in their home states, hoped the new government would abolish slavery or at least provide for its gradual demise. However, no document could be drafted and agreed upon without the support of southern delegates, whose state economies depended on the preservation of bondage. During the debates over the Constitution, the question quickly became not whether slavery should be abolished, but whether or not the northern and southern delegates could compromise on the issue.

The Constitution was more than a compromise; the document shocked northerners for its proslavery tone and content. Many of the southern delegates, including George Washington and James Madison, held significant numbers of slaves themselves. Yet even southerners like Thomas Jefferson (Jefferson was in France during the drafting of the Constitution and thus not directly involved in the convention proceedings) were keenly aware of the contradictions inherent in a democratic society that protected slavery, and Jefferson worried what Europeans would think about the continuance of the slave trade. In fact, the word "slavery" never appears in the Constitution proper. Some political leaders understood clearly the contradictions of a government based upon the will of "the people" yet simultaneously disfranchised and enslaved millions of human beings.

Without employing the word "slavery," the Constitution as ratified nonetheless clearly endorsed the institution. The Three-Fifths Clause (Article One, Section Two) counted slaves as three-fifths of a white person for purposes of political representation.

The Fugitive Slave Clause (Article Four, Section Two) stated that any "Person held to Service or Labour in one State" who had fled to a free state was still a slave, and that the free state was required to deliver the fugitive back to slavery. In Article One, Section Nine, the Constitution declared that a future Congress would have the right to end the African slave trade in 1808. Many northerners and southerners supported the continuance of slavery but were disgusted by the trafficking in human beings. Perhaps, moderates conjectured, if no more slaves were allowed to be imported from Africa beginning from 1808 then the existing slaves would naturally die out over many decades. Such thinkers, however, did not count on there being enough slaves in the nation already by 1808 to ensure a natural increase. Despite the end of the African slave trade in that year, on the eve of the Civil War in 1861 there were four million slaves living in the southern states.

Later supporters of the antislavery movement would damn the Constitution as a pact with the devil. Critics like Boston's William Lloyd Garrison would be so angered by the Constitution's protection for slavery that undermining, denouncing, and even setting the document afire would become a way for abolitionists to protest the federal government's dedication to sanctioning bondage. This is not to say that war between the North and South was inevitable or the result of "irrepressible conflict," to use the words of New York Senator William Henry Seward. But neither can we deny the central importance of slavery to the causes of the conflict. As we will see, throughout the first half of the nineteenth century northerners and southerners would argue intensely over slavery and its extension into new states brought into the Union. For decades, skillful politicians kept the Union together, but even they realized the precarious nature of a government that every decade erupted into crisis over the issue of slavery.

The Cotton Boom

The Northwest Ordinance, passed by Congress under the Articles of Confederation in the summer of 1787, laid out a plan for the territories south of the Great Lakes and north and west of the Ohio River to become states. In addition to laying down rules for the shift to statehood, the ordinance prohibited slavery in the northwestern territories, establishing the Ohio River as an important future boundary between slavery and freedom. Although the Confederation's life was short, the territorial precedents founded by the Ordinance would be followed even after a new Constitution was drafted in 1787. The Northwest Ordinance identified the Great Lakes region as one of freedom rather than slavery.

Slavery in the South, however, was bolstered significantly by the invention of the cotton gin in 1793. Developed by Eli Whitney, a northern schoolteacher who had moved to Georgia, the cotton gin removed the seeds from the thick raw cotton fifty times faster than it could be done by hand. With the invention of the gin, much more cotton could be grown because more could be processed. As historian Angela Lakwete has discovered, after the cotton gin's invention in the early 1790s, manufacturers built hundreds of the machines and they spread throughout the region. Southern farmers sold their increased tonnage of cotton to the rapidly expanding textile mills in Britain and the northern states. Cotton production rose from about 75,000 bales in 1800 to almost five million bales by 1860. And more cotton meant an increased demand for slaves. The explosive growth in the production of cotton ensured not only that slavery would continue to be used on southern plantations, but also that southerners would view slavery as vital to their interests. In fact, as historian Sven Beckert has shown, the rise and fall in the price of cotton was closely linked to the rise and fall in the value of slaves.

Cotton production began in South Carolina and Georgia, but spread rapidly to the Old Southwest and then into Texas. In the 1810s and 1820s thousands of southerners living in states

FIGURE 1.4 *Cotton gin: girds and saws exposed. Courtesy of the New York Public Library, 107472*

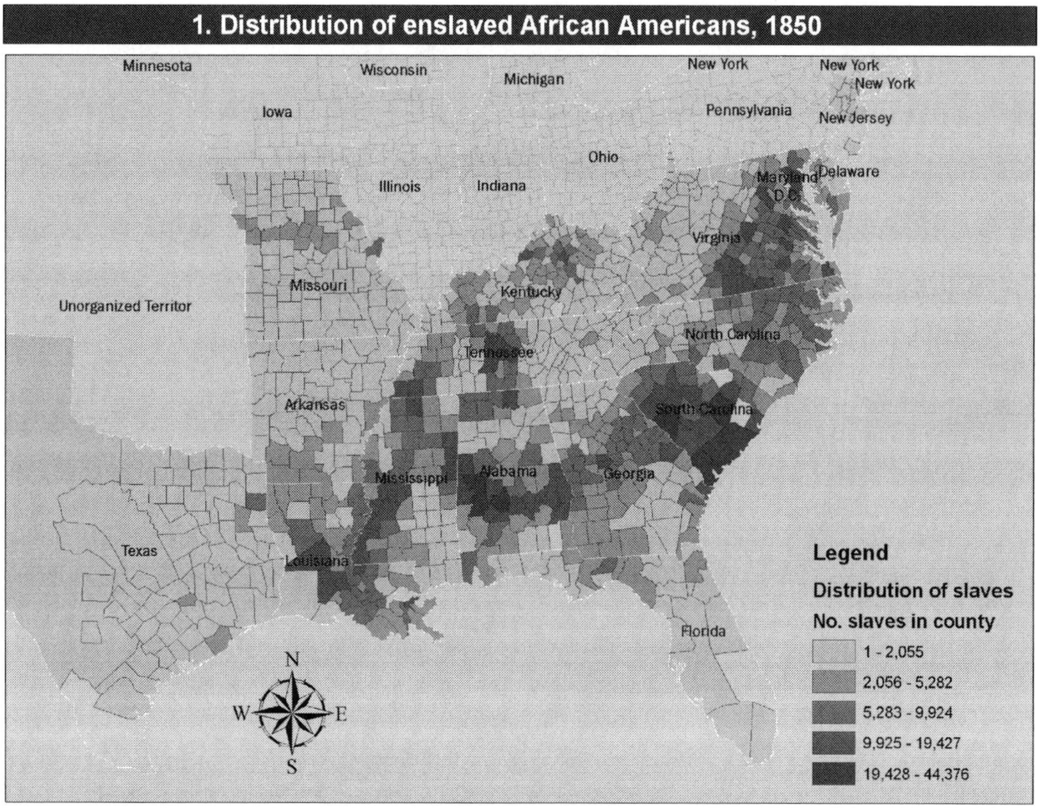

MAP 1.3 *Map of the slave south*

like the Carolinas, Virginia, and Georgia moved westward in search of good land on which to grow cotton, greatly increasing the populations of Alabama, Mississippi, Louisiana, Texas, and Arkansas. These migrants found that the soil in central Mississippi and Alabama was particularly fertile and in these regions, as scholar Edward Baptist has shown, slavery expanded with rapid and brutal force. One might draw a crescent shape in the southeast, called the Black Belt, a term that comes not from the color of the slaves there, but from the rich soil. In these regions, cotton production flourished and slavery became the main labor force. In some regions, slaves outnumbered whites more than ten to one, and on some plantations only a handful of whites controlled plantations harboring hundreds and even thousands of slaves.

The Plantation South

Although there was a great deal of variation, plantations in the South—whether in the seventeenth, eighteenth, or nineteenth century—shared some basic characteristics. In the Old South, plantations were scattered, particularly as one moved away from the Gulf and Atlantic coasts. Population was denser along the coastlines of the South because there the soil was especially fertile, and proximity to water facilitated trade. But inland planters often had no neighbors for five or ten miles or more in any direction. This scattered distribution not only made slave revolts more difficult, but it also created a great deal of anxiety among southern whites. Sometimes vastly outnumbered by the slaves on their plantations, whites constantly feared a revolt among their slaves, especially after the slave revolution in Haiti between 1791 and 1804, a revolt that reverberated with great force across the Caribbean and the American South.

The planters themselves often had little to do with the actual operation of the plantation. The master might handle the account books, purchase clothes for the slaves when needed, and occasionally supervise the operation of the farm. The day-to-day running of the plantation most often fell into the hands of an overseer, who was responsible for assigning work schedules and maintaining discipline. Usually overseers were white, but it was not uncommon to have trusted slaves serve in this role as well. The overseers, often guilty of the worst abuses, had great power to direct and punish slaves. Court records abound with examples of cruel punishments, maiming, and sexual abuse by overseers.

Yet few whites could have been classified as "planters" with twenty or more slaves. Historian James Oakes found that most masters owned fewer than five slaves, and many owned just one or two. If we take the wealthiest slaveowners in the South, those with fifty or more slaves, we find that about 1% of whites would fit into this class. Planters with twenty or more made up another 4% or so of southern whites. And those with between one and nineteen slaves, the vast majority of whom had only one or two, make up another 20% or so. So only about a quarter of the white population in the South had any direct connection with slavery. Most whites in the South were not planters; most were not even slaveholders. Most white southerners were either yeomen (small farmers who owned their own land), or landless. Despite their lack of slaves, however, poor and middle-class whites supported bondage with the same ferocity as their planter neighbors, in part because they too aspired to enter the slaveholding class.

Today scholars in fact marvel at the ways in which enslaved peoples were able to carve out lives for themselves and their loved ones under the most difficult of circumstances. Some masters allowed their slaves to marry, although many others prohibited it.

The truth is that there were some masters who were kind and relatively benign to their slaves and reluctant to sell off husbands and wives. Other masters cared nothing about the emotional or spiritual well-being of their slaves and broke up families at will. The point is that the law offered little or no protection; indeed court ruling after court ruling reestablished the idea that slaves were property. The slave's quality of life was completely dependent upon the whim of his master.

Although the lives of slaves varied greatly within the New World and within the southern United States, we might identify some chief general characteristics common to the experience of enslaved men and women. Slaves lived mainly on rations of cornmeal and salt pork distributed to them by the master. Together with vegetables they grew on small garden plots that many masters permitted and occasional catches of game and fish, slaves consumed a diet that provided ample calories but usually insufficient vitamins and nutrients. Intestinal disorders like cholera and dysentery were common. About 20% of the slaves on a plantation were sick at any given time. Infant mortality was twice as high among slaves as among whites in 1850. The life expectancy for slaves at birth was twenty-one or twenty-two years old, about half of what it was for whites.

Masters furnished their slaves with two sets of coarse clothing, one for summer and one for winter. Poor shoes were a constant complaint for slaves, as masters usually tried to get away as cheaply as possible and often bought shoes that did not fit. The clothes were rough, like the material used to make sacks for holding crops.

Despite these harsh working conditions, most slaves were able to form social bonds with other slaves. Often the slaves' quarters, a building or group of buildings on the plantation but apart from the master's "big house," was the location of dances, parties, or religious revivals, if the master allowed. Usually, field slaves lived in a fifteen-foot by fifteen-foot cabin built from logs. Five or six slaves lived in one cabin, often with no windows. Ironically, the fact that the slave cabins were set off from the master's house gave slaves some degree of autonomy. Slaves might hold religious meetings or join in prayer on Sundays. However, slaves who served as house servants usually lived with the master, providing opportunity for around-the-clock exploitation, especially of female slaves.

In one of the most famous slave narratives, or accounts of experiences under bondage by the slaves themselves, Harriet Jacobs told of the constant fear of sexual attack. To northern abolitionists such firsthand accounts added authenticity to claims of slavery's cruelty, and credence to arguments that bondage corrupted the master as well as the slave.

> **Even the little child, who is accustomed to wait on her mistress and her children, will learn, before she is twelve years old, why it is that her mistress hates such and such a one among the slaves. Perhaps the child's own mother is among those hated ones. She listens to violent outbreaks of jealous passion, and cannot help understanding what is the cause. She will become prematurely knowing in evil things. Soon she will learn to tremble when she hears her master's footfall. She will be compelled to realize that she is no longer a child. If God has bestowed beauty upon her, it will prove her greatest curse. That which commands admiration in the white woman only hastens the degradation of the female slave. I know that some are too much brutalized by slavery to feel the humiliation of their position; but many slaves feel it most acutely, and shrink from the memory of it. I cannot tell how much I suffered in the presence of these wrongs, nor how I am still pained by the retrospect. My master met me at every turn, reminding me that I belonged to him, and swearing by heaven and earth that he would compel me to submit to him. If I went out for a breath of fresh air, after a day of unwearied toil, his footsteps dogged me. If I knelt by my mother's grave, his dark shadow fell on me even there. The light heart which nature had given me became heavy with sad forebodings. The other slaves in my master's house noticed the change. Many of them pitied me; but none dared to ask the cause. They had no need to inquire. They knew too well the guilty practices under that roof; and they were aware that to speak of them was an offence that never went unpunished.[1]**

White plantation mistresses were forced to acquiesce to the sexual abuse of female slaves. Privately they might express disapproval to their husbands, but in most antebellum households the husband and father ruled. Yet, it was obvious when light-skinned children were born to slaves and looked much like the master's white children. "In this one particular aspect," Rebecca Latimer Felton, a white Georgian, later wrote,

slavery doomed itself. When white men put their own offspring in the kitchen and the cornfield and allowed them to be sold into bondage as slaves . . . the retribution of wrath was hanging over this country and the South paid penance in four years of bloody war.[2]

Census records indicate that thousands of "mulattos" lived in the antebellum South, data that provides statistical support for Felton's claims. The large number of mulattos, or those of mixed white and black ancestry, a number that swelled in the later antebellum period, is an obvious testament to the fact that a female slave was largely at the mercy of her white master. Even a white mistress who became aware of her husband's promiscuity had almost no legal or social recourse to question or thwart his behavior.

While sexual abuse existed alongside more general physical punishment of slaves in the Old South, historians debate the extent of actual whippings or killing of slaves. Virtually all scholars agree that such abuse and murder did occur throughout the South and throughout the time of slavery. In the 1970s, studies done by quantitative historians (those who use statistics and other data to study a time and place, often by using census records) seemed to suggest that whippings were lower in number and severity than scholars previously believed. In their widely debated book *Time on the Cross* (1974) Robert W. Fogel and Stanley L. Engerman were accused of manipulating data to show that whippings were not as common as other scholars had found, and that outright murdering of slaves was even more rare. Since the 1970s, however, historians have argued that plantation and legal records evince not only extreme and widespread physical abuse of slaves, including whipping and branding, but sexual violence as well. Regardless of the actual numbers of whippings, brandings, murders, and sexual exploitation, it is absolutely clear that such violence did occur often. It is equally clear that given the South's legal and political system, and its patriarchal society, slaves of both genders and of all ages were at the mercy of their masters, who had only their own consciences to control their behavior. Although nineteenth-century southerners and their latter-day defenders sometimes minimize white on black violence on the plantations and farms of the Old South, the historical record is rife with evidence that slavery was a brutal and frequently deadly system.

While the vast majority of enslaved men toiled in agricultural labor, some could be found in skilled positions on plantations and even in the few factories that existed in the South. Employed as stonecutters, blacksmiths, carpenters, or other skilled labor, these slaves were very controversial in the South. They could be "hired out" by their plantation master, or they might be owned directly by a factory or mill. If they were "hired out," a factory or mill manager would rent a slave who was not needed during a down time on the plantation. In this way southern masters could get something back for slaves who would otherwise remain idle and southern factory managers obtained cheap labor. As an incentive to work hard, factory managers might pay the slave a small wage. Although it was tiny compared to what a white laborer might earn, the wage was nonetheless a source of self-worth and pride for the slave who received it.

Divisions Within the South

The Black Belt and coastal regions of the South held the largest concentrations of plantations and slaves, and so here could be found the strongest, most vocal defenders of slavery. The South as a whole did not tolerate disagreements with slavery, especially after the early 1830s when Nat Turner's slave revolt led to heightened fears of abolition. But the Black Belt and coastal regions were especially vehement in asserting the justice and righteousness of slavery, and especially harsh in condemning anyone who dared to question the institution's legitimacy. Through political representatives in Congress, such as South Carolina's John C. Calhoun and Alabama's William Yancey, southern planters influenced political decisions disproportionate to their numbers. Planters, often defined by historians as those with twenty or more slaves, were often the leaders in southern communities. In rural areas, where larger farms and plantations could be found, the white population was scattered; schools and other community institutions were scarce, and wealthier families relied on private tutors, often young men and women from the North, to live with them and teach their children. Here large plantations were often communities unto themselves.

Despite the power of planters to control the political and economic systems in the eighteenth and early nineteenth centuries, the Old South was a complicated region with many class and geographical divisions. The towns and cities of the region, including New Orleans, Louisville, Baltimore, Charleston, Wilmington, Savannah, and Richmond, were smaller in size and population than northern behemoths like Boston, Philadelphia, and New York. But within southern towns and cities seeds of an economically and politically important middle class could be found as early as the 1820s. Comprising commercial folks like merchants, bankers, clerks, and shopkeepers as well as professionals like doctors, lawyers, editors, and dentists, this middle class increased in number and influence during the early nineteenth century. Its members formed organizations to promote their interests, such as chambers of commerce, medical associations, and bar associations. They shared much in common ideologically with their counterparts in northern towns and cities, including support for public schools and the promotion of an active role for the government in fostering economic growth through internal improvements. This southern middle class traveled to the North frequently, often admiring northern urban progress in establishing schools, creating lively cities, and encouraging cultural opportunities such as libraries and museums. Yet at the same time the white southern middle class was completely committed to slavery, unlike the northern middle class. In fact, middle-class white businessmen advocated using slaves as factory laborers to help grow the region's manufacturing base. Slave factory workers would never strike like many white workers had done in the antebellum North and some had done in the South. Indeed, in a few of the South's most celebrated factory disturbances slaves were brought in as scabs to break the strikes.

Despite agreeing with planters on the value of slavery, however, middle-class southerners reflected growing class divisions within the region. Professional and commercial southerners often blamed the planter class for failing to invest its considerable wealth in manufacturing enterprises or failing to support internal improvements. Historians have found that many planters did support more public investment in railroads, canals, and other improvements that facilitated economic growth. But the southern middle class went further, arguing that private investment was needed to remake the region with public schools and libraries, larger cities, centralized banking, and other signs of economic and cultural progress that planters did not always support, at least not to the satisfaction of the middle class. As a result professionals and merchants often criticized planters for what they considered to be the inadequate support of planters for modernizing the region and for their single-minded pursuit of profit through the cotton crop.

As scholars like William A. Link have demonstrated, white southerners who lived in the mountain areas tended to be less supportive of slavery. In the western sections of the Carolinas and Virginia, in the eastern sections of Tennessee, and in northeastern Alabama, mountainous terrain meant that the large, sprawling plantations of the Black Belt and coastal South were impossible to build. Mountain soil was not as rich as soil in the Lowcountry and cotton production not as ubiquitous. Smaller farms and plantations prevailed in the mountainous South and led to different social and economic characteristics. For example, in the mountains female slaves and their children were more often put to work, while male slaves might more often work in non-agricultural, skilled tasks such as blacksmithing. Even here, where the slave population was less dense than in the Lowcountry South, slaves were still able to form closely knit communities. While the South had little tolerance for opposition to slavery, southerners in the mountain regions came to believe that they had different interests from the slaveholding regions.

East–West conflicts within southern states were heated and powerful, but still other divisions could be found within the Old South. The slave population was less dense in the Upper South states of Maryland, North Carolina, Virginia, and Kentucky than it was in the Deep South. Only Mississippi and South Carolina had black populations that outnumbered whites, although in a given county in other states African Americans might comprise well over 50% of the overall population. Upper South whites usually supported slavery, but often not as vehemently as those in the Lower South. In fact, as late as the 1830s, white Virginians were still openly debating the merits of slavery, and throughout the antebellum period in the Upper South men like Hinton Helper and Benjamin Hedrick could be found criticizing the institution. The Upper South states were also more willing to invest public monies in promoting factories and other developments including railroads. One exception in the Lower South was Georgia, which spent considerable sums of public and private funds in industry, earning it the title "the Empire State of the South." In summary, it is important to note that the Old South, even as it broached little disagreement over the virtues of slavery, was nonetheless far from monolithic.

Northern Industrialization

Although the southern states were becoming increasingly industrialized over the course of the antebellum era, by 1861 at the start of the Civil War the region was still overwhelmingly agricultural. In contrast, northern cities and communities grew rapidly and changed dramatically even though there too agriculture remained paramount. Most apparent was the rapid growth of the population in northern cities. New York's population, which totaled just over 300,000 people in 1840, rose to more than 800,000 by 1860. The populations of Boston and Philadelphia doubled over the same period. Much of this increase was due to the dramatic influx of German and Irish immigrants beginning in the 1840s, when a potato famine decimated Ireland's crops and led to countless deaths from starvation and disease. Millions of Europeans immigrated to northern and midwestern cities, and the populations of New York, Chicago, Cincinnati, St. Louis, Philadelphia, and other cities expanded quickly. These immigrants faced discrimination and harsh working and living conditions; the Irish in particular faced prejudice because of their Catholic faith and because of widely held beliefs about the supposed laziness and drunkenness of Irishmen. They traveled across the Atlantic, however, because of the promise of high wages and economic independence, dreams that remained illusory for most. Adding to the influx of immigrants, thousands of rural northerners also moved from farms to towns and cities, swelling the urban population. Although hardly opposed to slavery or sympathetic to racial equality, urban northerners would prove important politically. At first strongly supportive of the Democrats, immigrants, particularly Germans, would prove vital components of the antislavery Republican Party in the late 1850s. Other midwestern cities like Detroit, Milwaukee, and Cleveland also grew substantially and helped to add people and political power to the free states.

Northern urbanization took place alongside industrialization in the early nineteenth century, a transformation that was due in part to advances in transportation. Canals and railroads were key to the transportation revolution, dramatically reducing the time and expense associated with moving people and goods. The Erie Canal, completed in 1825, stretched for more than 350 miles, linking the Hudson River with Lake Erie, and New York with midwestern cities like Chicago. Similar canal projects sprang up in Pennsylvania, Ohio, New York, and Indiana. Railroads flourished as well; the Baltimore and Ohio railroad was the first to operate fully in 1830. The laying of track took off after 1840, which nationwide consisted of about 3,000 miles. By 1860, however, 27,000 miles of tracks were functioning, mostly in the North and Midwest.

Other transportation and communication advances, especially the telegraph and the postal system, helped to spur the rapid industrialization of northern and midwestern states.

The building of canals and railroads, along with the dramatic new speed of communication brought about by the invention of the telegraph, led to increases in the number of factories and businesses in the antebellum North. The growing use of the corporation to spur investment and the rise of manufacturing began to transform the northern urban landscape. Advances in technology, especially in machinery, boosted industrialization. And the increase in population meant that an ample labor force was available to work in the new businesses. Young women often toiled in the clothing and textile industries; the Lowell Mills in Massachusetts were famous across the nation for their female workforce. Harsh working conditions and low pay led to the formation of labor unions in the antebellum North, a trend that would intensify after the Civil War.

Slavery and Sectionalism in the Early Republic

By the early 1800s every state north of Maryland had provided for the gradual abolition of slavery. As historians like Joanne Pope Melish have shown, the key term here is "gradual" because most states only provided for freedom for children born after the law was adopted, and only after they reached adulthood. New York's first emancipation law in 1799 stated that all existing slaves were to remain in servitude until they died; only their children were to be freed after they became adults. Even in the South some evidence of change was apparent. By 1790 in all states manumission (the freeing of slaves) became the prerogative of the owner. But such laws were temporary aberrations; most of the more radical laws in the South were repealed by a new wave of slave codes in the 1790s.

The Louisiana Purchase in 1803 proved another boon to slavery, but not without a great deal of controversy. Indeed, President Thomas Jefferson's support for the purchase, which stretched across most of the rest of the American continent, was based upon his belief that the nation's future lay with independent farmers. The vast expanse of new territory added to the United States would (Jefferson believed) ensure that enough land would be available for many generations to come. Yet almost as soon as Congress approved the purchase, the land became entangled

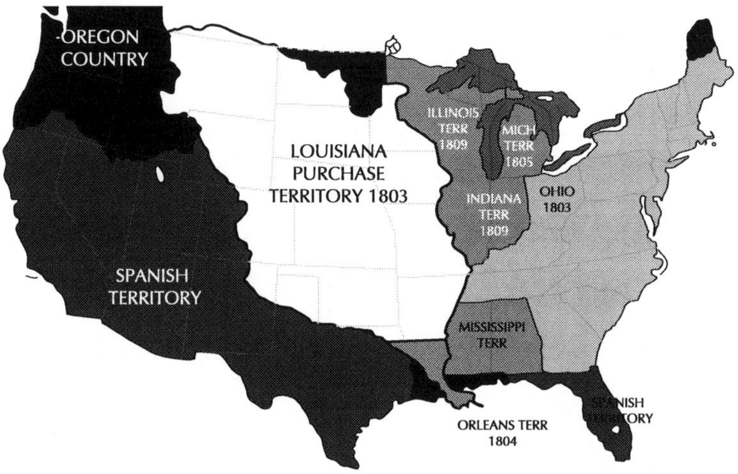

MAP 1.4 *Map of the Louisiana Purchase*

in conflict, primarily centered on two key questions: would new states admitted to the Union be slave or free, and how was this issue to be decided?

One of the first new states to derive from the Louisiana Purchase was Missouri, which followed the guidelines laid down by the Constitution and applied for statehood in 1819. At the time, the Union was divided evenly with eleven free states and eleven slave states, important because each new state brought two senators and a number of representatives based on the new state's population. In the northern states, many politicians sided with the slave South and claimed that the institution was protected by the Constitution and should therefore remain outside political debates. A growing number of northern politicians, even those not committed fully to slavery's immediate end, resented the possibility of slavery's expansion. These free-state politicians were concerned that the federal government was already under the control of proslavery presidents and congressional leaders, and while they wanted to maintain slavery in its present form, they were similarly determined that the institution would not spread to the new states emerging in the West. Pennsylvania's Senator Walter Lowrie, for example, was adamant that slavery remain a southern institution only, and that the breakup of the Union was preferable to permitting slaveholders an unlimited right to expand into the West. In fact, many northerners had come to believe, based on published travel accounts as well as their own travel to the largely agricultural South, that slavery retarded economic development, inhibited the growth of cities, and prevented cultural progress like schools and libraries. Widely available and popular accounts of travel in the slave states by the English novelist Frances Trollope and northern landscape architect Frederick Law Olmsted described primitive and dismal conditions wherever slavery was present. Such accounts confirmed for abolitionists the dangerous effects of slavery. Allowing slavery to expand into the newly organized states that would emerge from the Louisiana Purchase, the northern foes of slavery argued, would condemn these future states to economic, intellectual, and cultural backwardness.

White southerners responded angrily to the claims that slavery created a society and an economy inferior to the North's, and attacked the "wage slavery" that laboring whites experienced in northern cities like New York and Philadelphia. In sermons, pamphlets, newspapers, and political speeches white southern politicians denounced the crowded, dirty cities of the North, arguing vigorously that the Constitution protected bondage. They accused their northern opponents of seeking to wreck the document and the agreements upon which it was based. Southerners were right that northern laborers lived and worked under abominable conditions and "wage slavery" was a term not far from the mark. Child labor, long hours, unhealthy environments, and little freedom of choice governed the lives of millions of northern workers, many of whom were recent immigrants. But southern masters were similarly blind to the desires and sufferings of their slaves, choosing to believe that bondspeople were happy to be enslaved and that slaves were better off in the civilized Christian world than they were in "pagan" Africa. Therefore, even before abolitionism would become a powerful political force in the 1830s and 1840s, the contours of the debates over slavery were well established in the fight over Missouri's statehood.

In the midst of the Missouri debates in Congress, the bulk of which took place in the winter of 1819–1820, passions were inflamed by an amendment put forth by Representative James Tallmadge of New York. Tallmadge wished to prevent slavery's expansion into western territories, and his amendment made the prevention of slavery a condition of Missouri's statehood. In addition, Tallmadge proposed that all slaves who had already been brought into the Missouri territory be emancipated, or freed, at the age of twenty-five. Historian Elizabeth Varon has found that white politicians, ministers, and other leaders of southern public opinion denounced the proposal, and the word "disunion" was used often both as a threat and a concern. Leaders even employed the phrase "civil war" to describe what they saw as the logical outcome of these paralyzing debates over the legitimacy of slavery. Though it would not happen for more than four decades, such claims proved correct.

Disunion was thwarted during the Missouri Crisis by Kentucky's young Congressman Henry Clay, who helped to guide the nation through the predicament. A compromise allowed Missouri to enter the Union as a slave state, but Missouri's proslavery political power (including two new senators and a handful of representatives) would be balanced by the addition of the new free state of Maine. But politicians, worried about the effects of future similar crises over new states, added a stipulation that drew a line through the Louisiana Purchase Territory at 36° 30′, which was Missouri's southern border. Except for Missouri, slavery would be prohibited north of this line and permitted south of the border. While the Missouri Compromise of 1820 resolved the crisis, observers knew the controversy was far from permanently settled. Former President Thomas Jefferson, writing from his home near Charlottesville, Virginia, famously commented that the crisis rang "like a fire bell in the night," warning Americans that the debates over slavery might one day end in civil war.

As Jefferson feared, slavery did become a political wedge. Southern politicians like John C. Calhoun played on the voters' fears of northern dominance. The core ideas of political culture in the Early Republic were liberty and equality. In the South these twin doctrines were for whites only, and indeed, slavery guaranteed that African Americans would always remain at the bottom of the social ladder. Southern politicians played strongly on southern white worries of being forced into the kind of economic dependency that defined the lives of both slaves and the northern working class. For their part northern politicians used fears of a "Slave Power Conspiracy" that sought to elevate slavery to national status and control the federal government. In what would become known as the Second Party System, two parties, the Democrats and the Whigs, would battle over the sectional crisis engendered by slavery and consequently over which party was best suited to hold the Union together. As Jefferson would later famously remark, "we have the wolf [slavery] by the ear, and we can neither hold him, nor safely let him go. Justice is in one scale, and self-preservation in the other."

Please visit the companion website www.routledge.com/cw/wells for additional study aids including chapter overviews, interactive quizzes, and more.

COMPANION @ WEBSITE

Discussion Questions

- What were the long-term causes of the Civil War?
- How were sectional crises, such as the dispute over Missouri's admission into the Union, resolved?
- In what ways were the antebellum North and South distinctive? In what ways were they similar? Are there sectional differences today?
- The Old South is often depicted as monolithic, but historians have identified numerous divisions within the region. Discuss some of the ways in which the region was divided with regard to geography, class, and other factors.
- Was the United States Constitution drafted in 1787 a "proslavery" document as William Lloyd Garrison and many other abolitionists argued? Use evidence from the Constitution to support your answer.
- Historians have often turned to slaveholders' letters to find out more about slave life and work on the plantations. Why might letters written by planters be problematic when studying slave life and work?
- In the nineteenth century, many formerly enslaved people wrote autobiographies, which are known as slave narratives. What problems might these sources present for historical research? What benefits might they provide?

Notes

1 Harriet Jacobs, *Incidents in the Life of a Slave Girl* (Boston, 1861).

2 Rebecca Latimer Felton, *Country Life in the Days of My Youth* (1919), quoted in Lee Ann Whites, "The Civil War as a Crisis in Gender," in Catherine Clinton and Nina Silber, eds., *Divided Houses: Gender and the Civil War* (New York: Oxford University Press, 1992), 7.

Further Reading

Leslie M. Alexander, *African or American? Black Identity and Political Activism in New York City, 1784–1861* (Urbana: University of Illinois Press, 2008).

John Ashworth, *Slavery, Capitalism, and Politics in the Antebellum Republic* (volume 1: *Commerce and Compromise, 1820–1850*; Cambridge: Cambridge University Press, 1995).

Edward E. Baptist, *The Half Has Never Been Told: Slavery and the Making of American Capitalism* (New York: Basic Books, 2014).
Sven Beckert, *Empire of Cotton: A Global History* (New York: Knopf, 2014).
Ira Berlin, *Many Thousands Gone: The First Two Centuries of Slavery in North America* (Cambridge, MA: Harvard University Press, 1998).
Stephanie M.H. Camp, *Closer to Freedom: Enslaved Women and Everyday Resistance in the Plantation South* (Chapel Hill: University of North Carolina Press, 2004).
Wilma A. Dunaway, *Slavery in the American Mountain South* (Cambridge: Cambridge University Press, 2003).
Marc Egnal, *Clash of Extremes: The Economic Origins of the Civil War* (New York: Hill & Wang, 2009).
Robert W. Fogel and Stanley L. Engerman, *Time on the Cross: The Economics of American Negro Slavery* (Boston: Little Brown & Co., 1974).
Robert Pierce Forbes, *The Missouri Compromise and its Aftermath: Slavery and the Meaning of America* (Chapel Hill: University of North Carolina Press, 2007).
Lacy K. Ford, *Deliver Us from Evil: The Slavery Question in the Old South* (New York: Oxford University Press, 2009).
Elizabeth Fox-Genovese and Eugene Genovese, *Slavery in White and Black: Class and Race in the Southern Slaveholders' New World Order* (Cambridge, MA: Cambridge University Press, 2008).
William W. Freehling, *The Road to Disunion: Secessionists at Bay, 1776–1854* (New York: Oxford University Press, 1990).
Joanne B. Freeman, *Affairs of Honor: National Politics in the New Republic* (New Haven: Yale University Press, 2001).
Alan Gallay, *The Indian Slave Trade: The Rise of the English Empire in the American South, 1670–1717* (New Haven: Yale University Press, 2002).
Leslie M. Harris, *In the Shadow of Slavery: African Americans in New York City, 1626–1863* (Chicago: University of Chicago Press, 2003).
Daniel Walker Howe, *What Hath God Wrought: The Transformation of America, 1815–1848* (New York: Oxford University Press, 2007).
Walter Johnson, *Soul by Soul: Life Inside the Antebellum Slave Market* (Cambridge, MA: Harvard University Press, 2000).
Walter Johnson, *River of Dark Dreams: Slavery and Empire in the Cotton Kingdom* (Cambridge, MA: Harvard University Press, 2013).
Winthrop D. Jordan, *White Over Black: American Attitudes Toward the Negro, 1550–1812* (Chapel Hill: University of North Carolina Press, 1968).
Anthony E. Kaye, *Joining Places: Slave Neighborhoods in the Old South* (Chapel Hill: University of North Carolina Press, 2007).
Linda K. Kerber, *Women of the Republic: Intellect and Ideology in Revolutionary America* (Chapel Hill: University of North Carolina Press, 1980).

Peter Kolchin, *American Slavery, 1619–1877* (New York: Hill & Wang, 1993).

Barbara Krauthamer, *Black Slaves, Indian Masters: Slavery, Emancipation, and Citizenship in the Native American South* (Chapel Hill: University of North Carolina Press, 2013).

Angela Lakwete, *Inventing the Cotton Gin: Machine and Myth in Antebellum America* (Baltimore, MD: Johns Hopkins University Press, 2003).

Matthew Mason, *Slavery & Politics in the Early American Republic* (Chapel Hill: University of North Carolina Press, 2006).

Sally McMillen, *Seneca Falls and the Origins of the Women's Rights Movement* (New York: Oxford University Press, 2008).

Joanne Pope Melish, *Disowning Slavery: Gradual Emancipation and "Race" in New England, 1780–1860* (Ithaca: Cornell University Press, 1998).

Margot Minardi, *Making Slavery History: Abolitionism and the Politics of Memory in Massachusetts* (New York: Oxford University Press, 2010).

Edmund S. Morgan, *American Slavery, American Freedom: The Ordeal of Colonial Virginia* (New York: W.W. Norton, 1975).

Dylan C. Penningroth, *The Claims of Kinfolk: African American Property and Community in the Nineteenth-Century South* (Chapel Hill: University of North Carolina Press, 2003).

Marcus Rediker, *The Slave Ship: A Human History* (New York: Penguin Books, 2007).

Adam Rothman, *Slave Country: American Expansion and the Origins of the Deep South* (Cambridge, MA: Harvard University Press, 2005).

Joshua D. Rothman, *Flush Times and Fever Dreams: A Story of Capitalism and Slavery in the Age of Jackson* (Athens: University of Georgia Press, 2012).

Stephanie Smallwood, *Saltwater Slavery: A Middle Passage from Africa to American Diaspora* (Cambridge, MA: Harvard University Press, 2007).

James Brewer Stewart, *Abolitionist Politics and the Coming of the Civil War* (Amherst: University of Massachusetts Press, 2008).

George William van Cleve, *A Slaveholders' Union: Slavery, Politics, and the Constitution in the Early American Republic* (Chicago: University of Chicago Press, 2010).

Elizabeth R. Varon, *Disunion! The Coming of the American Civil War, 1789–1859* (Chapel Hill: University of North Carolina Press, 2008).

Jonathan Daniel Wells, *The Origins of the Southern Middle Class, 1800–1861* (Chapel Hill: University of North Carolina Press, 2004).

Sean Wilentz, *The Rise of American Democracy: Jefferson to Lincoln* (New York: W.W. Norton & Company, 2005).

Gordon S. Wood, *Empire of Liberty: A History of the Early Republic, 1789–1815* (New York: Oxford University Press, 2009).

THE SECTIONAL CRISIS, 1830–1850

Topics Covered in this Chapter:

- The Rise of the Second Party System
- The 1840s, Texas Annexation, and Manifest Destiny
- The Rise of Abolitionism and the Proslavery Defense
- Importance of Westward Expansion
- Crisis and Compromise in the Early 1850s

2

Introduction

By the 1830s, white southerners were already formulating arguments that they would later use to justify leaving the Union. With the tall and lanky John C. Calhoun leading the way, South Carolinians built the case for states' rights. Over the next three decades, from 1830 to secession in 1860–1861, white southerners continued to formulate their states' rights doctrines, believing that such ideas could counter antislavery sentiments building in the North. Although antislavery opinions could be found as far back as colonial America, and antislavery sentiments circulated even among white southerners in the early 1800s, abolitionism became a powerful reform movement in the 1830s. The rise of a visible and vocal abolitionist movement in the antebellum era was countered by an equally active proslavery faction.

Angry white southerners trumpeted proslavery and states' rights arguments and placed constant pressure on the national political system to meet their demands for the protection of slavery, especially the expansion of bondage into the new territories and states of the West. The two main political parties that formed the Second Party System of the antebellum era, the Democrats and Whigs, managed to endure until the 1850s despite growing divisions within their ranks. Southern Democrats and southern Whigs in the 1830s and 1840s strongly supported slavery, even while many northern Democrats and Whigs opposed it. How could members of the same party hold such different views? Politics in this period was highly localized; candidates for office could hold divergent opinions and still remain within the same party. Liberty and equality for whites only was the battle cry of southern politicians, both Democrat and Whig. But the power of the political parties could not stem the rising tide of abolitionist sentiment in the North, nor of proslavery passion in the South.

The Rise of the Second Party System

The Declaration of Independence had declared unequivocally, in language that has echoed around the world, that "all men are created equal." But while the rhetoric emanating from the Declaration, the American Revolution, and the Constitutional Convention would seem to have created a broad-based democracy, in reality American political culture in the 1790s and early 1800s was not rooted in popular participation. Of course, slaves, women, and free African Americans were excluded from voting and, in fact, from other forms of political engagement. During the Revolution, African Americans had served the cause of Independence with distinction. Women played key roles as patriots by holding rallies and organizing parades. Yet after the Revolution, nearly every state (except New Jersey) wrote constitutions that restricted suffrage to white men who were property holders, excluding not just women and African Americans from voting, but substantial numbers of poor white men as well. The first organized political groups, which historians and political scientists refer to as the First Party System, were the Federalists and the Republicans (also known as the Democratic-Republicans). So even when the first political parties formed in the 1790s American democracy was still far from fulfilling its promise.

FIGURE 2.1 *$1000 note showing John C. Calhoun (left) and President Andrew Jackson (right). The Granger Collection, NYC—All rights reserved*

Throughout the early 1800s the Federalists and Republicans battled for supremacy. The Federalists weakened significantly during the War of 1812 between America and Britain largely because Anglophile (or pro-British) Federalist Party leaders left themselves open to attacks of disloyalty. After 1815, the Federalists were no longer much of a political force, and for the next fifteen years, from about 1815 to about 1830, the Democratic-Republicans, soon to be known simply as the Democrats, were the only viable party. The election of Democrat Andrew Jackson as president in 1828 helped to focus the political opposition that led to a new party, the Whigs. From the early 1830s through the early 1850s the Democrats and Whigs competed in what scholars call the Second Party System, important for our purposes because during this period the sectional crisis worsened, abolitionism became a political force, and proslavery arguments made their way into national political discourse. Ultimately the Second Party System, though strong for more than two decades, would collapse under the weight of slavery and the sectional conflict.

Few voters knew precisely what Andrew Jackson stood for when he was elected in 1828, a victory largely dependent upon his success at the Battle of New Orleans in 1814–1815 during the War of 1812. Jackson could be overbearing, demanding, and aggressive; his political opponents accused him of being little more than a backwoods farmer who had no manners and a fiery temper. He had also acquired a somewhat dubious reputation as a tyrant in dealing with the Seminole Indians in Florida after the war and in fights and duels over the intervening years. Of course, these were the precise characteristics that frontier Americans valued, and the popularity of "Old Hickory" with common voters carried him into office and made him one of the most popular presidents of the antebellum era. Voters may have had little knowledge of Jackson's actual political views, but they identified with his rough demeanor, past military successes, and brash manner.

As president, Jackson was forced to take stands on important issues, positions that earned him supporters and detractors. One of the most challenging issues for Jackson arose with the emergence of sectionalism in the Nullification Crisis when the doctrine of states' rights first became a powerful political topic. Historians consider slavery the chief long-term cause of the Civil War, but the doctrine of states' rights also reflected the evolution of an increasingly assertive South that helped put the nation on the path to hostility and division. On the eve of the disunion in 1860, white southerners would harken back to ideas formed in 1830 about the power of states to secede from the Union because their individual state interests superseded that of the federal government. But by 1860 such arguments were already decades old, having first become prominent in 1828 in the Nullification Crisis. According to historian William W. Freehling, many of the arguments and justifications that southerners would employ in 1860 were formulated much earlier, and within this earlier crisis we can see the signs of the formation of a southern regional identity distinct from the North. In fact, one could go back even farther in time, to the Virginia and Kentucky Resolutions of 1798–1799, state laws that rejected the centralizing Alien and Sedition Acts. The resolutions emphasized the importance of retaining state powers in contrast to the federal government, notions at the heart of the Nullification Crisis.

At issue in the Nullification Crisis was the elevated tariff of 1828 (a tariff is a tax levied on imports and exports) passed by Congress. The tariff raised the prices of manufactured goods that southerners bought from Europe and elsewhere. Southerners thought that the high tariff was beneficial to New England manufacturers and unfair to them. The tariff drew anger throughout the South, but especially from South Carolina, where John C. Calhoun defended his region's interests by criticizing the higher tariff. He and like-minded southerners called it the "Tariff of Abominations." Calhoun wrote an essay entitled "South Carolina Exposition and Protest" in 1828 in which he argued that South Carolina (and other states) had a right to nullify federal laws opposed to their interests. In other words, Calhoun argued that states did not have to obey or abide by all federal laws. This was an early form of the states' rights argument, the notion that state laws and state governments should supersede the laws of the federal government.

In November 1832, a convention of South Carolinians met and officially and publicly declared the 1828 tariff "null and void" in the state, forbidding the collection of customs duties. A furious Jackson responded by getting Congress to pass the Force Bill in 1833, which authorized the president to use troops in South Carolina to enforce the law. At the same time Speaker of the House Henry Clay proposed a lower tariff. South Carolina was reluctant to give in but was virtually alone on the issue of nullification; no other southern state backed South Carolina publicly, and state leaders saw the lower tariff as an escape route. The Compromise of 1833, engineered by Clay, settled the Nullification Crisis. Once again, crisis was averted, and again, only temporarily.

Jackson thus created enemies among some extreme states' rights southerners, but his positions on economic issues and his eagerness to exercise executive authority also encouraged the formal development of a political opposition. Jackson and the Democrats had inherited from the Jeffersonian Democratic-Republicans a belief in the virtues of small government. In Congress Democrats opposed the use of public funds to pay for internal improvement projects. The Jacksonians were equally suspicious of bankers, whom they labeled "speculators" and "money-changers." They railed against paper money as illegitimate and argued in favor of using species such as gold and silver for exchange. In strongly worded vetoes of laws passed by Congress, the president reiterated the Jeffersonian distrust of businessmen, bankers, and capitalists, while reaffirming support for small government and a nation of independent farmers. As historian Michael F. Holt has shown, congressional leaders slapped Jackson with the nickname "King Andrew" for his willingness to veto laws passed in Congress, and by the early 1830s those leaders inside and outside Washington began to form the new Whig Party. Led in Congress by Henry Clay and Daniel Webster, the Whigs could soon claim support from all regions of the country. In opposition to the Democrats, Whigs generally supported an active role for government in encouraging economic growth and supported policies that would lead to internal improvements, industrialization, and urbanization. Historian Elizabeth Varon found that the more progressive Whigs permitted women greater involvement in party activities than did the rival Democrats. It is important to note that within the Democratic and Whig parties, northern and southern wings often held different views on slavery and yet remained in the same party. Northern Whigs, for example, included antislavery supporters such as future President Abraham Lincoln and former President John Quincy Adams. Yet southern Whigs remained staunchly proslavery and could never have achieved considerable power in states such as North Carolina without defending the institution. Thus, the Second Party System helped to tie the Union together, as both parties harbored northern and southern leaders and voters.

The 1840s, Texas Annexation, and Manifest Destiny

The 1840s began with healthy signs for democracy and for the Whig Party in particular. During the 1840 presidential campaign, the Whigs adopted their opponents' democratic flair and held rallies, marches, parades, and other popular campaign events. Symbolized by that enduring democratic symbol of humble beginnings—the log cabin—the victorious campaign of Whig candidate William Henry Harrison, whose early death would elevate Vice President John Tyler to the highest office, demonstrated a vibrant and healthy political culture. The log-cabin symbol appeared in newspaper mastheads, on parade banners, umbrellas, and medallions, and other campaign paraphernalia. Slaves and free African Americans were still unable to vote even in local elections, and women were confined to participating in campaign events without the ability to vote. Yet the 1840 campaign seemed to embody a livelier democratic politics.

While other territorial concerns distracted American leaders, including disputes over the Oregon Territory, Texas emerged as the greatest source of controversy. Difficulties between Mexico and America over Texas dated to the early years of the 1800s, but in 1824 Mexico rendered a decision that would profoundly alter the controversy. In that year Mexican leaders, hoping to spur development, offered American settlers financial incentives to come to Texas. During the 1820s, thousands of Americans, many of whom were southern planters who brought their slaves with

FIGURE 2.2 *[1840 Presidential campaign handkerchief] Log cabin with flag on top reading "Harrison and Reform." Library of Congress, LC-USZ62-43921*

them, settled in Texas, so many that a concerned Mexico tried to stop the influx of Americans in 1830. Yet throughout the 1830s people from across America journeyed to make their fortunes in the Mexican territory. Unable to stem the tide of foreign settlers, the Mexican government began using force in 1835, and the Americans responded in kind until outright fighting erupted in 1836. The leader of Mexico, General Antonio Lopez de Santa Anna, led troops into Texas, successfully subduing a group of ragtag Americans (including David Crockett) at the Battle of the Alamo in San Antonio. Sam Houston, a Virginia native who would later become the president of an independent Texas, ultimately led the American settlers in battle against Santa Anna. At the Battle of San Jacinto in April 1836, Houston and his army captured the Mexican general. Texas had won its independence from Mexico.

Attempts in the late 1830s and early 1840s to annex Texas failed, but fortunes changed when Tennessee Democrat James K. Polk was elected president in 1844. Historian Amy S. Greenberg found that the Democrats had been the loudest proponents of an idea that came to be known as "Manifest Destiny," that America was destined by God and by nature to occupy all of North America. "Manifest Destiny" had been popularized in newspapers and magazines by Democratic editors and writers such as John O'Sullivan. The democratic exuberance felt by many Americans in the early 1840s was embodied in the optimistic notion that expansion was not only good for America, but also good for the people it would come to rule. Polk had declared the importance of occupying both Oregon and Texas, a strategy that had helped him win the presidency. Now he was following through. Polk supported the annexation of Texas, and the former republic became a state near the end of 1845. Many northerners had opposed Texas annexation because they knew that the new state would be open to slavery, and thus elect two more proslavery senators and any number of proslavery congressmen, giving weight to abolitionist cries of a "Slave Power Conspiracy." But antislavery northerners were unable to prevent the admission of Texas.

The controversy over Texas is important to the coming of the Civil War for a number of reasons. First, westward territorial expansion sparked a fierce political battle between proslavery and antislavery forces. White southerners wanted the western territories and any new states admitted from them to be open to slavery. In the minds of many slaveholders, bondage needed to expand to endure, and the wide-open spaces of the West seemed to them

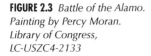

FIGURE 2.3 *Battle of the Alamo. Painting by Percy Moran. Library of Congress, LC-USZC4-2133*

to be ideally suited to plantation agriculture. Leading politicians such as South Carolina's John C. Calhoun argued that the West represented slavery's future. Tens of thousands of southern farmers and planters had already moved from the older Atlantic states of Virginia and the Carolinas to settle in Alabama, Mississippi, Arkansas, Texas, and Louisiana. The southwestern corner of the continent seemed the next logical destination for slavery's expansion.

Texas statehood and Manifest Destiny were also key factors in causing the war between the United States and Mexico from 1846 to 1848. Democratic Party expansionists coveted not only Texas but the New Mexico and California territories as well. Mexicans understandably bristled against the arrogant American assumption that the entire continent was destined for U.S. control and refused American efforts to purchase the territories. As historian Timothy J. Henderson has explained, Polk sent General Zachary Taylor across the Nueces River to set up camp along the Rio Grande River, deliberately provoking the Mexican government. Mexican soldiers eventually took the bait and reportedly crossed the Rio Grande to confront American soldiers. Seizing the opportunity, Congress declared war on Mexico in May 1846.

Not everyone favored war, however, especially antislavery northerners who charged that the battle was manufactured by a proslavery president simply to extend bondage. New England writer Henry David Thoreau refused to pay his taxes because of his opposition to the war and slavery and was briefly jailed. Profoundly affected by this turn of events, he delivered a groundbreaking lecture on individual conscience in 1848 entitled "The Rights and Duties of the Individual in Relation to the Government," which was later incorporated into his seminal work *Civil Disobedience*. John Quincy Adams and Abraham Lincoln questioned the war's necessity, as did abolitionist Joshua Giddings. Even John C. Calhoun, Robert Toombs, and other leading southern politicians questioned the wisdom of the war. Political rhetoric became especially heated when Pennsylvania Democratic Congressman David Wilmot introduced a proposal in 1846 to prohibit slavery from any land added to the U.S. as a result of the war.

What became known as the Wilmot Proviso never became law but it generated great controversy. Wilmot's strong antislavery proposal laid bare the tensions and divisions within the Democratic Party. Northern and southern wings of the party split over slavery and western expansion. "Barnburners," as the more strident Democrats were known, included Gideon Welles, Preston King, and Hannibal Hamlin, all of whom joined Wilmot in supporting his proposal. Conservative or "Hunker" Democrats sought to minimize the conflicts over slavery. Even more dramatic was the white southern reaction to the proviso.

Southerners responded with fury, claiming the proviso was an insult to their region. Newspapers, pamphlets, and fiery speeches railed against Wilmot's proposal. The "Alabama Platform," put forth with the support of the state's fire-eating editor and politician William Yancey, confronted the antislavery sentiments of the Wilmot Proviso with proslavery doctrines. Any new state, the Alabama Platform declared, should be open to slavery. Politicians and state legislatures throughout the South endorsed these principles. Although Polk had not intended to worsen sectional hostilities by going to war with Mexico, northern politicians who found in the war evidence of the "slave power" in action helped to stir anger in the South.

The war lasted longer than the enthusiastic administration believed it might, until a treaty was signed two years later. While the armies battled along the border with Texas and into Mexico, Polk also sent troops to capture California and the New Mexico territories. Shortly after the war began, Brigadier General Stephen W. Kearny captured Santa Fe and then combined forces in California with explorer (and later the first Republican Party candidate for president) John C. Fremont in the Bear Flag Revolt.

Before the end of 1846, California was firmly in American hands. The fighting lingered until February 1848 when, in the Treaty of Guadalupe Hidalgo, Mexico ceded claims to California and New Mexico to the United States. Although the United States grew in size, it paid a heavy price as the war significantly exacerbated sectional hostilities.

Finally, in regard to the importance of the Mexican–American War to the coming war between North and South, the battles in Mexico and the southwest became vital training grounds for many of the soldiers and officers who would come to play crucial roles in the Civil War. Robert E. Lee of Virginia served as a trusted aide to General Winfield Scott and from Veracruz marched with his army on Mexico City where he was wounded at a battle in Chapultepec. During the Civil War Winfield Scott commanded the Union army while Lee would emerge as the head of the Army of Northern Virginia. Braxton Bragg, later a Confederate general at Shiloh, Corinth, Chickamauga, and elsewhere during the Civil War, served at the Battle of Fort Brown and the Battle of Monterrey. Ulysses S. Grant served as a lieutenant during the Mexican–American War under Zachary Taylor and Winfield Scott, seeing action in numerous battles. Many other officers and soldiers who were veterans of the Mexican–American War fought for the Union or the Confederacy more than a decade later.

The Rise of Abolitionism and the Proslavery Defense

Antislavery sentiment had been a presence in America almost from its inception. But we must be careful not to conflate the terms "antislavery" and "abolitionist." Many northern whites were opposed to slavery not on the grounds of morality or justice but rather because they believed slavery led inevitably to an economy in which wealthy planters dominated the rest of white society. In what became known as "free labor ideology," white northerners worried that wherever slavery spread, low wages, the stunting of manufacturing and enterprise, and the denigration of labor soon followed. Abolitionists also believed that slavery warped the development of an economy and society but they also believed that on its face it was immoral and unjust to hold other human beings as property. Abolitionists were a small, often despised minority, even in the North, and were denounced as fanatical reformers by both northern and southern critics.

FIGURE 2.4 *Am I not a man and a brother? Courtesy of the New York Public Library, 427780*

During the American Revolution the egalitarian rhetoric of the era prompted many to join the abolitionist movement. The great radical of the period, Thomas Paine, whose best-selling *Common Sense* spurred the quest for independence, authored an important early antislavery tract entitled "African Slavery in America." Early abolitionists were heartened by the decision in the famous Somerset case in 1772 that declared slavery to be unsupported by common law in England. Quakers in Philadelphia and sympathetic radicals such as Paine continued to be active in abolitionism after the Revolution. The New York Manumission Society, founded in 1785, comprised leading statesmen including John Jay, Alexander Hamilton, and Aaron Burr. They pressured merchants and traders in New York to end their affiliations with bondage. Many of these wealthy and prominent New Yorkers conducted correspondence with abolitionists in England. Aided by the transatlantic movement against slavery, northerners formed abolitionist societies that published newspapers, printed pamphlets, and held meetings and conferences. Ultimately these eighteenth-century antislavery societies had little impact on southern slavery but were highly successful in encouraging northern state legislatures to outlaw bondage by the turn of the nineteenth century.

Abolitionists wanted to abolish slavery in America and the world; on this point most in the abolitionist movement agreed.

Beyond this basic point, however, there were significant disagreements among abolitionists over whether slavery should end gradually or quickly; whether slavery should be acknowledged as a *fait accompli* in the southeast and efforts focused instead on preventing its spread to other states; whether moral and religious objections to slavery were paramount; and what role if any the federal government should play in abolishing or limiting the spread of bondage.

Although the abolitionist movement by the early 1800s was diverse and embraced a range of opinions, the movement might usefully be divided into "gradualists" and "immediatists," depending upon one's approach to the problem of slavery. Until the 1960s, many historians tended to consider the more radical or immediate abolitionists as fanatical agitators who hastened the demise of the Union by uncompromisingly demanding the end of slavery. Beginning in the 1960s, however, scholars reconsidered the role of abolitionists and emphasized their principled commitment to ending slavery and racial injustice.

Of all the reform movements that circulated in antebellum America, including movements to expand rights for women, to reduce alcohol consumption, and to erect public school systems, the most controversial reform effort was the movement to end slavery. While many other reform movements found support among northerners and southerners alike, abolitionism was almost exclusively a northern movement, especially after 1830. Abolitionism helped to split the sections apart and therefore is crucial to understanding the coming of the Civil War.

The leading movement for gradual emancipation of slaves was called the colonization movement. The American Colonization Society was formed in 1816 to promote the gradual and voluntary freeing of slaves so that they could be sent back to Africa. The idea was the same that had been used for Indians: removal to a faraway place. This movement attracted a wide range of supporters from Quakers to legal and political leaders such as John Marshall and Henry Clay. The colonization movement was a safe, moderate position for southerners who wanted to end slavery. They could advocate the end of slavery without looking as though they were fanatics or antithetical the South's interests. By 1830, the colonization movement had transported more than one thousand African Americans to a colony in northwestern Africa called Liberia. Although the colonization movement began to lose steam in the 1840s, descendants of these immigrant former slaves from America continued to rule the African country of Liberia until the late twentieth century.

While the colonization movement garnered the support of prominent political leaders and even presidents, it was eventually overtaken by the immediatist approach, led by white abolitionists such as William Lloyd Garrison as well as African American opponents of slavery, most notably Frederick Douglass. Garrison, a fervent Boston abolitionist who began publishing the famous antislavery newspaper *The Liberator* in 1831, helped found the American Anti-Slavery Society in 1833 with Robert Purvis, a free black, and Theodore Weld, a minister. Although southern ministers were to play central roles in defending slavery, northern religious figures such as Weld often spoke in favor of abolitionism. Like them Garrison was moved by the moral and religious objections to bondage. Born in Massachusetts in 1805, Garrison was an early advocate of abolition, using his talents as a newspaper editor to promote the cause. He was unusually progressive and supported women's suffrage when even other abolitionists wanted to keep women from active participation in the movement. Strident in his views, he denounced the Constitution as a proslavery document, pointing out that the Declaration of Independence was a

FIGURE 2.5 *Frederick Douglass, head-and-shoulders portrait, facing right. Library of Congress, LC-USZ62-15887*

clearer statement of equality. He was widely reviled in the South and repeatedly condemned as a radical and fanatic by the southern press. He was denounced in Congress by southerners and scorned in political speeches. But few white men did more to promote the antislavery cause than Garrison.

Other antislavery activists would take paths different from Garrison's to engage in national party politics. The Liberty Party and the Free Soil Party were important third parties in the 1840s, running candidates for president who backed the elimination of the Fugitive Slave Clause of the Constitution and the immediate end of bondage. Though neither party garnered much support, a fact that reminds us of the limited popularity of abolitionism with the majority of northern voters, the Free Soil Party would later merge with the newly formed Republican Party in the mid-1850s.

At the top of the distinguished list of prominent African American antislavery activists was Frederick Douglass. In his voluminous writings, particularly *Narrative of the Life of Frederick Douglass, an American Slave*, published in 1845, Douglass passionately argued for the immediate end of slavery. Born into slavery, Douglass escaped to the North and became one of the most famous orators of nineteenth-century America. When he published his autobiography in 1845, skeptics scoffed that no black man could have authored such a moving and well-written work, but Douglass soon emerged on the public lecture circuit to tell his story of having been a slave. His *Narrative* sold thousands of copies in America and also reached a broad audience in Europe. In fact, Douglass traveled to England and Ireland and was pleased to find that he was generally treated well. Throughout the 1850s and the Civil War, Douglass pressured politicians to support abolition, and he developed a relationship with Lincoln that no doubt helped to influence the president to issue the Emancipation Proclamation.

Garrison and Douglass knew each other well through their support for women's suffrage and their direct involvement in the abolitionist cause. Despite an early collaboration and a friendship based upon mutual abhorrence for bondage, Garrison and Douglass divided over antislavery tactics, especially the use of violence in ending slavery. As a pacifist Garrison remained steadfast in his belief that slavery had to be denounced through moral persuasion, by making clear through peaceful means slavery's immorality. Douglass, on the contrary, came to believe that slavery was so deeply entrenched in the South that violence was sometimes an acceptable weapon in the abolitionist arsenal.

FIGURE 2.6 *Anthony Burns, in various scenes through his life as an abolitionist. "Anthony Burns," Boston: R.M. Edwards, 1855 Broadside Prints and Photographs Division, Library of Congress (50)*

Garrison harbored a hatred for slavery that often erupted into public spectacle and moral outrage, while Douglass was equally passionate in his abolitionism but also believed that founding documents such as the Declaration of Independence and the Constitution could be used in the fight against proslavery forces. Such differences in strategy were significant enough to cause a major rift between Garrison and Douglass in the 1840s, as abolitionism struggled to combat the southern slave power and to convince white northerners of the immorality of bondage. The rift between two leading abolitionists no doubt prevented the formation of a united antislavery front, but the forces of abolitionism (though never able to win over a majority of northern whites) were potent enough to attract the notice of proslavery southerners who defended their institutions against northern criticism.

Abolitionists met their match in proslavery southerners. Prior to about 1830, it was not uncommon to hear antislavery sentiments from white southerners themselves. The questioning of slavery on moral, religious, or economic grounds appeared in newspaper editorials, books, sermons, and political speeches. But in the 1830s this changed, and the South became virulently intolerant of abolitionism in any form. One reason was the fear and panic sparked by Nat Turner's rebellion in Virginia in 1831 that resulted in the murder of many whites. Reaction to the rebellion was powerful and quick, as southern state legislatures placed new limits on the mobility of even free African Americans. Another reason for the crackdown on dissent was a response to abolitionists. Southerners were put on the defensive, and believed that they had to defend the institution against northern and British criticism. As a result, historians have identified a broad "proslavery argument" that drew from history, the Bible, Christian tradition, economics, legal precedent, philosophy, and science to justify slavery. The proslavery argument was not just a defense of bondage, but a broader critique of free labor society and a far-reaching attempt at vindicating the South.

The invention of the cotton gin had contributed significantly to the explosion of the southern slave population, and southerners themselves realized that regional wealth and prosperity depended on the health of slavery. So southerners thought that any attack upon slavery was a direct attack on southern economic interests. But under the attack of northern abolitionists, southerners began to think that slavery was not just important to their economy, but to the structure of their entire society. Thus as abolitionism grew increasingly vocal, southerners grew increasingly aggressive in their defense of slavery.

By the 1830s, southern politicians and intellectuals began to form a collection of reasoned defenses of their region. Writer after writer in the South believed that if he or she could only make the North see the South's side of the argument rationally, if he or she could contribute to the debate one more piece of evidence from the Bible, or history, or philosophy, then perhaps the hostilities between the sections would subside. Southerners held on to this faith tenaciously. It was as if southerners were preparing a huge legal brief to defend slavery in the court of public opinion. It is hard to overestimate the strong feelings that many southerners had on the issue. They wrote pamphlet after pamphlet, book after book, and essay after essay to defend the institution.

Even as the North attacked slavery, southerners attacked northern society and culture with equal venom. Southerners often linked antebellum northern movements such as abolitionism to

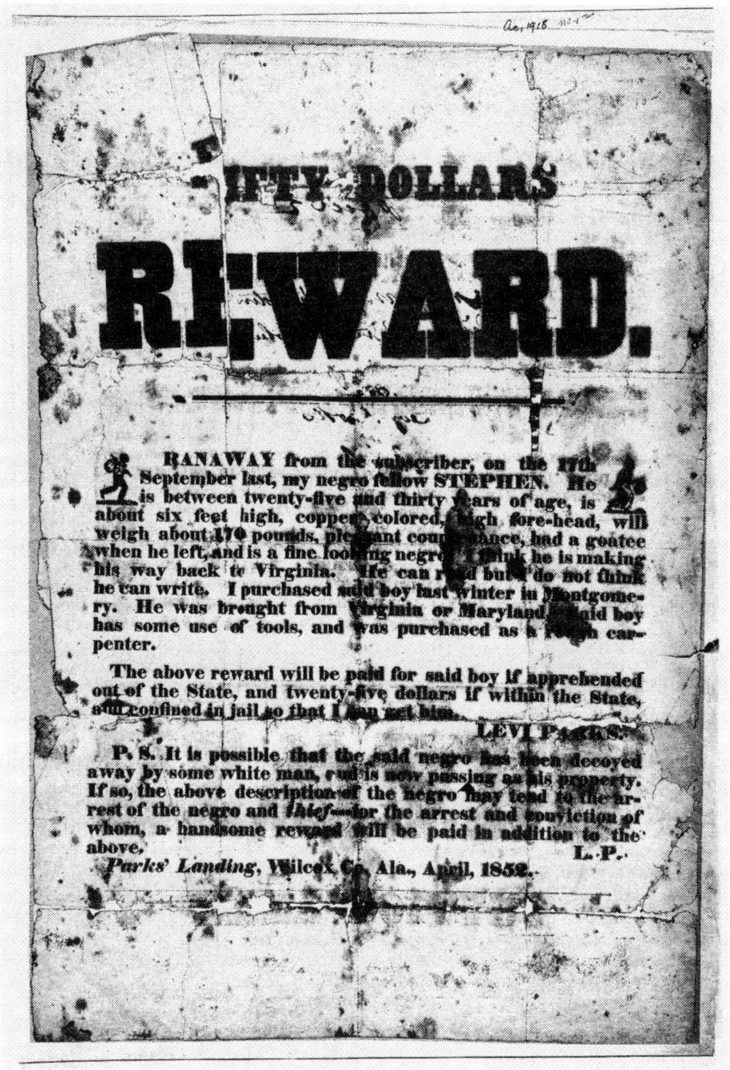

FIGURE 2.7 *Poster offering fifty dollars reward for the capture of a runaway slave.* Stephen. An American Time Capsule: Three Centuries of Broadsides and Other Printed Ephemera. *Courtesy of the Library of Congress*

the region's Puritan past. Like their abolitionist descendants, the Puritans were intrusive and obsessed with moral reform, "busybodies" who could not restrain themselves from interfering in other people's business. And like their Puritan ancestors, abolitionists were self-righteous, bullying, and consumed with misplaced philanthropy. As southerner George Fitzhugh wrote in *DeBow's Review*, "Misanthropy, hypocrisy, diseased philanthropy, envy, hatred, fanaticism, and all the worst passions of the human heart, were the ruling characteristics of the English Puritans; and they continue to be the ruling characteristics of New-England Yankees."

As Fitzhugh's quotation indicated, religious divisions between northerners and southerners were becoming acute by the 1840s.

As religious northerners, led by prominent preachers such as Henry Ward Beecher, moved toward the view that slavery was a sin, religious white southerners were concluding that slavery was part of God's plan. Among Baptists the schism over slavery permanently divided northern and southern members of the faith. In 1845 the Southern Baptist Convention split from the northern wing of the church. The Methodists, too, were deeply divided; in fact, fed up with white racism, Philadelphia's Richard Allen, an African American religious and intellectual leader, founded the African Methodist Episcopal Church in 1816. By the 1840s, however, white Methodists were also deeply divided. In 1845, the same year the Baptists split along sectional lines, the northern and southern Methodists went their separate ways, leading to the founding of the Methodist Episcopal Church, South.

As these dramatic religious schisms demonstrate, northerners and southerners were coming to view one another by the 1830s and 1840s as mirror opposites. Northerners viewed the South as an undemocratic region dominated politically by planter aristocrats made economically backward by immoral slavery. Slavery was much more than immoral, abolitionists argued; along with slavery came an attachment to rural life that impeded urban development and hindered economic growth. For these northerners, slavery became associated with decay, worn-out and discredited economic and social systems, and undemocratic politics.

Southerners held an equally damning view of northern society. Free labor, in the eyes of many southerners, was a failure and a fraud. Northern factory workers, or "wage slaves," as southerners referred to them, were not really free at all. In fact, said southerners, masters treated their slaves better than factory owners treated their employees. This led to a broader critique of northern society as dominated by filthy, crowded cities with immigrants, and by Yankee businessmen ready to slit throats in the name of competition. Financial panics in 1819, 1837, and 1857 generated suspicion among southerners that Yankee bankers and merchants were to blame for the national economic crisis. So while slavery divided North from South, each region expressed broader critiques of the other's society, economy, and culture. Historians have pointed out that painting an opponent or enemy as "the other," as somehow fundamentally different and even alien, is often a precursor to hatred and war. By the early 1850s, many northerners and southerners came to view each other with jealousy, suspicion, and even hatred. At the center of this mistrust was the fate of the new states and territories of the West.

Importance of Westward Expansion

The acquisition of California and New Mexico as a result of the Mexican–American War considerably expanded the size of the United States, and further developments in the late 1840s and very early 1850s hastened the process of western settlement. In the northwest, the Oregon Territory and its boundary were under dispute through the early 1840s. As the result of an early treaty between America and Britain, both of whom laid claims to the region, Oregon had been jointly occupied. Steady migration of eastern and midwestern settlers over heavily traveled paths such as the Oregon Trail swelled the territory's population. Seeking fresh lands to farm, many of these migrants were young families led by a paid guide who was charged with safely taking them through the perilous Rocky Mountain trails into modern-day California, Oregon, and Washington. The Oregon Trail was more than 2,000 miles long, stretching from Kansas City and snaking northwest to Portland and other destinations near the Pacific Coast. Boarding horse-drawn wagons piled with belongings, families endured

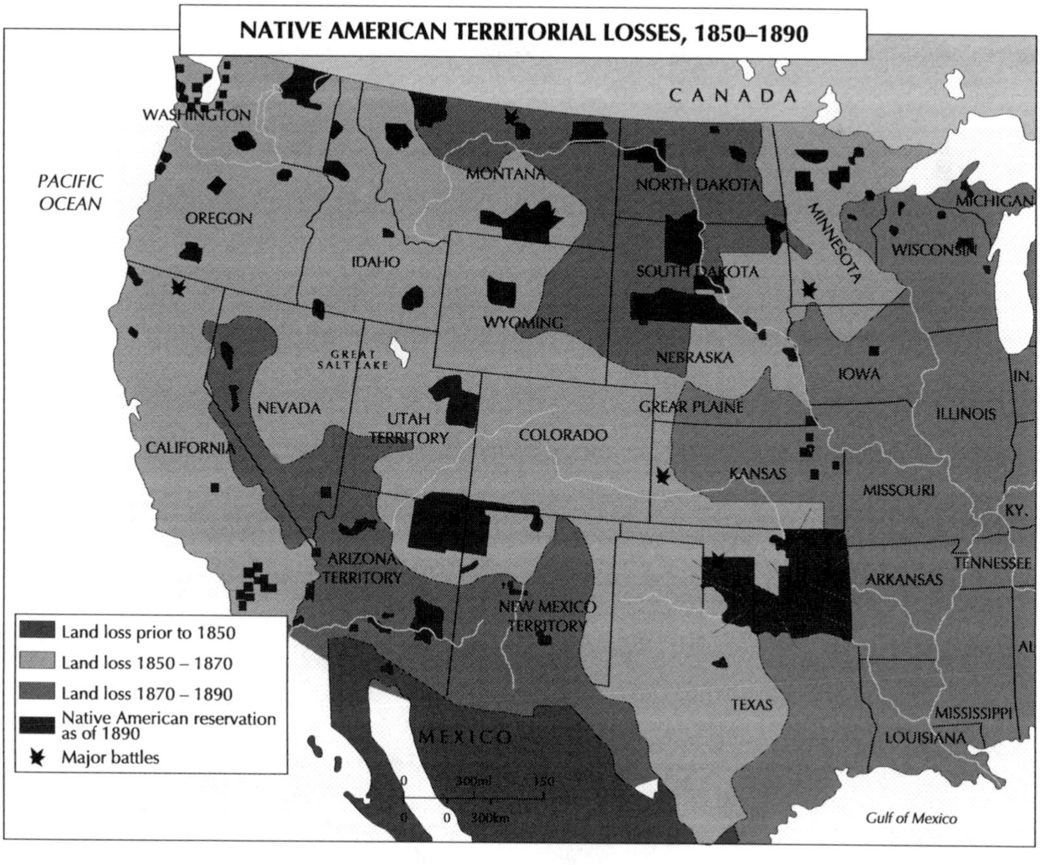

MAP 2.1 *Map of American West with Native Americans*

considerable hardship along the rough trails. Native Americans along the paths were more often helpful guides and traders than hindrances, but nonetheless the journey was arduous, often taking more than six months. Yet the pull of the West was powerful, and tens of thousands of families braved the rough terrain in the 1830s, 1840s, and 1850s.

While the promise of prosperity pulled families to western lands, the discovery of gold in California in the late 1840s drew thousands of young men eager to get rich quickly. After the discovery of gold at John Sutter's mill near the Sierra Nevada in early 1848, travel to California, Utah, and Oregon spiked dramatically. "Forty-niners" sought fortunes in the hills and valleys of California, and small towns seemingly sprang up overnight. Between 1848 and 1855 or so, emigration to the West spiked at 50,000–70,000 people per year. The population growth of the western territories had a number of important implications, both for western development and for the coming of the Civil War.

Migrants to the West traveled over and inhabited lands that had been the homes of Native Americans for thousands of years. Overland Trails split the Plains buffalo herds, imperiling Indians who depended on the animals for survival. Disease also hampered native tribes. In the Great Plains east of the Rocky Mountains, large tribes such as the Sioux were able to survive the diseases settlers brought with them to the West. Other tribes were decimated along the Pacific Coast, especially those who lived in villages and towns. The Sioux tended to travel in smaller groups and were less tied to a specific place so they were not hit as hard by disease. Numbering in the tens of thousands by the late 1840s, the Sioux were among the more powerful tribes inhabiting western lands. After the Indian Removal Act of 1830, one of the more egregiously cruel pieces of legislation of the Jacksonian era, Native Americans had been pushed out of the East and onto reservations in Oklahoma and other western regions. But the Indians living farther west were able to endure in part because other than fur traders from Russia, America, and Europe, the land along the Pacific Coast had escaped the worst effects of white settlement. Although the Great Plains fell into American hands as a result of the Louisiana Purchase in 1803, white settlers did not begin coming in large numbers until the 1830s and 1840s. Historians, anthropologists, and archaeologists estimate that between 300,000 and 400,000 Native Americans lived west of the Mississippi by the time American settlers began moving there in large numbers. While the eastern tribes tended to live in communities and settlements engaged in farming, western

FIGURE 2.8 *The council, Sioux tribe. Courtesy of the Library of Congress Prints and Photographs Division*

Native Americans, especially the Sioux and Cheyenne who lived on the plains, were more nomadic.

Many of these tribes, including the Sioux, would play small roles in the Civil War. In many ways the war militarized the West, as western volunteers replaced small regular garrisons and waged campaigns of unprecedented scale against the Plains tribes. Although they often avoided taking sides directly in the war, Native Americans fought federal troops in Utah, Colorado, Minnesota, and Arizona. Union soldiers grew wary of attacks by Native Americans and the conflicts led the federal government to construct western forts to protect the Union armies of the West. Other Native Americans did in fact join one side of the Civil War: Confederates successfully negotiated terms with the Cherokees (some of whom also owned enslaved people of African descent) and other tribes in the early stages of the war and as many as 8,000 Indians fought for the Union. Whether directly engaged in the fighting or not, Native Americans in the West were active players in American expansion and its political consequences.

Crisis and Compromise in the Early 1850s

American settlement and expansion shaped the course of national politics in the late 1840s and early 1850s. A number of issues came to a head at once, forcing political leaders such as Henry Clay and Stephen Douglas to seek a compromise that might stem the strident rhetoric coming from extremists in the North and the South. One issue of concern was the fact that the borders of the southwestern lands acquired during the Mexican–American War were ill-defined. Texas claimed a large swathe of land to its west, potentially adding tens of thousands of acres to its borders. The borders and future path to statehood for New Mexico and Utah were similarly open to question. With the admission of Texas into the Union as a slave state, northerners worried that all of the new lands and the states to come from the West would be proslavery as well.

Equally troubling to Americans was the admission of California into the Union. With the influx of settlers into California after the discovery of gold, the territory had a sufficient population to apply for statehood, a process laid down in the U.S. Constitution. White southerners believed they had an ally in the White House (then called the Executive Mansion) when the proslavery hero of the Mexican War, Whig Zachary Taylor, won the presidency in the election of 1848. Taylor, a southerner and a slaveholder, seemed to southerners an ideal protector of slavery and to many northerners he seemed to offer further evidence that a slaveholding conspiracy controlled the federal government.

Southerners were disappointed, however, when President Taylor took a contrary position on the admission of California into the Union. By 1850 there were not enough slaves within the territory to render likely its admission into the Union as a slave state, so southerners hoped the process would move slowly so as to gain time to increase the slave population. To their dismay, though, President Taylor backed the immediate admission of California into the Union, meaning almost certainly that it would dramatically increase land under free soil control.

Two other issues boiled to the surface as controversy over California's admission into the Union and the borders of the southwestern lands festered. Antislavery northerners had grown increasingly unhappy that slavery and the slave trade operated freely within the bounds of the U.S. capital. They argued that as the seat of the federal government, the buying and selling of human beings should be banned. Britain had banned slavery in the 1830s, and many abolitionists had traveled to London to attend antislavery meetings, becoming all the more painfully aware that in their own nation's capital the buying and selling of human beings was legal. The *Pearl* Incident, in which more than seventy slaves attempted to escape the capital in 1848, brought the issue of slavery in Washington, D.C. greater attention. Abolitionists were determined that if slavery was allowed to continue in the South, at least it should be banned in the same city where the Congress and the president resided.

Southerners responded to complaints about the slave trade in Washington with equally vehement complaints that the federal government was not doing enough to recapture enslaved people who had emancipated themselves by fleeing to the North. The Fugitive Slave Clause of the Constitution, reinforced by the Fugitive Slave Act of 1793, required the federal government to help slaveholders locate and capture slaves who had escaped to northern cities. But southerners believed that this law was not being adequately enforced, and that white and black northerners were complicit in helping slaves to run away and conceal their true identities.

During a meeting in Nashville, Tennessee in June 1850, delegates from throughout the South convened to debate a course of action if in fact the federal government prohibited slavery in the West or took any other antislavery actions. Having averted the official passage of the Wilmot Proviso, southern politicians were determined to thwart any other perceived legislative threats to slavery. Delegates included leaders such as Jefferson Davis of Mississippi, but moderates eventually prevailed and the convention took no direct action to authorize secession. Still, the Nashville Convention was further evidence that tensions ran high in the summer and fall of 1850.

As the results of the Nashville Convention showed, many Americans in 1850 favored compromise over civil war. The key question was how to resolve the various hot-button issues while getting enough support from both sides for passage in Congress. Clay and Douglas, leaders of the Whig and Democratic parties, respectively, helped to shepherd five bills through Congress that, taken together, are known as the Compromise of 1850. Making the compromise possible was the death of President Taylor and the accession to the office by Millard Fillmore, who supported the compromise. Passed and signed into law by President Fillmore, the Compromise of 1850 sought to calm sectional tensions, but it sowed seeds of discord that would reappear in short order.

Clay, Calhoun, and Webster, the aging triumvirate, delivered influential speeches in favor of the compromises. The laws passed in part because of the support provided by these respected statesmen. In one of the more famous of the speeches delivered in favor of the compromise, Webster lent his support. Although a senator from Massachusetts, a hotbed of abolitionism, Webster gave his famous "Seventh of March Speech" in support of compromise, saying in part that:

It is not to be denied that we live in the midst of strong agitations, and are surrounded by very considerable dangers to our institutions and our government. The imprisoned winds are let loose. The East, the North, and the stormy South combine to throw the whole sea into commotion, to toss its billows to the skies, and disclose its profoundest depths. I do not affect to regard myself, Mr. President, as holding, or as fit to hold, the helm in this combat with the political elements; but I have a duty to perform, and I mean to perform it with fidelity, not without a sense of existing dangers, but not without hope.

Webster paid a heavy political price for backing the compromise. He was vigorously attacked by northerners, especially abolitionist intellectuals such as Theodore Parker, James Russell Lowell, and Ralph Waldo Emerson. Webster died two years later in 1852, his popularity still suffering in Massachusetts.

Although politically costly to Webster, the chances of compromise increased with his support, and the laws passed in September. The Compromise of 1850 allowed for the settlement of the boundaries of Texas and the organization of New Mexico and Utah, the admission of California as a free state, and the continuation of slavery in Washington, D.C. but the abolition of the slave trade within the bounds of the capital city. The status of slavery in the future states of New Mexico and Utah would be decided by "popular sovereignty," or a democratic election that would theoretically express the will of the states' citizens. In addition, a long-simmering dispute between Texas and New Mexico was settled in favor of the latter state; in compensation, the federal government promised to absorb Texas's debt.

The most controversial piece of the compromise was the Fugitive Slave Act, one of the most controversial laws ever passed by Congress. The law demonstrated an important truth about antebellum America: even though they could not vote or hold political office, African Americans placed unceasing pressure on the American political system by seeking liberty by running away from slavery. White southern anger over the constant stream of fugitives escaping bondage and making their way through the Underground Railroad to freedom in the North or Canada continued to build throughout the early 1800s. The Constitution had included a "Fugitive Slave Clause" that appeased southerners who feared that runaways who made it to free states would never be returned. Yet southerners quickly deemed the clause a failure, and a new Fugitive Slave Law passed in 1793 required free states to return accused runaways to their masters. Still, throughout the early nineteenth century enslaved men and women continued to resist bondage by running away, and northern states refused to return suspected fugitives. Pennsylvania, Massachusetts, and other northern states passed "personal liberty laws" designed to protect escaped slaves, to the great frustration of white southerners who demanded the return of their property. Newspapers of the era contain numerous advertisements demanding the return of runaways and promising rewards.

The new Fugitive Slave Act of 1850 passed as part of the compromise reaffirmed the federal government's responsibility to pursue fugitive slaves more vigorously by creating for the first time a federal bureaucratic apparatus to hear cases of accused fugitives. But as northerners soon found out, the 1850 law went further. It required any federal officer to arrest a suspected runaway slave, and threatened to fine him the substantial sum of $1000 if he failed to do his duty. Even worse, the law required ordinary citizens to aid in the process. Citizens were required to form a posse when needed and to hunt down and capture runaways. The legal wrangling over the Fugitive Slave Law continued into the Civil War, and the 1850s witnessed dozens of emotionally powerful cases of the attempted rescue or recapture of runaway slaves.

In February 1851 a coffeehouse waiter named Shadrach Minkins who had escaped slavery in Virginia and settled in Boston was discovered by agents representing his former master. One can just imagine the constant state of fear in which runaways such as Minkins lived. Although the Massachusetts capital harbored hundreds of black and white abolitionists who might come to the aid of an accused fugitive, Minkins was terrified of being discovered. Unbeknownst to Minkins, two of the men in the coffeehouse were a deputy marshal and a former constable. They arrested Minkins for being a runaway and rushed him to the courthouse.

Boston's African American community was keenly aware of the Fugitive Slave Law, and abolitionists of both races had spent much of the fall and winter of 1850–1851 denouncing the law. African American conventions condemned the law and harkened back to the Declaration of Independence's claim that "all men are created equal." From the perspective of white and black abolitionists, the worst feature of the law was that a slaveholder merely had to give his word and the case was nearly won; there was little room for the presentation of evidence or the calling of witnesses

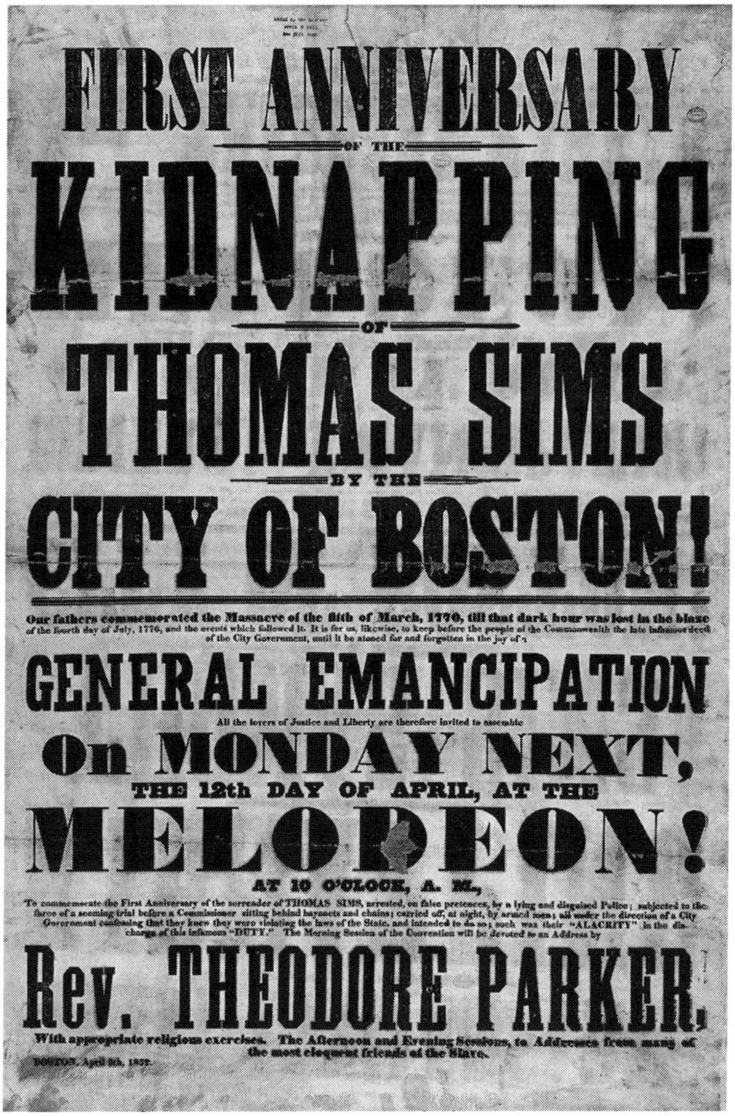

FIGURE 2.9 *Call to a meeting at the Melodeon to be addressed by Rev. Theodore Parker to memorialize the arrest of the fugitive slave, Thomas Sims, and to express outrage at the action. Courtesy of Boston Public Library, Rare Books & Manuscripts Department*

to testify. As word spread of the federal government's determination to enforce the law, hundreds and perhaps thousands of African Americans fled northeastern and midwestern cities for Canada.

It should not have been a surprise, therefore, when ordinary African Americans took the matter of Minkins's arrest and his possible return to slavery in Virginia into their own hands. Shortly after his arrest, more than one hundred black men had gathered outside the courthouse. Inside, five abolitionist lawyers, including prominent African American Robert Morris and white antislavery lawyer Richard Henry Dana, Jr., succeeded in adjourning the case so that they could prepare Minkins's defense. At noon, African

Americans who had gathered outside rushed into the courtroom, seized Minkins and, before the stunned judge and lawyers, whisked him away into the streets of Boston. No one was harmed in the affair, but according to legend the emboldened black mob paused briefly to remember Crispus Attucks, a mixed-race victim of the Boston Massacre and a freedom-fighting symbol of American independence. With the aid of the Underground Railroad, Minkins escaped to Canada and joined other former slaves who were living in freedom and no longer fearing the slave hunter's steps.

Abolitionists such as Frederick Douglass and William Lloyd Garrison praised Minkins's rescue, but political leaders in Washington considered the affairs in Boston profoundly humiliating. A black mob had openly defied federal law and officials were powerless to stop the transgression. Two months after Minkins's rescue, federal marshals seized another Boston fugitive slave, Thomas Sims, but this time the overwhelming demonstration of federal military might ensured that no black mob rushed in to save him. As Sims was marched through the city streets by well-armed militiamen, black and white citizens shouted "Shame! Shame!" and asked "Is this Boston?" or "Is that Charlestown and Bunker Hill?" It seemed unimaginable to Bostonians that the city at the forefront of revolutionary freedom had become, in the words of the abolitionists, one vast hunting ground for slave catchers.

To many northerners this smacked of conscription and in their minds they were being made accomplices to a system they detested. The law further established fines for anyone who abetted a fugitive slave. The law became a rallying cry for northerners, many of whom did not consider themselves abolitionists but who also hated the idea of helping slave traders. New York Whig Senator William Henry Seward claimed famously that there was a "higher law" than the Constitution, a commitment to justice and morality that should supersede unjust laws passed by man.

By 1850 the sectional dispute had reached the point of crisis. Both political parties were damaged by infighting between their northern and southern wings. The localized politics of the early nineteenth century had given way to a national political discourse. Northerners and southerners read each other's newspapers and magazines, read speeches by politicians in other regions, and studied pamphlets published by antislavery and proslavery partisans. Rather than help bind the Union together, the expansion and speeding up of communication via the telegraph and the postal system only hastened the breakup of the Union. Transportation advances, which greatly reduced the time needed to travel from one section to another, encouraged familiarity but also contempt. Added to long-term trends were the sharpening of abolitionist claims against the South, and the subsequent unwavering defense of slavery by southern intellectuals and politicians. The Mexican War significantly worsened sectional relations by pushing the issue of slavery's expansion into the West to the forefront of political debate.

As bleak as the prospects appeared in 1850, there were still powerful Americans, not the least of them Henry Clay, who believed civil war might be avoided. If only compromise could be reached, the preservation of the Union was still possible in their eyes. Even the faith of optimists would be tested, however, during the debates in the summer of 1850 over a series of compromises to end the sectional controversy once and for all. As often happens, political compromise pleased almost no one, North or South.

Please visit the companion website www.routledge.com/cw/wells for additional study aids including chapter overviews, interactive quizzes, and more.

Discussion Questions

- What were the chief characteristics of the Second Party System?
- What were the key components of the Compromise of 1850? To what extent did it hasten or delay the onset of civil war?
- How were westward expansion and the Mexican–American War important to the origins of the Civil War?
- Why was the Fugitive Slave Act so controversial and what role did it play in the sectional crisis?
- How did the abolitionist and proslavery movements contribute to the sectional crisis? What evidence do we have that these movements hastened the coming of the Civil War?
- Many historians have argued that the United States provoked Mexico into war to take advantage of a less powerful country and to expand territory available for slavery. Do you agree or disagree? Support your answer with evidence.
- If you wished to know what were the political views of the Democratic and Whig Parties, what primary sources might you use in your research? Where might you find these sources?

Further Reading

Susanna Ashton, *I Belong to South Carolina: South Carolina Slave Narratives* (Columbia: University of South Carolina Press, 2010).
Daina Berry, *"Swing the Sickle for the Harvest Is Ripe": Gender and Slavery in Antebellum Georgia* (Urbana: University of Illinois Press, 2010).
Christopher Leslie Brown, *Moral Capital: Foundations of British Abolitionism* (Chapel Hill: University of North Carolina Press, 2006).
Ron Chernow, *Alexander Hamilton* (New York: Penguin, 2004).
Jeannine Marie DeLombardo, *Slavery on Trial: Law, Abolitionism, and Print Culture* (Chapel Hill: University of North Carolina Press, 2007).
Martin Dugard, *The Training Ground: Grant, Lee, Sherman, and Davis in the Mexican War, 1846–1848* (New York: Little Brown & Co., 2008).
Anne Farrow, *Complicity: How the North Promoted, Prolonged, and Profited from Slavery* (New York: Ballantine Books, 2005).
Drew Gilpin Faust, *A Sacred Circle: The Dilemma of the Intellectual in the Old South, 1840–1860* (Baltimore: Johns Hopkins University Press, 1977).
Lacy K. Ford, *Deliver Us from Evil: The Slavery Question in the Old South* (New York: Oxford University Press, 2009).
Amy S. Greenberg, *Manifest Manhood and the Antebellum American Empire* (Cambridge: Cambridge University Press, 2005).
Holman Hamilton, *Prologue to Conflict: The Crisis and Compromise of 1850* (Lexington: University of Kentucky Press, 2005, new edition).
Stanley Harrold, *Border War: Fighting over Slavery before the Civil War* (Chapel Hill: University of North Carolina Press, 2010).
Timothy J. Henderson, *A Glorious Defeat: Mexico and its War with the United States* (New York: Hill & Wang, 2007).
Michael F. Holt, *The Rise and Fall of the American Whig Party: Jacksonian Politics and the Onset of the Civil War* (New York: Oxford University Press, 1999).
James Oliver Horton, *In Hope of Liberty: Culture, Community and Protest among Northern Free Blacks, 1700–1860* (New York: Oxford University Press, 1996).
Daniel Walker Howe, *The Political Culture of the American Whigs* (Chicago: University of Chicago Press, 1984).
Mason I. Lowance, Jr., *A House Divided: The Antebellum Slavery Debates in America, 1776–1865* (Princeton: Princeton University Press, 2003).
Henry Mayer, *All on Fire: William Lloyd Garrison and the Abolition of Slavery* (New York: St. Martin's Press, 1998).
William S. McFeely, *Frederick Douglass* (New York: W.W. Norton, 1991).
Joanne Pope Melish, *Disowning Slavery: Gradual Emancipation and Race in New England, 1780–1860* (Ithaca: Cornell University Press, 1998).
Michael Morrison, *Slavery in the American West: The Eclipse of Manifest Destiny* (Chapel Hill: University of North Carolina Press, 1997).

Merrill D. Peterson, *The Great Triumvirate: Webster, Clay, and Calhoun* (New York: Oxford University Press, 1987).

Raul A. Ramos, *Beyond the Alamo: Forging Mexican Ethnicity in San Antonio, 1821–1861* (Chapel Hill: University of North Carolina Press, 2008).

Patricia Roberts-Miller, *Fanatical Schemes: Proslavery Rhetoric and the Tragedy of Consensus* (Tuscaloosa: University of Alabama Press, 2009).

Adam Rothman, *Slave Country: American Expansion and the Origins of the Deep South* (Cambridge, MA: Harvard University Press, 2005).

Phillip J. Schwarz, *Slave Laws in Virginia* (Athens: University of Georgia Press, 1996).

Joel H. Silbey, *Storm over Texas: The Annexation Controversy and the Road to Civil War* (New York: Oxford University Press, 2005).

John Stauffer, *The Black Hearts of Men: Radical Abolitionists and the Transformation of Race* (Cambridge, MA: Harvard University Press, 2002).

Larry E. Tise, *Proslavery: A History of the Defense of Slavery in America, 1701–1840* (Athens: University of Georgia Press, 1990).

Elizabeth Varon, *We Mean to Be Counted: White Women & Politics in Antebellum Virginia* (Chapel Hill: University of North Carolina Press, 1998).

Anthony Wallace, *The Long, Bitter Trail: Andrew Jackson and the Indians* (New York: Hill & Wang, 1993).

Harry Watson, *Liberty and Power: The Politics of Jacksonian America* (New York: Hill & Wang, 2006, second edition).

Deborah Gray White, *Ar'N't I A Woman? Female Slaves in the Plantation South* (New York: Norton, 1999).

THE 1850s AND SECESSION

Topics Covered in this Chapter:

- The Fury over *Uncle Tom's Cabin*
- Continued Controversy Over the Fugitive Slave Act of 1850
- Bloody Kansas
- A New Political Party
- The Dred Scott Supreme Court Case
- The Lincoln–Douglas Debates
- John Brown's Raid
- The Presidential Election of 1860
- Secession
- Lincoln and the Start of the War

3

Introduction

As the 1850s opened, the Union was in peril. The Mexican–American War worsened the sectional crisis by laying bare northern fears that the federal government would use its military might to expand territory for slaveholders. Antislavery northerners such as author Henry David Thoreau and politician William Henry Seward argued that a "slaveholder conspiracy" had taken control of Congress and the presidency and that northern free-labor advocates had to fight the conspiracy at every turn. Yet, as pivotal as the Mexican War was in aggravating hostility between North and South, with political leaders often mentioning dangerous words such as "disunion" and "civil war," the majority of southerners remained opposed to secession. War continued to be unthinkable for ordinary Americans in both sections. The dramatic events of the 1850s helped convince many Americans that war was not only conceivable but perhaps inevitable.

If John Brown's raid in October 1859 rendered any chance for a peaceful resolution to the sectional crisis unlikely, Abraham Lincoln's election as the sixteenth president in November 1860 shifted the prospects for peace from unlikely to improbable. Throughout the presidential campaign of 1860, fire-eating southerners threatened to leave the Union if an antislavery Republican president was elected. Just a few weeks after Lincoln's victory, South Carolina became the first state to secede, followed by ten other southern states by early 1861. Yet, even after North Carolina became the last southern state to secede in the spring following Lincoln's election, some still harbored hope that full-scale war could be avoided. April 1861 saw those hopes dashed forever as Union and Confederate soldiers fought in the first major battle of the Civil War at Fort Sumter, South Carolina.

The Fury over *Uncle Tom's Cabin*

Although Henry Clay, Daniel Webster, John C. Calhoun, Stephen Douglas, and other national political leaders believed that the Compromise of 1850 would calm sectional tensions, the compromise only inflamed southern and northern activists. Northern abolitionists were incensed by the Fugitive Slave Law, especially since the legislation denied runaways the right to a trial by jury and permitted their return to slavery merely on the word of a slaveholder. Worst of all perhaps was a stipulation in the law that denied the accused fugitive the right to a proper defense. Antislavery northerners angrily proclaimed that they were forced to become complicit in supporting an institution they despised. Antislavery passions in the North, sentiments never sustained by a large majority of northerners, were heightened by a novel published in 1852 by a previously little-known New England woman writer.

Among the abolitionists outraged over the Fugitive Slave Act of 1850 was Harriet Beecher Stowe, a white woman from Connecticut who hailed from a well-known New England family. When Stowe sat down to write an antislavery novel, she could not have known the furor it would create. Part of the novel's popularity was the sentimental way in which characters and incidents were depicted. As the title character, Uncle Tom was an older slave of strong values who reflected the Christian ideals so important to Stowe and other abolitionists. But much of the novel tells the story of slaves such as Eliza and George who, after their small child is sold to another master, run away to keep the family intact. The three escape to Canada and eventually move to Africa. Another character, Eva, is a small child of a white master who befriends Tom and other slaves. One of the younger slaves, Topsy, believes she is worthless and Eva convinces Topsy that all people are God's children and of value. Eva tries to persuade her father to free Tom but this never happens. Finally, perhaps the most reviled character is Simon Legree, a brute whose occupation reflected the most hated aspect of slavery: the trafficking of human beings.

Serialized initially in the abolitionist periodical *National Era* in 1851 and 1852, *Uncle Tom's Cabin* attracted immediate and remarkable attention when published in book form in 1852, selling more than a quarter of a million copies in America in its first year. The popular response to the novel in the North and in Britain, where the novel sold nearly as well as it did in the U.S., reflected the anger with which northerners had greeted news of the Fugitive Slave Act. Stowe herself claimed that the Fugitive Slave Act was a major impetus for writing the novel. But *Uncle Tom's Cabin* would

FIGURE 3.1A *H.B. Stowe and* Uncle Tom's Cabin. *Library of Congress, African American Odyssey, LC-USZ62-10476*

FIGURE 3.1B *The publication of Harriet Beecher Stowe's* Uncle Tom's Cabin *was the inspiration for many cultural products, including the Garden City Quartette, pictured here. Library of Congress, African American Odyssey, LC-USZC4-6171*

never have become such a popular success if it had not struck a chord with ordinary northerners. In fact, there is evidence that both the novel and the runaway slave legislation intensified antislavery sentiment among northerners; in 1854 a Boston mob, aroused by abolitionist speeches, killed a courthouse guard in an attempt to rescue fugitive slaves being held for their return to slavery.

Uncle Tom's Cabin caused equally strong reactions in the South, whose leading intellectuals denounced the book in reviews and whose writers penned their own novels to demonstrate slavery's supposedly positive effects on the slaves. Readers such as South Carolina's wealthy and white Mary Boykin Chesnut chastised Stowe for proclaiming that northern women were more moral than their southern counterparts. Reviews in southern newspapers and magazines claimed that Stowe's novel was false and malicious, and that it was written by a northerner who had no direct knowledge of the South's people or institutions. It was read widely in the South and almost all reaction was negative. In the 1850s, southern authors countered with more than two dozen proslavery novels, none of which even approached the popularity of *Uncle Tom's Cabin*. Interestingly, southern women novelists and poets, many of whom had earned considerable fame in the region by the 1850s, engaged in the debate with their own refutations of

Stowe. Caroline Lee Hentz's *The Planter's Northern Bride* and Mary Henderson Eastman's *Aunt Phillis' Cabin*, for example, rejected Stowe's negative depiction of bondage and argued that the institution fed, clothed, Christianized, and civilized the slave. At the same time that the literary war of words over slavery paralleled the sectionalized political debates of the 1850s, the literary battles also asserted a new role for women in both southern and northern society. While women could not yet vote or hold political office, they could exercise moral and political influence through their talents as writers. Other women would become personally involved in reform movements such as temperance (the movement to limit or prohibit altogether alcohol consumption), but women authors demonstrated that they could employ their intellectual talents and participate actively in the political storm over slavery.

Continued Controversy Over the Fugitive Slave Act of 1850

Throughout the 1850s, the Fugitive Slave Act that had prompted Stowe to pen *Uncle Tom's Cabin* continued to incite northern and southern activists to new levels of rage. The horrifying tale of Margaret Garner, an enslaved woman who crossed the frozen Ohio River into freedom in the winter of 1856 only to be recaptured in her cousin's Cincinnati cabin, was perhaps the most publicized case of a female runaway. When she heard the slave catchers outside her cabin, Garner panicked and killed one of her daughters with a knife rather than witness the child's return to bondage. Word of the recapture and the child's killing reached newspapers throughout the nation. Abolitionists pitied Garner and said her actions were evidence of slavery's evil and corrupting nature. Proslavery forces argued that the killing demonstrated that blacks were inherently uncivilized and fit only for control under slavery. Ultimately, Garner was brought back to slavery in Kentucky, but Americans continued to debate the case well into the late 1800s.

Although the Garner case is perhaps the best-known fugitive slave affair involving a female runaway, there were many others. One of the most moving fugitive slave cases involved Jane Johnson. As a slave owned by North Carolina diplomat John Wheeler, she had already experienced the horrifying trauma of watching one of her sons sold away. Wheeler, who sported a bushy mustache that matched his graying hair and a thick southern accent, was a low-level but active Democratic politician. When Wheeler took Johnson and her two young sons with him to Philadelphia, en route to his new post as ambassador to Nicaragua via New York, Johnson and her sons escaped in a harrowing tale of desperation and courage. Although Wheeler had locked Johnson and her sons in their Philadelphia hotel room, with specific instructions not to talk to the all-black hotel staff, Johnson managed to inform a porter that she wanted to escape her master. The porter notified the local vigilance committee, a group of black and white abolitionists who offered protection to runaways. Word then spread to the Philadelphia Antislavery Society offices nearby and a white abolitionist named Passmore Williamson met Wheeler, Johnson, and the young slave boys as they were about to board a ship to New York.

At the Philadelphia docks, Williamson told Wheeler that Johnson and her sons were now free under Philadelphia state law, and Williamson had brought with him five burly black dockworkers to restrain the loudly protesting Wheeler. William Still, a prominent African American abolitionist and member of the

FIGURE 3.2 *Jane Johnson, 1872. From* The Underground Railroad, *by William Still, Courtesy of the Library of Congress*

vigilance committee, quickly took Johnson and her sons to a waiting carriage and into hiding in the attic of his Philadelphia home. Ultimately Johnson and her sons settled in Boston with the help of suffragette Lucretia Mott, and until her death in 1872 Johnson relished the freedom she and her sons had won.

For the Philadelphia abolitionists who had arranged her escape, however, the aftermath of the rescue lingered. The diplomat Wheeler used his political influence to press his case, and Passmore Williamson and William Still were jailed for contempt for failing to divulge Johnson's whereabouts. Leading abolitionists such as Harriet Tubman and Frederick Douglass visited Williamson in jail and abolitionists everywhere paid close attention to the courtroom dramas surrounding the case. Protests snowballed until Judge Kane finally relented and released Williamson from prison.

The federal government's resolve was also tested in one of the more dramatic fugitive slave stories from the Midwest. Joshua Glover escaped slavery in St. Louis in 1852 and made his way to Racine, Wisconsin, realizing that if he were ever discovered he would be closer to freedom in Canada. Glover lived for two years in Racine, earning respect in the small frontier town for his hard work and character. But in 1854 agents of Glover's former master tracked him down after slinking around the town and asking questions. They subdued the panicked Glover and with the help of local officials jailed him in Milwaukee. Glover's white and black neighbors, incensed by the "kidnapping" of one of their own, boarded the next ship to Milwaukee. Numbering over 100 strong, and led by abolitionist Sherman Booth, the mixed-race mob overtook the jailers, broke through the prison, and freed Glover.

While Glover crossed the border and settled in Canada, members of the mob who had rescued the runaway felt the full brunt of federal determination to enforce the Fugitive Slave Law. Booth was a newspaper editor and prominent member of the Free Soil Party, a small third party that advocated the immediate abolition of slavery; his political activism and his visible role in rescuing Glover made him a prime target for prosecution. Yet the charge was not obstruction of justice or another lesser charge; in its quest to show resolve the government charged Booth with treason for inciting a mob that thwarted federal law. Throughout the country, several other fugitive slave cases also led to treason charges and prosecutions, but the Booth case was unique. The legal wrangling went on throughout the 1850s, going back and forth between conviction and acquittal until the Wisconsin Supreme Court boldly declared the Fugitive Slave Act unconstitutional. This unprecedented move shocked the political and legal worlds. Not until 1859, in the famous decision in *Abelman v. Booth*, would the U.S. Supreme Court finally rule that state courts could not declare federal laws unconstitutional. The fact that cases were spread across the North, from Wisconsin and Iowa, to Michigan and Indiana, and throughout the northeast, reminds us that the sectional crisis did not just pit the northeast against the Deep South, but also generated passionate debates in the Midwest and West.

Bloody Kansas

The Compromise of 1850 reflected the fact that the issue of slavery, and specifically its possible spread to the western territories, now weighed heavily on the two parties, the Democrats and Whigs. But the northern and southern Whigs, even more so than the Democrats, were fatally split over the issue of slavery. In fact, the 1852 presidential election was the last one pitting a Whig candidate against a Democratic one. Although the Democrats survived the sectional division until 1860, the Whigs did not. Democratic candidate Franklin Pierce of New Hampshire handily won the election against Whig candidate Winfield Scott, a U.S. Army general who had served in both the War of 1812 and the Mexican–American War. In nominating a proslavery northern candidate the Democrats were able to keep the party from dividing fatally between its northern and southern wings. The Whigs were not as sturdy. They lost the popular vote to Pierce 51% to 44% and the Electoral College vote 254 to 42. But the loss in the presidential election was just the beginning of problems for the Whigs. By the 1852 congressional elections, the Whigs had lost eleven seats in the House of Representatives and two years later in 1854 the party disbanded. The early 1850s marked the end of the Second Party System between the Democrats and the Whigs that had endured for two decades, replaced by new political battles between a weak Democratic Party, a new Republican Party opposed to slavery's westward expansion, and a short-lived anti-immigrant American Party.

On the heels of the election of a proslavery northerner in the 1852 presidential campaign and the anger sparked by *Uncle Tom's Cabin*, the Kansas and Nebraska territories applied for statehood. Few controversies of the tumultuous 1850s contributed so much to the causes of the Civil War. The crisis over Kansas's statehood in particular erupted into armed conflict in which proslavery and antislavery forces killed one another. War was still unimaginable in the minds of many Americans, but the fact that white men were willing to fight and die for the free soil and proslavery causes certainly awoke in the minds of dubious Americans that war was quite possible if not yet likely. Just as Missouri, Texas, and California ignited conflicts over statehood, so too did the storm over Kansas inflame the passions of proslavery and free soil disciples.

Toward the end of 1853, farmers in the Midwest wanted to organize the Nebraska territory for statehood. Champions of a transcontinental railroad who saw the Kansas and Nebraska territories as the best route to the Pacific also promoted statehood, hoping that western development would speed the development of an east–west route. The problem was that Nebraska lay north of the Missouri Compromise line (see Chapter 1) that marked the northern most boundary of slavery's reach. Southerners did not want another free state in the Union, especially when California had been admitted as a free state just a few years before. Free soil advocates were equally determined to keep Kansas and Nebraska closed to what they perceived as the debilitating and immoral effects of slavery. How would this crisis be solved?

Illinois Senator Stephen Douglas, a popular Democrat and a leader in Congress, proposed a compromise. The line drawn at the 36°30′ as part of the Missouri Compromise of 1820 would be declared null and void, superseded by popular sovereignty in which a vote of citizens within the new states would determine the status of slavery. In addition, Congress would divide the territory into two states, Kansas and Nebraska, with the latter almost certainly becoming a free state but with Kansas open to bondage. These stipulations became the Kansas–Nebraska Act of 1854, but like previous compromises, it failed to stem the tide of anger rising among antislavery and proslavery forces.

The trouble erupted even before Kansas officially petitioned for statehood. Many northerners had come to Kansas with hopes of settling in a free state. They did not want slavery in Kansas and did not want to have to compete with slave labor. But in an election in March 1855, thousands of proslavery supporters from Missouri flooded over into Kansas to vote to make Kansas a slave state. The territorial capital of Lecompton, Kansas thus became proslavery. It seemed that, although the election was decided by fraudulent voting, Kansas would enter the Union as a slave state. But in the summer of 1855, supporters of a free Kansas set up a rival state government in Topeka. In the ensuing skirmish between proslavery and antislavery forces, many people died, creating a sense among many Americans that "Bloody Kansas" was merely a prelude to civil war.

Popular sovereignty proved a miserable failure in Kansas, and events in Congress lent further credence to claims that only violence would settle the dispute. During the crisis, Massachusetts Republican Senator Charles Sumner, well known as a fierce opponent of slavery, delivered a speech in which he criticized the South for supporting slavery, and specifically attacked South Carolina Senator Andrew Butler for making "the harlot, slavery" his mistress. Two days later a relative of Butler's, South Carolina Representative Preston Brooks, strode into the Senate chamber and proceeded to beat Sumner with his cane. Sumner was badly hurt, and took years to recover from the beating. Brooks was hailed as a hero in the South, and people from all over the region sent him canes imprinted with slogans such as "hit him again" and "take a hit for me." This incident demonstrates the hostility that had arisen between the sections, even generating violence in the halls of Congress.

A New Political Party

The rise of the Republican Party is perhaps the most remarkable ascendance to power in American political history, chronicled by historians such as William Gienapp and Eric Foner. Begun in 1854, the party won the presidency just six years later with Abraham Lincoln, and won every presidential election from 1860 until 1884. Few, however, would have predicted such success in 1854 and 1855 when the party was getting off the ground. The Republicans were united on one issue: opposition to the extension of slavery into the western territories. The Republican Party was thus almost completely a northern party. Republicans had almost no support in the South.

The Republican Party began to form in reaction to the Kansas–Nebraska Act of 1854, when the questions of statehood and the status of slavery for Kansas and Nebraska were troubling the nation. The Whigs were collapsing as a result of their poor showing in the 1852 elections and seemed incapable of representing northern interests in the debate. Former Whigs in search of a new political home met in states such as Michigan and Wisconsin, where delegates were charged with formulating a party structure and platform. By the start of 1856 Republicans had managed to organize in only half of the northern states, and had no national organization. But the issues surrounding "Bloody Kansas" galvanized the party. Northerners who wanted a free soil Kansas and Nebraska backed the Republicans. By the end of 1856, as the smoke of the Kansas crisis began to clear, the Republicans had become a major national party and emerged as the main challengers to the Democrats in what scholars call the Third Party System.

The presidential election of 1856 demonstrated the new party's appeal to northern and western advocates of free soil. After nominating California explorer John C. Fremont, a vocal opponent of bondage and its spread to the western territories, to represent their party, the Republicans could not have expected any support among white southerners. Even so, Fremont fared well in the campaign, winning the northeast and the upper Midwest under the slogan "Free Soil, Free Men, Free Labor." Northern antislavery adherents could now rally under the "free labor" banner, a kind of political shorthand that meant opposition to the spread of slavery and to the economic backwardness, cultural deficiencies, and planter dominance that northern Republicans saw in the slave South. The Democratic Party ran on the principle of popular sovereignty, a doctrine that seemed to many moderates a middling position that left the status of slavery in the new states up to the voters in those states. As the election debacle in Kansas showed, however, popular sovereignty was better in theory than in practice.

Democrats in the 1850s had become adept at appealing both to northern and southern voters at the same time. Since politics was often highly localized, candidates for office could offer different views to voters in different regions of the country. Southern Democrats might emphasize the party's role in defending slavery, while northern Democrats stressed the importance of protecting the Union and the Constitutional safeguards for state autonomy. This strategy proved successful in the presidential elections of 1852 and 1856, in which northern Democrats who promised to defend the Constitution (widely interpreted among southern voters as the protection of slavery) received electoral votes in all regions. These northern Democrats, often termed "doughfaces" for their pro-South sympathies, won presidential and congressional elections. But one could not deny the success of the political maneuvering. In the 1852 campaign, New Hampshire native Pierce defeated Mexican War hero Winfield Scott and in 1856 the antislavery Fremont lost to Pennsylvania Democrat James Buchanan 45% to 33%. Eventually the Democrats' strategy would falter and

FIGURE 3.3 *1860 Campaign Poster. Library of Congress, Rare Book and Special Collections Division, Alfred Whital Stern Collection of Lincolniana*

they too would witness the collapse of the party along sectional lines in the presidential campaign of 1860.

The Dred Scott Supreme Court Case

The formation and early success of the Republican Party, whose platform was unabashedly opposed to slavery's expansion, generated anger and fear in the white South. Yet many southerners still held that the conflicts over slavery would subside, and a Supreme Court decision handed down in 1857 gave them reason to hope that their cherished institution would be protected. The case, officially titled *Dred Scott v. Sanford*, pivoted on whether Scott, a fugitive slave in the eyes of southerners, should be returned to his master. During the 1830s, his master had taken Scott with him as he traveled from slave state Missouri to the free state of Illinois and the free territory of Wisconsin. After his master's death, Scott sued for his freedom on the grounds that he became free after crossing into free soil. The court, led by Chief Justice and Marylander Roger B. Taney, ruled that Scott could not sue for his freedom because slaves had no legal rights in court and could not become citizens. Taney further declared that the Missouri Compromise Line was unconstitutional because slavery was a national institution that could only be prohibited by local laws:

A free negro of the African race, whose ancestors were brought to this country and sold as slaves, is not a "citizen" within the meaning of the Constitution of the United States . . . When the Constitution was adopted, they were not regarded in any of the States as members of the community which constituted the State, and were not numbered among its "people or citizens." Consequently, the special rights and immunities guaranteed to citizens do not apply to them. And not being "citizens" within the meaning of the Constitution, they are not entitled to sue in that character in a court of the United States, and the Circuit Court has no jurisdiction in such a suit . . . It is difficult at this day to realize the state of public opinion in regard to that unfortunate race which prevailed in the civilized and enlightened portions of the world at the time of the Declaration of Independence, and when the Constitution of the United States was framed and adopted; but the public history of every European nation displays it in a manner too plain to be mistaken. They had for more than a century before been regarded as beings of an inferior order, and altogether unfit to associate with the white race, either in social or political relations, and so far unfit that they had no rights which the white man was bound to respect.

Taney hoped that the court's decision would resolve the conflict over whether new states would enter the Union with or without slavery, but the ruling served only to inflame northern free soil supporters further. Taney's ruling seemingly overturned the precarious compromise reached in the crisis over Bloody Kansas that popular sovereignty would decide the status of slavery south of the 40th parallel. Republicans reacted with an uproar of

FIGURE 3.4 *Chief Justice Roger B. Taney. Library of Congress, LC-USZ62-107588*

opposition, claiming that the court's decision proved that the federal government was dominated at all levels by the slave power. Lincoln referred to the case in his famous "House Divided" speech in 1858. Frederick Douglass declared the court's ruling an "open, glaring, and scandalous issue of lies." On the other hand, southern newspapers such as the *Richmond Examiner* praised the decision as "emphatically in favor of the advocates and supporters of the Constitution and the Union, the equality of the States and the rights of the South." As a result Taney's decision worsened sectional discord and hastened secession.

The Lincoln–Douglas Debates

Since the Republicans could only find support in the northeast and midwest, the only truly national political party by the late 1850s was the Democratic Party. Increasingly divided between

FIGURE 3.5 *The political quadrille. Music by Dred Scott. Library of Congress, LC-USZ62-14827*

northerners and southerners like the Whigs before them, the Democratic Party successfully navigated the controversies over slavery and its westward expansion; but even this venerable party was significantly weakened heading into the latter years of the 1850s. There were many prominent northern Democrats who, like New York's James Kirke Paulding, supported the South's constitutional right to own slaves. The party won the presidential elections of 1852 and 1856 by putting forth northern candidates who promised to protect slavery. In addition, there were a few whites who publicly opposed slavery despite earning scorn from their fellow southerners. Benjamin Hedrick, for example, supported John C. Fremont for president in 1856, but then paid for this support by being fired from his position as a University of North Carolina professor. White southerner Hinton R. Helper wrote the widely read *The Impending Crisis of the South*, which sought to demonstrate the ill effects of bondage on the South's economic development and culture. But there was almost no tolerance for dissent in the Old South on the issue of slavery, and thinkers like Helper were shunned. Both the proslavery and antislavery sides of the debate remained unwilling to compromise and grew increasingly intolerant of opposing views.

FIGURE 3.6 *Lincoln & Douglas in a presidential footrace. Library of Congress, LC-DIG-ppmsca-15777*

Yet there were occasions in the 1850s when the debate over slavery was elevated to an intellectual, rather than a rhetorical discussion, and the debates between Illinois Republican Senate candidate Abraham Lincoln and incumbent Democrat Stephen A. Douglas are one such example. The Lincoln–Douglas Debates have become part of American lore, not just because the arguments reflected the broader national arguments over slavery, but also because the American people followed the debates closely as they were reprinted in newspapers across the nation.

A former Whig congressman from his native state of Kentucky, Lincoln was not well known when the first of the seven debates began in August 1858, but his intellectual challenges to Douglas and his oratorical skills won him national attention. Douglas continued to trumpet the doctrine of popular sovereignty, pointing to the Compromise of 1850 and the Kansas–Nebraska Act of 1854 as examples of the doctrine's successful implementation. Lincoln harkened back to the Northwest Ordinance of 1787 to argue that slavery should be kept out of the upper Midwest. Although Douglas would recapture his Senate seat in the fall election (at that time senators were chosen by state legislatures, not by the voters at large), the attention Lincoln earned catapulted him two years later into a position where he became a leading candidate for the Republican Party presidential nomination in 1860.

By the time of the debates in the summer and fall of 1858, Lincoln was already becoming known for his eloquence as a writer. Upon accepting the Republican Party's nomination as a Senate candidate in June 1858, Lincoln delivered one of the most famous speeches in American history. Reflecting the threat of disunion that historian Elizabeth Varon has found to be at the heart of the sectional crisis, Lincoln (drawing from the Book of Matthew in the Bible) presciently warned that:

A house divided against itself cannot stand. I believe this government cannot endure, permanently, half slave and half free. I do not expect the Union to be dissolved—I do not expect the house to fall—but I do expect it will cease to be divided. It will become all one thing or all the other.

Either the opponents of slavery will arrest the further spread of it, and place it where the public mind shall rest in the belief that it is in the course of ultimate extinction; or its advocates will push it forward, till it shall become alike lawful in all the States, old as well as new—North as well as South.

The phrase "a house divided" comes originally from the Book of Matthew, but it has been used ever since by Americans to reflect the breakup of the Union.

Viewing transcripts of the debates today, the modern reader can see the race-baiting strategy behind Douglas's campaign for reelection as well as Lincoln's attempt to assure white voters that he was not veering too far in the direction of protecting African Americans. As Douglas put it:

I ask you, are you in favor of conferring upon the Negro the rights and privileges of citizenship? Do you desire to strike out of our State Constitution that clause which keeps slaves and free Negroes out of the State, and allow the free Negroes to flow in, and cover your prairies with black settlements? Do you desire to turn this beautiful State into a free Negro colony, in order

that when Missouri abolishes slavery she can send one hundred thousand emancipated slaves into Illinois, to become citizens and voters, on an equality with yourselves? If you desire Negro citizenship, if you desire to allow them to come into the State and settle with the white man, if you desire them to vote on an equality with yourselves, and to make them eligible to office, to serve on juries, and to adjudge your rights, then support Mr. Lincoln and the Black Republican party, who are in favor of the citizenship of the Negro.

Douglas's strategy was a political maneuver that had worked well for northern Democrats since the emergence of the antislavery Republican Party in 1854. Democrats painted their opponents as overly sympathetic, pro-black abolitionists whose election threatened to overthrow white rule. Lincoln responded somewhat defensively at the same debate that:

I agree with Judge Douglas he [the African American] is not my equal in many respects—certainly not in color, perhaps not in moral or intellectual endowment. But in the right to eat the bread, without the leave of anybody else, which his own hand earns, he is my equal and the equal of Judge Douglas, and the equal of every living man.

In the second debate, Douglas tried to walk a middle ground between proslavery and antislavery viewpoints by reemphasizing the importance of popular sovereignty. In what became known as the Freeport Doctrine, Douglas argued that the question of slavery's existence would be decided by the new western states themselves. Douglas would emerge victorious in the campaign but Lincoln's performance during the debates earned him a national reputation.

John Brown's Raid

The year after the Lincoln–Douglas Debates another event proved to be one of the major factors in leading the South to secession. At the center of this new controversy sat an enigmatic figure named John Brown. Brown, born in Connecticut in 1800, had failed at a number of occupations prior to 1850, including farming, tanning, and business. But he had always been deeply moved by the injustice of slavery. After hearing of the murder of abolitionist Elijah P. Lovejoy in Alton, Illinois in 1837, Brown proclaimed that "Here, before God, in the presence of these witnesses, from this time, I consecrate my life to the destruction of slavery!" By the time of the crisis over Bloody Kansas, Brown was determined at all costs to thwart the state from falling into the proslavery column. His passion was fueled by the destruction in Lawrence at the hands of proslavery "Border Ruffians" in early May 1856.

Once in Kansas, Brown took action. At what became known as the Pottawatomie Massacre in late May 1856, Brown, some of his sons, and other followers came upon the home of James P. Doyle, who Brown suspected of being a proslavery settler. Taking Doyle and two of his grown sons outside, Brown and his sons proceeded to murder the three captives. The murderous band then moved on to kill more suspected proslavery activists. The method of the murders, which consisted of stabbings and hacking the victims to death with swords, was particularly gruesome. Yet Brown continued his rampage at nearby Osawatomie and other towns. When the crisis subsided later in the year, Brown came back to the East realizing that to fight slavery he would need more money.

For two years Brown traveled throughout New England seeking funds to support his plan to fight slavery with arms. Although historians debate the extent to which these northern abolitionists knew about Brown's past actions or his full intentions for the future, wealthy New Englanders did give him substantial sums. While in the northeast, Brown met William Lloyd Garrison, Theodore Parker, Henry David Thoreau, Frederick Douglass, and other leading abolitionists, but most of the money he would use on the raid at Harper's Ferry came from a small band of well-off antislavery advocates (Thomas Wentworth Higginson, Samuel Howe, Theodore Parker, Franklin Sanborn, Gerrit Smith, and George Stearns) who became known as the "Secret Six." Although their commitment to Brown's antislavery violence is unclear, the Secret Six were radical abolitionists steadfast in their dedication to ending slavery.

Brown met frequently with members of the Secret Six in 1858 and 1859, hatching a plan to free southern slaves by force and to help them found a new state for which he drafted a constitution. But he kept the details of his plan largely secret, and came unnoticed to Harper's Ferry, Virginia just before July 4, 1859. He selected Harper's Ferry because of a government weapons cache there that Brown believed could be used to arm slaves for rebellion. Brown waited for reinforcements that were supposed to arrive but he never received the level of support promised by his conspirators. Impatient, he decided to attack the armory on October 16, 1859. At first, Brown, his sons, and their associates experienced little opposition, but shooting soon broke out and several people were killed, including Brown's sons. Word spread via telegraph throughout the country, and white southerners responded to the news with hysteria and fear.

Brown and several of his men were caught and held. Two days later, on October 18, Brown was questioned by Virginia Governor Henry A. Wise and others. After a week-long trial, a jury found Brown guilty.

In his final speech, given at court on November 2, Brown said:

In the first place, I deny everything but what I have all along admitted, the design on my part to free the slaves. I intended certainly to have made a clean thing of that matter, as I did last winter, when I went into Missouri and there took slaves without the snapping of a gun on either side, moved them through the country, and finally left them in Canada. I designed to have done the same thing again, on a larger scale. That was all I intended. I never did intend murder, or treason, or the destruction of property, or to excite or incite slaves to rebellion, or to make insurrection . . . This court acknowledges, as I suppose, the validity of the law of God. I see a book kissed here which I suppose to be the Bible, or at least the New Testament. That teaches me that all things whatsoever I would that men should do to me, I should do even so to them. It teaches me, further, to "remember them that are in bonds, as bound with them." I endeavored to act up to that instruction. I say, I am yet too young to understand that God is any respecter of persons. I believe that to have interfered as I have done as I have always freely admitted I have done on behalf of His despised poor, was not wrong, but right. Now, if it is deemed necessary that I should forfeit my life for the furtherance of the ends of justice, and mingle my blood further with the blood of my children and with the blood of millions in this slave country whose rights are disregarded by wicked, cruel, and unjust enactments, I submit; so let it be done!

Brown was hanged for treason on December 2, but before he died he had one final observation. "I, John Brown," he wrote, "am now quite certain that the crimes of this guilty land will never be purged away but with blood." He was right, and his actions had helped the premonition to come true. Brown's raid frightened southerners who saw it as evidence that abolitionists were now willing to use violence and force to end slavery. They blamed Republicans and abolitionists for inciting and supporting Brown. The raid, though a failure, convinced many in the South that if slavery and southern interests were to be protected, then it would have to be under a separate government. Many northerners, meanwhile, did not know how to respond to Brown's actions. Some thought him insane and a murderer, while others proclaimed him a martyr. New England poet and abolitionist John Greenleaf Whittier penned a poem entitled "Brown of Osawatomie" shortly after his execution. In part the poem read:

John Brown of Osawatomie, they led him out to die;
And lo! a poor slave-mother with her little child pressed nigh:
Then the bold, blue eye grew tender, and the old harsh face grew mild,
As he stooped between the jeering ranks and kissed the negro's child!

While many abolitionists struggled with the justice and morality of Brown's actions, Frederick Douglass later commented that:

John Brown began the war that ended American slavery and made this a free Republic. His zeal in the cause of freedom was infinitely superior to mine. Mine was as the taper light; his was as the burning sun. I could live for the slave; John Brown could die for him.

The Presidential Election of 1860

John Brown's raid had a profound effect on the presidential election that took place roughly twelve months after his guilty verdict, a campaign that promised to be contentious aside from the hysteria caused by the raid. In 1860 the Democrats were suffering badly from internal division and party unity finally succumbed to the same internal split over slavery that caused the Whig Party to collapse in the early 1850s. Historian Frank Towers has reminded us that urban areas in the South significantly complicated the attempt of the national Democratic Party to keep its various factions under control. In cities like Baltimore, New Orleans, and St. Louis, white laborers posed a threat to planter dominance in state and local politics. Though these workers were proslavery, they did not fall in line with unquestioning support of the planter class. Wrought by internal divisions, the southern Democrats by the late 1850s no longer could be counted on to stay united.

This split became fatal in April 1860 when the Democrats met for their convention in Charleston. Failing to win a platform guaranteeing federal protection for slavery in the territories, delegates from Alabama, Louisiana, Georgia, Texas, Mississippi, Florida, and South Carolina stormed out. Led by Alabama fire-eater William Lowndes Yancey, the Lower South delegates wanted the platform to reflect the strongest proslavery sentiment possible. Frustrated by their failure to nominate a candidate after taking almost sixty votes, the delegates adjourned and met in Baltimore where another conflict emerged about whether or not to replace the Lower South delegates who had walked out. When the convention decided to replace those delegates with potentially antislavery northern delegates, the Upper South members of the party walked out. What remained of the original convention delegates then nominated Stephen Douglas of Illinois as their presidential candidate.

While not as divided as the Democrats, the Republicans also struggled at their convention in Chicago to arrive at a decision on who would carry the banner for their party. One leading candidate was New York Governor William H. Seward, who was widely despised among white southerners for making the argument that a "higher law" should guide the nation on the issue of slavery. Proslavery southerners and northern Democrats had argued throughout the antebellum era that the Constitution protected slavery and its expansion into the western territories. But in a speech that was disseminated in newspapers and pamphlets, Seward claimed that there were laws above even the Constitution that should guide policy. Southerners howled that Seward and his fellow abolitionists sought to subvert the nation's founding document. He was reviled throughout the slave states as a dangerous radical, but among Republicans Seward was considered the leading candidate to become the party's nominee for president.

Other potential Republican nominees included former congressman Abraham Lincoln of Illinois, Pennsylvania's Simon Cameron, and Salmon P. Chase of Ohio. Cameron and Chase were unable to muster enough support at the convention, and many delegates began to consider Seward too radical to attract broad support. Although the Republicans had little hope of winning over many white southerners, party leaders harbored hopes of picking off northern Democrats who resented the stridently proslavery elements of their party. So although Seward came to the convention as the front-runner to secure the Republican nomination, delegates turned to the more moderate Lincoln. He had won wide respect in the North for his performance in the 1858 debates with Douglas, and he offered the possibility of carrying western states such as his home state of Illinois. Although he was considered to be an antislavery moderate, Lincoln was also firmly opposed to the expansion of slavery into the western territories, an important free-labor stance that became a key plank in the Republican Party platform. Hannibal Hamlin of Maine was nominated for vice president.

Although Republicans considered Lincoln a moderate, white southerners lumped him in with the radical Republican group of Seward, Garrison, and Douglass. During the presidential campaign many southern politicians warned that if Lincoln was elected the South would have no choice but to secede from the Union. Passionately proslavery "fire-eaters" such as Edmund Ruffin advocated secession if a Republican was elected to the nation's highest office. Southern and northern Democratic newspapers vilified Lincoln, depicting him as an ape or chimpanzee to highlight his unusual facial features and also link him to African Americans in the minds of racist voters. Douglas was hailed by

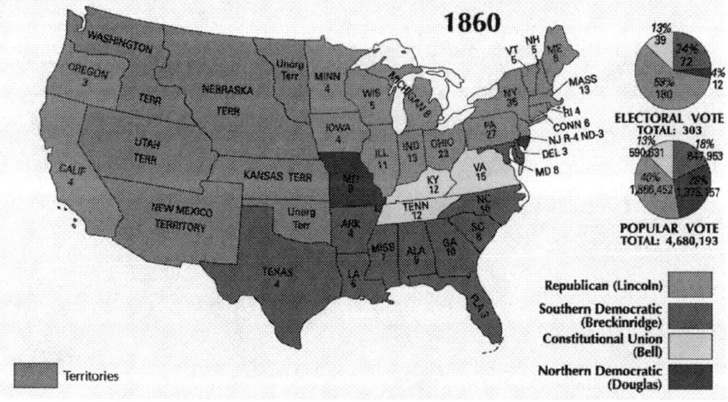

MAP 3.1 *1860 electoral map. From the National Atlas of the United States, www.nationalatlas.gov*

northern Democrats as the compromise candidate who would support "popular sovereignty" as the only legitimate way to end the conflict over the future of slavery and the West.

In addition to the two major party candidates, two other campaigns vied for public attention. Southern Democrats, believing a bolder pronouncement in favor of slavery's expansion was needed, chose John C. Breckinridge as their standard bearer. A Kentucky native, Breckinridge was the incumbent vice president and earned President Buchanan's backing. Rounding out the pool of major candidates was John Bell of Tennessee. Bell was nominated by the short-lived Constitutional Union Party, whose brief platform excoriated the other parties and pledged to uphold the Constitution. The party's platform argued that "Experience has demonstrated that Platforms adopted by the partisan Conventions of the country have had the effect to mislead and deceive the people, and at the same time to widen the political divisions of the country, by the creation and encouragement of geographical

FIGURE 3.7 *Edmund Ruffin, said to have fired first shot against Fort Sumter. Library of Congress, LC-USZ62-123816*

and sectional parties." Not all southerners were extremists on the slavery issue; in the Upper South states of Tennessee, Maryland, and Virginia, pro-Union sentiment was particularly common. During the summer of 1860 these moderates banded together and formed the Constitutional Union Party. But the relatively low percentage of the vote won by the Constitutional Unionists indicated the absence of a compromising mood among the voters. In the end, Lincoln won with only 40% of the vote but by far the most electoral votes (180), while Douglas received 30% but only twelve electoral votes, winning only Missouri and New Jersey. Bell attracted just 13% of the popular vote, with much of his support originating in the Upper South states of Tennessee, Virginia, and Kentucky. Breckinridge earned significant support in the Deep South, totaling 18% of the popular vote and seventy-two electoral votes. The South's worst fears were realized: a Republican, openly antislavery candidate was now president of the United States.

Secession

Even after Lincoln's election, white southerners were deeply divided over the proper response. Moderate southerners such as South Carolina newspaper editor Benjamin F. Perry still believed the Union could and should be saved, and that compromise with the North over the protection of slavery could be reached. Others, such as the passionately secessionist Virginian Edmund Ruffin, had been calling for the southern states to leave the Union since 1850 and saw Lincoln's victory as the chance to convince fellow southerners of secession's necessity. Most historians have concluded that even after the Republican triumph the majority of white southerners opposed secession, especially in the Upper South states of Virginia, Tennessee, North Carolina, and Maryland. But a series of events that unfolded in the early months of 1861 eventually convinced a total of eleven southern states to leave the Union and form a new confederation.

White southern politicians and intellectuals had long argued that states had the right to withdraw from the Union based upon the fact that the Constitution was ratified or approved by individual states that thus had the right to rescind ratification. Leading statesman and thinker John C. Calhoun had helped to develop the case for the right of secession during the Nullification Crisis three decades earlier. He had argued in his essay entitled "Exposition and Protest" that states could declare federal laws null and void if they deemed such laws unconstitutional. The notion of a "concurrent majority" lent credence to the argument that in a federalist system, states reserved powerful rights in opposing federal laws. During the 1830s, 1840s, and 1850s, what became known as the "states' rights" argument was further embellished by leading white southerners who came to believe that northern antislavery forces dominated the federal government.

Not surprisingly, the first state to take action was South Carolina, the same state that had declared federal law "nullified" during the Nullification Crisis. On December 20, 1860, South Carolina became the first state to declare it was no longer part of the Union in the "Declaration of the Immediate Causes" written by Christopher Memminger, who would later become Secretary of the Treasury in the new Confederate States of America. Memminger declared that:

> **the Union heretofore existing between this State and the other States of North America, is dissolved, and that the State of South Carolina has resumed her position among the nations of the world, as a separate and independent State; with full power to levy war, conclude peace, contract alliances, establish commerce, and to do all other acts and things which independent States may of right do.**

Fully aware of the magnitude of their secession from the Union, South Carolinians now waited for the reaction of the other southern states as well as the response of the newly elected President Lincoln.

Other states in the Lower South quickly followed suit, reflecting the Deep South's commitment to protecting slavery. After South Carolina left the Union in December 1860, Alabama, Mississippi, Florida, Georgia, Louisiana, and Texas all voted to secede within the next two months. On February 4, 1861, delegates from these seven states met in Montgomery, Alabama to establish the Confederate States of America and chose its first president, Jefferson Davis of Mississippi.

At first, the Upper South states of Tennessee, Virginia, North Carolina, Arkansas, Missouri, Kentucky, and Maryland rejected secession as a radical and extreme move. They still held out hope that the crisis could be averted. These states were also more economically dependent and tied to the North than were the Lower South states. In addition, states such as Virginia and North

Carolina knew that if civil war erupted, their towns and farms would be in the middle of the conflict.

Lincoln and the Start of the War

In his inaugural address, President Lincoln struck a firm but conciliatory tone. He still harbored hope that war could be avoided and tried to convince southerners that he was not their adversary. In his beautifully worded speech he declared that:

We are not enemies, but friends. We must not be enemies. Though passion may have strained it must not break our bonds of affection. The mystic chords of memory, stretching from every battlefield and patriot grave to every living heart and hearthstone all over this broad land, will yet swell the chorus of the Union, when again touched, as surely they will be, by the better angels of our nature.

He made clear that while he opposed the extension of slavery into the western territories, "I have no purpose, directly or indirectly, to interfere with the institution of slavery in the States where it exists. I believe I have no lawful right to do so, and I have no inclination to do so." Yet Lincoln was also adamant that secession was neither legal nor warranted, proclaiming:

that no State upon its own mere motion can lawfully get out of the Union; that resolves and ordinances to that effect are legally void, and that acts of violence within any State or States against the authority of the United States are insurrectionary or revolutionary.

As one of the most eloquent writers among American presidents, Lincoln carefully crafted his inaugural address to alleviate the concerns of white southerners. But southerners, particularly those in the seven states that had already seceded, were in no mood to be assuaged.

When Lincoln delivered his address, he already had a rebellion on his hands. Lincoln promised to hold on to federal property—the forts, arsenals, ports, and military hardware—that remained in the seceding states, including Fort Sumter in Charleston. Begun in the early nineteenth century, Fort Sumter was constructed on a man-made island to protect Charleston, South Carolina and its valuable harbor. There were only a few such southern forts that remained in federal hands, and in fact U.S. Army Major Robert Anderson abandoned another fort and moved his forces to Fort Sumter in case of attack by the newly formed Confederacy. Attempts to keep the island fort supplied were troubled by South Carolina's demands for its surrender. Lincoln, still hoping to thwart the secession of the Upper South, wanted to avoid provoking moderate southerners. He also realized upon becoming president that the soldiers at Fort Sumter would likely run out of supplies, including food, in the middle of April 1861. In early April, taking a moderate approach, Lincoln sent ships merely to resupply the fort. He tried to appear conciliatory by sending only food, clothing, and other necessities, not guns or ammunition. But South Carolina saw the fort as its territory now, and threatened to attack Fort Sumter if Lincoln sent supplies. Through intermediaries South Carolina General P.G.T. Beauregard demanded the fort's surrender but was rebuffed by Major Anderson. Believing negotiation to be futile, Beauregard and his soldiers began bombarding the fort in the early morning hours of April 12, 1861, in what is widely regarded as the beginning of the Civil War. Although only one soldier perished in

FORT SUMTER, SEEN FROM THE REAR, AT LOW WATER.

FIGURE 3.8 *Fort Sumter, seen from the rear, at low water. Courtesy of the New York Public Library, 809326*

the fighting, killed by a misfired cannon, southern forces outlasted Anderson, who ran out of ammunition and surrendered the fort the following day.

Lincoln was determined to restore federal authority and he called for 75,000 militia for ninety days to enter the South and retake what he believed to be federal government property. The president's call for troops convinced southern states that had not yet seceded to declare their allegiance with the Confederacy. Virginia withdrew from the Union a few days after the Battle of Fort Sumter, while in May 1861 Arkansas, Tennessee, and North Carolina became the last of eleven states to join the Confederate States of America.

Please visit the companion website www.routledge.com/cw/wells for additional study aids including chapter overviews, interactive quizzes, and more.

COMPANION @ WEBSITE

Discussion Questions

- Which events or crises of the 1850s exacerbated sectional tensions the most?
- After John Brown's raid in October 1859, do you think war was inevitable or do you believe that armed conflict could still be avoided? Be sure to support your answer with evidence.
- What were the central ideas of the Republican Party in the 1850s?
- How did the Democrats deal with a sectional crisis that divided the nation as well as the party?
- New York politician William Henry Seward argued that the sectional crisis was an "irrepressible conflict." Do you think civil war was inevitable? Why or why not? Be sure to provide evidence in support of your argument.
- To what extent was the demise of the Whig and Democratic Parties a symptom or cause of the sectional crisis?
- What evidence did northerners have that a "slave power conspiracy" was behind the perpetuation of slavery?
- Historians have argued that *Uncle Tom's Cabin* helped exacerbate hostilities between the North and South. What primary sources might be employed to make the case that the novel shaped Americans' attitudes toward slavery? What kinds of data would be useful in making the case?

Further Reading

Shearer Davis Bowman, *At the Precipice: Americans North and South during the Secession Crisis* (Chapel Hill: University of North Carolina Press, 2010).

David Detzer, *Allegiance: Fort Sumter, Charleston, and the Beginning of the Civil War* (Orlando: Harcourt, 2001).

Charles B. Dew, *Apostles of Disunion: Southern Secession Commissioners and the Causes of the Civil War* (Charlottesville: University of Virginia Press, 2001).

Tom Downey, *Planting a Capitalist South: Masters, Merchants, and Manufacturers in the Southern Interior, 1790–1860* (Baton Rouge: Louisiana State University Press, 2006).

Don E. Fehrenbacher, *The Dred Scott Case: Its Significance in American Law and Politics* (New York: Oxford University Press, 2001).

Eric Foner, *Free Soil, Free Labor, Free Men: The Ideology of the Republican Party before the Civil War* (New York: Oxford University Press, 1995, new edition).

Eric Foner, *Gateway to Freedom: The Hidden History of the Underground Railroad* (New York: Norton, 2015).

William W. Freehling, *The Road to Disunion, Volume I: Secessionists at Bay, 1776–1854* (New York: Oxford University Press, 1990) and *The Road to Disunion, Volume II: Secessionists Triumphant 1854–1861* (New York: Oxford University Press, 2007).

William W. Freehling and Craig Simpson, eds., *Showdown in Virginia: The 1861 Convention and the Fate of the Union* (Charlottesville: University of Virginia Press, 2010).

William E. Gienapp, *The Origins of the Republican Party, 1852–1856* (New York: Oxford University Press, 1987).

Michele Gillespie, *Free Labor in an Unfree World: White Artisans in Slaveholding Georgia, 1789–1860* (Athens: University of Georgia Press, 2000).

Allen C. Guelzo, *Lincoln and Douglas: The Debates that Defined America* (New York: Simon & Schuster, 2008).

Stanley Harrold, *Border War: Fighting over Slavery before the Civil War* (Chapel Hill: University of North Carolina Press, 2010).

Michael F. Holt, *The Fate of Their Country: Politicians, Slavery Extension, and the Coming of the Civil War* (New York: Hill & Wang, 2004).

Harold Holzer, *Lincoln President-Elect: Abraham Lincoln and the Great Secession Winter 1860–1861* (New York: Simon & Schuster, 2008).

Anthony E. Kaye, *Joining Places: Slave Neighborhoods in the Old South* (Chapel Hill: University of North Carolina Press, 2007).

Maury Klein, *Days of Defiance: Sumter, Secession, and the Coming of the Civil War* (New York, Vintage, 1999).

William A. Link, *Roots of Secession: Slavery and Politics in Antebellum Virginia* (Chapel Hill: University of North Carolina Press, 2003).

Forrest McDonald, *States' Rights and the Union: Imperium in Imperio, 1776–1876* (Lawrence: University of Kansas Press, 2000).

James Oakes, *The Scorpion's Sting: Antislavery and the Coming of the Civil War* (New York: Norton, 2014).

David S. Reynolds, *John Brown, Abolitionist: The Man Who Killed Slavery, Sparked the Civil War, and Seeded Civil Rights* (New York: Knopf, 2005).

Heather Cox Richardson, *To Make Men Free: A History of the Republican Party* (New York: Basic Books, 2014).

James F. Simon, *Lincoln and Chief Justice Taney: Slavery, Secession, and the President's War Powers* (New York: Simon & Schuster, 2006).

Kenneth M. Stampp, *America in 1857: A Nation on the Brink* (New York: Oxford University Press, 1990).

Frank Towers, *The Urban South and the Coming of the Civil War* (Charlottesville: University of Virginia Press, 2004).

Elizabeth Varon, *Disunion! The Coming of the American Civil War, 1789–1859* (Chapel Hill: University of North Carolina Press, 2008).

Eric H. Walther, *The Shattering of the Union: American in the 1850s* (Wilmington: SR Books, 2004).

Eric H. Walther, *William Lowndes Yancey and the Coming of the Civil War* (Chapel Hill: University of North Carolina Press, 2006).

THE WAR BEGINS

Topics Covered in this Chapter:

- Importance of Upper South Secession
- Battles and Military Maneuvering in the Spring and Summer of 1861
- Mobilizing for War
- Military Maneuvering in the West
- The Eastern Theater in Early 1862
- Naval Warfare
- Literary Responses to the Beginning of the Civil War

4

Introduction

Americans North and South had to come to terms with what the Civil War would mean for their families and communities, an adjustment that did not truly begin until the first real battles of the war. Immediately after the brief Battle of Fort Sumter in April 1861, Americans were still struggling with what war portended. After discussing the formation of the Confederate States of America, this chapter deals with the early fighting of the war, the intellectual and psychological transformations necessary to fight and kill, and the gearing up militarily, culturally, and politically for all-out war. Confronting the first battles to the Second Battle of Bull Run in August 1862, this chapter presents perspectives on the battles while relating as well the slow realization by Americans, both North and South, that the war would last far longer than nearly all had anticipated, despite elaborate Union plans to strangle the Confederacy by land and sea.

As Americans struggled to grasp the full meaning of civil war, they turned to art and literature to express their pain and suffering. A rich and evocative literature emerged during the war to which men and women, North and South, contributed. As important as battles are to understanding the nature of the Civil War, so too does wartime literature reveal thoughts and feelings that deepen our abilities to understand the war itself.

Importance of Upper South Secession

Throughout the early months of 1861 President Lincoln endeavored to keep the Upper South states of Virginia, Maryland, Delaware, North Carolina, Tennessee, Missouri, and Kentucky in the Union. While the Gulf South states had clearly withdrawn from the Union and presented a dire threat, President Lincoln concentrated his full attention for the moment on keeping other states from seceding and thus compounding the already troublesome dilemma. Such hopes were dashed when all of the Upper South states, except for Maryland, Delaware, Kentucky, and Missouri, announced their intentions to leave the Union, portending a dark future for Lincoln and the nation.

Just as the secession of the Lower South drained talented officers from the Union military, so too did Upper South secession remove experienced men such as Virginia's Robert E. Lee. Lee was widely respected in political and military circles, and had served in both the Mexican War and in the suppression of John Brown's ill-fated rebellion at Harper's Ferry. A quiet and effective leader, Lee was so admired that Lincoln asked the Virginia general to head the growing federal army, for which the president had just recruited 75,000 militia. Lee, electing to side with his native Virginia, declined the president's offer, resigned from the United States Army, and would eventually take command of the Army of Northern Virginia.

In addition to depriving the U.S. Army of some of its most experienced leadership, the secession of the Upper South kept tens of thousands of potential soldiers from joining Lincoln's volunteers and at the same time greatly deepened the pool of potential fighters for the Confederacy. As Lincoln had suspected, the secession of the Upper South significantly strengthened the Confederacy in terms of manpower, agriculture, industry, and wealth. In addition, Upper South secession rendered the suppression of the rebellion more complicated and costly, and most likely prolonged the Civil War by months if not years. In the 1860 census Virginia's free population numbered well over one million, North Carolina's nearly 700,000, and Tennessee's 800,000. The addition of these states allowed the Confederacy to call for 400,000 volunteers in late May 1861 after Lincoln had called for half a million to join the Union forces earlier in the month. On the other hand, the Upper South states that remained in the Union, along with West Virginia, a mountainous, pro-Union region that split off from secessionist Virginia, also supplied the Union forces with considerable support. Those states provided nearly a quarter of a million white and black soldiers for the North. Thus the decisions of Border States to secede from the Union played important roles in determining the strength of the Confederate and Union armies, as well as in ensuring that the Border States would see the worst of the fighting.

Like the other Upper South states, Virginia well knew that its geographical location would mean many of the battles would take place in its towns and farms. In May 1861 the Confederate Congress, meeting in Montgomery, Alabama, accepted Virginia's offer to move the southern capital to Richmond, where it would remain for the duration of the war. There were a number of reasons to move the capital to Richmond, but the primary factor was Virginia's symbolic importance to the Confederacy. As the home of Washington, Jefferson, Madison, and other statesmen, Virginia had long been known as a cornerstone of the Union. That state's decision to secede gave legitimacy to the Confederate government, an important step that was rewarded by seating the capital in Richmond. For the state's residents, however, the relocation of

MAP 4.1 *Map of Upper Virginia*

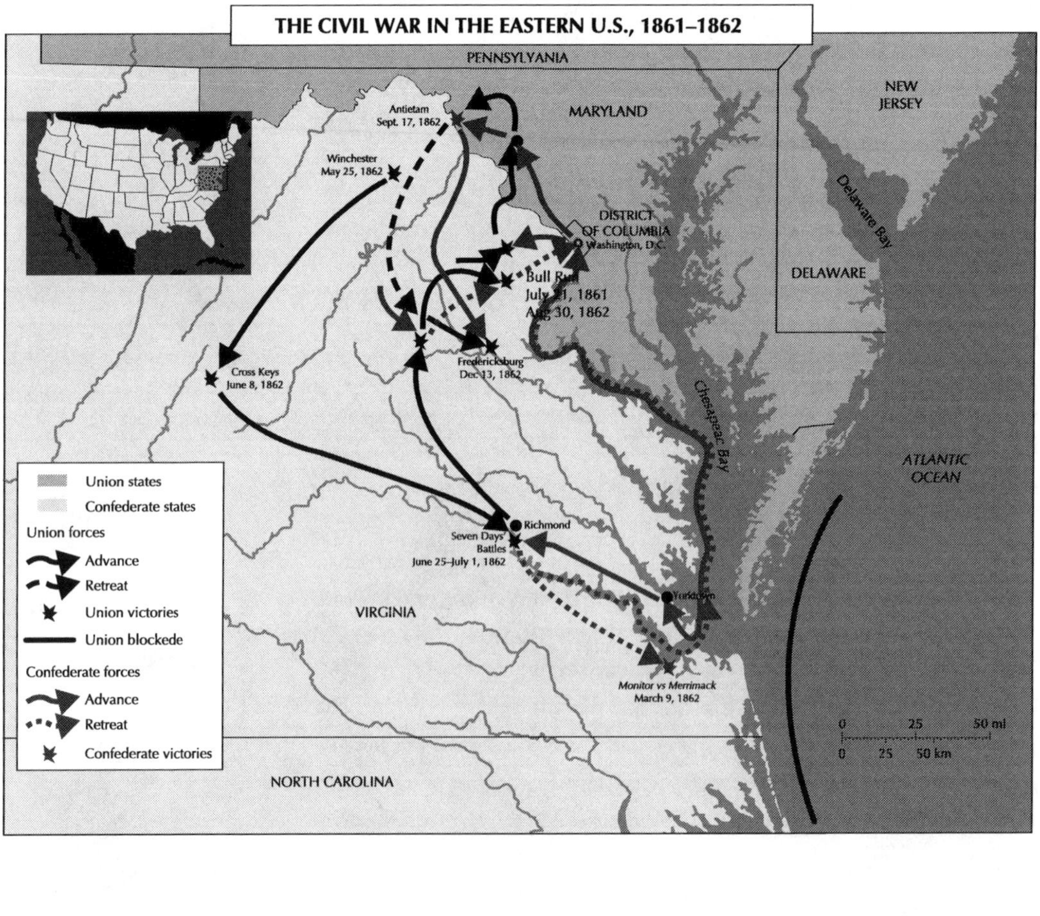

the Confederate capital would prove costly, as many battles would be fought within a 150-mile radius of Richmond.

Battles and Military Maneuvering in the Spring and Summer of 1861

The First Battle of Bull Run, fought on July 21, showed President Lincoln, as well as the nation, merely a glimpse of what lay before them. Near the town of Manassas, Virginia, just miles from Washington, D.C., more than 20,000 Confederate troops serving under the command of General P.G.T. Beauregard were encamped. Lincoln, determined to seize momentum for the Union cause, ordered Irvin McDowell and his 35,000-strong army to attack the Confederate encampment. Before McDowell could take advantage of his superior numbers, however, southern forces were bolstered by the arrival of more than 10,000 additional troops under Joseph Johnston. Much of the important fighting took place around Henry House Hill, which the Confederates controlled despite Union attempts to take it. Confederate General Thomas Jackson, who would earn the nickname "Stonewall" for thwarting Union advances, helped to turn the battle in favor of the South. What could have been an important early victory for the Union instead turned into an embarrassing defeat, made worse by stories of inexperienced and disorganized Union forces. The first major battle of the war, therefore, boosted Confederate morale and demonstrated to Union supporters that hopes for a quick suppression of the rebellion were illusory.

Lincoln not only had to fight the Confederacy militarily, which by necessity meant sending Union troops into southern towns and farms to put down the rebellion, but also faced the challenge of preventing the South from obtaining additional resources from within the nation as well as from other nations. In fact, prominent voices in Europe did support the Confederacy as a conservative counterrevolution against the growing forces of democracy. Equally vehement supporters of the Union, especially in the popular press and among working-class Europeans, saw the North as a bastion of free labor.

Europe, particularly Britain and France, watched the events of early 1861 unfold with great interest; a divided America greatly weakened the nation's ability to influence matters around the world. With the help of key abolitionists such as William Wilberforce, Britain had outlawed the slave trade in 1807 and abolished slavery altogether in 1833. Wilberforce and other British antislavery activists provided aid to American abolitionism throughout the late eighteenth and early nineteenth centuries. But Britain's expansive textile industry also relied heavily on southern raw cotton, a fact that led many Confederate politicians to believe aid from Britain would be forthcoming.

In what became known as "cotton diplomacy," the Confederacy decided in 1861 to embargo cotton exports to Europe. Southerners hoped that by refusing to send cotton to British textile mills in particular Europeans would be forced to recognize officially the legitimacy of the Confederate government. Initially cotton diplomacy seemed to work. When cotton exports dropped dramatically textile mills across Europe closed, throwing vast numbers of people out of work in English cities such as Manchester and Liverpool. However, European textile manufacturers quickly regrouped and imported cotton from other regions, especially India and Egypt.

Lincoln and the Union leadership was similarly concerned about France. The cotton embargo hurt France just as it hampered Britain's economy. French textile factories, unable to obtain southern cotton, closed their doors and massive unemployment led to widespread suffering. Just as Britain had financial interests in many southern cities, so too did many French businessmen have investments and interests in the Confederacy. French Emperor Louis Napoleon III was widely believed to be sympathetic to the southern war effort, and through diplomat John Slidell the Confederate government made repeated overtures to the French leader. Slidell, a Louisiana politician, later died in an explosion aboard a ship and France never officially recognized the Confederacy.

In November 1861 the Trent Affair laid bare the precarious nature of Europe's relations with an America embroiled in Civil War. Charles Wilkes, a well-known maritime explorer, captained the Union warship USS *San Jacinto*. On patrol in the Caribbean, Wilkes boarded the British ship, the *Trent,* and discovered Confederate diplomats James Mason and John Slidell aboard. Wilkes, acting alone, seized the envoys and took them to Boston where they were jailed. Wilkes's actions sparked an international crisis as Britain reacted angrily to the incident. War between Britain and the Union was avoided only when the crisis was defused by an acknowledgment from the State Department that Wilkes's actions were unauthorized. In the end, the crisis demonstrated the dangers faced by both the Confederate and Union governments in dealing with other nations. The South's wooing of the European powers, and Lincoln's determined attempts to keep other nations on the sidelines, would continue until 1863 when the Emancipation Proclamation virtually closed the door on possible international involvement in the Civil War.

While concerned that European countries might take advantage of America's divisions to support the Confederacy, Lincoln also recognized the importance of cutting off or at least limiting the South's ability to move soldiers and weapons through southern port towns, via river systems, and via the region's nascent but growing railroad network. Union General Winfield Scott, one of the leaders behind America's victory in the Mexican War, devised what critics called the "Anaconda Plan," which like a snake was to smother southern trade. The president saw early on in the war the necessity of blockading southern ports along the Atlantic and Gulf coasts and of taking control of the Mississippi River, and approved Scott's Anaconda Plan in May 1861.

In ordering a naval blockade in the spring of 1861, Lincoln knew that the Union naval forces were ill equipped to keep southern and foreign ships from entering the thousands of miles of coastline along the Atlantic Ocean and the Gulf of Mexico. In fact, British traders used small and fast runners to penetrate the blockade. At the start of the war, the Union ships numbered only a few dozen, but rapid production increased that number to nearly 100 in the summer and nearly 300 by December. While the effectiveness of the blockade is debated among historians, the Union warships likely did prevent large ships from entering most southern ports, leaving runners to rely on smaller ships that could carry only light loads. Equally significant, the blockade meant that naval forces had to capture southern port towns. The capture of Port Royal, South Carolina in November 1861 not only provided the Union with an important morale boost after the defeats at Fort Sumter and the First Battle of Bull Run, but also gave Union forces a base from which to attack the Confederacy. Ultimately the blockade would prove effective in limiting southern access to foreign goods and to the movement of resources within the Gulf States.

Mobilizing for War

Neither the Confederate nor the Union governments were fully mobilized for war in the first six months of 1861. At the beginning of the fighting, the North possessed significant advantages over the South in nearly every category relevant to winning the war: numbers of factories, factory production, numbers of banks, miles of railroads, size of the skilled workforce, and many other factors. To take full advantage of its superior numbers and productive capacity, the Union ramped up industrial production, which, perhaps more than any other single factor, led to victory. Yet it should always be remembered that the South had the advantage of needing only to maintain a defensive posture, an advantage made even more powerful by the use of rifled weapons.

To pay for the tremendous costs of conducting the war, the Union and Confederate governments employed a number of different strategies. Taxes on property and income were levied to raise badly needed funds, although the latter did not raise significant revenue. More effective was the issuance of paper money. Before the war the national economy was hampered by a dizzying number of banks that issued their own paper money, a situation that, as historian Stephen Mihm has demonstrated, encouraged counterfeiting. But in early 1862 the U.S. Congress passed the Legal Tender Act, which authorized the government to issue paper money, called "greenbacks," that could be used to settle public or private debts. This system, which laid the foundation for America's current monetary policies, smoothed the payment of war debts and helped the Union fund the tremendous costs associated with fighting the war. In addition, Lincoln and his cabinet authorized generous payments to any northern factories and businesses that aided the Union effort. Although southern towns also geared up for the war and dramatically increased their productive capacities, the South throughout the war suffered from spiraling and devastating inflation, which harms an economy by reducing the value of money and increasing prices on goods, including food. Southerners suffered from rapid and dramatic inflation in the latter half of the war, rendering even the most basic needs increasingly scarce. The longer the war lasted, the more the Union's significant industrial and economic advantages became increasingly important.

While the financial advantages were clearly and overwhelmingly on the Union's side, when it came to military leadership and experience the Union and Confederate forces were more evenly matched. Officers such as Virginia's Robert E. Lee gained leadership experience during the Mexican–American War in the late 1840s. Both sides at the start of the Civil War could boast of West Point graduates, talented leaders, and capable military strategists.

FIGURE 4.1 *General Robert E. Lee. Library of Congress, LC-USZC2-2409*

The emergence of Lee as the commander of Confederate forces in eastern Virginia proved fortuitous for the South. Lee has fascinated historians who have studied his personal character, military experience, and strategic thinking. Born at Stratford Hall, Virginia in 1807, Lee seemed destined to become a military icon. His father, Henry "Light-Horse Harry" Lee, was a hero during the American Revolution, while other relatives had also served in important political and military capacities. Although not wealthy, the family inculcated the values of a southern gentleman into young Robert E. Lee, and he enrolled at West Point in 1825. While there, Lee earned respect for integrity and hard work and finished second in his class. Classmates affectionately dubbed him the "Marble Model" because he supposedly never committed a disciplinary infraction.

Lee played a pivotal role in the Mexican–American War. In 1847 he aided General Winfield Scott in the preparation for an assault on Vera Cruz. Scott and the U.S. Army succeeded in capturing the Mexican capital, earning Lee the admiration of Scott.

After the war, he worked in the military in engineering and served in Texas. Coincidentally, Lee was in Virginia when John Brown attacked Harper's Ferry, and the general was sent to subdue Brown and his followers. Shortly after the raid Lee captured Brown and later helped to convict him.

Like many southern military leaders, Lee was torn when his state seceded from the Union. After all, in 1861 he had already served the United States military for more than thirty years. He opposed secession generally and initially rejected overtures from the nascent Confederate government. But when Virginia voted to leave the Union, Lee elected to resign his commission and join the Confederacy. His reputation and character would serve the southern army well, for organization and strategic planning were sorely needed. Lee helped in all respects, and shortly after Virginia seceded on April 19, 1861, he shaped tens of thousands of Virginians into a raw fighting force.

Although he has become an icon of American history, Lee was not without faults. He could be aggressive and stubborn, and scholars have faulted him for several strategic errors made during the war. The victories he won were often costly, with losses of men that the Confederacy could ill afford. In fact, rebels revered Stonewall Jackson more than Lee until the summer of 1862. But the Confederacy likely lasted longer than it otherwise would have without Lee in command. Equally significant, as historian Gary Gallagher has pointed out, Lee became for the South a symbol of the Confederate cause in a way that President Jefferson Davis

FIGURE 4.2A *General George B. McClellan. Library of Congress, LC-DIG-cwpbh-00537*

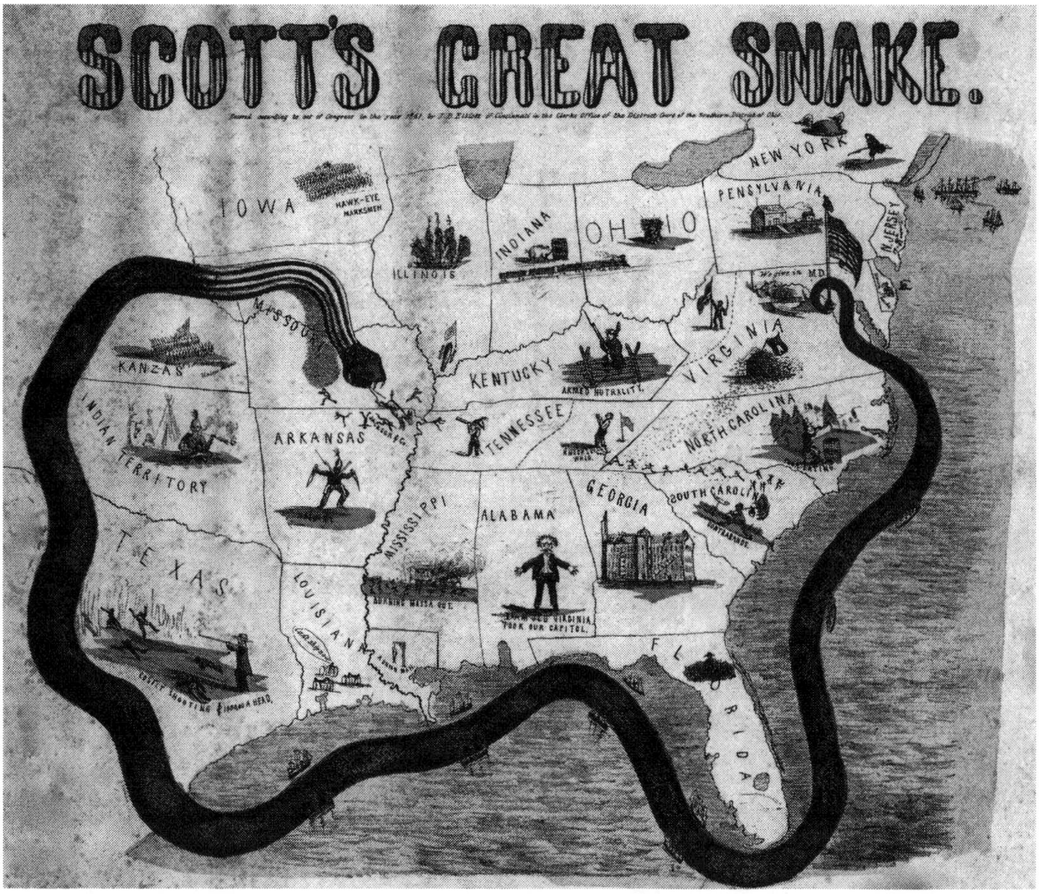

never did. While Lincoln remained a controversial figure among northerners, and only after his assassination became a powerful symbol for the Union and the abolition of slavery, Lee served early on in the Civil War as the symbolic leader of the Confederacy.

FIGURE 4.2B *General Scott and his Anaconda Plan. Buyenlarge/Getty Images*

Chief among the Union's early military leaders was George B. McClellan, who was born in Philadelphia and graduated from West Point. Like Lee, McClellan served in the Mexican–American War, arriving on the scene too late to participate in the Battle of Monterrey, but nonetheless aiding the American victory as an engineer. In the 1850s, he continued studying military tactics while actively engaged in the railroad business. Given his business and military experience, McClellan was destined to assume a leadership role for the Union, with a rapid rise through the officer ranks that began with service in Ohio in the spring of 1861. In his early thirties, McClellan benefited from key connections with Union political leaders, including Secretary of the Treasury Salmon P. Chase. He turned these connections into increasing levels of command, until he was second in military leadership only to Winfield Scott and President Lincoln himself. Eventually he had Scott pushed into retirement.

McClellan, however, would prove no match for Lee, and the only Union general who would be compared favorably to the Virginian was Ulysses S. Grant. Born in 1822 in Point Pleasant, Ohio, Grant would demonstrate the military boldness and daring that eluded McClellan and other Union leaders. Like others, Grant graduated from West Point and gained experience during the war with Mexico, where he served as a lieutenant and captain under Scott and Zachary Taylor. Although Grant would later denounce the war as an unjust attack on a weaker nation in the interests of extending slavery, his wartime experience in Mexico shaped his views on both leadership and strategy. In the early years of the Civil War, the Union military leadership struggled mightily, as McClellan and other officers fell short. Grant's success in the Western Theater of the war earned him great respect from Lincoln, and helped turn the war in the Union's favor.

Military Maneuvering in the West

Just months into the war, significant victories in the West and to some degree in the East buoyed Union hopes of victory. While fighting spread in the Eastern Theater of the war, from the initial battle at Bull Run to other areas of northern Virginia and along the Atlantic Coast, key battles took place further west under the command of aggressive leaders like Grant. At the end of 1861, Kentucky found that its attempts to remain neutral during the war were futile, as Confederate forces crossed into the state and took over the small town of Columbus. Grant then felt fully justified in occupying Paducah, Kentucky and from there he moved into Missouri and western Tennessee. Grant then set his sights on Confederate forts near the Cumberland River.

By early 1862, the Confederacy's lack of resources and centralized authority became apparent in southern Kentucky and northern Tennessee. The Confederate forces in the West were under the command of General Albert Sidney Johnston, who was not given sufficient resources to protect the important lines guarding access to the Tennessee and Cumberland Rivers. In fact, it might be argued that even considerably greater resources could not have defended the Confederacy's vast frontier. Given the thousands of square miles in the southern frontier, perhaps the task was impossible.

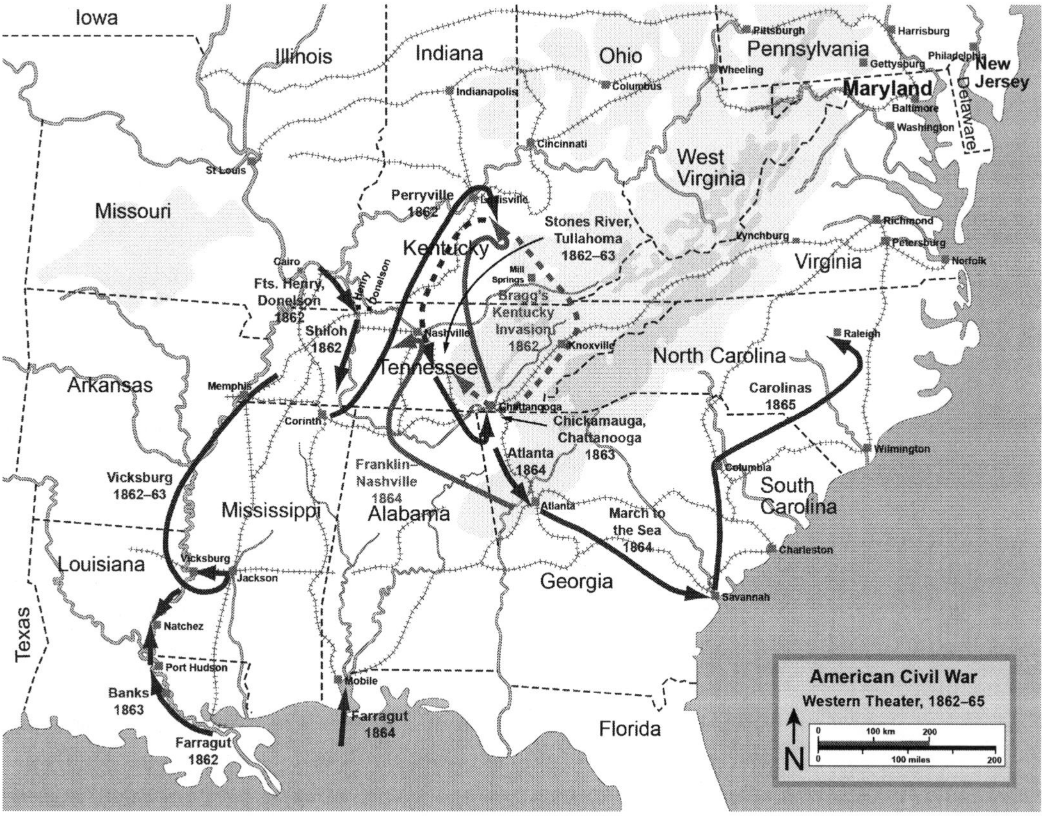

MAP 4.2 *American Civil War, Western Theater, 1862–1865. Black lines represent Union movements, while gray lines indicate Confederate movements. Map by Hal Jespersen, www.posix.com/CW*

Fort Henry and Fort Donelson were ill equipped to handle a Union attack in late January and early February 1862. Federal forces under Grant's command, combined with naval gunboats under the leadership of Andrew H. Foote, first assaulted Fort Henry and won access to the Tennessee River, followed by the capturing of Fort Donelson, which opened the Cumberland River to Union armies. Northerners searching desperately for good news saw Grant as a determined and relentless leader. His demand that Confederate forces cede Fort Donelson with an "unconditional and immediate surrender" attracted the notice of northern newspapers as well as of Lincoln himself. Grant's successful and determined prosecution of the war contrasted sharply with General George B. McClellan's slow and conservative maneuvering in the East. Grant, little known before the war, would win fame and admiration throughout the North, especially in Republican circles, ultimately leading to his assumption of command over the entire Union army.

Still, the Confederacy was hardly ready to concede defeat in the West, and its armies coalesced once again into an effective fighting force after the defeat in Tennessee and the fall of Nashville. In early April 1862 at the Battle of Shiloh, Grant's forces clashed with the Confederate army, leading to a deadly affair that saw more than 20,000 casualties. The extent of the casualties at Shiloh shocked the nation, especially since the losses at this single battle represented more casualties than the country had seen in the entire fighting of the Mexican–American War. One of the most important battles of the war, Shiloh changed many Americans' perceptions of the conflict.

Under the leadership of Albert Sidney Johnston, P.G.T. Beauregard, and Braxton Bragg, the Confederacy's Army of the Mississippi attacked Union soldiers at Pittsburg Landing, Tennessee on April 6, 1862. With fighting continuing in northern Mississippi and southern Tennessee, Henry W. Halleck would take command as the Union's leading officer in the Western Theater, but he proved as reluctant to move quickly as McClellan did in the East. Although Halleck's army numbered 120,000 he proceeded slowly, seemingly reticent to confront directly the opposing force of only 70,000 Confederate troops under Beauregard, a delay that provided the Confederacy with valuable time to regroup. The rebels, however, were unable to overcome Union advantages and the North won an important victory. Perhaps more importantly, Shiloh revealed to both sides the truly deadly nature of the war as no previous battle had. Grant later remarked on the Battle of Shiloh, realizing with hindsight how significant the fighting there had been:

The position of our troops, as here described, made a continuous line from Lick Creek, on the left, to Owl Creek, a branch of Snake Creek, on the right, facing nearly south, and possibly a little west. The water in all these streams was very high at the time, and contributed to protect our flanks. The enemy was compelled, therefore, to attack directly in front. This he did with great vigor, inflicting heavy losses on the Federal side, but suffering much heavier on his own.

The Confederate assaults were made with such disregard of losses on their own side, that our line of tents soon fell into their hands. The ground on which the battle was fought was undulating, heavily timbered, with scattered clearings, the woods giving some protection to the troops on both sides. There was also considerable underbrush. A number of attempts were made by the enemy to turn our right flank, where Sherman was posted, but every effort was repulsed

with heavy loss. But the front attack was kept up so vigorously that, to prevent the success of these attempts to get on our flanks the Federal troops, we were compelled several times to take positions to the rear nearer Pittsburg Landing. When the firing ceased at night the Federal line was more than a mile in rear of the position it had occupied in the morning . . .

Shiloh was the most severe battle fought at the West during the war, and but few in the East equaled it for hard, determined fighting. I saw an open field, in our possession on the second day, over which the Confederates had made repeated charges the day before, so covered with dead that it would have been possible to walk across the clearing, in any direction, stepping on dead bodies, without a foot touching the ground . . . Contrary to all my experience up to that time, and to the experience of the army I was then commanding, we were on the defensive. We were without [e]ntrenchments or defensive advantages of any sort, and more than half the army engaged the first day was without experience or even drill as soldiers. The officers with them, except the division commanders, and possibly two or three of the brigade commanders, were equally inexperienced in war. The result was a Union victory that gave the men who achieved it great confidence in themselves ever after. The enemy fought bravely, but they had started out to defeat and destroy an army and capture a position. They failed in both, with very heavy loss in killed and wounded, and must have gone back discouraged and convinced that the "Yankee" was not an enemy to be despised. After the battle I gave verbal instructions to division commanders to let the regiments send out parties to bury their own dead, and to detail parties, under commissioned officers from each division, to bury the Confederate dead in their respective fronts, and to report the numbers so buried.

Grant felt compelled to explain his actions during the battle for he came under criticism when the maneuvering was reported in the northern newspapers. The press questioned his decision-making and some intimated without proof that he was drunk on April 6, the first day of the fighting. Yet the Confederate army's defeat was important. Johnston was unable to achieve one of his chief aims and the Union forces were able to join their efforts in Tennessee.

By the end of the summer of 1862, Union supporters could point to significant advances in the West. Not only had the Tennessee and Cumberland rivers fallen under Union control, forcing the rebels to evacuate Nashville, but so too had most of the highly significant Mississippi River. Finally, the capture of New Orleans in June 1862, by far the Confederacy's most populous and economically important city, meant that the Union controlled most of the key ports and that Lincoln's plan to strangle the South in part by controlling maritime trade had been realized.

The Eastern Theater in Early 1862

While both sides spent much of the spring and summer of 1861 skirmishing in small-scale battles, the early months of 1862 proved shockingly deadly. Lincoln, anxious for the Union army to attack the Confederate capital at Richmond, ordered General McClellan to move his 100,000-man army from Washington into Virginia, which the general finally did in March. But McClellan still hesitated to advance even after getting underway, and he has been faulted by historians ever since for failing to confront Confederate forces north of Richmond, which numbered only about half of his large army. The president had ordered McClellan to advance on Confederate troops directly, but the general had other ideas. His reluctance was due in large part to his mistaken belief that the Confederate forces around Richmond numbered more than 180,000 soldiers, when in fact the total was much less than half that. The president wrote McClellan a lengthy letter on April 9, 1862 urging him to act: "The country will not fail to note—is now noting—that the present hesitation to move upon an [e]ntrenched enemy, is but the story of Manassas repeated." McClellan elected to attack the Confederate capital by maneuvering around the James-York Peninsula via the James River to attack Richmond. The Peninsula Campaign, instead of fulfilling Union hopes for an early end to the war, demonstrated that despite superior numbers, the Union armies, encumbered by McClellan's reticence, would suffer bitter and prolonged fighting. While much has been made of McClellan's reluctance to fight aggressively, it is important to remember that McClellan, like many northerners, believed that the war should leave the South intact as much as possible. He took

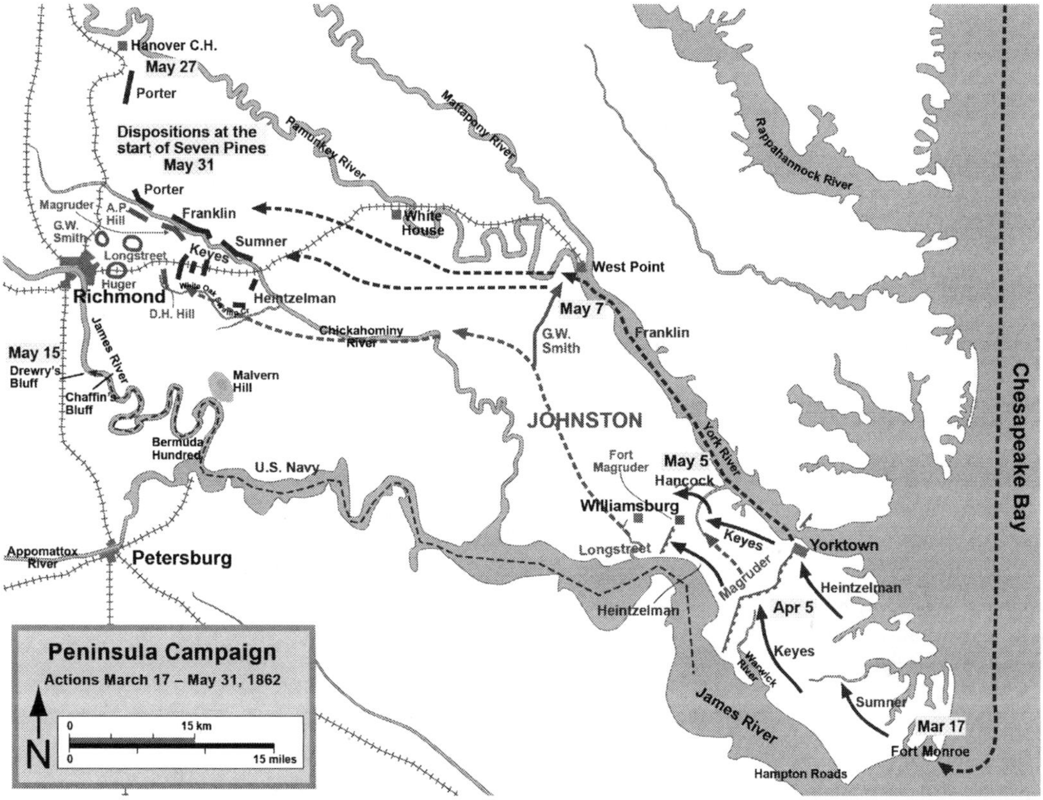

MAP 4.3 *The Peninsula Campaign, Actions from March 17–May 31, 1862. Map by Hal Jespersen, www.posix.com/CW*

a politically conciliatory approach and this conservatism was reflected in his cautious approach to fighting.

In preparation for the Peninsula Campaign, Lincoln assumed control over the overall strategy of the war and divided the Union army into five commands. McClellan was thus free to mobilize his army and focus his energies on the campaign against Richmond. He was opposed by Confederate forces under the commands of John Magruder and Joseph Johnston that together numbered about 55,000, seemingly no match for McClellan's army of more than 100,000. Indeed, Union soldiers captured Yorktown in early May 1862 followed by the port town of Norfolk. McClellan's attempts to reach Richmond were turned back by Confederate batteries, but his forces were so close to the southern capital that the Confederate government contemplated evacuating the city. At the nearby Battle of Seven Pines on May 31 and June 1, 1862, the first battle of considerable casualties of the Peninsula Campaign, the combined Confederate forces numbered more than 80,000 men while McClellan had cobbled together nearly 100,000 soldiers. Johnston was wounded and replaced by Robert E. Lee, who would lead the Confederate forces for the remainder of the war and who renamed his command the Army of Northern Virginia. Lee marshaled as many troops as he could, putting together an army of about 75,000 to combat McClellan. It was enough to protect Richmond and stave off McClellan, who retreated to the James River in June 1862. Combined Union and Confederate casualties numbered more than 11,000.

While both sides claimed victory at the Battle of Seven Pines, the Seven Days Battles between June 25 and July 1, 1862 ended the Peninsula Campaign with little to show for the Union's massive casualties, which numbered more than 15,000. Yet neither was the fighting during the Seven Days Battles an unqualified success for Lee and his army, whose casualties mounted to more than 20,000 after the battles. After the first several days saw fighting near Richmond between Lee's force of about 90,000 men and McClellan's 100,000 plus-strong Army of the Potomac, the two sides fought to a draw at the Battle of Malvern Hill on July 1. As Lee thwarted McClellan's assaults on Richmond, he and the Confederacy missed opportunities to pursue heavily damaged Union forces, and McClellan's army successfully gained a

FIGURE 4.3 *Confederate camp, Warrington Navy Yard, Pensacola, Florida, 1861. Library of Congress, LC-DIG-ppmsca-35444*

(Lot 4210) Confederate camp, Warrington Navy Yard, Pensacola, Florida, 1861.

defensive position at Malvern Hill, which Lee attacked unsuccessfully. Lee was confident that Richmond was safe for now, and McClellan's Peninsula Campaign had failed.

Naval Warfare

At the start of the war, neither the Union nor the Confederacy could boast of substantial navies. Yet both sides realized the importance of naval warfare in winning the war. In addition to the ability to import goods from European trading partners along its Atlantic Coast, southerners also viewed ships as vital to protecting river ports such as New Orleans and Vicksburg, and to the transportation of troops and supplies within the interior. Resources were scarce however, and the Confederacy had only two shipyards—in Norfolk, Virginia and Pensacola, Florida, neither of which had a significant impact on the war's outcome. Fortunately for the South the Confederate Secretary of the Navy, Stephen Mallory, was innovative and adept. Mallory experimented with new technology, including a primitive submarine, the *CSS Hunley*. He also helped grow the Confederate navy from almost nothing to a significant array of vessels, including new ironclads to combat the Union blockade. Even Mallory, however, could not overcome the South's disadvantages in resources, skilled labor, and money.

Union leaders were equally keen to blockade southern coastal and river ports to cut off supply and transportation routes, but this was no easy task. The Confederate coastline stretched for some 3,500 miles and even after gearing up for war the Union Navy could not hope to blockade it all. Yet, although harassed by Confederate ships, Union vessels did succeed in disrupting southern shipping routes. Led by Secretary of the Navy Gideon Welles, the Union Navy proved remarkably proficient at shipbuilding. Numbering only about forty-five seaworthy ships in early 1861, the Union Navy grew to more than 650 vessels by the end of the war, rivaling the great British Empire in sea power.

Although both the Union and Confederate navies were still gearing up in the spring of 1862, an important battle in naval history, the first battle between two ironclad ships, took place in March while McClellan was moving on Richmond. Confederate Navy Secretary Mallory realized the potential of ironclads to close the huge gap between the numbers of southern and northern vessels. The Union, too, built ironclads and sent them into battle.

FIGURE 4.4 *The Hunley. MPI/ Stringer/Getty Images*

Off the Virginia Coast, in an area known as Hampton Roads, the CSS *Virginia* (formerly known as the USS *Merrimack* and refitted by the Confederate navy) confronted the USS *Monitor* in an epic battle fought to a draw. Armed with an iron ram, the *Virginia* successfully attacked a number of wooden ships in Hampton Roads, leading many in the South to believe that they had found a way to defeat the Union blockade and attack northern ports. But the arrival of the *Monitor* from New York thwarted Confederate hopes of naval superiority and kept the *Virginia* contained near Norfolk. When that port city was captured in May, Confederate forces scuttled their ironclad ship. This key confrontation between two ironclad ships, however, is an important historical marker, for the tendency in future wars would be to use ironclad rather than wooden ships.

Literary Responses to the Beginning of the Civil War

The costly Peninsula Campaign, the fighting in western battles such as Shiloh, and the deadly early naval battles of the war deeply affected American culture. Northerners and southerners in the first year of the war had witnessed more suffering and death than many would have imagined. American towns, rivers, creeks, roads, and mountains became battlefields, and by 1862 thousands of families in both the North and South had lost loved ones. The trauma of the war and all of the suffering that came with it profoundly shaped the lives of an entire generation. Americans did this in countless ways, some through faith and religion, others through the daily routine of the home front, still others through art and literature.

Despite the scarcity of paper and ink supplies, as well as the significant disruption in trade and mail caused by the war, southerners and northerners continued to publish books, magazines, and newspapers during the war, providing modern observers with a valuable window on life during war. Until the 1850s, northern and southern intellectuals had managed to put aside differences over slavery and form friendships and professional relationships. Such comity permitted the emergence of a national literature before the war, and intellectuals often visited each other across the sectional divide. Northern writers such as New York's James Kirke Paulding visited friends in South Carolina, and southern writers such as William Gilmore Simms traveled to the North to visit literary colleagues. In the 1850s these literary friendships began to break down, a collapse caused in part by the rage over *Uncle Tom's Cabin*. By the 1850s Nathaniel Hawthorne was widely respected in the North for such novels as *The Scarlet Letter* (1850) and *The House of the Seven Gables* (1851). But when Hawthorne dedicated his 1863 book *Our Old Home* to his friend Franklin Pierce, the former president commonly regarded as a southern sympathizer and advocate of slavery, a storm of criticism erupted from northern readers. Many northern booksellers boycotted the volume and critics charged Hawthorne with insulting the Union cause.

Both the Union and the Confederacy could boast of writers and thinkers who saw the beginning of the war as an opportunity to use art in support of a sectional cause and to probe the meaning of death. In the North, prominent writers such as Ralph Waldo Emerson, Henry David Thoreau, and Walt Whitman had considered the war a chance to end slavery. Southern writers such as William Gilmore Simms and Margaret Junkin Preston penned prose and poetry in support of the Confederate cause. Few novels of quality came out of the war. In fact, the greatest Civil War novel was produced by a writer who had not been born by the war's end—*The Red Badge of Courage* by Stephen Crane.

While novels were perhaps less commonly produced during the war, by the second year of the war newspapers and magazines in the North and South were publishing large numbers of poems, most of which were amateur endeavors but which gave heartfelt expressions to anger, grief, and patriotism. Not surprisingly the three greatest poets of the age, Walt Whitman, Herman Melville, and Emily Dickinson, were motivated to express their varied reactions to the war and the national and personal suffering it brought to everyone's daily life. Each of the three sought, in his or her own characteristic way, to understand the war, its impact, and its legacy.

Whitman was born on Long Island in 1819 and spent much of his early adult life working in the printing business. As a teenager, he began writing poetry for newspapers such as the *New York Mirror* and by the early 1850s was working on his most important work, a collection of poems entitled *Leaves of Grass*, which was privately published in 1855. Praised by Emerson, the volume earned Whitman attention in and around New York, and when the Civil War erupted Whitman was caught up in the patriotic fervor. One of his Civil War-era poems captured the sentiment felt by many northern soldiers as they headed off to battle:

Beat! beat! drums!—blow! bugles! blow!
Through the windows—through doors—burst like a ruthless force,
Into the solemn church, and scatter the congregation,
Into the school where the scholar is studying;
Leave not the bridegroom quiet—no happiness must he have now with his bride,
Nor the peaceful farmer any peace, ploughing his field or gathering his grain,
So fierce you whirr and pound you drums—so shrill you bugles blow.

Such poetry, widely read in the North, put into verse the complex mix of sentiments felt by families whose sons, fathers, and husbands were marching into battle. Although Whitman would also support the northern war effort by helping to nurse wounded soldiers, he continued his active literary support. For example, in *Leaves of Grass*, Whitman painted a portrait of life on the battlefield that northern readers back home could appreciate. In "An Army Corps on the March," Whitman captured the movement of troops in a tone much more somber than the bombastic lines quoted above:

With its cloud of skirmishers in advance,
With now the sound of a single shot snapping like a whip, and now an irregular volley,
The swarming ranks press on and on, the dense brigades press on,
Glittering dimly, toiling under the sun—the dust-cover'd men,

In columns rise and fall to the undulations of the ground,
With artillery interspers'd—the wheels rumble, the horses sweat,
As the army corps advances.

Whitman's response to the war became personal when he became a nurse in the dozens of army hospitals in and around Washington, D.C. In the poem "The Wound-Dresser" Whitman recalls his efforts at helping to heal the injuries of soldiers on both sides while at the same time poetically hoping to help bind the wounds of the fractured nation:

(Arous'd and angry, I'd thought to beat the alarum, and urge relentless war,
But soon my fingers fail'd me, my face droop'd and I resign'd myself,
To sit by the wounded and soothe them, or silently watch the dead;) . . .
Thus in silence in dreams' projections,
Returning, resuming, I thread my way through the hospitals,
The hurt and wounded I pacify with soothing hand,
I sit by the restless all the dark night, some are so young,
Some suffer so much, I recall the experience sweet and sad,
(Many a soldier's loving arms about this neck have cross'd and rested,
Many a soldier's kiss dwells on these bearded lips.)

For poets like Whitman, the prevalence of death during the war became a common theme. The ever-present nature of death for Civil War-era families meant that grieving took many forms, especially in literature. For nineteenth-century Americans North and South, the primitive state of medicine and the poor understandings of disease meant that death could come at any moment, even without war. The beginning of the battles of course added greatly to Americans' thinking about death and its meaning, as historians have recently pointed out.

For Melville the war evoked irony and pity, as men were transformed into fighting machines that kill and frightened machines that are killed. Combatants always sit precariously at the end of someone else's weapon, as seen in the ironically titled "At the Cannon's Mouth," in which one very brave or very foolish man battles an ironclad:

Palely intent, he urged his keel
Full on the guns, and touched the spring;
Himself involved in the bolt he drove
Timed with the armed hull's shot that stove
His shallop—die or do!
Into the flood his life he threw,
Yet lives—unscathed—a breathing thing
To marvel at.
He has his fame;
But that mad dash at death, how name?

Is heroism real? Or is it madness? Is the war a moral necessity or a dash into chaos? Is it all of these things and more? Such was Melville's state of mind as he analyzed the effects of war on America throughout his collection *Battle-Pieces; and Aspects of the War*.

FIGURE 4.5 *Herman Melville, head-and-shoulders portrait, facing left. Library of Congress, LC-USZ62-135949*

FIGURE 4.6 *Walt Whitman, 1887. Library of Congress, LC-DIG-ppmsca-07550*

Dickinson, like Whitman and Melville, was often consumed in her poetry by thoughts of death and dying. The war only increased her interest in these themes. Born in Amherst, Massachusetts in 1830, Dickinson published little during her lifetime, but her most productive years paralleled the early years of the war. Appreciation for her poetry came posthumously, but her writing nonetheless reflected the contemporary national concern with death, and more specifically the guilt felt by those who lived on the home front while innocent young men died on the battlefield. In one of her poems, Dickinson powerfully related such feelings:

It feels a shame to be Alive—
When Men so brave—are dead—
One envies the Distinguished Dust—
Permitted—such a Head—
The Stone—that tells defending Whom
This Spartan put away
What little of Him we—possessed

In Pawn for Liberty—
The price is great—Sublimely paid—
Do we deserve— a Thing—
That lives—like Dollars—
must be piled
Before we may obtain?
Are we that wait—sufficient worth—
That such Enormous Pearl
As life—dissolved be—for Us—
In Battle's—horrid Bowl?
It may be—a Renown to live—
I think the Man who die—
Those unsustained—Saviors—
Present Divinity—

Southern authors, too, produced a wartime literature to express the South's suffering and to propagandize the Confederate cause. In this literary tradition, southern women were conspicuous and active. One of the most prolific female Confederate writers was Margaret Junkin Preston, sometimes referred to as "the poet of the Confederacy." The sister-in-law of Stonewall Jackson, Preston benefited from private tutors while growing up in Virginia. Her father, a Presbyterian minister and college president, instilled in Preston the importance of education but did not always approve of his daughter entering the public world of publishing. Yet, during the war Preston did publish poems in southern newspapers and magazines, and near the end of the war published a book-length poem entitled *Beechenbrook: A Rhyme of the War*. One of her most famous poems took a cue from Stonewall Jackson's dying words:

What are the thoughts that are stirring his breast?
What is the mystical vision he sees?
—"Let us pass over the river, and rest
Under the shade of the trees."
Has he grown sick of his toils and his tasks?
Sighs the worn spirit for respite or ease?
Is it a moment's cool halt that he asks
"Under the shade of the trees."

The death of Jackson and his poignant last words were later explored by other southern writers, including the native Georgian poet Sidney Lanier. Like many writers of the Confederacy, Preston continued writing poetry after the war, lending her pen to new causes: the justification of secession and the glorification of the South's Lost Cause.

The most prolific writer of the antebellum South was South Carolina's William Gilmore Simms, who had published numerous novels and poems before the war. An ardent southern partisan, Simms had been a strong supporter of slavery and the Confederate cause. In the 1850s he wrote a refutation of *Uncle Tom's Cabin* entitled *The Sword and the Distaff.* During the war, he continued to write, but he often found it difficult to concentrate. As he wrote to a southern editor in the fall of 1862:

You have well adverted, in your editorial department, to the difficulty of engaging now in literary composition. To do justice to the public, or to one's self, in letters, implies a perfectly calm mind, much leisure, and freedom from distracting occupation . . . But who can give his whole mind to [writing] when the whole country is heaving with the throes of a mighty revolution—when we are arming our sons for battle?

Yet Simms and other authors managed to write despite the wartime disruptions. Indeed, many found new inspiration from the war.

Known as the "Poet Laureate of the Confederacy," Henry Timrod provided the South with unabashedly bold writings that proclaimed the virtues of the new Confederacy. Born in Charleston, South Carolina, Timrod became a lawyer and published poems in Richmond's magazine *The Southern Literary Messenger* in the early 1850s. In "Ethnogenesis" Timrod declared after secession that the South was destined for a golden age and he praised the region's people and culture. During the war he continued to publish poems in southern newspapers and magazines, including "Graves of the Confederate Dead":

Sleep sweetly in your humble graves,
Sleep, martyrs of a fallen cause;
Though yet no marble column craves
The pilgrim here to pause.
In seeds of laurel in the earth
The blossom of your fame is blown,
And somewhere, waiting for its birth,
The shaft is in the stone!
Meanwhile, behalf the tardy years

Which keep in trust your storied tombs,
Behold! your sisters bring their tears,
And these memorial blooms.
Small tributes! but your shades will smile
More proudly on these wreaths to-day,
Than when some cannon-moulded pile
Shall overlook this bay.
Stoop, angels, hither from the skies!
There is no holier spot of ground
Than where defeated valor lies.

African American poets and writers contributed significantly to the literature produced during the war. Susie King Taylor, born to slave parents in Georgia in 1848, attended school clandestinely in Savannah since strict laws limited teaching to black children. With this modest education though, she became literate at a young age, an experience that would lead her to pen perhaps the only Civil War memoir published by an African American woman. In the spring of 1862, as Union forces began seizing southern ports along the Atlantic Coast, Taylor entered a Union camp at St. Simons Island. There she became a teacher for black children and adults who yearned to read. Throughout much of the war she traveled with a black regiment, aiding the Union cause by performing a range of domestic duties and teaching soldiers to read and write. Her memories of these experiences were published near the turn of the century in the form of a memoir entitled *Reminiscences of My Life in Camp with the 33d United States Colored Troops*. In this valuable memoir, Taylor dramatized how black soldiers faced racism and violence from white southerners. In one particularly powerful passage Taylor related the capture of Charleston by Union forces:

On February 28, 1865, the remainder of the regiment were ordered to Charleston, as there were signs of the rebels evacuating that city. Leaving Cole Island, we arrived in Charleston between nine and ten o'clock in the morning, and found the "rebs" had set fire to the city and fled, leaving women and children behind to suffer and perish in the flames. The fire had been burning fiercely for a day and night. When we landed, under a flag of truce, our regiment went to work assisting the citizens in subduing the flames. It was a terrible scene. For three or four days the men fought the

fire, saving the property and effects of the people, yet these white men and women could not tolerate our black Union soldiers, for many of them had formerly been their slaves; and although these brave men risked life and limb to assist them in their distress, men and even women would sneer and molest them whenever they met them.

Taylor's reminiscences and similar books have helped historians to understand in greater detail the wartime experiences of enslaved and free African Americans. In the late nineteenth century numerous slave narratives appeared that confirmed for former abolitionists the true nature of slavery's cruelty as did Harriet Jacobs's *Incidents in the Life of a Slave Girl* (1851) and Solomon Northup's *Twelve Years a Slave* (1853). But other important slave narratives were printed only after the war ended. Together these works shed light on the painful antebellum and wartime experiences of male and female slaves.

The writings of Taylor, Preston, Dickinson, and other northern and southern writers demonstrate that war is experienced in the pages of novels and poems as well as on the battlefield. When a society endures war, all aspects are affected, from family life, to technology, to military strategy, to literature. It is only by exploring the totality of war that we fully appreciate the experiences of the men, women, and children who suffered in the midst of unimaginable death and destruction.

Please visit the companion website www.routledge.com/cw/wells for additional study aids including chapter overviews, interactive quizzes, and more.

COMPANION @ WEBSITE

Discussion Questions

- Why did Lincoln consider the secession of the Upper South states to be of utmost significance?
- What did northerners and southerners do to mobilize for war?
- How did the Western and Eastern Theaters of the war differ?
- How did northern and southern poets respond to the war? How were their responses to war similar? How were they different?

- Assess the Union and Confederate strategies for military success in 1861 and 1862. What were the strengths and weaknesses of these strategies?
- How does war affect the political, economic, social, and cultural life of a society? How were northerners and southerners responding to civil warfare in the early years of the Civil War?
- To understand Confederate citizens' morale after the defeat of the Peninsula Campaign in July 1862, what primary sources might you examine?
- If you were studying the wartime experience of free African Americans in the North in the early years of the war, what sources could you use?

Further Reading

Daniel Aaron, *The Unwritten War: American Writers and the Civil War* (New York: Random House, 1973).

Stephen E. Ambrose, *Halleck: Lincoln's Chief of Staff* (Baton Rouge: Louisiana State University Press, 1996).

Michael T. Bernath, *Confederate Minds: The Struggle for Intellectual Independence in the Civil War South* (Chapel Hill: University of North Carolina Press, 2010).

R.J.M. Blackett, *Divided Hearts: Britain and the American Civil War* (Baton Rouge: Louisiana State University Press, 2000).

Diane Mutti Burke, *On Slavery's Border: Missouri's Small Slaveholding Households, 1815-1865* (Athens: University of Georgia Press, 2010).

Mary Price Coulling, *Margaret Junkin Preston: A Biography* (Winston-Salem: John F. Blair, 1993).

Susan Coultrap-McQuin, *Doing Literary Business: American Women Writers in the Nineteenth Century* (Chapel Hill: University of North Carolina Press, 1990).

William C. Davis, *Battle at Bull Run: A History of the First Major Campaign of the Civil War* (New York: Doubleday, 1977).

David Detzer, *Dissonance: The Turbulent Days between Fort Sumter and Bull Run* (New York: Houghton Mifflin Harcourt, 2006).

Alice Fahs, *The Imagined Civil War: Popular Literature of the North and South, 1861–1865* (Chapel Hill: University of North Carolina Press, 2001).

Drew Faust, *This Republic of Suffering: Death and the American Civil War* (New York: Knopf, 2008).

George M. Frederickson, *The Inner Civil War: Northern Intellectuals and the Crisis of the Union* (New York: Harper & Row, 1965).

Randall Fuller, *From Battlefields Rising: How the Civil War Transformed American Literature* (New York: Oxford University Press, 2010).

Gary W. Gallagher, *The Richmond Campaign of 1862: The Peninsula and the Seven Days* (Chapel Hill: University of North Carolina Press, 2000).

Charles M. Hubbard, *Burden Of Confederate Diplomacy* (Knoxville: University of Tennessee Press, 1998).

Howard Jones, *Union in Peril: The Crisis over British Intervention in the Civil War* (Chapel Hill: University of North Carolina Press, 1992).

Stacey Jean Klein, *Margaret Junkin Preston: Poet of the Confederacy* (Columbia: University of South Carolina Press, 2007).

Louis P. Masur, *The Real War will Never Get in the Books: Selections from Writers during the Civil War* (New York: Oxford University Press, 1993).

Stephanie McCurry, *Confederate Reckoning: Power and Politics in the Civil War South* (Cambridge, MA: Harvard University Press, 2010).

W. Caleb McDaniel, *The Problem of Democracy in the Age of Slavery: Garrisonian Abolitionists and Transatlantic Reform* (Baton Rouge: LSU Press, 2013).

James M. McPherson, *Tried by War: Abraham Lincoln as Commander in Chief* (New York: Penguin Press, 2008).

Frank J. Merli, *The Alabama, British Neutrality, and the American Civil War* (Bloomington: Indiana University Press, 2004).

Stephen Mihm, *A Nation of Counterfeiters: Capitalists, Con Men, and the Making of the United States* (Cambridge, MA: Harvard University Press, 2007).

David Hepburn Milton, *Lincoln's Spymaster: Thomas Haines Dudley and the Liverpool Network* (Mechanicsburg: Stackpole Books, 2003).

Phillip E. Myers, *Caution and Cooperation: The American Civil War in British–American Relations* (Kent: Kent State University Press, 2008).

James Oakes, *The Radical and the Republican: Frederick Douglass, Abraham Lincoln and the Triumph of Antislavery Politics* (New York: Norton, 2007).

Paul Quigley, *Shifting Grounds: Nationalism and the American South, 1848–1865* (New York: Oxford University Press, 2011).

Stephen W. Sears, *To the Gates of Richmond: The Peninsula Campaign* (Gettysburg: Stan Clark Military Books, 1992).

Stephen W. Sears, *George B. McClellan: The Young Napoleon* (New York: Da Capo Press, 1999).

Stephen R. Wise, *Lifeline of the Confederacy: Blockade Running During the Civil War* (Columbia: University of South Carolina Press, 1989).

ORGANIZING AND MOBILIZING FOR WAR

Topics Covered in this Chapter:

- Formation of the Confederate Government
- Organization of the Union and Confederate Military
- War in the Pacific Coast and Southwest
- Native Americans in the Civil War
- Communications and the Telegraph
- Railroads During the War
- Lincoln and Race at the Start of the War
- Port Royal and Other Experiments with Freedom During the War

5

Introduction

As the reality of the war set in after Shiloh and other early bloody battles, Confederate and Union forces mobilized. Soldiers were organized to maximize fighting ability and industries were called upon to aid the war effort. The telegraph and railroads were used extensively by both sides, though the Union could boast many more miles of railroad track and telegraph wires than the Confederacy. Historians have pointed out that the reluctance of many southern political leaders to surrender their states' authorities to the new Confederate central government hampered the South's ability to mobilize effectively. Historian John Majewski has argued effectively that the Confederate government became more centralized and exercised more authority than would have been thought possible in early 1861. Yet the South faced considerable organizational hurdles, including the fact that railroad gauges—the width of the tracks—were not uniform throughout the region.

The Civil War is often depicted as merely an eastern phenomenon. But many important developments occurred in the Far West. Native Americans in the West found themselves in the midst of brutal fighting, and some decided to join the Union or Confederate causes. Southern California in particular witnessed significant fighting between Union and Confederate sympathizers.

As the military forces braced for prolonged combat, Lincoln began rethinking his earlier positions regarding slavery in the South. As historian Eric Foner has argued, before the war, Lincoln actually adhered to the principles of the American Colonization Society, and in the 1860 presidential campaign he repeatedly declared that he would not interfere with slavery as it existed in the South, only prevent slavery's expansion to the West. As president, however, Lincoln's views on race and the continuation of slavery began to shift.

Formation of the Confederate Government

By January 1861, seven Deep South states (South Carolina, Florida, Louisiana, Alabama, Mississippi, Georgia, and Texas) had left the Union, and representatives from these states soon met to begin writing a Constitution and electing leaders. As it turned out the Confederate Constitution made few changes to the existing United States Constitution and many of the politicians who were senators or representatives before secession served in the same capacity under the new Confederacy.

The Provisional Congress of the Confederate States of America met in Montgomery, Alabama on February 4, 1861 to begin writing the new Constitution. Led by South Carolina's Robert Barnwell Rhett, delegates spent several weeks hammering out the document. Rhett was a fire-eating politician who had long championed secession, and now he was rewarded with the honor of chairing the committee to draft the new Constitution for the Confederacy. The resulting document shared a great deal with the older United States Constitution, only with more explicit protection for slavery and states' rights. Slavery was protected by a stipulation that "the right of property in negro slaves" could not be abridged and the freedom to move with slaves in tow into free territories or states was acknowledged. States' rights ideology was enshrined in the document as well; instead of a preamble announcing the desire to establish "a more perfect union," the Confederate Constitution emphasized the "sovereign and independent" power of the individual states. Though some reactionaries wanted to reopen the slave trade and others wanted a weaker federal system in which the central government would have little to no power

FIGURE 5.1 *R.B. Rhett. Library of Congress, LC-DIG-cwpbh-01450*

over the states, the southern Constitution certainly reflected the proslavery and pro-states' rights positions that had led to secession in the first place. The new document was adopted by the provisional Congress on March 11, 1861. Praise from southern voters and the press was far from unanimous. Some thought the Confederate Constitution was too similar to the Constitution of old, while others complained that it did not go far enough in protecting slavery. Such reactions foreshadowed the political and ideological divisions that would plague the Confederate government throughout the rest of the war.

The provisional Congress elected Jefferson Davis of Mississippi as president of the Confederacy. In early 1861, Davis was a nationally known politician and prominent defender of slavery and the South. Nearly fifty-three years old, with narrow, sharp cheekbones and a thin frame, Davis was initially opposed to secession but joined the cause when Mississippi seceded. After graduating from West Point, he fought in the Mexican–American War, landed a seat in the United States Senate, and then served as President

Franklin Pierce's Secretary of War in the 1850s. He was inaugurated as the first and only president of the Confederacy for a six-year term (a change from the United States Constitution, which granted the president a four-year term) on February 18, 1861. The new government chose Georgia's Alexander Stephens, a prominent southern Whig representative who had opposed the war with Mexico, as vice president. Known as a political moderate, Stephens held out the possibility of uniting fire-eaters and lukewarm secessionists into a powerful governing coalition. Instead, almost from the moment they took office, Davis and Stephens suffered from political attacks from within the South, including from the Confederate Congress.

Shortly after taking office, Davis wrote a letter to President Lincoln. The February 1861 letter introduced an envoy to the Union, who would begin to formulate treaties and establish parameters for diplomatic relationships between the two nations. Lincoln, of course, did not see the Confederacy as a separate nation but rather as a collection of rebellious states. In the letter, Davis claims he was "animated by an earnest desire to unite and bind together our respective countries by friendly ties." Davis had to know that Lincoln would not treat the Confederacy as a legitimate and independent nation, since Lincoln himself had referred to the South as rebellious states. The lack of such formal ties, however, would later prove problematic on issues such as the exchange of prisoners.

The Confederate Constitution kept the bicameral legislative branch envisioned in the United States Constitution. The representatives and senators of the southern Congress were largely familiar faces, many of whom had been advocating secession for a decade or more, but the Confederate capital was moved from Montgomery to Richmond after Virginia's secession in April 1861. Established election rules were re-adopted for the first Confederate political campaigns in November 1861. The winners were by and large the members of the provisional Congress that had drawn up the new Constitution. The first session of the new Congress convened in February 1862, and immediately it began issuing bonds and notes to raise money for the southern cause. However, the Congress would not play the role of rubber-stamp to the policies recommended by Davis and his cabinet. On the contrary, as we will later see, dissatisfaction with the course of the war and the plight of southern citizens away from the battlefield generated bold criticism of the Davis administration within the halls of the Confederate Congress.

FIGURE 5.2 *Confederate Capitol Building, Richmond. Photo by Buyenlarge/Getty Images*

Organization of the Union and Confederate Military

The Confederate and Union militaries were organized along similar lines and followed long-held custom. The basic unit for both the infantry—foot soldiers—and the cavalry—horse-mounted soldiers—was the regiment; the basic unit of the artillery—soldiers in charge of cannons and other weaponry—was the battery. The regiments were supposed to have about 1,000 men each, and these regiments were grouped into brigades, brigades into divisions, divisions into corps (pronounced "core"), and corps into armies.

In reality, however, the regiments rarely counted the traditional 1,000 or so men, and sometimes they were able to muster only a few hundred. While stories of bravery and courage certainly pervade the experiences of both sides, so too do reports of absentee soldiers and deserters. In fact, many soldiers drifted back and forth between home and the fighting, leaving because of homesickness or to tend crops. A captain knew how many men in his company answered the morning roll call, but an army commander did not always know how many of his men might desert the night before a battle, a fact rendered more troubling for historians trying to recreate the numbers 150 years later. So when historians write of the number of soldiers on each side of a battle, rarely are those numbers determined with precision. Needless to say, absenteeism and desertion were constant complaints for Union and Confederate generals, particularly for southern officers who did not have men to spare. From the soldiers' perspective though, volunteering to fight was just that: a voluntary commitment that might be withdrawn or reconsidered.

Early in the war an informal organizing of the regiments and brigades gradually gave way to a more rigid structure. Volunteer regiments were raised by states and then taken into national service. The large numbers of soldiers in the Union army by 1862—the Army of the Potomac counted more than 100,000 men—meant that officials had to reorganize the commands. The cavalry was similarly organized by General Joseph Hooker, and became an important force for the Union in the latter years of the war. The Confederacy was likewise organized and reorganized during the war. Names of armies took the form of their origins as state militia; the Army of Tennessee under General Braxton Bragg in the West and the Army of Northern Virginia led by General Robert E. Lee in the East were two of the Confederacy's most important forces.

Both sides realized the debilitating effects of desertion, and if caught deserters were treated harshly. Traditionally the punishment for desertion in wartime was execution, but this was rarely enforced, much to the chagrin of Union and Confederate generals who believed that only firm discipline could keep soldiers in the armies. Yet on many occasions, deserters were in fact dealt with harshly. One African American woman in camp with Union soldiers remembered many years later the punishment for desertion:

While at Camp Shaw, there was a deserter who came into Beaufort. He was allowed his freedom about the city and was not molested . . . On his return to Beaufort a second time, he was held as a spy, tried, and sentenced to death, for he was a traitor. The day he was shot, he

was placed on a hearse with his coffin inside, a guard was placed either side of the hearse, and he was driven through the town. All the soldiers and people in town were out, as this was to be a warning to the soldiers. Our regiment was in line on dress parade. They drove with him to the rear of our camp, where he was shot. I shall never forget this scene.[1]

While soldiers left the battlefield for many personal reasons, others deserted for financial gain. Since the armies often provided a financial bonus for enlisting, some soldiers deserted only to rejoin under a different name to claim another bonus. Bounty jumping mainly affected the federal armies after the implementation of the Enrollment Act of 1863. Both sides also provided incentives for enemies to desert their armies; the Confederacy seduced Union soldiers with promises of financial rewards and land grants.

Deserters combined with anti-war activists throughout the nation to form pockets of resistance. Quakers in the North formed pacifist communities who opposed killing even in times of war. Also known as the Religious Society of Friends, the Quakers were influential in states such as Pennsylvania and had been leaders in conducting the Underground Railroad before the war. Some still fought in the war despite the pacifist standing of the faith, while other Quakers aided the war effort through peaceful means.

Many northerners and southerners opposed to the war took to the Appalachian Mountains where they sought isolation. Deserters flocked to the mountains to escape capture, but elsewhere islands of resistance became famous. Federal troops had to disperse a camp of about 1,000 draft resisters in Ohio. In southeastern Mississippi, Jones County and its neighboring counties earned infamy within the South for its opposition to secession and the Confederacy. What became known as the "Free State of Jones" was led by the irascible Newton Knight, a white southerner who lived with, and had children with, a slave. Knight and his supporters defended themselves against Confederate officials sent to arrest them for desertion and treason, but Jones County remained an anti-war holdout until the end of the war. Although Jones County was perhaps the most famous of the desertion "colonies," it was hardly the only one. Desertion and absenteeism were painful thorns in the sides of Union and Confederate officers alike.

War in the Pacific Coast and Southwest

The Pacific Coast Theater of the war consisted of California, Oregon, and Washington, and though few battles were fought in the region, the stakes were significant. Southern California, especially the area in and around Los Angeles, was known as a bastion of Confederate support and the state was deeply divided in the first months of the war as Unionists took control of northern California in the first weeks after the Battle of Fort Sumter. Many southerners were stationed in forts along the West Coast, including Kentucky native Albert Sidney Johnston, who resigned his post at the Presidio in San Francisco as head of the Department of California and Oregon. Johnston went to southern California and then to the East where he became an important Confederate general until his death at the Battle of Shiloh in Tennessee during April 1862. As a result of resignations by Johnston and other Confederate sympathizers, the North was deprived of western leaders who might have helped combat rebels in the West.

In May and June 1861, the Far West was still very much in play, but quick action by Union military leaders secured the state for the North by the summer. General Edwin Vose Sumner, a Boston native who was in his early sixties, took over the Department of California and Oregon when Johnston resigned, and seized control of the state militia. He sent troops from Ft. Tejon in south central California to subdue Confederate sympathizers in Los Angeles in early May. Many Mormons in the Utah Territory and the few settlers in western Nevada remained neutral during the war. Some of Utah's Mormons fought with the Union's territorial government, and internal divisions led to the Morrisite Rebellion in the early years of the war. President Lincoln had to devote time and resources to this troublesome region throughout the war, but fighting did not rise above the level of minor skirmishes. California, on the other hand, was a primary recruiting state for the Union, and Bay Area "California Volunteers," also known as the "California Column," headed to the southwestern territories, where they prevented the Confederates from gaining control of the southwest.

Western Texas contained important garrisons, including Forts Bliss and Quitman along the Rio Grande River, and Fort Davis just to the East of the river. In early 1861, secessionists took control of the forts, which then became key launching points for Confederate attempts to take over the Arizona and New Mexico territories, which were divided at the 34th parallel. In and around Santa Fe and Albuquerque, Unionists were in control, but further to the

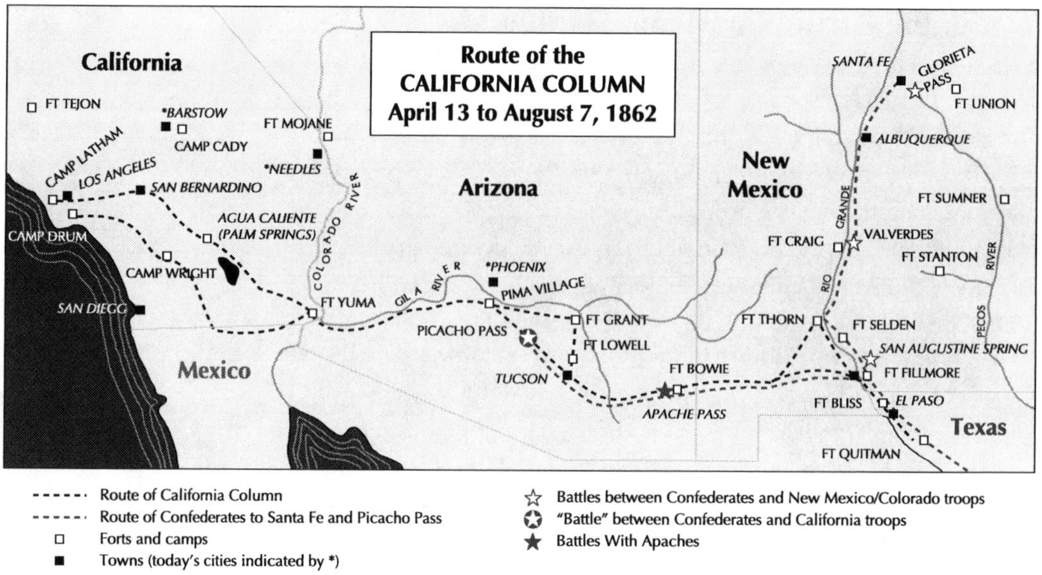

MAP 5.1 *Map of the American West. Photo by Buyenlarge/ Getty Images*

south in Arizona, Confederate sympathizers could be found in Tucson and Mesilla. During the summer of 1861, Confederates made steady progress in expanding their control of southeastern Arizona with the help of Texas forces. Lieutenant Colonel John Robert Baylor led Confederates in victory at the Battle of Mesilla in July 1861, leading Confederates to take over Fort Fillmore a few days later. This string of successes, combined with secessionist control of Tucson and the evacuation of Union troops from Arizona, led the Confederacy to declare its jurisdiction over the Arizona Territory.

The Union would attempt to regain control over Arizona using California volunteers, who began flooding into Camps Latham and Drum and Fort Yuma in the fall of 1861. The New Mexico Campaign began in early 1862 with rebel movements led by Confederate Brigadier General Henry Hopkins Sibley, a man with deep roots in New England but southern sympathies. Sibley began his campaign in January 1862 by moving north along the Rio Grande River in an effort to wrest control of Santa Fe and Albuquerque, especially Fort Union, from the Federals. Sibley's hope was to then take over mines in Colorado and then to move west to attack California. In March at the Battle of Glorieta Pass, the two sides met, with the heaviest fighting occurring on March 28. Companies from the Texas Mounted Rifles led by Charles Pyron and William Read Scurry nearly succeeded in defeating the Union soldiers at Apache Canyon. But Unionists disrupted the Confederate supply lines, forcing the secessionists back to camp in Santa Fe. Ultimately, the

Battle of Glorieta Pass would prove important; the fighting marked the gradual return of the entire southwest to Union control and the end of Confederate hopes to hold the valuable lands of the region. The battle also doomed any lingering hopes the Confederacy might have had about conquering California. Yet in the summer and fall of 1862, Unionists still had work to do. Confederates relinquished authority over its last southwestern stronghold at Mesilla, but Unionists had to contend with Native Americans who asserted their own interests in the midst of wartime chaos.

Native Americans in the Civil War

Central to Unionist concerns in the southwest were the powerful Apaches. In July 1862, as Union soldiers from California marched into the southwest, they were ambushed by Apache raiders. This raid foreshadowed fighting for the remainder of the war, for as Union forces prevented Confederates from reasserting authority in the southwest, they had to contend with rising tribes of Native Americans. During the fighting between Native Americans and the Union soldiers, many individuals would win fame. Christopher Houston "Kit" Carson, already a famous frontier scout, brutally subdued the Navajo Indians during the war, and earned notoriety as a frontiersman and Indian fighter. The fighting between Native Americans and Union soldiers in the West during the Civil War began decades of bitter fighting that endured to the end of the nineteenth century, when land-hungry settlers conflicted with Native American tribes who had made their homes in the western territories for centuries.

Before the war, Native Americans and European settlers already had more than two centuries of mutual history, a past riddled with mistrust and warfare. Many of the tribes along the Atlantic Coast had been decimated by European diseases and conflicts by the late 1700s, but in the early 1800s many tribes in the interior regions away from the coast remained. But as Europeans continued to encroach upon lands to the west of the Atlantic Coast, Native Americans were forcibly moved to reservations further west to places such as southwestern North Carolina and the Oklahoma Territory. In the 1830s, many members of the Cherokee, Choctaw, Seminole, and Creek were marched to the West in the Trail of Tears during which many Indians died. So before the war the decades of mistrust between Native Americans and the federal government would seem to leave little room for cooperation between the Indians and either the Confederate or Union sides of the war.

Conflict and death characterized much of the Native American experience during the war, but many Indians did serve in the Union and Confederate military. In some cases entire tribes sided with the North and South; in the case of the Cherokee, they were deeply divided as to which side to support. Some 30,000 or so Native Americans served in the war as soldiers, engineers, scouts, guides, laborers, or spies; a few, such as Seneca Ely S. Parker, became leaders in the military. Both the Confederate and Union governments realized the importance of Indians, and both tried earnestly to recruit Native American leaders to their side. While most tribes joined the Union cause, such as the Delaware people who declared their alliance with the North in October 1861, many Creeks and Choctaws owned hundreds of slaves and sided with the Confederacy.

Union officials actively recruited Native American volunteers, issuing a call in early 1862 for recruits. Thousands formed the 1st and 2nd Indian Home Guard. Company K of the 1st Michigan sharpshooters earned renown for their bravery and skill while serving under Ulysses S. Grant and the Army of the Potomac, when they joined in battles at Spotsylvania and Petersburg. Tribes throughout Virginia and North Carolina also joined the Union, as did many of the Iroquois tribe. Some Native American Union soldiers also served in African American regiments. Generally Native American soldiers received overwhelmingly positive reports from their Union commanders.

Among the most prominent Native Americans to serve the Union was Ely S. Parker, a member of the Seneca nation who became an engineer for the North and a close confidant of Ulysses S. Grant. Born in New York in the Tonawanda Reservation, Parker studied law but was not permitted to practice since he was a Native American. He then became a skillful engineer. While serving in this latter capacity, Parker met Grant in Galena, Illinois, and the two men became friends. The professional relationship would survive the war and, as president, Grant would appoint Parker to the post of Commissioner of Indian Affairs. As soon as the war began, Parker volunteered to recruit Iroquois for the Union but was rejected. This was also true of African Americans early on in the war, as black soldiers volunteered only to be turned down by Union officials until later in the war. Lincoln would insist upon open recruitment of black soldiers, and he similarly welcomed Native Americans who wished to fight for the North. Grant agreed

FIGURE 5.3 *City Point, Virginia. Lt. Col. Ely S. Parker (General Grant's military secretary), General John A. Rawlins, Chief of Staff and others at Grant's headquarters. Library of Congress, LC-DIG-cwpb-02956*

with the president, and Grant intervened to get Parker commissioned as a captain in 1863. Parker played a key role later at Vicksburg, Mississippi as Grant and the Union army took the river town. Parker then became Grant's military secretary and handled much of the general's correspondence as a lieutenant colonel.

Native Americans also joined the Confederacy. Albert Pike trained Confederate cavalry regiments made up of Native Americans from the "Civilized Tribes" and helped negotiate treaties between the rebels and the Cherokee. In addition to Pike's efforts, the rebels could count important Native American leaders among their ranks. William Holland Thomas was born to white parents in western North Carolina, but he maintained close ties with the Cherokee and even learned their language. Adopted into the Cherokee tribe with the nickname "Little Will," Thomas earned the trust of the Cherokee and they responded favorably to his call for Confederate volunteers. He raised about 400 soldiers who harassed Union forces in western North Carolina and eastern Tennessee all the way to May 1865. Holland's success in organizing members of the Cherokee belies the internal divisions the tribe suffered. In fact, the Cherokee would suffer terribly during the war, losing more than one-third of their number by 1865. While

Holland led tribal Confederates in the East, Stand Waite and John Ross joined the Confederacy further west in the Oklahoma Territory. In October 1861 the Cherokee signed a treaty with the Confederacy, promising to contribute soldiers to the Confederate army in return for protection. After the Battle of Pea Ridge, however, the Confederacy could no longer offer firm protection for the Cherokee. Fought in northwest Arkansas on March 7 and 8, 1862, the battle was a key victory for Union troops under Brigadier General Samuel Curtis. After Pea Ridge, Missouri would no longer be threatened by Confederate forces and the Cherokee lost a key means of support.

Communications and the Telegraph

Until the antebellum period, news traveled slowly across America. Before the invention of communication devices such as the telegraph and telephone, the only way for news to spread was through the postal system or by word of mouth. In cases of emergency, fast riders mounted horses to deliver news. But although, as historian Richard John has written, the national postal system made important advances by the 1830s, mail still required travel over land or sea. Improvements in transportation, such as the construction of plank roads, canals, and railroads, helped immensely in speeding travel for early nineteenth-century Americans and also improved the pace of mail delivery. News from Europe was even slower, since mail had to be delivered by ships. So by the early 1800s progress in transportation had quickened the spread of mail, news, and information of all kinds, but mail could still take weeks to reach its destination. The invention of the telegraph by Samuel B.F. Morse changed the spread of information from days and weeks to mere minutes.

Born in Massachusetts in 1817, Morse began experimenting with a device that could send electronic signals over wires in the early 1830s. Although a northerner, Morse himself supported slavery as an institution ordained by God and denounced abolitionists as meddlesome fanatics:

My creed on the subject of slavery is short. Slavery per se is not sin. It is a social condition ordained from the beginning of the world for the wisest purposes, benevolent and disciplinary, by Divine Wisdom. The mere holding of slaves, therefore, is a condition having per se nothing of moral character in it, any more than

the being a parent, or employer, or ruler . . . When the relation of Master & Slave is left to its natural workings under the regulations divinely established, and unobstructed by outside fanatic busybodyism, the result, on the enslaved and on society at large, is salutary and benevolent. When resisted, as it is by the abolitionism of the day, we have only to look around us to see the horrible fruits, in every frightful, and disorganizing, and bloody shape.

Such views were quite common among northerners, even on the eve of the Civil War. Conservative northerners such as Morse believed strongly that the union between North and South was more important than whatever evils slavery might represent, and they worried that abolitionist agitation would anger southerners and force them to secede from the country. Morse's conservative ideology can also be seen in his strident anti-immigrant and anti-Catholic sentiments. Yet Morse was to be credited with one of the greatest inventions of the nineteenth century. His electromagnetic telegraph was no less than a revolution in human communication.

With insights contributed by other inventors and scientists adding to the telegraph's power, signals could be sent several miles, and by the 1840s signals were powerful enough to be transmitted from New York to Mississippi. Eventually an elaborate system of wires crisscrossed the country and cable was laid to connect America with Europe. The instant transmission of signals using Morse code fundamentally and permanently altered the spread of news and information even before the Civil War began.

Both the Union and Confederate forces recognized the need for fast communication over great distances, and both sides made wide use of the telegraph and relied heavily upon the cooperation of private telegraph companies. The Confederacy incorporated their telegraph corps into the broader Signal Corps, while the Union created a new department, the Military-Telegraph Corps, which was part of the Quartermasters Department. Confederate telegraphs were used in cities and in the field with the help of private telegraph companies. The Union, however, struggled mightily to maintain clear lines of authority between the military and the largely independent employees of private businesses such as the American Telegraph Company. Although considerable hostility developed between field commanders and telegraph employees over authority, the Union used the telegraph to great effect, laying down thousands of miles of wire that was strung

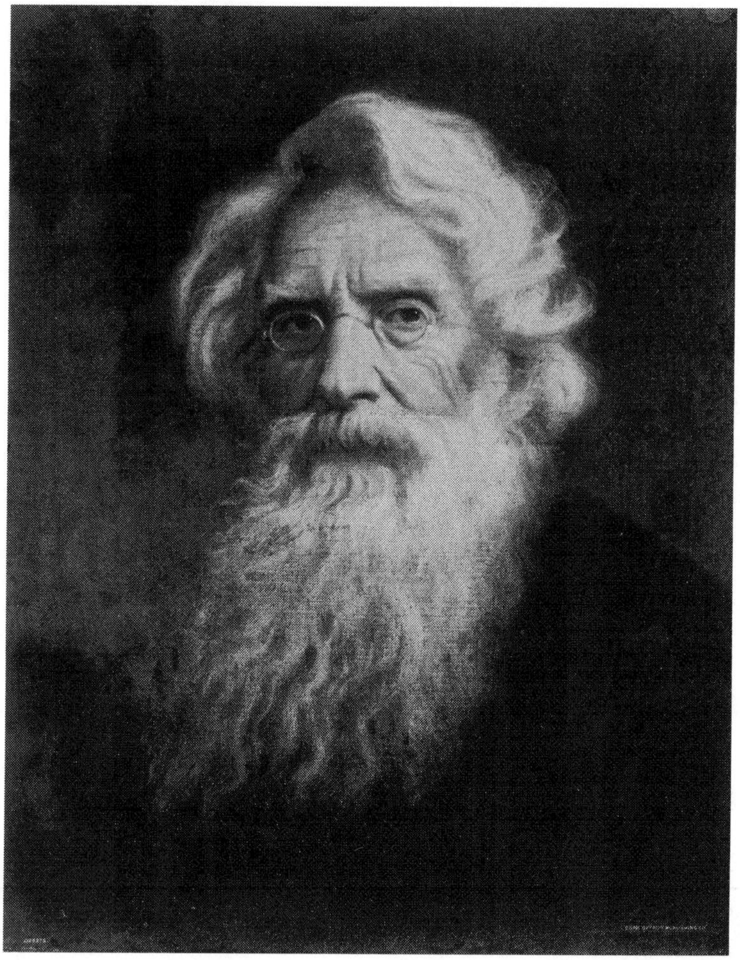

FIGURE 5.4A *Samuel F.B. Morse. Library of Congress, LC-DIG-det-4a28540*

on often hastily raised wooden poles. The U.S. government solved some of the problems with lines of authority by ordering the government take-over of lines in and around Washington, D.C. shortly after the war began and, in 1862, it assumed control over all lines in the Union. President Lincoln realized the importance of the telegraph and he could often be found in the telegraph office in Washington waiting for the latest news from the field.

The telegraph system was far from foolproof, however. Lines could be wiretapped and generals on both sides worried constantly that messages were being intercepted. So Union and Confederate telegraph operators developed an elaborate ciphering system to thwart eavesdroppers. New operators had to be trained to code messages, which often led to confusing communications. Women stepped in to help with the ciphers, and as telegraph operators for the Union, women served valuable roles in addition to their duties as nurses, spies, and even occasionally as soldiers.

FIGURE 5.4B *Telegraph Machine. Library of Congress, LC-USZ62-57414*

Another important means of military communication was the Signal Corps, founded just before the war by Albert James Myer. Myer was a doctor and former telegraph operator who had worked on creating a sign language for the deaf. In the 1850s he patented a signal system using a single flag that could be displayed and waved in different ways to communicate messages over long distances. After a series of trials, the U.S. Department of War authorized the new Signal Corps and placed Myer in charge of it. The new system employed a square flag four feet long (often called a "wig wag") that could be seen from up to fifteen miles away during the day. Myer trained many hundreds of recruits to use the new signaling system, including Edward Porter Alexander. Once the Civil War broke out, Alexander, a native Georgian, joined the Confederacy and helped to establish its Signal Corps. Alexander would go on to serve in many important battles during the war, and his skills as an officer, engineer, and signaler were important to the southern cause. His mentor, Albert Myer, helped the Union develop a code for transmitting signals that was equally important to the Union war effort.

Railroads During the War

Both Confederate and Union forces made use of the telegraph and signal corps, and both turned to the nation's developing railroad system to ferry troops and supplies to the battlefield. In the case of the railroad, however, the Confederacy was at a significant disadvantage. While northern states had begun building an extensive rail system by the 1830s, with thousands of miles of track linking the northeast to the Midwest, the South had really only begun focusing on developing a rail system in the 1850s. Southern states made considerable progress during the final antebellum decade in increasing the number of railroad companies and by building a broader system of tracks. Prior to 1850, the South could boast of few railroads outside of Georgia. During the 1850s, southern communities competed with one another for the next rail link, printed pamphlets announcing new companies and partnerships, and hosted politicians who promised to devote vast funds to new tracks. They had made much headway by 1860, and the rail system looked far more advanced than it had been even in 1850.

Despite southern railroad advances in the 1850s, the region's rail system was paltry compared with the sophisticated networks of the northeast and Midwest. In addition, while the northeast and Midwest had largely agreed on a standard gauge (the gauge is the width of the railroad track), generally 4 feet and 8.5 inches, the South had a patchwork of different gauges. Southern rails ranged up to 6 feet, with many at 5 feet and 5 inches, while others were 5 feet. This meant that each time a different gauge was confronted, the cargo would have to be unloaded and then reloaded onto the next track. This cumbersome and time-consuming problem hampered the Confederacy's ability to move men and resources throughout the war.

The Confederacy was slow to deal with the problem. Robert E. Lee and other Confederate leaders realized the importance of a reliable rail system. In June 1861, Lee tried to prod the government to devote greater resources to building a more extensive network:

> **I consider it very important to the military operations within Virginia that proper and easy connections of the several railroads passing through or terminating in Richmond should be made as promptly as possible. The want of these connections has seriously retarded the operations so far, and they may become more important.**[2]

Lee was pointing to another problem for the South: the fact that many railroads terminated in towns and did not extend to other areas. In his classic study of Confederate railroads, Robert C. Black III argues that the poor condition of the southern rail network, conditions that only deteriorated during the war due to overuse, contributed significantly to the South's defeat. As one Confederate officer, General G. Moxley Sorrel, later recalled regarding the use of railroads in Tennessee in 1863:

Never before were so many troops moved over such worn-out railways, none first-class from the beginning. Never before were such crazy cars—passenger, baggage, mail, coal, box, platform, all and every sort wobbling on the jumping strap-iron—used for hauling good soldiers.[3]

Iron resources that could have and perhaps should have been used to build a more complex rail system were instead diverted to build ironclad ships for the Confederate navy.

By contrast, the Union's extensive railroad network was used wisely to move men and supplies to battlefields. Numbering nearly 25,000 civilians, the Union's Construction Corps was responsible for building and maintaining railroads used by the military. In addition, they built bridges and even developed a way to build trusses for bridge supports quickly and efficiently. Confederate raiders sabotaged Union rails at every opportunity, and Union raiders did the same to Confederate rails. The destruction of a bridge or track could significantly ruin supply chains, and both sides devoted considerable effort and resources to building and repairing tracks and bridges.

FIGURE 5.5 *Engine W.H. Whiton, and President's car, Alexandria, January, 1865. Library of Congress, LC-DIG-ppmsca-08257*

Lincoln and Race at the Start of the War

Americans in both the North and South spent a great deal of time thinking about and discussing the meaning of race. Few whites considered the races to be intellectually equal, just as they doubted that women were the intellectual equals of men. Writers and thinkers believed for the most part that peoples of African descent were more suited to agricultural and mechanical labor that required endurance and strength. Scientists such as Alabama's Josiah Nott provided "evidence" that the races were fundamentally different and pseudo-scientific movements such as phrenology and even scientifically accurate works such as Charles Darwin's *On the Origin of Species* (1859) seemed to confirm what white Americans thought they witnessed in their everyday experience: that few African Americans had achieved literary or scientific success or other notable intellectual accomplishments. Of course, we know today that differences in scholarly attainments between men and women or between Europeans and Africans were not a result of biological differences but differences in education, expectations, and experience. Yet in the nineteenth century the opinion that African Americans were inferior to whites of European descent was widely held in all regions of the country.

Such prejudice was the basis for enslaving African Americans in the South and for widespread discrimination in the North and West. Although northerners had put slavery on the path to abolition by the turn of the nineteenth century, very few northerners (even Republicans) advocated full social or political equality between whites and African Americans. In fact, each time voting rights or other political responsibilities were contemplated for free blacks, white northern voters reacted strongly against such sentiments. Schools, hotels, eating establishments, trains, and other public facilities were segregated by race, and even many abolitionists doubted whether the races could coexist peacefully.

In the slave states, elaborate state legal codes were devised to limit the ability of bondspeople to earn an education, work as skilled labor, travel freely, or engage in other normal daily activities taken for granted by whites. In the North, although slavery was mostly abolished by the turn of the nineteenth century, even free African Americans saw their ability to live and work independent of social control severely circumscribed. Because by far the vast majority of northerners opposed radical abolitionism, and because the Democratic Party warned northerners that Lincoln and the Republicans were determined to undermine the Constitution and battle the South to end slavery, the president and his party had to be careful when crafting policies against slavery.

Some historians have faulted Lincoln for failing to pursue an aggressive antislavery path during the war, criticizing him for being too timid in his suppression of the southern rebellion. Because Lincoln was active politically long before the Civil War, including stints in the Illinois state legislature in the 1830s and in the U.S. Congress in the 1840s, we have a good sense of the future president's views on race and slavery. For the most part Lincoln struck a moderate tone. In 1837 he registered his views on slavery as a state representative, the earliest example we have of his opinions. With another legislator, Lincoln argued that "the institution of slavery is founded on both injustice and bad policy, but that the promulgation of abolitionist doctrines tends rather to increase than to abate its evils." This moderate position, criticizing slavery as unjust while also denouncing the abolitionists, was a common one. In the 1850s Lincoln made clear his opposition to bondage, referring to slavery in 1854 as a "monstrous injustice." Yet he also refused to believe that the two races could live together peacefully in the same nation, an opinion that led him to embrace the colonization movement.

FIGURE 5.6 *Abraham Lincoln. Photograph by Joseph E. Baker. Library of Congress, LC-DIG-pga-03412*

Upon taking the oath of office on March 4, 1861, Lincoln decided that caution and calculation would be needed. The power of Democrats who sympathized with white southerners remained significant, even after the 1860 elections, and the midterm 1862 congressional elections would be hotly contested between the two parties. For all of his virtues as an orator and statesman, Lincoln was a politician who had to remain keenly aware of northern political sentiments. In his estimation, northern and Border State white voters were not prepared to accept radical abolitionism before late 1862, and in any event the president doubted he had the authority under the Constitution to abolish slavery in Union states such as Maryland and Kentucky. In the first year and a half of his presidency, Lincoln emphasized that his chief goal was to end the rebellion, not to end southern slavery. Even during the 1860 campaign and in the early months of his administration, his main objective was to end the rebellion and reunite the sections with or without slavery intact. He did seem to believe, harboring opinions that reflected Republican Party ideology, that in the long term slavery was doomed to fail in the face of competition with free labor. In his famous speech at the Cooper Union in New York City in February 1860, Lincoln not only claimed that he and his party had no interest in interfering with slavery within the South, he also supported enforcement of the Fugitive Slave Act. He affirmed his opposition to bondage and disagreed with white southerners that slavery was part of the natural order. Yet, in his presidential campaign and in the first year of his presidency Lincoln balanced precariously the antislavery sentiments of himself and his party with his fear of upsetting Upper South and Border slave states.

While the president feared that too strident an antislavery path would alienate moderate northerners and pro-Union forces in the Border States, Lincoln was also criticized on the other side of the political spectrum by those who considered him too hesitant to attack slavery head-on. As much as anyone, African American abolitionist Frederick Douglass continued to press the president to undermine slavery more vigorously. In fact, Douglass said at one point during the 1860 campaign to fellow abolitionist Gerrit Smith: "I cannot support Lincoln." However, the president seems to have respected Douglass and even invited the abolitionist to the White House. Lincoln, both before and after he became president, most likely believed that African Americans were naturally and biologically inferior to whites. But he also believed that slavery was morally wrong and destined to fail. Historian James Oakes has argued that over time, Douglass seems to have influenced the president in moving more directly to end slavery, but Lincoln (as Douglass himself would later acknowledge) was bound by political and military calculations that prevented him from moving more quickly on slavery. Even after Upper South states such as Virginia, Tennessee, and North Carolina seceded, the president had to worry about angering the Union slave states, especially Maryland, Missouri, and Kentucky. In addition, northern Democrats who questioned the need for war and urged compromise with the Confederacy, so-called Peace Democrats or Copperheads, constantly pressured Lincoln to end the fighting. In the 1862 congressional elections the Democrats fared well politically, demonstrating clearly to Lincoln and moderate Republicans the dangers of pursuing a bold antislavery strategy during the early stages of the war.

As abolitionists noted, Lincoln had numerous opportunities in the early months of the war to strike blows against slavery, but in such cases he urged caution. For example, in August 1861, General John C. Fremont, the Republican Party candidate for president in 1856 and now commanding Union troops in Missouri, declared martial law and directed his troops to free rebels' slaves. Lincoln encouraged Fremont to obey more strictly the directives of the Confiscation Act and not to venture beyond the law's limitations. Such restraint worried abolitionists such as Douglass, who questioned the president's commitment to ending slavery.

Yet, in part because of the activism and agitation of men such as Douglass, and in part because of his own predilections, by the summer and fall of 1862 the president was beginning to show signs of an antislavery strategy that would culminate in the Emancipation Proclamation and the Thirteenth Amendment. Republicans in Congress also helped to push the president to take such actions against slavery. The First Confiscation Act of 1861, for example, authorized soldiers and officers to seize slaves employed by their masters or the Confederacy in sustaining the rebellion. Previously Union forces were obligated to return slaves to their masters, but now viewed as contrabands of war these slaves could be taken from their masters. Although a modest step, the act changed Union policy toward slaves and foreshadowed further legislation and military actions that would lead to the end of slavery.

As the war progressed, however, more opportunities came for the president and his party to demonstrate their *bona fides* on abolitionism. Republicans in Congress passed another confiscation act in the summer of 1862, authorizing Union forces to seize all slaves of rebellious masters, not just slaves employed in support of the Confederacy. This was a much bolder step that foreshadowed the Emancipation Proclamation. At about the same time, Congress passed the Militia Act, which granted African Americans the right to serve as Union soldiers, another crucial step in the direction of equality and emancipation. Eventually both laws proved central to the Union war effort, as both free African Americans and self-emancipated formerly enslaved people not only bolstered the Union armed forces, but also made significant contributions as laborers in aiding the Union cause. Even more galling was the fact that the Militia Act called for African Americans to serve in manual labor positions in the Union army rather than in combat. Although clearly limited, wartime legislation such as the Militia Act and the Confiscation Act helped move the nation in the direction of outlawing slavery.

While the confiscation acts and other laws heralded shifts in Union policies on slavery, the most important decree issued in the first years of the war was the Emancipation Proclamation. Since the late nineteenth century, historians have debated whether the proclamation was a radically antislavery move by Lincoln or a timid response to the southern rebellion. As we will see, there are merits to both sides of the argument. When the president decided to put forth the proclamation in the summer of 1862, he had no doubt been influenced by the arguments of abolitionists such as Frederick Douglass and Gerrit Smith, who had been urging the president to offer a bold gesture against slavery. In newspaper editorials, widely distributed pamphlets, and public speeches, abolitionists scorned Lincoln for taking mere baby steps in the direction of emancipation. Insistent, too, were the calls in Congress for more forceful action. Radical Republicans in the House and Senate faulted the president for timidity. Public figures such as Horace Greeley, editor of the influential newspaper *New York Tribune*, openly criticized the president for not going further to end slavery and in particular for not enforcing existing federal laws meant to weaken the institution during the war. Lincoln had to weigh such criticisms from abolitionists and from leaders in his own party against the very real possibility that a broad policy of emancipation might force the Upper South states into the arms of the Confederacy. The president also reiterated that his overriding goal—more important than ending slavery—was the end of the rebellion and the restoration of the Union. In a letter to Greeley shortly before he issued the Emancipation Proclamation, the president underscored his fundamental beliefs when it came to the goals of the war:

I would save the Union. I would save it in the shortest way under the Constitution . . . If there be those who would not save the Union, unless they could at the same time save slavery, I do not agree with them. If there be those who would not save the Union unless they could at the same time destroy slavery, I do not agree with them. My paramount object in this struggle is to save the Union, and is not either to save or destroy slavery.[4]

Like most Americans, Lincoln had been struggling with the meaning and significance of race for many years. Were there fundamental and divinely ordained differences between blacks and whites? Or were the observable differences between the races a product of education, culture, and upbringing? Most Americans, even abolitionists, believed that there were basic differences between the races aside from skin color. But even if there were differences did they matter? Such questions plagued Lincoln, but the longer the war endured the more open he became to the notion of racial equality. Although Lincoln naturally reflected on these important questions because of his intelligence and thoughtful nature, circumstances during the war forced him to consider and reconsider the future of blacks in America. African Americans themselves demanded attention, as they left southern plantations and farms behind to find freedom and protection behind Union lines.

Port Royal and Other Experiments with Freedom During the War

As Union soldiers took control of southern areas early in the war, few knew what do to with the large numbers of slaves who flocked to the Union lines, seeking freedom and protection. Frustrated Union officers wanted direction from Washington. What were they to do with the thousands of slaves who sought Union protection? In July 1861 General Benjamin Butler wrote to Union Secretary of War Simon Cameron, requesting guidance:

In the village of Hampton there were a large number of negroes, composed in great measure of women and

children of the men who had fled thither within my lines for protection . . . Indeed it was a most distressing sight to see these poor creatures, who had trusted to the protection of the arms of the United States . . . The questions which this state of facts presents are very embarrassing. *First,* What shall be done with them? and *Second,* What is their state and condition?

Butler wanted to know if the slaves were to be considered property, and therefore "contrabands of war." Despite his pleas, Butler and other Union officers did not get clear direction from the administration. This ambiguity provided room for experiments and ad hoc decision making. At Port Royal, South Carolina the Union army established farms where ex-slaves could work and live. These experiments, especially the community at Port Royal, were important for later debates over the fate of the freedpeople.

As early as 1861, just months after the war began, slaves pressured the legal, military, and political system to compromise. At first Union officers showed malice toward the freedmen and women; former slaves who had fled to Union armies in the South were put into positions of hard labor. Other runaway slaves were returned by Union forces to their masters' plantations and forced to work for low wages. But the slaves themselves ensured that they would not be carelessly neglected.

Port Royal, part of the Sea Islands under Union control since November 1861, was the site of one of the more unusual wartime experiments with emancipation. Union Secretary of the Treasury Salmon P. Chase authorized northern philanthropists to employ former slaves to help farm vast plantations in Port Royal. Harriet Tubman traveled to many of these camps, including Port Royal, where she assisted African Americans. The slaves themselves, of course, much preferred to work their own land, realizing the independence land ownership brought to black families. But their work on the Port Royal plantations for small wages proved to many abolitionists and northern political leaders that free African Americans could and would work, contradicting widely held racist opinions among northerners that blacks were inherently lazy.

Abolitionists agreed that one of the most important and immediate needs among the freedmen was education. The vast majority of enslaved men and women were illiterate and even before the war ended policies were enacted that sought to redress this

Entered according to Act of Congress, in the year 1862, by BARNARD & GIBSON, in the Clerk's Office of the District Court of the District of Columbia.

FIGURE 5.7 *Contrabands at headquarters of General Lafayette. Library of Congress, LC-DIG-ds-05120*

deficiency, putting into practice what would become established federal policy after the war. For example, Union General Grant appointed New Hampshire native John Eaton to oversee a Department of Negro Affairs. Eaton's authority extended over Tennessee and the surrounding region, and with this power he established nearly seventy-five schools for black adults and children. Similarly, General Benjamin Butler helped to erect schools in North Carolina and Virginia. In addition to teaching reading and writing, the schools taught skilled trades to former slaves in hopes of encouraging their economic independence. Some of these early experiments with freedom allowed former slaves to farm the lands abandoned by whites. A few African Americans earned money by selling crops and used the funds to buy their own land. With the help of northern Republicans and abolitionists, more teachers numbering into the thousands ventured to Union-occupied areas to instruct former slaves how to read and write. Such wartime initiatives to aid the southern freedpeople were preludes to massive efforts after the war to educate and support the four million formerly enslaved people.

Please visit the companion website www.routledge.com/cw/wells for additional study aids including chapter overviews, interactive quizzes, and more.

Discussion Questions

- What role did improvements in transportation and communication play during the war?
- How effective were Confederate and Union leaders in dealing with problems of absenteeism and desertion in the armies?
- Why would Native Americans choose to fight for the Confederacy or the Union? What did they have to gain by joining one side or the other?
- Union generals were perplexed by the problem of how to deal with the thousands of former slaves who fled behind Union lines. How did Union leaders deal with this important issue? How else might they have confronted the issue of escaped slaves?
- How did Lincoln's views on race and slavery change over time?

Notes

1 Susie King Taylor, *Reminiscences of My Life in Camp* (1902), Chapter V.

2 Lee quoted in Gary W. Gallagher's foreword to the 1998 republication of Robert C. Black, *The Railroads of the Confederacy* (Chapel Hill: University of North Carolina Press, 1952), xi.

3 G. Moxley Sorrel, *At the Right Hand of Longstreet: Recollections of a Confederate Staff Officer* (originally 1909, reprinted New York: Bison Books, 1999), 189.

4 Lincoln to Horace Greeley, August 22, 1862; reprinted in Cole C. Kingseed, *The American Civil War* (Westport: Greenwood Press, 2004), 135.

Further Reading

Annie Heloise Abel, *The American Indian as Slaveholder and Secessionist* (Lincoln: University of Nebraska Press, 1992).

Annie Heloise Abel, *The American Indian and the End of the Confederacy, 1863–1866* (Lincoln: University of Nebraska Press, 1993).

William H. Armstrong, *Warrior in Two Camps: Ely S. Parker, Union General & Seneca Chief* (Syracuse: Syracuse University Press, 1978).

David W. Baird, *A Creek Warrior for the Confederacy: The Autobiography of Chief G.W. Grayson* (Norman: University of Oklahoma Press, 1988).

Robert C. Black, *The Railroads of the Confederacy* (Chapel Hill: University of North Carolina Press, 1952).

Victoria Bynum, *The Free State of Jones: Mississippi's Longest Civil War* (Chapel Hill: University of North Carolina Press, 2002).

John Elwood Clark, *Railroads in the Civil War* (Baton Rouge: Louisiana State University Press, 2001).

Clarissa W. Confer, *The Cherokee Nation in the Civil War* (Norman: University of Oklahoma Press, 2007).

William C. Davis, *Rhett: The Turbulent Life and Times of a Fire-Eater* (Columbia: University of South Carolina Press, 2001).

John Ehle, *Trail of Tears: The Rise and Fall of the Cherokee Nation* (New York: Doubleday, 1989).

W. Craig Gaines, *The Confederate Cherokees: John Drew's Regiment of Mounted Rifles* (Baton Rouge: Louisiana State University Press, 1989).

Thom Hatch, *The Blue, the Gray, & the Red: Indian Campaigns of the Civil War* (Mechanicsburg: Stackpole Books, 2003).

Laurence M. Hauptman, *Between Two Fires: American Indians in the Civil War* (New York: Free Press, 1995).

David M. Henkin, *The Postal Age: The Emergence of Modern Communications in Nineteenth-Century America* (Chicago: University of Chicago Press, 2006).

Sally Jenkins and John Stauffer, *The State of Jones* (New York: Random House, 2009).

Richard R. John, *Spreading the News: The American Postal System from Franklin to Morse* (Cambridge, MA: Harvard University Press, 1995).

John Majewski, *Modernizing a Slave Economy: The Economic Vision of the Confederate Nation* (Chapel Hill: University of North Carolina Press, 2009).

Kenneth Noe, *Reluctant Rebels: The Confederates Who Joined the Army after 1861* (Chapel Hill: University of North Carolina Press, 2010).

Theda Perdue, *Cherokee Women: Gender and Culture Change, 1700–1835* (Lincoln: University of Nebraska Press, 1998).

Steven Ramold, *Baring the Iron Hand: Discipline in the Union Army* (Dekalb: Northern Illinois University Press, 2009).

Robert Sandow, *Deserter Country: Civil War Opposition in the Pennsylvania Appalachians* (New York: Fordham University Press, 2009).

Brian D. Schoen, *The Fragile Fabric of Union: Cotton, Federal Politics, and the Global Origins of the Civil War* (Baltimore: Johns Hopkins University Press, 2009).

William Shea, *Pea Ridge: Civil War Campaign in the West* (Chapel Hill: University of North Carolina Press, 1992).

Kenneth Silverman, *Lightening Man: The Accursed Life of Samuel F.B. Morse* (New York: Knopf, 2003).

David H. Stone, Jr., *Vital Rails: The Charleston & Savannah Railroad and the Civil War in Coastal South Carolina* (Columbia: University of South Carolina Press, 2008).

Mark A. Weitz, *A Higher Duty: Desertion among Georgia Troops during the Civil War* (Lincoln: University of Nebraska Press, 2000).

Tom Wheeler, *Mr. Lincoln's T-Mails: The Untold Story of How Abraham Lincoln used the Telegraph to Win the Civil War* (New York: Harper Business, 2006).

IN THE GRIP OF WAR

Topics Covered in this Chapter:

- Women and Gender During the War
- War in the Summer of 1862
- Emancipation Proclamation
- Politics and Parties

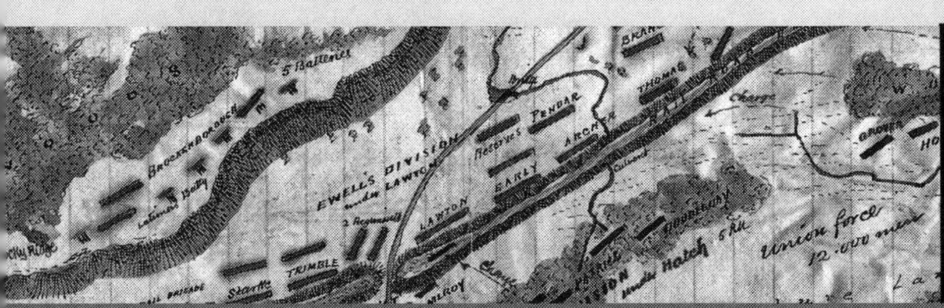

6

Introduction

While wartime writers such as Emily Dickinson, Herman Melville, and Henry Timrod used literature to explore the meaning of war, women and African Americans were trying to determine whether the war would lead to a shift in gender roles or to the end of slavery. Although many women—and some men—had begun making the case for expanding women's roles in society before the war, exemplified by the famous meeting at Seneca Falls, New York in 1848, whether or not the upheavals caused by the Civil War would include new rights and responsibilities for women was not at all clear. For free African Americans, including those who had challenged Union racial ideology by escaping slavery and seeking protection behind Union lines, the meaning of the war was equally unclear, at least until Lincoln declared emancipation a war goal by issuing the Emancipation Proclamation.

While women and African Americans were still determining the meaning of the war for them, the summer and fall of 1862 would prove difficult for Lincoln, his party, and the Union cause. On the battlefield, failures at the Second Battle of Bull Run and the Peninsula Campaign, and George McClellan's unwillingness to pursue Robert E. Lee after Antietam, demonstrated both southern intransigence and conservatism in Union military leadership. Union strategy remained cautious, mirroring the political conservatism of Democratic generals such as McClellan, who continued to believe that restoration of the Union and an end to the southern rebellion, rather than a revolutionary remaking of the South, was the primary war goal. Risking a political backlash from northern white moderates and conservatives, and perhaps even from Democratic Party-leaning Union soldiers themselves, Lincoln issued the Emancipation Proclamation in hopes of recasting the meaning of the war. But in the congressional elections in the fall of 1862, the president and the Republicans suffered defeat at the hands of rival Democrats.

Yet the South, too, suffered from internal divisions. Dissenters—those who disagreed with or rebelled against orthodox views—appeared throughout the South and significantly hampered the Confederacy's ability to win the war. Some southern dissenters resented the policies of the Confederate government, while others simply grew weary from the fighting and all of the death and disruptions it caused. Whatever their motives, southern dissenters shaped their region's wartime experience. In fact, some historians argue that the prevalence of dissent among white southerners was a major factor in the Confederacy's defeat.

Women and Gender During the War

Despite prohibitions against women serving in battle, northern and southern women played vital roles in the war. As we have seen, in the antebellum era white women had made progress in gaining attention for expanded rights and responsibilities; yet those advocating female suffrage and broader career options for women were a small minority of Americans before the war. In the magazines and novels women read, domestic duties were paramount with women taking charge of managing the home and raising the children. The vast majority of men and women embraced such traditional gender roles.

Still, southerners and northerners alike believed that when it came to gender roles they lived in an enlightened age. By the 1850s, teaching was shifting from a predominantly male occupation to a female one. Hundreds of young women, educated in normal schools in the North, ventured to the southern states to tutor wealthy and middle-class students. Single women were permitted limited property rights in the North and South as early as the 1830s, but during the war women advanced into more prominent public roles even in the South. Historian George C. Rable, who has written extensively on southern women during the war, argues that Confederate women often questioned the necessity of war even as they failed to question the racial and class dynamics of the South. Alas, most people accept without a second thought the injustices around them, and southern white women were no different. In language commonly found in the nineteenth-century South, a contributor to the New Orleans magazine *De Bow's Review* proclaimed at the beginning of the war that:

> **The beginning of our career as an independent nation, a career destined, we believe, to be prosperous beyond all comparison in the annals of history, ought to be signalized by the beginning of a nobler, loftier career for women. Let her but use well the advantages within her grasp, and in future ages it will be the proudest boast ever permitted a woman to utter—that she is a citizen of the Southern Republic of America.[1]**

As Nina Silber, Elizabeth D. Leonard, and other scholars have argued, while rhetoric such as that expressed in *De Bow's Review* proved overly optimistic, women did indeed find new duties and responsibilities during the war from new positions on the home front as teachers to serving the war effort as nurses and even spies.

In the early years of the war, women found that they could aid their section's cause while also remaining true to their traditional roles in society. Women on the home front seized the opportunity to educate children on the importance of the Confederate and Union causes. White women in all sections of the country helped to sew uniforms and flags for the troops. Historian Bettye Collier-Thomas has shown that even before the war, African American women trumpeted the cause of freedom in northern churches.

Before the Civil War nursing had become an important career for women. England's Florence Nightingale earned fame for organizing and training nurses during the Crimean War in the 1850s, and she set up a nursing school to offer formal training to women. Nursing allowed women to participate in the war effort while remaining within the traditional bounds of the woman as caretaker. Still, it was highly unusual for respectable Victorian women to engage in such close contact with strange men of all classes. During the Civil War, nurses helped soldiers to cope with injury, death, and suffering, often simply by sitting next to a wounded or dying soldier, holding his hand and engaging in conversation. Civil War veterans often remembered years after the war the comforting sound of a woman reading to them from the Bible or another book. Nurses such as the Union's Hannah Ropes complained of poor resources and inadequate supplies while in camp, while others complained that too few women were willing to make sacrifices for the war effort. Confederate nurse Kate Cumming asked, "Are the women of the South going into the hospitals? I am afraid candor will compel me to say they are not! It is not respectable, and requires too constant attention, and a hospital has none of the comforts of home!"[2] Ultimately women on both sides joined the war effort in large numbers, including 20,000 or so who served as nurses. White women of middling means were more apt to join the war as nurses because they could afford leisure time. Some had several children whom they carried with them to the hospitals.

Two of the best-known Civil War women were Dorothea Dix and Clara Barton. A Maine native, Dix was born in 1802, taught in Boston schools, and by the 1840s was nationally known as an advocate for the mentally ill. She had traveled throughout the antebellum North and South, pressing her case for improving the care and treatment of the insane. When the war broke out, she was nearly sixty years old and still active; her record of achievement led to an appointment as Superintendent of Union Army Nurses. Clara Barton, who after the war would help found the American Red Cross, was a Massachusetts native born in 1821.

FIGURE 6.1A *Dorothea Lynde Dix. Library of Congress, LC-USZ62-9797*

FIGURE 6.1B *Clara Barton. Courtesy of Library of Congress Prints and Photographs Division, LC-USZ62-69290*

During the war Barton worked hard to move badly needed medical supplies to the battlefield, enduring dangerous conditions as she crisscrossed the front lines.

Hundreds of women served as nurses in organized societies as well. Northern women formed the U.S. Sanitary Commission to ameliorate the condition of wounded soldiers by organizing drives to collect blankets, clothes, shoes, Bibles, and other items for the Union forces. Although less formally organized, southern women also conducted drives to gather medicine, clothes, and food for the Confederate army. At the battlefronts, Union and Confederate women helped doctors by administering medicine and assisting in amputations. A few women served the army as doctors, including Esther Hill Hawks, a northerner who traveled to the South during the war to tend to wounded Union soldiers and freedmen.

On rare occasions, women served as spies or even as combatants. Since women were prohibited from fighting, as many as 250 women, by one scholar's estimate, had to pretend to be men in order to serve in battle. Somewhat more commonly, women became spies including two of the most famous

Confederate spies, Belle Boyd and Rose O'Neal Greenhow. Born into a prominent southern family, Greenhow became well known in and around Washington, D.C. Early in the war she used her connections with the rich and powerful to relay intelligence to the Confederacy. Even more importantly, Greenhow became a Confederate diplomat, venturing across the Atlantic to encourage British support for the southern cause. Elizabeth Van Lew, who hailed from a wealthy Richmond family, opposed slavery and secession in 1861. When the war began, she operated a sophisticated spy network that utilized both black and white Union sympathizers.

Women on the home front hardly escaped the trials and traumas of the war. As Drew Faust has shown, southern white women faced the daunting task of overseeing farms and plantations, and all of the stressful and back-breaking work that entailed, from managing slaves to harvesting crops. Such "Mothers of Invention," as Faust called them, endured the hardships of new burdens placed on them by absent sons, husbands, and fathers. In the South, slaves often took advantage of this breakdown in management by refusing to work or by running away, but many southern women directed their slaves effectively, managing to eke out a living under significantly disrupted economic conditions. White women in the North often managed stores and businesses for their merchant husbands and assumed other tasks traditionally reserved for men. But Faust also argued that northern middle-class women were more effective in adjusting to the new roles expected of them during the war, while white elite southern women had a more difficult time adapting to the demands of war.

One of the most famous confrontations over gender took place in New Orleans in the spring of 1862, when Union General Benjamin Butler occupied the city. White women responded to the occupation with contempt for Union soldiers, wearing Confederate emblems, spitting on the soldiers, and expressing their outrage in other ways. Butler responded in turn by issuing General Orders, No. 28:

As the officers and soldiers of the United States have been subject to repeated insults from the women (calling themselves ladies) of New Orleans in return for the most scrupulous non-interference and courtesy on our part, it is ordered that hereafter when any female shall by word, gesture, or movement insult or show contempt for any officer or soldier of the United States she shall be

regarded and held liable to be treated as a woman of the town plying her avocation.

Southern leaders responded to Butler's order with fury, claiming that the general had declared open season on white women. The mayor of New Orleans responded angrily but was forced to back down in the face of Butler's stubbornness. Anger quickly spread throughout the South as word of Butler's order reached every Confederate town and city. Confederate General Beauregard, then in northern Mississippi, issued a call of his own, appealing to notions of manhood to defend white southern women:

MEN OF THE SOUTH: Shall our mothers, our wives, our daughters, and our sisters be thus outraged by the ruffianly soldiers of the North, to whom is given the right to treat at their pleasure the ladies of the South as common harlots? Arouse, friends, and drive back from our soil those infamous invaders of our homes and disturbers of our family ties.[3]

African American women were caught between worlds, and as a result precious few writings from them survived the war. Most black women before the war were illiterate because of strict southern laws that rendered any attempts to teach slaves to read and write illegal. One important exception is Susie King Taylor, born a slave in 1848 near Savannah. When Union soldiers captured Fort Pulaski in the spring of 1862, Taylor was only a teenager but she managed to flee her master and run behind the Union lines. There Taylor became an aid to the cause of freedom by washing clothes, working as a nurse, and cooking for the Union army. Much later, Taylor recorded her remarkable experiences with the 1st South Carolina Volunteers in *Reminiscences of My Life in Camp* (1902). As Taylor recalled, she sought food and resources even as she aided the Union soldiers:

While the fighting was on, a friend, Lizzie Lancaster, and I stopped at several of the rebel homes, and after talking with some of the women and children we asked them if they had any food. They claimed to have only some hardtack, and evidently did not care to give us anything to eat, but this was not surprising. They were bitterly against our people and had no mercy or sympathy for us.

Taylor went on to describe life in the camps and the extensive maneuvering the soldiers endured. Her recollections, while reflecting her unique experiences during the war, must have been repeated thousands of times in different forms. Masses of slave women and children fled slavery at the earliest opportunity under the umbrella of Union protection, defying centuries of claims by white southerners that their slaves were contented with bondage.

Notions of masculinity and manhood were also central to the war, as scholars such as Lorien Foote have found. Much of the bravado of disunionists in the 1850s emanated from masculine rhetoric about the need to protect home and family. Politicians painted their opponents as cowardly and womanly in the heated partisan discourse of the prewar period. During the war this masculine rhetoric rose to new levels. Private wartime diaries are filled with references to soldiers whose experiences with death quickly turned them from boys into men. The very act of volunteering for battle was a mark of manly assertiveness and acceptance of responsibility for both black and white men. Massachusetts Governor George Briggs urged volunteers to "show yourselves to be *men* and *New England men*."[4]

Much of the prewar and wartime rhetoric about manhood highlighted honor, a complex concept that, Bertram Wyatt-Brown and others have shown, weighed heavily on nineteenth-century Americans, especially in the South. The practice of dueling emanated from cultural attitudes that considered honor worth defending, even at great cost. All classes of white southerners embraced the concept of honor, granting whites a shared cultural trait to the exclusion of African Americans, free or slave. The war was a prime opportunity for a new generation of young men to demonstrate their honor on the battlefield, one that southern and northern soldiers seized with equal vigor. Such eagerness, though, often became bravado as southern soldiers bragged about their hopes to whip a hundred Yankees, and northern soldiers boldly threatened to thrash the Confederates into submission and back into the Union. Such rhetoric diminished as the war progressed, as both sides realized that the enemy would not be so easily intimidated.

War in the Summer of 1862

Facing calls to undermine slavery, and satisfied that the Border States were firmly in Union control, Lincoln had decided by July

1862 to strike at the foundation of the Confederacy by issuing a proclamation freeing slaves in rebellious states. But Lincoln did not wish to issue the proclamation from a position of weakness or defeat, so the president and his cabinet agreed that the announcement of the new policy would have to await a Union battle victory. That victory took longer to accomplish than Lincoln had hoped.

The disappointing losses in the Peninsula Campaign, especially the Confederate victories at the Seven Days Battles in late June and early July 1862, convinced Lincoln and his commanders that a tougher line of attack was needed. Any hopes for a quick Union victory, or of a southern white internal uprising that might weaken the Confederate government, were now dashed. The Emancipation Proclamation would be an integral component of this new harder line but the president thought triumphs on the battlefield necessarily came first.

Lincoln reworked both strategy and command. In early July the president issued a call for 300,000 more volunteers and he placed John Pope, who had helped achieve Union victories in the West, in charge of the new Army of Virginia. Whether true or not, Pope believed that the soldiers of the Eastern Theater were not as accustomed to hardship as his forces in the West, and he immediately set his new command on a different footing in Culpepper, Virginia near but to the west of both Washington and Richmond. Pope instructed his soldiers to take food and supplies from southern civilians when needed, and to treat harshly any white southerners who thwarted the Union army. Pope's main tasks in Virginia were to utilize the more than 55,000 men under him to engage southern soldiers while also destroying as much of the Confederate infrastructure, particularly railroads, as possible. Although Nathaniel P. Banks, under Pope's command, lost to Stonewall Jackson's forces at Cedar Mountain in early August 1862, Pope seemed tenacious and bold where General McClellan had been shrinking and timid.

Lincoln also brought western General Henry Wager Halleck to the East in July to provide a fresh approach to the overall command structure. McClellan was no longer the man for the job. Historians have given McClellan credit for his skills at training soldiers and for his ability to coordinate action. He was attentive to detail and often seemingly consumed with minutiae in his preparation. But the general was not adept at leading troops into battle. Lincoln's frustration with McClellan's poor leadership at Seven Days was compounded by the general's insubordination, worsened by his

Democratic Party loyalties. McClellan appeared unwilling to accept unconditionally the president's constitutional authority as commander in chief, and regarded Lincoln as a politician inexperienced in military matters. He worried that information he related to Lincoln and his cabinet was leaked to the press. McClellan criticized superiors as being little more than fools, complaining of their incompetence in letters to the Executive Mansion. Soon after Seven Days, McClellan wrote a bold letter to the president questioning his strategy for defeating the South. Lincoln replaced McClellan with Halleck, who had been successful in capturing Corinth in Mississippi in May 1862, as general in chief. Halleck was now charged with reworking military strategy to take the war more directly to the Confederacy and its citizens. At the same time, Lincoln appointed Grant as head of the District of West Tennessee in a strategically important area between the Mississippi and Tennessee Rivers.

The first real test of the revised Union strategy came during the Second Battle of Bull Run in late August 1862. Shortly before the battle, Lee directed Jackson and his nearly 25,000-strong army to cut off Pope's supply line to the capital. After marching more than fifty miles, Jackson successfully isolated Pope from resupplies, allowing Lee to assail Pope from the flank. Lasting three days, from August 28–30, the Second Battle of Bull Run sent a defeated Pope back to encampments at Washington. Lee, Jackson, and the Confederates were victorious in northern Virginia.

Meanwhile, further west, Major General Edmund Kirby Smith made headway for the Confederacy in Tennessee. From Knoxville, Smith marched toward the Cumberland Gap with troop reinforcements from Confederate leader Braxton Bragg and others. After capturing several garrisons in south-central Kentucky, Smith defeated Union forces in battle at Richmond, Kentucky at the same time that eastern Confederate forces emerged victorious at the Second Battle of Bull Run. Smith would continue to retain a firm grip on central Kentucky through September. Victories in Virginia and Kentucky bolstered gains along the Red River and the Mississippi River, allowing the Confederacy to control strategically important garrisons at Vicksburg, Mississippi and Baton Rouge, Louisiana.

Union forces were not completely devoid of triumphs in the summer and fall of 1862. By August, Union forces were firmly in control over the key Border State of Missouri. Curtis had also marched across northern Arkansas to take Helena on the Mississippi River. Cracks were opening in the wall of white southern unity; in

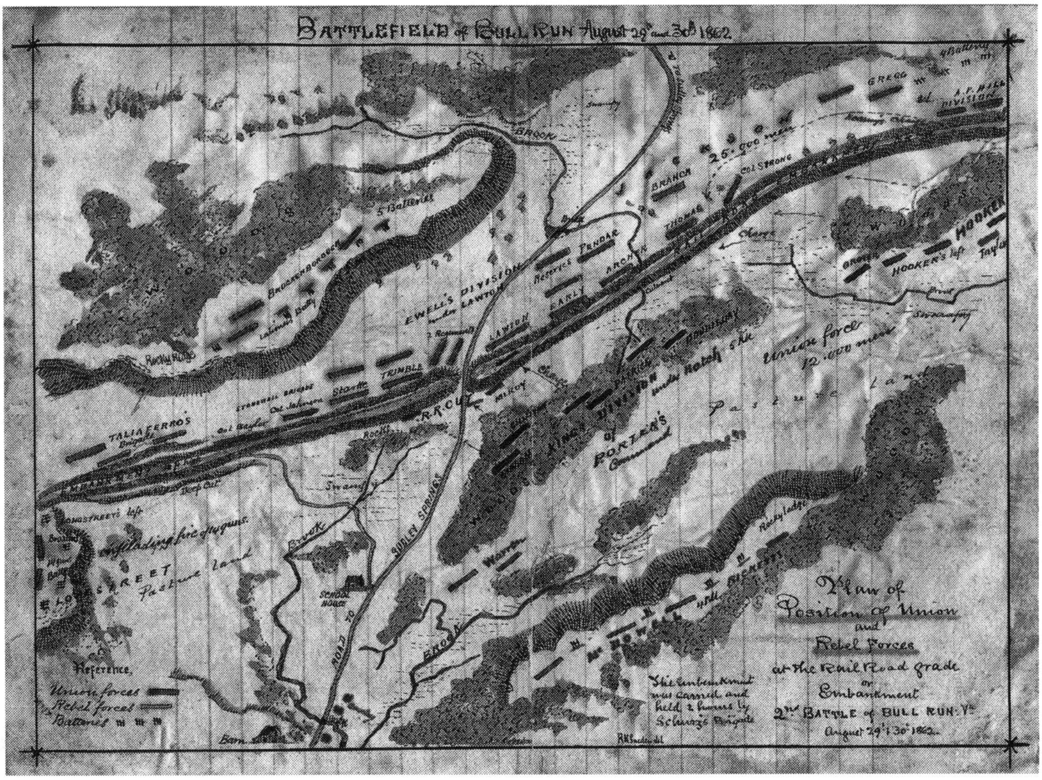

FIGURE 6.2 *Battlefield of Bull Run August 29th and 30th 1862. Library of Congress, Geography and Map Division*

western Virginia, mountain folks not enamored of either slavery or the rebellion split off to form their own state, while dissenters in northern and central Texas, many of them German immigrants, flouted Confederate rule and opposed secession. Most notably, sporadic but bold dissenters cropped up in such places as Jones County, Mississippi, a hotbed of anti-secession and pro-Union sentiment. Open dissent remained largely on the margins but nonetheless significantly weakened the Confederate war effort there.

Even with his victory at Second Bull Run, Lee realized that privation in the South might lead to more vigorous dissent and he knew that with each month the war lasted, the southern economic and military disadvantages would become increasingly painful. Determined to benefit from the successes in northern Virginia, Lee pushed into Union territory for the first time in September 1862. Entering Maryland with about 40,000 troops, Lee hoped to rally support from pro-Confederate Marylanders as well as earn credibility in the eyes of the European powers. He still sought European recognition of the Confederacy and the trade ties such recognition would bring. The ensuing battle would be shaped in part by a remarkable mistake on the part of the Confederate army. Before the full battle took place, Lee's orders to Jackson were discovered by Union forces wrapped around three cigars, providing McClellan with details of southern troop movements. Again McClellan hesitated, believing Lee's forces to be much stronger than they were. McClellan's delay allowed Lee and Jackson to bolster their numbers and fortify their defenses. Meanwhile, Longstreet occupied the southern flank on Antietam Creek and Jackson took the northern flank on the Potomac River, awaiting the Union attack.

The attack came on September 17, and the fighting at the Battle of Antietam, named after the creek near Sharpsburg, Maryland where most of the action took place, turned out to be the most deadly single day of the entire war. At dawn, Union officer Joseph Hooker and his more than 8,000 men attacked the Hagerstown Turnpike defended by Jackson, who had nearly the same number of troops. The battle soon spilled into a nearby cornfield, generating terrible losses by a sustained exchange of artillery fire, with fire coming from Union batteries in the North Woods and near Antietam Creek and answered by Confederate batteries under the commands of Jeb Stuart and Stephen Lee. Both sides received reinforcements in the first two hours of the fighting with little progress made by either despite heavy casualties, especially in the cornfield. By the middle of the day, casualties continued to mount. Some of the worst killing occurred in and around a sunken road, which would become known as "Bloody Lane."

By afternoon, the battles had shifted to the South, but General Ambrose Burnside, apparently angry at what he perceived to be disrespectful actions by McClellan, seemed distracted. His four divisions would meet Confederate forces on and around a formidable stone bridge, which would later become known as "Burnside's Bridge." McClellan neglected to oversee directly the tactical arrangements on the battlefield, meaning that valuable time was lost. Intense fighting here and at Cemetery Hill added to the casualties. At the end of the day, Union and Confederate forces had suffered a combined 23,000 men dead or wounded. As George Thomas Stevens, a New York volunteer, wrote in a letter to his family:

The scene on the battlefield was past description. The mangled forms of our own comrades lay stretched upon the ground, side by side with those of the rebels. On almost every rod of ground over one hundred acres, the

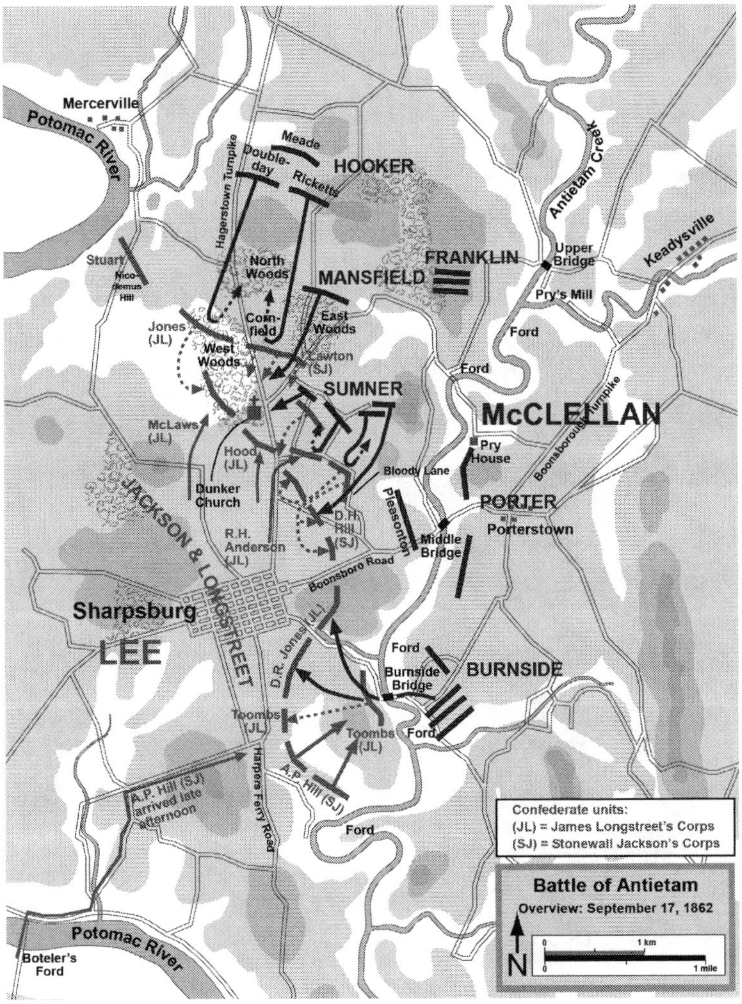

MAP 6.1 *Battle of Antietam, September 17, 1862. Map by Hal Jespersen, www.posix.com/CW*

dead and wounded, some clad in the Union blue and some in the Confederate gray, were lying . . . the dead and dying were scattered thickly among the broken cornstalks, their eyes protruding and their faces blackened by the sun . . . Broken caissons, wheels, dismounted guns, thousands of muskets, blankets, haversacks, and canteens, were scattered thickly over the field; and hundreds of slain horses, bloated and with feet turned toward the sky, added to the horror of the scene.[5]

In the end Lee's forces, though badly mauled, were allowed to slip back into Virginia across the Potomac River as McClellan again failed to pursue a weakened enemy. Once again frustrated

FIGURE 6.3 *Two unidentified Civil War soldiers in Union uniforms, seated in a photographer's studio; one is holding a saber. Library of Congress, LC-USZ62-65089*

with McClellan's hesitant leadership, the president wrote to his general in October 1862 politely but firmly questioning McClellan's decision making:

> **You remember me speaking to you of what I called your over-cautiousness. Are you not over-cautious when you assume that you cannot do what the enemy is constantly doing? Should you not claim to be at least his equal in prowess, and act upon the claim?**

Yet Lincoln did not normally micro-manage strategy and tactics. Although the president offered suggestions to McClellan, he ended the above criticism with the note that "this letter is in no sense an order." Lincoln made his wishes clear and his thoughts known, but deferred to the judgments of his military leaders. In political matters, however, the president took the lead. Although the Battle of Antietam was hardly a resounding Union victory, and Lee was allowed to cross back over the Potomac River and regroup in northern Virginia, the battle was sufficiently successful to permit Lincoln to announce to the nation a preliminary Emancipation Proclamation on September 22, 1862.

Emancipation Proclamation

Effective on January 1, 1863, the Emancipation Proclamation declared that all slaves of the rebellious states were now free. In addition, Lincoln again backed the gradual emancipation of slaves in Union states, perhaps with some form of compensation paid to owners. But the heart of the proclamation, reflecting a policy shift that had been building for many months, asserted that "on the first day of January in the year of our Lord, one thousand eight hundred and sixty-three, all persons held as slaves within any state, or any part of a state, the people whereof shall then be in rebellion against the United States shall be then, thenceforward, and forever free." This was not the beautifully worded oratory that had come to mark the president's speeches and documents during his presidency, but the point was clear: slaves in any state still in rebellion as of January 1, 1863 would, in the eyes of the federal government, be free.

Of course, Jefferson Davis, not Lincoln, was the president of the southern states and he, not the Union commander in chief, had authority over the slave states. Historians have rightly pointed out that Lincoln therefore did not free any slaves via the proclamation, since the document did not declare slaves in Union states free. Lincoln had authorized the Union army to free slaves and each Union advance would liberate thousands of slaves. The Emancipation Proclamation was a war measure justified as punishment for rebellion and so it did not apply to slave states remaining in the Union. Despite its practical limitations, the Emancipation Proclamation was vitally important. For the first time in American history a president had publicly proclaimed a substantial group of slaves, millions of them, in fact, free. Lincoln himself realized the historical significance of the proclamation, remarking that "If my name ever goes into history, it will be for

FIGURE 6.4 *Emancipation Proclamation. Library of Congress, LC-DIG-pga-02040*

this act." The Emancipation Proclamation has indeed marked Lincoln's role in American history. To say that Lincoln was a politician and that political calculations were important factors in deciding when to announce the proclamation is not to diminish the importance of the document. As Lincoln reminded northerners in the proclamation, the new policy did not change the overall objectives of the war, which were to end the rebellion and to reunite the country. Yet, many observers knew well the importance of the document and what it portended for the Union cause, the morale of Union soldiers, and the future of slavery in the South once the war was over. Despite criticisms at the time and since, many slaves and free African Americans themselves realized the implications of the proclamation. In a speech in Rochester, New York, the great abolitionist Frederick Douglass joyfully exclaimed at the end of 1862:

We stand today in the presence of a glorious prospect. This sacred Sunday . . . is the last which will witness the existence of legal slavery in all the Rebel slaveholding States of America. Henceforth and forever, slavery in those states is to be recognized . . . as an unmitigated robber and pirate, banded as the sum of all villainy, an outlaw having no rights which any man white or colored is bound to respect.

In echoing the language of Judge Taney's decision in the *Dred Scott* case, Douglass drew attention to the fact that the beginning of the end of slavery had come just five years after that infamous ruling. He no doubt felt vindicated, upholding the Emancipation Proclamation as both a culmination of decades of abolitionist activism and a harbinger of slavery's final destruction.

Like Douglass, other northerners recognized the significance of the proclamation, though not all praised it. Ralph Waldo Emerson wrote a lengthy article in one of the most popular magazines of the era, the *Atlantic Monthly*, asserting that he now viewed the president in a different light. Like many, Emerson had doubted Lincoln's commitment to abolition; the proclamation helped destroy such doubts forever. Of Lincoln, Emerson declared,

He has been permitted to do more for America than any other American man. He is well entitled to the most indulgent construction. Forget all that we thought shortcomings, every mistake, every delay. In the extreme embarrassments on his part, call these endurance, wisdom, magnanimity, illuminated, as they now are, by this dazzling success.

But longtime abolitionist Lydia Maria Child, who had written *An Appeal in Favor of that Class of Americans Called Africans* back in 1833, was considerably more muted in her assessment of the document. In an 1862 letter she revealed that:

As for the President's Proclamation, I was thankful for it, but it excited no enthusiasm in my mind . . . The ugly fact cannot be concealed from history that it was done reluctantly and stintedly [and that it] was merely a war-measure, to which we were forced by our own perils and necessities . . . This war has furnished many instances of *individual* nobility, but our *national* record is mean.

While Child wished for a purer declaration of emancipation, the reality was more complicated because Lincoln had to factor in politics and public opinion. Most northerners disagreed with Child's reservations and praised the Emancipation Proclamation.

In assessing the factors that led Lincoln to issue the Emancipation Proclamation, historians have recently stressed not just the political pressure abolitionists and Radical Republicans placed on the president, but also the pressure enslaved people themselves levied on the American political system. Early on in the war, it was clear that when given the chance slaves would flee their masters' plantations, often at great personal peril, to reach Union soldiers in hopes of becoming free. By the end of the war, tens of thousands of former slaves had left their masters to live behind Union lines, generating significant pressure on Union leaders to somehow accommodate the growing numbers of refugees seeking freedom and protection. In escaping slavery, men and women were at the same time forcing the Union's hand; simply by running behind Union lines, ex-slaves refused to be mere pawns in the white man's game of chess. The military and political leadership had to deal with them whether it wanted to or not. In the early years of the war, before Lincoln and Union military and political leaders devised consistent and firm policies, the confusion over how to deal with the logistics of thousands of freed slaves led to wartime experiments that sowed the seeds for full emancipation after the war.

Finally, the Proclamation had the added benefit of uniting the Republican Party. As the 1862 congressional elections approached and the 1864 presidential election appeared on the horizon, the president and his political advisors were well aware of the continued power of their Democratic opponents. Although both parties in the North had rallied around the Union cause, by 1862 considerable opposition to the president's handling of the war led to open and bold criticism from Democrats.

Politics and Parties

The Civil War reversed the antebellum Democratic dominance and ensured that Republicans would be the majority party for the rest of the century. For many northerners the Democratic Party was forever tainted with the southern rebellion. After all, the Democratic presidents of the 1850s, northerners Franklin Pierce and James Buchanan, pandered to southern slaveholders by promising to protect bondage in the South, and Democrats supported the

Fugitive Slave Act that was roundly denounced in the North. In addition, the southern Democrats were key to the rebellion, and Jefferson Davis himself was a Democratic leader and cabinet member before assuming the Confederate presidency. Thus, from the outbreak of the war, the Democratic Party became identified as the party of secession, rebellion, and treason, labels that would be hard to shake after the war and into the early twentieth century. In a reversal of prewar political culture, the Republicans would remain the dominant party in the latter decades of the nineteenth century, winning every presidential contest until 1912 except Grover Cleveland's victories in 1884 and 1892.

Yet the Democratic Party remained a force in southern and northern politics throughout the war. In the South, since there were no Republicans and no real opposition to Democratic dominance, that party would retain a firm grip on southern politics not only during the war, but also for the next hundred years. One-party rule characterized southern political culture from the 1860s to the 1960s, with Democratic candidates competing with one another in all city, county, and state elections. Not until the 1970s would Republicans make serious inroads into the Deep South.

In the North during the Civil War, the Democratic Party remained a loyal opposition to Lincoln's conduct of military and political affairs, although Republicans—with some justification—often accused the Democrats of becoming more opposition than loyal. Democratic dissatisfaction with Lincoln came for a number of different reasons. First, northern Democrats could point to serious lapses in the prosecution of the war that left the president, his cabinet, and his military leadership open to stinging criticism. The two failures of Union forces at the First and Second Battles of Bull Run, the collapse of the Peninsula Campaign, and the horrors at Antietam were just some of the military shortcomings upon which Democrats jumped, charging that Lincoln's poor management of the war reflected weaknesses in leadership, experience, and strategy. Democrats vehemently denied in 1861 and 1862 that they were disloyal to the goals of the war, but they cautioned that in order to save the Union and end the rebellion, new presidential leadership was needed.

Democrats, however, walked a fine line between criticism of Lincoln and the Union cause. Republican politicians and newspapermen sought to portray their rivals as always on the verge of treason, even though the Republicans themselves were also divided on the best ways to prosecute the war. Labeled "Copperheads" by their Republican critics, northern Democrats

FIGURE 6.5 *A newspaper cartoon from 1864 showing the Union threatened by political serpents wearing the hats of Midwest Democratic congressmen. Photo by MPI/ Hulton Archive/Getty Images*

loudly pointed to the administration's failures on the battlefield while arguing to voters that if given the reins of power they would bring a swift and successful end to the war. As the important 1862 congressional elections approached in November, Democrats appeared to possess considerable momentum.

While Democratic congressional candidates used the administration's military failures to highlight the need for a change in leadership, they also focused on Lincoln's wartime domestic policies. The Democratic Party harkened back to its antebellum roots and emphasized limited government and state power, principles that to Democratic minds were jettisoned by Lincoln. Candidates attacked such Republican policies as the issuance of greenback currency and the consolidation of the banking system. They condemned with particular vehemence the president's suspension of *habeas corpus*. An important legal doctrine that protects individuals from capricious government power, *habeas corpus* has a long history of securing the rights of individuals against arbitrary arrest and imprisonment. During wartime, however, political leaders, even democratically elected ones, have had to weigh the exigencies of war with legal precedent. Lincoln was no different, and his training as a lawyer and his respect for the Constitution made the prosecution of dissent and treason exceedingly difficult. How does a leader in a democracy allow for legitimate criticism of the government and freedom of the press during war? Are the legal precedents the same during peace and war? The president struggled mightily with such questions and ultimately decided to suspend *habeas corpus* at times during the Civil War, allowing him to imprison particularly harsh critics of his prosecution of the war. Although the president did not make these decisions lightly, he realized that politically he left himself open to attack, and the Democrats obliged.

Finally, in the fall 1862 congressional contests, Democrats disparaged the president and the Republicans for turning the war into a crusade against slavery. Northern Democrats, including those who joined Republicans in a pro-Union faction, supported the war when the goal was to end the rebellion and bring the South back into the Union. But the Emancipation Proclamation seemed to confirm the Democrats' charge that Lincoln was a radical abolitionist who had entered the war with the secret intent of ending slavery in the South. Although both parties shared a belief in the inferiority of African Americans and rejected any hint of social equality between blacks and whites, the Democrats were particularly loud and blunt in their denunciations of abolitionism and radical programs for black political equality. They appealed to the northern working class by playing up fears that the Emancipation Proclamation would eventually lead to mass black migration to the North, forcing white workers to compete with black laborers who were likely to accept much lower wages.

While Lincoln faced an emboldened Democratic Party in the fall of 1862, he confronted equally challenging divisions within his own Republican ranks and, indeed, within his own cabinet. Chief among his "team of rivals" were Secretary of State William Seward and Secretary of the Treasury Salmon P. Chase. From the earliest stages of the war, Chase wanted to take a harder line against the South than Seward. Throughout 1861 and 1862, Chase and Seward competed for Lincoln's favor, and the president proved adept at managing the strong personalities that populated his cabinet.

The final results of the 1862 elections worsened the divisions within the Republican Party and within the Lincoln Administration. While Republicans lost only a few seats, the number of seats controlled by the regular Democrats rose from forty-two to seventy-seven. Republicans lost support across the northeast and Midwest, including the president's home state of Illinois. These embarrassing losses led Republican Party leaders to worry whether they could hold on to the presidency with the 1864 election only two years away. Lincoln seemed to be weakened in the wake of the 1862 congressional results, and leaders such as Chase and Seward, while not openly campaigning for the party's nomination, did not overtly dissuade followers from maneuvering behind the scenes to assume the party's mantle if Lincoln's support collapsed. Chase in particular considered himself a more effective leader, and he and his followers presented a formidable challenge to the president from within the Republican Party.

For their part the Democrats were even more emboldened after their gains in the 1862 elections. Into the winter and spring of 1863 the Democrats continued to charge that the president had violated the Constitution by suspending *habeas corpus*, drafting citizens into the Union army, and imprisoning dissenters. They repeated claims that the Emancipation Proclamation would weaken the Union war effort as well as harm northern white labor by lowering wages. Skilled white workers were especially concerned that an influx of black labor would reduce their ability to strike when necessary. Thus, Democratic Party slogans against Lincoln and the Republicans seemed to resonate with northern white voters. As Lincoln awaited the day that the Emancipation Proclamation would take effect on January 1, 1863, he simultaneously faced a revitalized Democratic opposition and the internal factions within his own party.

COMPANION @ WEBSITE

Please visit the companion website www.routledge.com/cw/wells for additional study aids including chapter overviews, interactive quizzes, and more.

Discussion Questions

- What roles did women play on the home front and the battlefront?

- Characterize the views of white Americans in the North and South regarding race.
- How successful were the Union military campaigns of the summer and fall of 1862? What could Union leaders have done differently?
- Discuss the significance of the Battle of Antietam and its aftermath.
- Historians have debated the significance of the Emancipation Proclamation. How did the proclamation affect the Union cause? How did it affect Lincoln politically? In the end, how important was the proclamation to the ending of slavery?
- Why were the 1862 congressional elections significant?
- How did Lincoln deal with divisions within his cabinet and within the Republican Party?
- During the Civil War, Lincoln suspended *habeas corpus* and curtailed freedom of speech, actions for which he has been criticized by later observers. In your view, was Lincoln justified in these actions? How does a democratic nation protect civil liberties during wartime? Should freedom of speech and press, including the right to criticize the government, be abridged during wartime? Why or why not?
- Historians often struggle to appreciate and understand the views of those who were less educated, since they are less likely to have left behind written primary sources such as letters and diaries. What sources might you use to learn about African Americans' reactions to the Emancipation Proclamation? How might you trace the evolution of African American attitudes toward Lincoln over the course of the war?

Notes

1 "Education of Southern Women," *De Bow's Review* n.s. 6 (October/November 1861), 390.

2 Cumming quoted in Richard B. Harwell, ed., *Kate: The Journal of a Confederate Nurse* (Baton Rouge: Louisiana State University Press, 1959), 135–136.

3 Beauregard quoted in Crystal N. Feimster, "Benjamin Butler & the Threat of Sexual Violence during the American Civil War," *Daedalus* 138 (Spring 2009), 130.

4 Briggs quoted in David W. Blight, "No Desperate Hero: Manhood and Freedom in a Union Soldier's Experience," in Catherine Clinton and Nina Silber, eds., *Divided Houses: Gender and the Civil War* (New York: Oxford University Press, 1992), 57.

5 George Thomas Stevens, *Three Years in the Sixth Corps* (Albany: SR Gray, 1866), 153–154.

Further Reading

Jeanie Attie, *Patriotic Toil: Northern Women and the American Civil War* (Ithaca: Cornell University Press, 1998).

James Alex Baggett, *The Scalawags: Southern Dissenters in the Civil War and Reconstruction* (Baton Rouge: Louisiana State University Press, 2004).

Jean H. Baker, *Affairs of Party: The Political Culture of Northern Democrats in the Mid-Nineteenth Century* (Ithaca: Cornell University Press, 1983).

Ann Blackman, *Wild Rose: The True Story of a Civil War Spy* (New York: Random House, 2005).

De Ann Blanton, *They Fought Like Demons: Women Soldiers in the Civil War* (New York: Vintage, 2003).

Thomas J. Brown, *Dorothea Dix: New England Reformer* (Cambridge, MA: Harvard University Press, 1998).

John R. Brumgardt, ed., *Civil War Nurse: The Diary and Letters of Hannah Ropes* (Knoxville: University of Tennessee Press, 1980).

Victoria E. Bynum, *The Long Shadow of the Civil War: Southern Dissent and its Legacies* (Chapel Hill: University of North Carolina Press, 2010).

Catherine Clinton and Nina Silber, eds., *Divided Houses: Gender and the Civil War* (New York: Oxford University Press, 1992).

Bettye Collier-Thomas, *Jesus, Jobs, and Justice: African American Women and Religion* (New York: Knopf, 2010).

Peter Cozzens, *Shenandoah 1862: Stonewall Jackson's Valley Campaign* (Chapel Hill: University of North Carolina Press, 2008).

Kate Cumming, *Kate: The Journal of a Confederate Nurse* (Baton Rouge: Louisiana State University Press, 1998).

O. Edward Cunningham, *Shiloh and the Western Campaign of 1862* (El Dorado Hills: Savas Beatie, 2007).

Don H. Doyle, *The Cause of All Nations: An International History of the American Civil War* (New York: Basic Books, 2014).

Edmund L. Drago, *Confederate Phoenix: Rebel Children and their Families in South Carolina* (New York: Fordham University Press, 2008).

Drew Faust, *Mothers of Invention: Women of the Slaveholding South in the American Civil War* (Chapel Hill: University of North Carolina Press, 1996).

Lorien Foote, *The Gentlemen and the Roughs: Violence, Honor, and Manhood in the Union Army* (New York: New York University Press, 2010).

Douglas Southall Freeman, *Lee* (New York: Scribner's, 1997).

Gary W. Gallagher, *The Antietam Campaign* (Chapel Hill: University of North Carolina Press, 2007).

Judith Giesberg, *Army at Home: Women and the Civil War on the Northern Home Front* (Chapel Hill: University of North Carolina Press, 2009).

Doris Kearns Goodwin, *Team of Rivals: The Political Genius of Abraham Lincoln* (New York: Simon & Schuster, 2006).
John J. Hennessy, *Return to Bull Run: The Campaign and Battle of Second Manassas* (Norman: University of Oklahoma Press, 1993).
Frank L. Klement, *The Limits of Dissent: Clement L. Vallandigham and the Civil War* (New York: Fordham University Press, 1998).
Elizabeth D. Leonard, *Yankee Women: Gender Battles in the Civil War* (New York: W.W. Norton, 1994).
Donald E. Markle, *Spies and Spymasters of the Civil War* (New York: Hippocrene Books, 1994).
James M. McPherson, *Crossroads of Freedom: Antietam* (New York: Oxford University Press, 2002).
Katherine Shively Meier, *Nature's Civil War: Common Soldiers and the Environment in 1862 Virginia* (Chapel Hill: UNC Press, 2013).
Mark E. Neely, Jr., *The Union Divided: Party Conflict in the Civil War North* (Cambridge, MA: Harvard University Press, 2002).
Mark E. Neely, Jr., *The Boundaries of American Political Culture in the Civil War Era* (Chapel Hill: University of North Carolina Press, 2005).
James Oakes, *The Radical and the Republican: Frederick Douglass, Abraham Lincoln, and the Triumph of Antislavery Politics* (New York: W.W. Norton, 2007).
Michael D. Pierson, *Mutiny at Fort Jackson: The Untold Story of the Fall of New Orleans* (Chapel Hill: University of North Carolina Press, 2008).
John Michael Priest, *Antietam: The Soldiers' Battle* (New York: Oxford University Press, 1994).
George C. Rable, *Civil Wars: Women and the Crisis of Southern Nationalism* (Urbana: University of Illinois Press, 1989).
James A. Rawley, *The Politics of Union: Northern Politics during the Civil War* (Hinsdale: Dryden Press, 1974).
James Robertson, *Stonewall Jackson: The Man, the Soldier, the Legend* (New York: Macmillan, 1997).
Hyman Rubin III, *South Carolina Scalawags* (Columbia: University of South Carolina Press, 2006).
Gerald Schwartz, ed., *A Woman Doctor's Civil War: Esther Hill Hawks' Diary* (Columbia: University of South Carolina Press, 1984).
Nina Silber, *Daughters of the Union: Northern Women Fight the Civil War* (Cambridge, MA: Harvard University Press, 2005).
Margaret M. Storey, *Loyalty and Loss: Alabama's Unionists in the Civil War and Reconstruction* (Baton Rouge: Louisiana State University Press, 2004).
Elizabeth Varon, *Southern Lady, Yankee Spy: The True Story of Elizabeth Van Lew, A Union Agent in the Heart of the Confederacy* (New York: Oxford University Press, 2003).
Jennifer L. Weber, *Copperheads: The Rise and Fall of Lincoln's Opponents in the North* (New York: Oxford University Press, 2006).

Jonathan W. White, *Abraham Lincoln and Treason in the Civil War: The Trials of John Merryman* (Baton Rouge: Louisiana State University Press, 2011).

LeeAnn Whites and Alecia P. Long, *Occupied Women: Gender, Military Occupation, and the Civil War* (Baton Rouge: Louisiana State University Press, 2009).

Bertram Wyatt-Brown, *Southern Honor: Ethics and Behavior in the Old South* (New York: Oxford University Press, 1982).

TURNING POINTS

Topics Covered in this Chapter:

- The Eastern Theater in Early 1863
- Ethnicity and Immigrants During the War
- African American Soldiers and Sailors
- The Battle of Gettysburg
- Death and Medicine During the War
- Prisoners and Prison Camps
- New York Draft Riots and Class Conflict
- The Western Theater in Early 1863

7

Introduction

The year 1863 is often considered crucial in determining the war's outcome. In the West, Vicksburg, a Confederate bastion on the Mississippi River, absorbed Union blows for weeks but ultimately succumbed to Grant's successful maneuvering. In the East, the Battle of Gettysburg in Pennsylvania helped to turn the war slowly to the Union's favor. The three-day battle at Gettysburg thwarted Lee's incursions into Union territory and provided Lincoln with a battlefield venue for his famous address.

While armies and navies struggled for the upper hand, trouble at home threatened to divide both the Union and the Confederacy. Political and class divisions in the northeast led to deadly draft riots in New York City, while white southerners similarly questioned whether the burdens of war were spread evenly across all social groups. As Union and Confederate political leaders sought a united war effort, ordinary citizens experiencing the privation and suffering of the fighting unleashed their anger and frustration.

African Americans joined the Union war effort in great numbers, often despite deep-seated racism that kept them in positions as laborers. Lincoln, however, remained determined to use black soldiers, believing strongly that African Americans would make good soldiers because they had reason to fight. Famous black forces, such as the Massachusetts 54th, have earned fame in Hollywood films, but about 200,000 African Americans fought for the Union, and served in a range of roles. The visibility of black soldiers also made them a special target of the Confederacy.

Black and white soldiers on both sides of the war died in great numbers. The deadly nature of the war lay partly in improved weaponry, an industry that advanced significantly over the course of the war. But many tens of thousands of soldiers also died from disease, and Union and Confederate camps struggled with lack of food, poor sanitation, and primitive medicine. Soldiers held in prison camps remained particularly vulnerable to poor sanitation and lack of food. Although doctors were beginning to understand the role of microbes in causing disease, science and medicine could offer little help to badly wounded soldiers. The great writer Walt Whitman later remarked that "Future years will never know the seething hell and the black infernal background" of the battles. "The real war," Whitman claimed, "will never get in the books." Death, whether the result of fighting or disease, reached all corners of the nation, and soldiers and their families had to come to grips with the possibility that death could come at any time.

The Eastern Theater in Early 1863

The early months of 1863 were devastating to Union morale. The Army of the Potomac experienced battlefield reversals, but perhaps equally damaging to the Union cause was the growing dissension within the northern populace.

The Union reversals of early 1863 came on the heels of one of the Union army's darkest moments: the defeat at Fredericksburg, Maryland in mid-December of the previous year. Substantial Confederate forces occupied the town and the surrounding area. On December 13, 1862, Union General Burnside launched an attack employing more than 100,000 against Confederate forces totaling a little over 70,000. Lee's men occupied an impregnable position but Burnside attacked them anyway. In the clash, the Union right moved against southern soldiers under James Longstreet's command, while the Union left battled Stonewall Jackson and his corps. Union efforts failed and the defeat at Fredericksburg boded ill for the Federals as 1863 began. After Burnside failed once again in January 1863 in an ill-advised

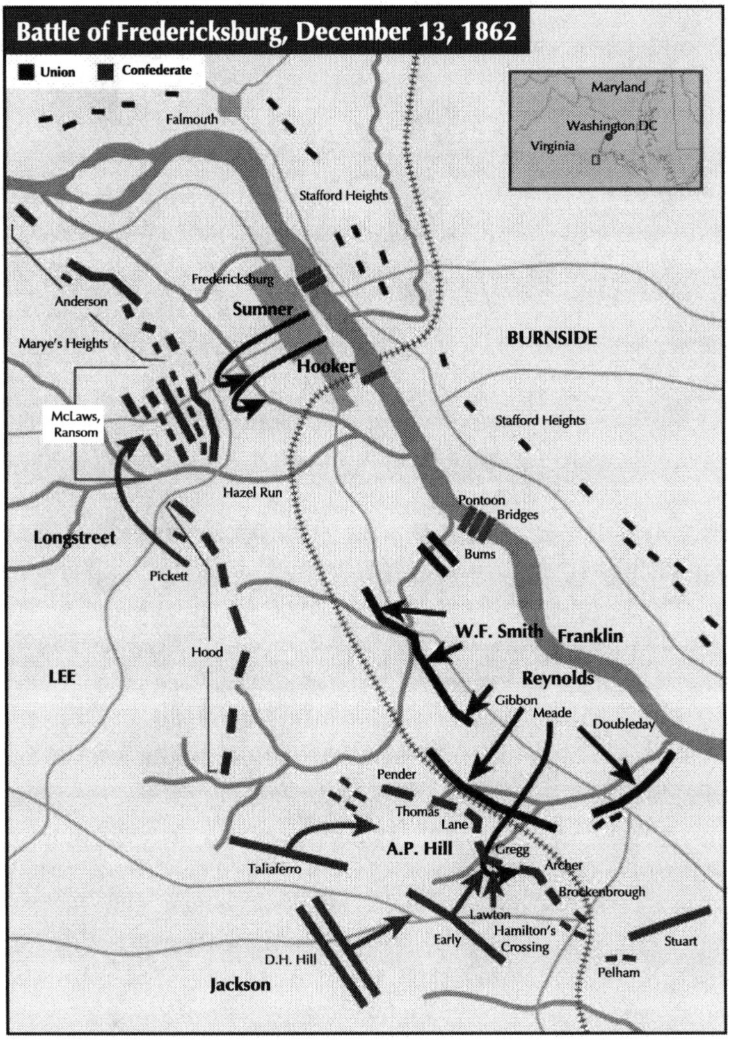

MAP 7.1 *Battle of Fredericksburg, 1862*

maneuver on the Rappahannock that became known as the "Mud March," Lincoln replaced him with General Joseph Hooker. Meanwhile the United States Congress passed the Federal Enrollment Act in February to add soldiers to the ranks. The draft act signed into law by Lincoln set the draft age for men at twenty to forty-five, but also allowed draftees to send substitutes or pay a $300 fee to avoid fighting. This latter provision would prove particularly galling to northern citizens, who could claim with justification that such a law allowed the rich to escape the fighting.

The Enrollment Act damaged Union morale but so too did military defeat at Chancellorsville, Virginia in May 1863. At the beginning of the month, Hooker first flanked Lee, catching him against the Rappahannock; but then Lee pulled off a devastating counterattack when Hooker balked. Lee attacked Hooker's substantial forces near Chancellorsville in Spotsylvania County, a maneuver that added to Lee's reputation as a military strategist. In the face of the much larger Army of the Potomac, Lee divided his forces. Confederate losses were significant, including the mortal wounding of General Stonewall Jackson, which Lee likened to losing his right arm. But Lee's expert maneuvering combined with Hooker's confusion and timid leadership resulted in a Confederate victory. Upon learning of the defeat, Lincoln is supposed to have lamented, "My God! My God! What will the country say?"

The answer to Lincoln's lament was already developing in the form of heightened criticism for his wartime leadership. Northern Democrats, emboldened by gains in the congressional elections in the fall of 1862, stepped up their attacks on the Republican president. Ohio's Clement Vallandigham, leader of the Copperheads and Democratic candidate for governor, lambasted the president and his party as the fighting at Chancellorsville was getting underway; to an Ohio audience he denounced "King Lincoln" and the northern war effort. In Vallandigham's mind, the South had a right to secede and the Federals had no business forcing the rebellious states back into the Union. But to Lincoln, the Ohio Copperhead had gone too far. On May 5, Vallandigham was arrested for violating General Order Number 38 that warned against sympathizing with the Confederate enemy. Denied the traditional peacetime right to *habeas corpus*—by which a person can protest what might be deemed an illegal detention—Vallandigham was convicted and eventually exiled to the South. Such bold suppression of the freedom of speech earned Lincoln much criticism at the time, and scholars have since also faulted the president for violating basic freedoms. Lincoln's defenders claimed that wartime exigencies demanded the curtailment of peacetime liberties. Although Republicans praised Vallandigham's arrest, many copperhead Democrats saw the president's move as an act of political folly that evinced weak and desperate leadership. Fortunately for Lincoln and the Union cause, victory at the Battle of Gettysburg in Pennsylvania would chasten northern political critics.

Ethnicity and Immigrants During the War

Even while fighting political battles at home, Lincoln remained ever conscious of the need for men and supplies on the field, which could be augmented by waves of new immigrants. Most immigrants settled in the northern states in hopes of landing factory jobs at good wages. Although the South began to welcome an influx of white immigrant laborers in the late 1850s, it could not compete with the millions of Europeans who had been settling in the northeast and Midwest since the 1840s. As one historian has pointed out, about one in every six residents of the North had been born outside the United States; about one in thirty southerners came from outside the country.[1]

In 1860, about a quarter of residents in Boston and New York City were Irish, numbers that would aid the Union cause. Historian David Gleeson found that a series of crop failures in Ireland in the early 1860s led many Irish citizens to consider immigrating to the United States. A $500 bonus encouraged them to enlist. The tactic worked, as the number of Irish immigrants in the Union army rose from about 40,000 in 1862 to about 100,000 in 1863. Actually, some of these immigrants were recruited directly from Ireland into the Union army, and by 1863 many resented the fact that they were fighting for a country that they had barely lived in. They died in great numbers at battles such as Antietam in 1862. Irish soldiers endured this suffering even as anti-Catholic sentiments circulated in the North and even as stereotypical caricatures depicting the Irish as drunken and lazy appeared in popular magazines such as *Harper's Weekly*. Irish resentment of the war, historian Susannah Ural Bruce has argued, became more powerful when Lincoln issued the Emancipation Proclamation and immigrants, especially the Irish in New York City, angrily rejected the idea that they might fight and die to end slavery. Their anger would erupt in a series of deadly riots in New York City in July 1863.

Although the Irish were among the largest immigrant groups to join the Union army, Germans, Jews, and Canadians fought in large numbers. Like the Irish, Germans had been coming to settle in significant numbers in the free states since the 1840s, but Germans in Texas were divided over whether or not to support secession. When calls came for Confederate volunteers, German immigrants in Texas such as Charles A. Leuschner enlisted. The Union, however, could count far more German regiments than could the southern states. Jewish Americans were largely welcomed in southern cities before the war; Jews in Charleston played prominent roles in city life throughout the colonial and antebellum eras. Although small in number relative to other ethnic groups, southern Jews avidly joined the Confederacy and a few, like Judah

P. Benjamin, became important Confederate leaders. The Union had important Jewish support and Lincoln counted many Jews among his key allies and friends, such as Isachar Zacharie. Lincoln and Abraham Jonas, a Jewish resident of Illinois, carried on a lengthy correspondence after he became president.

During the Civil War, Canada was not an independent nation. Canadians, however, contributed to the Union victory, many lured by the $200 signing bonus offered by the North. More than 30,000 Canadians served in the Civil War, and around 5,000 died in the conflict. Only a few hundred Canadians fought for the Confederacy, but according to one account, Montreal became a covert base of operations for Confederates. In the October 1864 affair known as St. Albans Raid, Confederate spies crossed over the border from Canada and robbed three banks in Vermont, returning to Canada with more than $150,000. A diplomatic crisis ensued when the U.S. government requested extradition for the Confederate sympathizers, a request ultimately denied in Canadian courts.

African American Soldiers and Sailors

While immigrants added significantly to Union numbers, Lincoln became aware soon after the war began that the Union would need to tap the large numbers of free African Americans in the North, as well as the ex-slaves who sought protection behind Union lines. Unofficial organization of black soldiers began in 1862 when General David Hunter formed the First South Carolina Volunteers from ex-slaves and free blacks. The Second South Carolina Volunteers, under the command of abolitionist James Montgomery, added ex-slaves from Florida and Georgia. In an 1863 letter to General Grant, Lincoln implored his officer to recruit black soldiers:

General [Lorenzo] Thomas has gone again to the Mississippi Valley, with the view of raising colored troops. I have no reason to doubt that you are doing what you reasonably can upon the same subject. I believe it is a resource which, if vigorously applied now, will soon close this contest. It works doubly—weakening the enemy and strengthening us.

In the Emancipation Proclamation, Lincoln had hinted that the time was approaching when the Union army and navy would enlist African American soldiers and sailors. In May 1863, the Union established the Bureau of Colored Troops, but with the stipulation that most of these black soldiers would serve under white officers. Equally discriminatory was the fact that black soldiers were paid $10 per month, $3 less than white privates, and another $3 was deducted from their pay for their uniforms. All black soldiers received the same $10 per month, regardless of rank. Whites of higher rank made more money than white privates. Perhaps most importantly, black Union soldiers and sailors faced harsh attacks from Confederate armies, who promised to be especially brutal in dealing with blacks. In fact, in 1863 the Confederacy threatened to kill or enslave African American soldiers and sailors.

At first, African Americans in northern cities such as Philadelphia and Boston were turned away when they tried to enlist. The Emancipation Proclamation had endorsed enlistment by blacks, but once accepted as soldiers, they were given substandard pay and resources. Still, they contributed significantly to the Union effort.

Eventually, nearly 200,000 black soldiers served the Union cause, making up more than 160 regiments, including the famous Massachusetts 54th, comprised of free black men. Established as a model black regiment, with officers from prominent families and men recruited from the free states, a young white officer named Robert Gould Shaw led the 54th. Shaw and his regiment played an important part in the attempted retaking of Fort Sumter in Charleston

FIGURE 7.1 *District of Columbia. Company E, 4th U.S. Colored Infantry, at Fort Lincoln. Library of Congress, LC-B817- 7890 [P&P]*

Harbor. The fort was protected by Confederate defenses known as the Battery Wagner, and Shaw led his men in a direct assault on the battery during the evening of July 18, 1863.

The 54th regiment suffered devastating casualties while failing in an attempt to retake the fort. As one doctor on the scene reported,

> **150 of the brave boys from the 54th . . . were brought to us and laid on blankets on the floor all mangled and ghastly. What a terrible sight it was! It was 36 hours since the awful struggle at Ft. Wagner and nothing had been done for them. We had no beds, and no means even of building a fire, but the colored people came promptly to our aid.**

Formerly enslaved men and women in the area brought food and water to the hospital to aid the wounded black soldiers, and

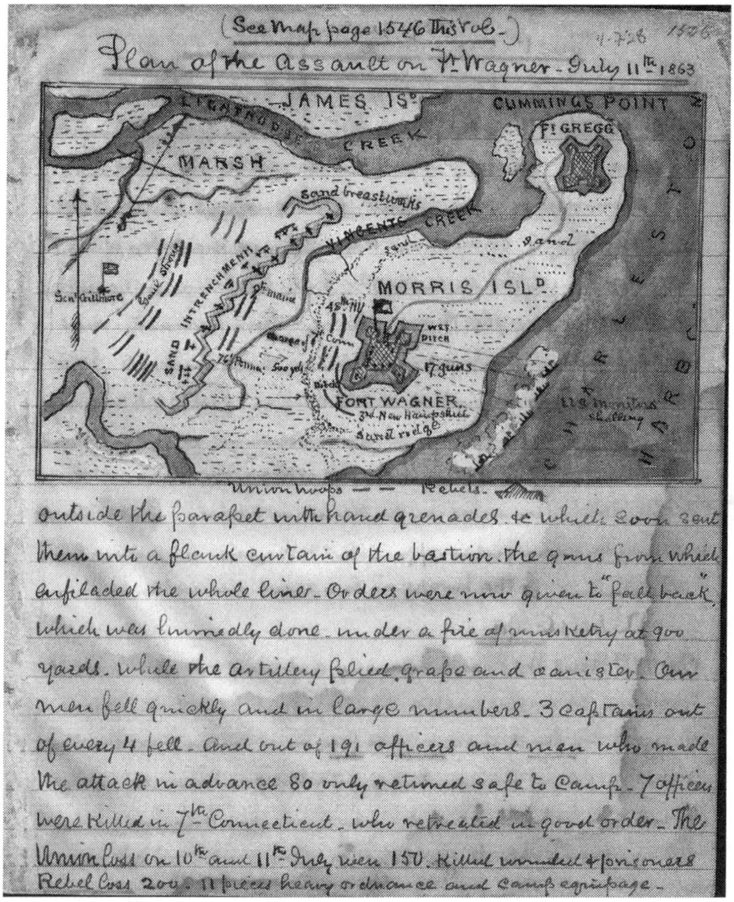

FIGURE 7.2 *Plan of the assault on Fort Wagner, July 11th 1863. http://www.loc.gov/item/gvhs01.vhs00151/*

they took pride in the soldiers' courage. Quickly word spread in northern papers of the bravery of Shaw and his men.

More than 20,000 African Americans served in the Union naval forces, which was on the whole more equitable than the army in its treatment of black sailors. Partly this was due to the difficulty of segregation on crowded ships, but black sailors were paid on par with whites and were generally provided with resources and food equal to that of white sailors. One of the most prominent black Union sailors was Robert Smalls, a Charleston slave who escaped during the war in dramatic fashion. Born in 1839 to a generally kind master named John McKee, Smalls served the Confederacy in the early months of the war as a hand on the ship *The Planter*, a private vessel that had been pressed into service once war broke out. He had gained extensive knowledge as a seaman before the war, and he knew the inlets and harbors around Charleston well. In May 1861, Smalls used that knowledge to escape with his family and other slaves. So confident were the white officers that on the night of May 13 they left the ship under the control of its black crewmen, including Smalls, who had already hatched a plan for escape. After the whites left the ship, Smalls took control of *The Planter* and sailed to a nearby dock where his wife and children were waiting with the families of the other black crewmen. However, the danger was just beginning.

Charleston harbor was well protected, and passing ships had to run a gauntlet of forts and lookouts. Smalls knew all of the appropriate signals to give the lookouts, and he dressed in the captain's uniform to deceive the Confederates under cover of darkness. Smalls even reportedly walked the deck of the ship and mimicked the real captain's walk. The ruse was successful, but Smalls and his collaborators then had to meet up with the Union fleet outside Charleston harbor without drawing fire. The escapees lowered the Confederate flag from the ship and hoisted a white bed sheet in its place, and the Union ships allowed *The Planter* to approach. Smalls and his men were greeted with fanfare, not only because of their gutsy escape, but also because the ship and its ammunition were great prizes for the Union. In addition, Smalls had detailed knowledge of the waterways around Charleston, as well as its defenses. The dramatic story of his escape appeared in newspapers throughout the North, and his heroism earned him duty with the Union navy. After the war, Smalls returned to South Carolina and became an important Republican politician.

While African Americans such as Robert Smalls served the Union cause, free blacks and slaves were also forced to serve

FIGURE 7.3 *Robert Smalls. Library of Congress, Prints and Photographs Division, LC-USZ62-99507*

the Confederacy. A few states, including Tennessee and Louisiana, drafted blacks into state militia. But because of the Confederate government's reluctance to arm slaves and free African Americans until very late in the war, conscripted blacks could not be deployed to the battlefield. Instead, they were used as laborers to construct bridges and buildings, dig trenches, and other activities requiring physical labor, work that freed up whites to fight.

Eventually, the Confederacy was desperate enough to reconsider arming black soldiers. In early 1864, Confederate General Patrick Cleburne recommended that "we immediately commence training a large reserve of the most courageous of our slaves, and further that we guarantee freedom within a reasonable time to every slave in the South who shall remain true to the Confederacy in this war." The government was slow to consider Cleburne's plan, a plan that Lee did not initially support. Not until March 1865, just weeks before the war itself ended, did the Confederate government officially call for the drafting of African Americans. Even then, few signed up, obviously unwilling to aid the government that enslaved them. But many African Americans did serve, although their numbers pale in comparison to the black soldiers who joined the

Union army. Ultimately, whether it was because of the promise of freedom or their loyalty to a particular master, black Confederates numbered only in the hundreds.

The Battle of Gettysburg

Buoyed by military success at Fredericksburg and Chancellorsville, Lee began to prepare for an ambitious new plan for crossing into federal territory. His first attempt to penetrate Union territory had resulted in the bloody Battle of Antietam, but the Virginian wanted to continue to pressure Union forces. He also wanted to gather food and supplies for his troops from the Pennsylvania countryside. As historian Peter Carmichael points out, although Lee had told his soldiers to spare private property, not all of them obeyed. One Virginia officer wrote to his wife that "Genl. Lee may order private property to be respected, but I don't mean to obey & the Army will not." Lee's army suffered from both hunger and broken or ill-fitting shoes. Some even believed that the need for shoes brought Lee's forces close to Gettysburg. Lee's Gettysburg Campaign culminated in the battle fought from July 1 through July 3, 1863, which many historians argue increased the likelihood of Union success in the war. Glorified in Hollywood films and in novels such as Michael Shaara's *Killer Angels*, Gettysburg produced the most casualties of any of the war's battles, each side suffering about 23,000 killed or wounded.

The battle began with promise for Lee and the Confederates. To confront Lee and his Army of Northern Virginia, Lincoln sent the newly appointed George Gordon Meade, commander of the Army of the Potomac. On July 1 the opposing sides clashed along the small ridges to the northwest of Gettysburg, a small town that was home to Gettysburg College (then called Pennsylvania College). Union Brigadier General John Buford commanded a cavalry division while Major General John F. Reynolds, one of Meade's wing commanders, committed infantry corps to the front. Buford intended merely to hold off Confederate forces until Union reinforcements could arrive and secure the hills south of the town. Challenged by Confederate forces attacking from the northwest under Henry Heth, the fighting began early in the morning of July 1, and continued throughout the morning hours with Heth's soldiers pushing the Union cavalry to the East. The line of the Union's XI Corps collapsed; the same troops who broke at Chancellorsville. At the end of the first day of battle, the Union

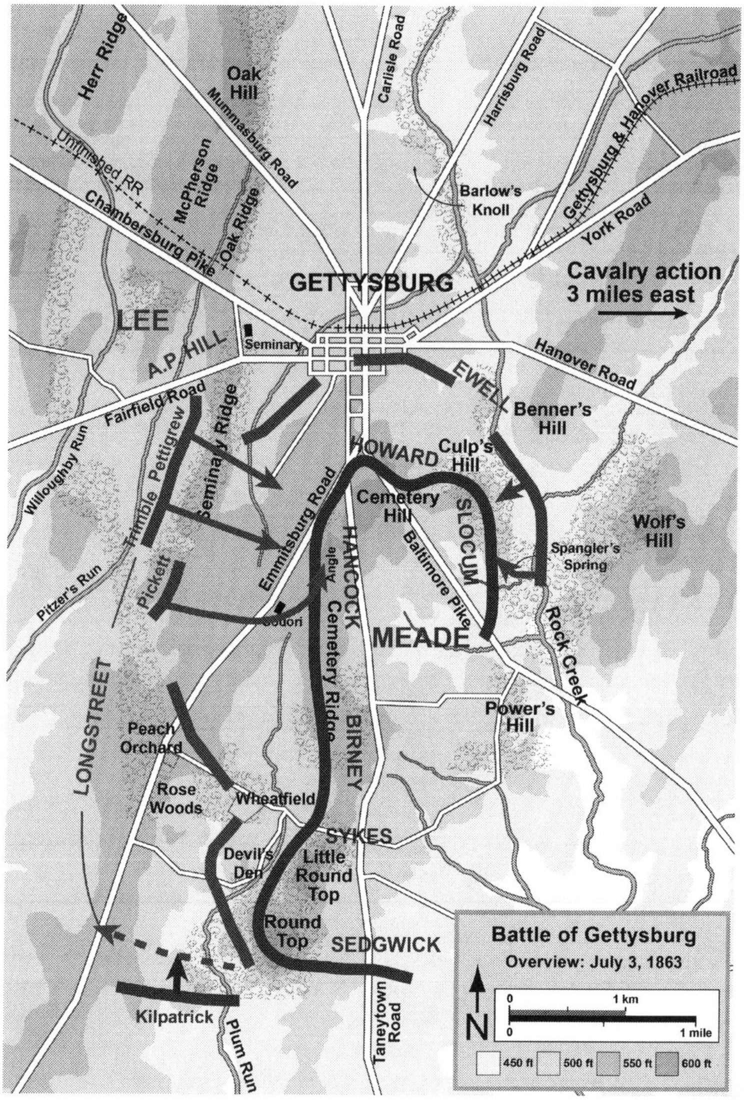

MAP 7.2 *Battle of Gettysburg, July 3, 1863. Map by Hal Jespersen, www.posix.com/CW.*

forces had retreated to Cemetery Hill to the south of the town. Later southern interpreters of the battle's history, especially those invested in smoothing over Lee's miscues, laid blame at the feet of Confederate Lt. General Richard S. Ewell for missing an opportunity to force Meade's army off the high ground. Apparently Ewell was in fact willing to advance with proper support, which Lee did not provide. Throughout the night both armies added to their infantry numbers, setting up the fighting for the next day.

Union control included Culp's Hill and much of Cemetery Hill and Cemetery Ridge to the south and southeast of the town of Gettysburg. In a kind of fishhook-shaped line, the Union forces arrayed against the Confederate lines on Seminary Ridge. The armies grew to epic proportions; the Confederate line alone was about five miles long. Almost 175,000 men clashed over the next two days.

Although Lee had not planned to fight at Gettysburg, once the battle started he hurled his forces against the Union left flank and challenged the center of Union lines to no avail. The 20th Maine Volunteer Infantry Regiment repelled a substantial Confederate effort to turn the Union left flank at Little Round Top. Reversing the struggles of the first day of the battle, Union defenses had largely held their ground against potent Confederate attacks. At the end of the first day of battle on July 1, Confederates had reason to believe that the Battle of Gettysburg would end in their favor, but by nightfall on the second day the outcome was far less clear.

The third and final day of the battle came on Friday, July 3 and would long be remembered for acts of folly and bravery. Lee intended to continue his plan of having General Longstreet's forces attack the Union left flank while Ewell confronted Union troops at Culp's Hill. Hoping to soften Union resolve, Lee ordered massive artillery bombing of northern defenses that began in the early afternoon. The artillery fire did not have the effect Lee had hoped for. Lee ordered Longstreet to assault the Union center on July 3. Three Confederate divisions attacked in what has become known—somewhat as a misnomer—as "Pickett's Charge." Led by Major General George E. Pickett of Virginia, thousands of Confederate soldiers died while attacking Cemetery Ridge. Of the thousands of men in the charge, nearly 70% were lost to death, injury, or capture. By the end of the third day, Union and Confederate losses totaled about 50,000 casualties, making Gettysburg the deadliest battle of the entire war. Lee's army had suffered defeat in its second foray into northern territory, and he and his army retreated southward, as Meade failed to pursue. President Lincoln despaired that Meade had missed a crucial chance to deal the death-blow to the Army of Northern Virginia. After pushing Meade to pursue Lee, an exasperated Lincoln remarked that "Our army held the war in the hollow of their hand and they would not close it!"

Although Gettysburg was a Confederate defeat, the battle's significance was not clear at first. Historian George C. Rable suggests that misleading reports in southern papers convinced many readers that they had won at Gettysburg and only gradually did they learn of the defeat. At the time, few southerners thought the defeat insurmountable; for most it was a temporary setback. Union newspapers initially thought their victory would bring the war to a rapid conclusion, but soon realized that the fighting was far from over. Historians have often considered the battle as an important turning point in the war. After Fredericksburg and Chancellorsville, Confederate victory appeared possible, although the victories were costly. After the damage suffered at Gettysburg, however, hopes for a southern triumph dimmed. The magnitude of the losses destroyed Lee's offensive capacity. After Gettysburg and Vicksburg, battles that occurred almost simultaneously, the Union's superior numbers and resources became more apparent with each month of fighting.

Throughout the rest of the summer and early fall of 1863, the corpses of men and horses lay in the harsh sun. What would become Gettysburg National Cemetery was in the works, and Lincoln uttered his famous "Gettysburg Address" at the ceremony dedicating the cemetery on November 19. Demonstrating Lincoln's remarkable talents for writing incisive, powerful prose, the address has become one of the key documents, along with the Declaration of Independence and the Constitution, of the nation. As scholar Gary Wills has argued, although fewer than 300 words comprise the address, it powerfully articulates the importance of the war and the justice of the Union cause.

Death and Medicine During the War

Nineteenth-century Americans were accustomed to death. The primitive state of medicine and the poor understanding of the underlying causes of disease meant that death could come at any time. Children often died before their first birthday, and the average life expectancy for white Americans was about forty years, while much lower for black Americans. Common maladies that are little more than nuisances to modern Americans could spell death or disfigurement for those in the 1860s. Despite their familiarity with death, Americans were ill prepared for the massive suffering of the Civil War. Especially deadly battles such as Antietam and Gettysburg brought death to nearly every town and village, and many families lost all of their male relatives, creating what historian Drew Faust has called "a broader republic of shared suffering."

The high rate of casualties during the war was due in part to improvements in all kinds of weapons. For the infantry, the basic weapon was the rifled musket, often known among Union soldiers as "Springfields," which fired a range of bullets such as the Minie ball. Shaped like a cylinder with a pointed front, the Minie ball had gained wide use just before the war. Other bullets of varying shapes and sizes were also tried, including the Brunswick, Picket, and Whitworth bullets. However, soldiers often loaded the rifles incorrectly, leading to misfiring or explosions. Soldiers experienced with rifles might be able to hit targets up to 300 yards away, while sharpshooters could hit targets from two or three times as far. But poor training, the chaos of the battlefield, and malfunctioning weapons reduced the effectiveness of even the best-intentioned soldier. More than one and a half million rifles were used by Union soldiers, especially models made in 1861, 1863, and 1864. Other guns widely employed on the battlefield included the Sharps breech-loading rifle, the Spencer repeating rifle, and the Colt revolving rifle. Soldiers also carried pistols and revolvers, and the fast-repeating Gatling gun was used to a lesser extent. Bayonets were fitted at the ends of weapons on both sides, but they were seldom used in fighting; more often the knife-like bayonets were used as tools for digging, carving, or opening objects.

Cavalry and artillery soldiers also employed a wide range of weapons to inflict as much damage on the enemy as possible. Cavalry soldiers normally used carbines, a lighter and shorter gun well suited to firing from atop a horse. Some examples used by Union and Confederate cavalrymen included the Smith percussion carbine, the Burnside percussion carbine, and the Gallager percussion carbine. Artillerymen, of course, fired large ordnance and they played a significant role in numerous battles, beginning with Fort Sumter in April 1861. Guns fired shells of six, twelve, or twenty-four pounds. Visitors today at Fort Sumter can still see large shells embedded in the walls of the fort. Cannons, many of which weighed hundreds of pounds, were pulled into place by horses or men, and could be fired from miles away. Mortars fired heavy shells at high trajectories, while hybrids such as the "Napoleon" fired twelve-pound smoothbore shells. Like the Minie ball and other bullets, artillery shells screamed as they sailed across the sky, leading soldiers to fear their distinctive sound.

While advances in weaponry increased casualty rates in the field, tens of thousands of soldiers also died from disease. Bacteria had been discovered in the seventeenth century, but it was not until the late nineteenth century that scientists and physicians understood the diseases caused by viruses and bacteria. That discovery would spur new efforts to create sanitary working and living conditions, especially in large cities. But in the 1860s little was known about the causes of malaria, typhoid, measles, smallpox, dysentery, cholera, tuberculosis, and other common

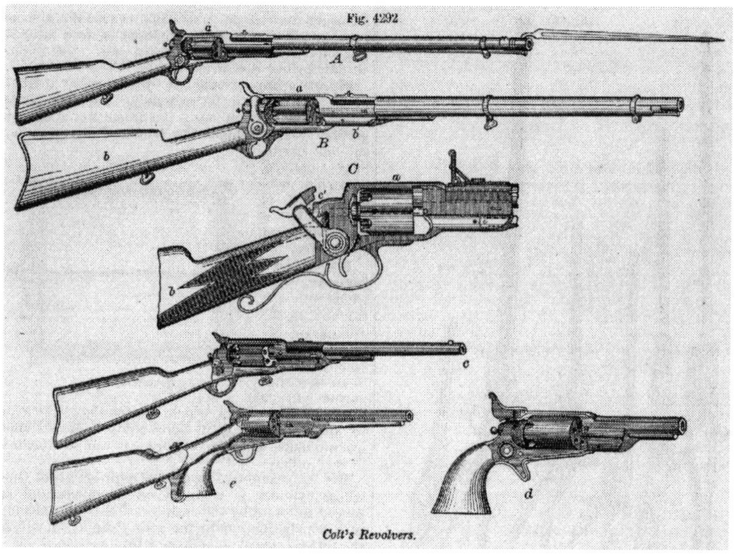

FIGURE 7.4 *Colt's revolvers. Courtesy of the New York Public Library, 835119*

diseases. Soldiers were more susceptible to these maladies because of the poor state of nutrition on the battlefield. Food often consisted of little more than hardtack, a stale bread. As one Union observer wrote:

> **The plates were of tin, badly marked by knives, and blackened by use; the coffee cups were common tin cups; the spoons were tin, the knives were poor iron, the forks were cast iron, and with many tines broken. The breakfast, or whatever meal it was I was invited to join them at, consisted of fried pork or bacon, swimming in grease. The coffee was black and muddy, the bread was hard tack.[2]**

Soldiers feared death by disease not only because great suffering usually accompanied disease, but also because such a death replaced the "good death" on the battlefield.

A "good death" happened in the midst of fighting, and soldiers wanted to be remembered for falling in the glory of battle. They often uttered last words that were passed on in letters to family as recorded by a fellow soldier. Death in battle sometimes occurred weeks after the initial damage was done; limbs amputated by rusty saws unwashed between uses led to horrible and painful cases of gangrene from which many soldiers eventually died. In addition, battlefield deaths were often compounded by the weeks and sometimes months it took to bury the dead. For example, the Battle of Gettysburg ended in early July 1863, but when Lincoln arrived to deliver his brief but memorable address the following November, hastily buried bodies filled the landscape. Even if they were destined for a "good death" on the battlefield, soldiers worried that their bodies would be subject to scavenging animals. Some soldiers were laid to rest in wooden coffins, but others were buried with no coffin at all in unmarked or mass graves.

Back home, news of a soldier's death might not reach his family for several weeks, if at all. Widows engaged in an elaborate ritual of mourning which might last years, including wearing dark clothing, writing on black-bordered stationery, and refusing to leave home. Families avidly sought news of loved ones, and letters from soldiers that managed to make it back home were dear. The wartime postal system was unreliable at best, and letters often failed to reach their destinations. Newspapers were similarly relied upon for news of the war, but the press frequently reported inaccurate information. Since neither the Union nor Confederate armies took the initiative in informing families of fallen soldiers, such relay of information often fell to fellow soldiers, who carried out dying wishes to report the "good death" to loved ones back home.

The tremendous loss of life from disease and combat was partly due to the primitive state of medicine. Medical colleges sprang up in the antebellum period in both the North and South. Georgia, South Carolina, Virginia, and other southern states harbored both public and private medical colleges well before the war, but many wealthy white southern men sought training in Philadelphia and other northern cities. Doctors and dentists throughout the North and South tried to persuade state governments to establish professional standards and licensing, and professional journals such as the *Southern Medical and Surgical Journal* chastised amateur practitioners who lacked college training, used professional degrees to elevate their status and provide access to wealth, protected earnings potential by limiting access to clients, and established means to discipline those who failed to uphold standards. State, county, and town societies created ethics codes and licensing boards to draw distinctions between themselves and laypeople and to establish rules that only group members knew and followed. They lobbied political bodies to support their interests, and they gathered frequently in state conventions and regional meetings to encourage the development of training guidelines and the expansion of knowledge.

Despite considerable energy devoted to raising professional medical and dental standards, by the Civil War those efforts had made little headway, and average citizens had little faith in doctors or their knowledge. "Quack" physicians were everywhere and even well-trained doctors seemed unable to thwart common diseases. Fallen soldiers were carried to makeshift battlefield medical camps and treated with a range of implements and medicines. Opium and other medicines could dull the pain of a bullet wound or amputated limb, but with no understanding of the importance of antibiotics, infection was the likely result.

Still, doctors did realize that whenever possible soap and water could help speed recovery. Esther Hill Hawks, a northern doctor who went South in 1862 to help African Americans at Port Royal, South Carolina, remarked that "the first thing to be done when a patient is admitted into a hospital is to make him thoroughly acquainted with soap and water." Although almost all the doctors were men, a few women like Hawks served as physicians during the war. More often women became nurses, who, because of the unfortunate prognosis for many injured soldiers, helped comfort the dying.

Soldiers held varying conceptions of God, heaven, and the afterlife, but by far the majority of leaders and soldiers on both sides were Christian. The First Great Awakening in the mid-1700s and the Second Great Awakening of the early 1800s increased greatly the numbers of Americans who joined the Baptist, Methodist, and Presbyterian denominations. Added to

FIGURE 7.5 *Confederate soldiers killed in the trenches at Petersburg April 2, 1865 [at Fort Mahone]. Courtesy of the New York Public Library, G92F256_022F*

these Christians were Catholic Irish and German immigrants mostly in the Union army as well as Episcopalians and smaller religious sects, including adherents to the newly formed Mormon faith. Jewish northerners and southerners served the Union or Confederate cause. In the South, Jews were often embraced in towns such as Charleston, where they played important roles in the economic, intellectual, and political lives of their cities. David Yulee of Florida became the first Jewish senator in the United States Congress and then served in the Confederate government.

The vast majority of the combatants were "Christian soldiers," and Union and Confederate men read the same Bible, interpreted in largely the same ways, and held fast to the view that all the suffering of the war was part of God's broader plan. Ministers such as Henry Ward Beecher constantly reminded churchgoers that God's omnipotence meant that death and war were part of providential design. Ministers and political leaders from both sides called for fasting days and prayers to aid their respective causes.

Yet camp life, as the historian George C. Rable argues, harbored the exact opposite of behaviors that ministers and chaplains hoped for. The dullness of camp life led soldiers to play cards, gamble, break the Sabbath, and swear. Poorly trained chaplains exercised little control over soldiers' behavior, although they tried to conduct religious services, scripture readings, and prayer meetings within the camps. Despite these efforts, vice pervaded the soldiers' camps, with prostitution and drinking among the most prominent offenses. As Rable points out, the "nearly 200,000 cases of syphilis and gonorrhea in the Union army" kept doctors and chaplains busy.[3]

Soldiers held elaborate conceptions of heaven and the afterlife. Generally Americans believed that paradise awaited them in the afterlife, especially as a reward for a "good death" on the battlefield. In the nineteenth century many Americans also believed that the dead could be contacted through various mediums. Such spiritualists, as those supposedly able to contact the dead were called, could be men or women; in 1848 Margaret and Kate Fox, sisters living in a small town in New York, became famous for their claims to be able to communicate with the dead. Part of the popularity of spiritualism came from the underlying assumption that the dead were still somehow reachable and not gone forever. It is no surprise that in the midst of the suffering and widespread death of the Civil War loved ones turned to spirit guides or mediums to contact fallen soldiers.

Lincoln himself was not a particularly religious man, although he knew the Bible well and often inserted biblical stories and phrases into his speeches and writings. In 1846, Lincoln had asserted that he was not "an open scoffer at Christianity," although he did admit that "I am not a member of any Christian Church." During the war, the president became more introspective in his beliefs. Early in the war, he wrote that:

> **The will of God prevails. In great contests each party claims to act in accordance with the will of God. Both *may* be, and one *must* be wrong. God can not be for, and *against* the same thing at the same time. In the present civil war it is quite possible that God's purpose is something different from the purpose of either party—and yet the human instrumentalities, working just as they do, are of the best adaptation to effect His purpose. I am almost ready to say this is probably true—that God wills this contest, and wills that it shall not end yet.**

Just like Union soldiers, southern soldiers and their chaplains prayed to God for survival, glory in battle, and victory for the Confederate cause. Religious revivals swept through many rebel units during winter encampments and soldiers carried Bibles with them into battle with the belief that killing in wartime did not violate the Ten Commandments.

Prisoners and Prison Camps

Deaths on the battlefield and in disease-ridden camps were compounded by the thousands of soldiers who died in prisoner-of-war camps in the North and South. Neither the North nor the South had well-established practices for holding or exchanging captured soldiers. Early in the war, holding pens sufficed for captured enemies, and informal exchanges were conducted on the battlefield. In July 1862 an agreement known as the Dix–Hill cartel was reached to facilitate the exchange of prisoners, but the agreement soon collapsed. Difficulty in tracking numbers of parolees meant that neither side was satisfied with one-to-one exchanges. Mistrust was exacerbated by events such as the Fort Pillow Massacre in April 1864, in which Confederate General Nathan Bedford Forrest, a former slave trader and a future leader of the Ku Klux Klan, was blamed for killing more than 200 black and white soldiers who were trying to surrender.

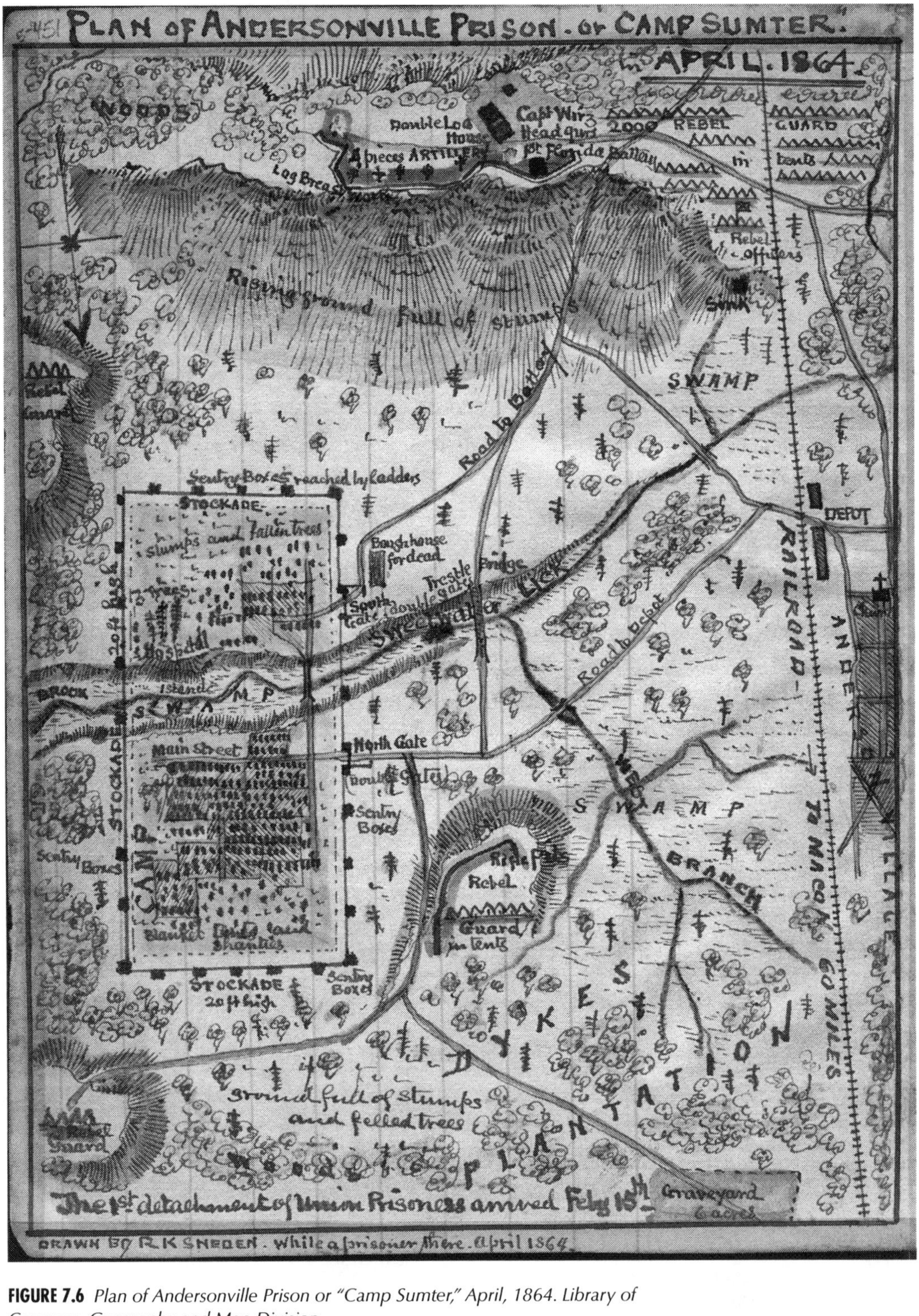

FIGURE 7.6 *Plan of Andersonville Prison or "Camp Sumter," April, 1864. Library of Congress, Geography and Map Division*

Lincoln and his administration did not wish to grant the Confederacy legitimacy by entering into formal agreements for exchanges, but by the summer of 1862 it had become clear that some kind of system was needed. In July of that year, an official agreement was reached that freed prisoners and essentially relieved both sides of having to care for large numbers of captured soldiers. These early efforts proved problematic in no small part because paroled prisoners often reappeared on the battlefield within weeks of their release. Perhaps the most important reason the exchanges broke down, however, was the Confederacy's decisions in May 1863 to enslave captured black Union troops and execute their white officers. This dramatic change in policy greatly upset the northern public and led to outcries in Union newspapers. Southern refusal to renounce this policy led once again to the holding of captured soldiers.

As the war continued, converted buildings and holding pens for captured soldiers proved insufficient, and larger, more elaborate prisoner-of-war camps had to be built. Yet, even in the last years of the war, the camps were horribly unsanitary, and soldiers were given little food on which to subsist. The ever-present problem of disease, as bad as it was in the army camps, was worse in the prison camps. During the war and ever since, observers and historians have identified the prison camps as one of the worst features of an inhumane war.

Union prison camps included more than a dozen facilities that ranged from small, converted buildings to newly constructed and more modern prisons. By the end of the war, some 200,000 Confederate soldiers had been incarcerated in Union prisons, with about 10% dying while there. Under the authority of Colonel William Hoffman, Union officials greatly expanded prisons beginning in 1863. Camp Douglas in Chicago began housing Confederates captured at Fort Donelson in early 1862 and from there the inmate population rose to several thousand. Constructed in a swampy area, the camp harbored many diseases due to poor sanitation and drainage, and the barracks were shabby. Colonels James Mulligan and Joseph Tucker failed to manage the prison well, and large numbers of soldiers died while many others escaped. Later officers managed the prison more effectively. Like Camp Douglas, Camp Morton in Indiana began as an unhealthy facility with poor sanitation but became more elaborate over the course of the war. Officials converted buildings on the Indiana State Fairgrounds to prison barracks, but for much of the war Camp Morton was infamous for unhealthy conditions. Perhaps the most notorious Union prison was Elmira Prison in New York state, which Confederates called "Hellmira." Opened in July 1864, the prison would hold more than 10,000 men. Limited food led to hundreds of cases of scurvy and even starvation. Nearly a quarter of the prisoners housed at Elmira died.

As bad as conditions were at Union military prisons, scholars believe that the Confederate prisons holding captured Union soldiers were worse, if only because the lack of resources and transportation breakdowns in the southern states meant that prisoners were housed in poorly constructed facilities with limited access to food, water, clothing, and medical care. The most notorious Confederate military prison was Andersonville in rural southwestern Georgia. Open from February 1864 until May 1865, the prison was designed to hold about 10,000 prisoners but at one time kept three times that many men. In total more than 45,000 soldiers were held at Andersonville, and about 13,000 of them died there, by far more than any other prison on either side. One of the reasons Andersonville was so deadly was its construction: the prison was little more than a stockade hastily built by slaves with pine logs for fencing. Soldiers slept, ate, and went to the bathroom in the open, creating a stench that made prisoners, guards, and citizens in the surrounding area sick. Using scavenged pieces of wood and cloth, prisoners built small shelters, called "shebangs," that offered limited protection from the elements. Soldiers suffered from scurvy and general malnutrition, and deadly fights often broke out among the prisoners. Soldiers especially blamed Captain Henry Wirz, responsible for life inside the camp, for the prison's conditions. The hated Wirz was tried for the inhumane conduct of the prison and in November 1865 was hung for his crimes.

Equally horrific was the treatment of Union prisoners at Libby Prison in Richmond. Located in the tobacco warehousing area of the city, Libby became synonymous with cruel treatment of captured soldiers. As at Andersonville, overcrowding and poor sanitation led to high death rates at Libby Prison. As one Union doctor reported on the prisoners' conditions:

Meat is no longer furnished to any class of our prisoners except to the few officers in Libby hospital, and all sick or well officers or privates are now furnished with a very poor article of corn bread in place of wheat bread, unsuitable diet for hospital patients prostrated with diarrhea, dysentery and fever, to say nothing of the

balance of startling instances of individual suffering and horrid pictures of death from protracted sickness and semi-starvation we have had thrust upon our observation. The first demand of the poor creatures from the island was always for something to eat. Self-respect gone, hope and ambition gone, half clad and covered with vermin and filth, many of them are too often beyond all reach of medical skill. In one instance the ambulances brought sixteen to the hospital, and during the night seven of them died. Again, eighteen were brought, and eleven of them died in twenty-four hours. At another time fourteen were admitted, and in a single day ten of them died. Judging from what we have ourselves seen and do know, we do not hesitate to say that, under a treatment of systematic abuse, neglect and semi-starvation, the numbers who are becoming permanently broken down in their constitutions must be reckoned by thousands.

Life in the camps, while usually miserable and often deadly, was not always so grim. Soldiers imprisoned at a camp in Salisbury, North Carolina played baseball to pass the time. Other soldiers found time to write letters to let loved ones know of their condition. Yet, such leisure was an aberration and in the years after the war the prison camps became grounds for recriminations on both sides. Throughout the Reconstruction years immediately after the war and throughout the rest of the nineteenth century, veterans on both sides claimed that the conditions of the prisons were brutal and inhumane.

Even for soldiers who escaped death and disease, the war meant personal discomfort, a longing for home, and unprecedented trials. The physical strain for many was unbearable. Confederate soldier Eugene Blackford sent a letter back home that expressed the miserable conditions he faced:

While we were looking over the field, an order came for us to go back to our batteries ten miles off, and defend them from the enemy who were advancing upon them, so we had to go back, tired as we were, to our holes, where we arrived half dead at twelve o'clock last night, having marched twenty-six miles heavily loaded. We have no protection against the rain, which has been falling all day. I have no blanket, not having seen my

baggage since leaving Fairfax; I never was so dirty before in my life and besides I have scurvy in my mouth, not having anything but hard bread and intensely salty meat to eat, and not enough of that.[4]

Many soldiers and officers on both sides of the war were not prepared for the physical toil of marching, camping, and fighting. Other soldiers, farmers or laborers back home, were more accustomed to physical labor. Regardless of their backgrounds, though, all soldiers experienced the burdens of miserable living conditions and separation from loved ones.

As word spread of the soldiers' sufferings, and as casualties mounted, many northerners began to question the reasons for fighting. Some resented the fact that wealthier citizens could escape combat; others were angry that Lincoln had made emancipation a war measure. Still others, including many New Yorkers, grew weary of the financial and personal costs of the fighting. The resentment rose to the surface in July 1863 just after the Battle of Gettysburg in a series of unprecedented anti-war riots in New York City.

New York Draft Riots and Class Conflict

Despite the successes at Gettysburg, Lincoln and his allies could not revel in battlefield victory for long. In mid-July 1863, anti-war and anti-draft riots quickly turned into malicious and murderous attacks on the city's African Americans. The New York City Draft Riots—July 13 through July 16, 1863—not only wounded Union morale, but also cast doubt on abolitionist claims that blacks and whites could coexist peacefully in the same communities. New York in particular harbored copperhead sentiments; extensive trading ties between the city and southern merchants led many of the city's businessmen and politicians to side with white southerners and defend slavery. They called pro-Union meetings intended to persuade southerners that New York businessmen meant the South no harm, and denounced fellow New Yorkers such as William H. Seward. It is no surprise then that, as historian Jennifer Weber has argued, the city was a hotbed of copperhead activism. In 1862, copperhead New York Governor Horatio Seymour, a harsh critic of Lincoln, won an election by scorning the war. A vigorous undercurrent of copperhead activism ran through the state's politics.

Strong copperhead sentiments boiled over in early 1863 when Lincoln signed into law the Enrollment Act. Especially damned in the eyes of New York's working class was the law permitting wealthy northerners to send a substitute if drafted, or pay a fee to avoid service. This angered many laborers, especially recent Irish immigrants who resented fighting in a war that, thanks to the Emancipation Proclamation, was now being fought to liberate at least some slaves. On July 13, 1863, as draft numbers were being drawn, an angry mob gathered and soon numbered in the hundreds. The mob soon directed their frustration at city police and political officials; the mayor's house and numerous police stations were looted and burned. Unprepared for the attacks, city authorities stood nearly helpless as the crowd turned on African Americans. The Fifth Avenue Colored Orphanage was destroyed, and blacks caught on city streets were beaten. A precarious order was restored on July 16, but not before more than a hundred whites and blacks laid dead, with many hundreds more injured.

Although riots erupted in other cities, including Buffalo, the New York riots were more violent and disruptive than any other wartime protests. Class conflict, in which the lower or working classes strongly protest their economic plight by denouncing the rich and powerful, has appeared sporadically throughout American history, and it is not surprising that the pressures of war would bring such resentments to the surface. Cries of a "rich man's war, but a poor man's fight" emerged especially during the draft riots. While class conflict certainly motivated many during the draft riots, scholars have also highlighted the anti-black rage of the Irish mobs during the draft riots, denouncing the rage as racist and hate-filled. As historian Iver Bernstein points out in his study of the riots, the disturbances were not just about racism among New York's Irish working class, although racism certainly played an important role in the brutal and cruel attacks on the black orphanage and on innocent African American victims of the violence. According to Bernstein, the "unprecedented scope, audacity, and violence of the insurrection" revealed the long-simmering ethnic tensions within New York City, as well as northern frustration with the demands of a long war.[5]

The end of the New York City draft riots did not diminish northern criticism of Lincoln and his prosecution of the war. Emboldened by their success in the fall 1862 congressional elections, northern Democrats continued to challenge the president. The issuance of the Emancipation Proclamation added new grounds for criticizing Lincoln, and the president chafed against claims that he had shifted the focus of the cause by announcing the proclamation. In a letter shortly after the draft riots, Lincoln wrote to James C. Conkling of Illinois, who had argued that the proclamation was unconstitutional. Lincoln responded in a letter he expected would be made public:

You say you will not fight to free negroes. Some of them seem willing to fight for you; but, no matter. Fight you, then, exclusively to save the Union . . . I thought that whatever negroes can be got to do as soldiers, leaves just so much less for white soldiers to do, in saving the Union . . . [N]egroes, like other people, act upon motives. Why should they do any thing for us, if we will do nothing for them?

Such resolve led Democrats to claim that Lincoln had established a dictatorship in which the Constitution and especially the Bill of Rights were being sacrificed for wartime exigencies. Under attack from political opponents, Lincoln took heart from battlefield successes in the West, particularly the capture of key points on the Mississippi River.

The Western Theater in Early 1863

Both northern and southern political leaders recognized the importance of the western battlefields, especially the Union attempts to take control of the Mississippi River. But Confederate leaders criticized Jefferson Davis for paying insufficient attention and devoting too few resources to defense of the southwestern states. Like Lincoln, Davis faced a constant barrage of criticism for his conduct of the war, and both presidents had to keep one eye on internal political maneuvering even as they oversaw military strategy. In part to counter these attacks, Davis embarked on a tour of the southwestern states at the very end of 1862. His travels brought him to Tennessee, Alabama, and Mississippi as Davis tried to show southwestern Confederates that they were vital to the war effort even though the Confederate capital lay far to the north and east in Richmond.

Davis's southwestern tour ended in early January 1863, but the battlefield clashes were beginning to heat up in the first months of that year. The Tennessee and Cumberland rivers were now under Union control, and New Orleans had fallen to the Yankees in

June 1862. Most importantly, thanks in large part to General Grant, the northern army controlled most of the Mississippi River. Grant and his 40,000-strong army landed at Bruinsburg, Mississippi near the end of April 1863 and then attacked the towns of Port Gibson and Raymond to the south and east of the key stronghold of Vicksburg. On May 14, Grant continued to move southward to control the great waterway by capturing Jackson, Mississippi. Now only Vicksburg stood between Grant and Union domination of the river.

Situated on a high bluff above the Mississippi River and bordered by strong defenses and nearly impenetrable terrain, Vicksburg would prove difficult to capture. Some 30,000 Confederates in the Army of Mississippi under John C. Pemberton's command added to Vicksburg's existing natural defenses, but Vicksburg eventually fell to the patient and determined Grant. The Union forces attacked the city beginning on May 19 but suffered substantial casualties. On May 25 Grant placed the city under a siege that would last for the next several weeks. Grant's now 70,000-strong army prevented supplies from reaching the town and Vicksburg's inhabitants suffered greatly from lack of food. Supporting the siege were navy ships under David Porter's command shelling the city from the river. As Grant later wrote, "I now determined upon a regular siege—to 'out-camp the enemy,' as it were, and to incur no more losses." Confederate soldiers and civilians caught in the siege were afflicted with scurvy (a deadly disease caused by a lack of Vitamin C), dysentery, and starvation. Pemberton finally surrendered the city on July 4, along with thousands of rifles and cannons. When Port Hudson, Louisiana fell on July 9, 1863, the Union had attained a vital and early goal: complete control over the Mississippi River.

July 1863 was a crucial month for the Union. The two victories at Gettysburg and Vicksburg helped turn the war in the North's favor, although fighting during the summer of 1864 would be another severe trial for Lincoln and the Union. The Union victory at Helena, Arkansas on July 4 opened the door for the capture of Little Rock. By September three southern capitals lay in federal hands: Nashville, Baton Rouge, and Little Rock. The Union had reclaimed West Virginia and Charleston, South Carolina was under siege. The war would endure for almost two more years, and many deadly battles remained to be fought. But after July 1863, Lee would never again penetrate into Union territory and the Confederacy would never regain control over the Mississippi River. These successes would be followed near the end of the year, when Union forces would badly damage Braxton Bragg's Army of Tennessee at Chattanooga. But as we will see in the next chapter, the Union experienced key reversals as well, and both sides would suffer greatly from internal dissension and division.

Please visit the companion website www.routledge.com/cw/wells for additional study aids including chapter overviews, interactive quizzes, and more.

Discussion Questions

- Discuss the state of the war by June 1863. What reasons did Confederates have to expect victory? What advantages still lay with the Union?
- How could Democrats during the war oppose the Lincoln Administration without appearing disloyal to the Union war effort?
- What role did class conflict play during the war? Did lower-class whites in the Union and the Confederacy have reason to be angry? Why or why not?
- Discuss the role of African Americans in the war. How important were black soldiers and sailors to Union victory?
- What mistakes did Union and Confederate leaders make on the battlefields in 1863?
- Why do historians consider the Battle of Gettysburg to be an important turning point in the Civil War? Do you agree or disagree with the importance assigned to this particular battle?
- Why did some African Americans fight for the Confederacy?
- Americans often avoid the subject of class and class conflict, but the draft riots demonstrate that the war was controversial among segments of the population. What does "class" mean? Why do many historians believe class is an important subject to consider?
- Visit two websites that address the issue of Civil War prisoner-of-war camps. Do you detect any bias in the history presented on these sites?
- Andersonville during and immediately after the war was known for its awful conditions. What is the site used for today?

Notes

1 Anne J. Bailey, *Invisible Southerners: Ethnicity in the Civil War* (Athens: University of Georgia Press, 2006), 1.

2 William G. Le Duc, *This Business of War: Recollections of a Civil War Quartermaster* (St. Paul: Minnesota Historical Society Press, 1963), 78.

3 George C. Rable, *God's Almost Chosen Peoples: A Religious History of the American Civil War* (Chapel Hill: University of North Carolina Press, 2010), 105.

4 Eugene Blackford letter to his father, July 22, 1861, quoted in Annette Tapert, *The Brother's War: Civil War Letters to their Loved Ones from the Blue and Gray* (New York: Times Books, 1988), 11.

5 Iver Bernstein, *The New York City Draft Riots: Their Significance for American Society and Politics in the Age of the Civil War* (New York: Oxford University Press, 1990), 6.

Further Reading

Stephen V. Ash, *Firebrand of Liberty: The Story of Two Black Regiments that Changed the Course of the Civil War* (New York: W.W. Norton & Co., 2008).

Anne J. Bailey, *Invisible Southerners: Ethnicity in the Civil War* (Athens: University of Georgia Press, 2006).

Michael B. Ballard, *Vicksburg: The Campaign that Opened the Mississippi* (Chapel Hill: University of North Carolina Press, 2003).

Ira Berlin, *Freedom's Soldiers: The Black Military Experience in the Civil War* (Cambridge, UK: Cambridge University Press, 1998).

Iver Bernstein, *The New York City Draft Riots: Their Significance for American Society and Politics in the Age of the Civil War* (New York: Oxford University Press, 1990).

Susannah Ural Bruce, *The Harp and the Eagle: Irish–American Volunteers and the Union Army, 1861–1865* (New York: New York University Press, 2006).

William L. Burton, *Melting Pot Soldiers: The Union's Ethnic Regiments* (Ames: Iowa State University Press, 1988).

Dudley Taylor Cornish, *The Sable Arm: Black Troops in the Union Army, 1861–1865* (Lexington: University of Kentucky Press, 1987).

Larry J. Daniel, *Shiloh: The Battle That Changed the Civil War* (New York: Simon & Schuster, 1997).

Robert Scott Davis, *Ghosts and Shadows of Andersonville: Essays on the Secret Social Histories of America's Deadliest Prison* (Macon: Mercer University Press, 2006).

Russell Duncan, *Where Death and Glory Meet: Colonel Robert Gould Shaw and the 54th Massachusetts Infantry* (Athens: University of Georgia Press, 1999).

Lorien Foote, *The Gentlemen and the Roughs: Violence, Honor, and Manhood in the Union Army* (New York: New York University Press, 2010).

Douglas Southall Freeman, *Lee* (New York: Scribner, 1997).
Gary W. Gallagher, *The Fredericksburg Campaign: Decision on the Rappahannock* (Chapel Hill: University of North Carolina Press, 1995).
Gary W. Gallagher, *A Savage Conflict: The Decisive Role of Guerrillas in the American Civil War* (Cambridge, MA: Harvard University Press, 2011).
James M. Gillispie, *Andersonvilles of the North: The Myths and Realities of Northern Treatment of Civil War Confederate Prisoners* (Denton: University of North Texas Press, 2008).
David T. Gleeson, *The Irish in the South, 1815–1877* (Chapel Hill: University of North Carolina Press, 2001).
Allen C. Guelzo, *Gettysburg: The Last Invasion* (New York: Knopf, 2013).
Earl J. Hess, *The Rifle Musket in Civil War Combat: Reality and Myth* (Lawrence: University Press of Kansas, 2008).
Michael Horigan, *Elmira: Death Camp of the North* (Mechanicsburg: Stackpole Books, 2002).
Claire Hoy, *Canadians in the Civil War* (Toronto: McArthur & Company, 2004).
Bertram Wallace Korn, *American Jewry and the Civil War* (Philadelphia: Jewish Publication Society of America, 1951).
Greg Marquis, *In Armageddon's Shadow: The Civil War and Canada's Maritime Provinces* (Montreal: McGill-Queen's University Press, 1998).
William Marvel, *Andersonville: The Last Depot* (Chapel Hill: University of North Carolina Press, 2004).
James M. McPherson, *Hallowed Ground: A Walk at Gettysburg* (New York: Crown, 2003).
James M. McPherson, *The Negro's Civil War: How American Blacks Felt and Acted during the War for the Union* (Urbana: University of Illinois Press, 1982).
Edward A. Miller, Jr., *Gullah Statesman: Robert Smalls from Slavery to Congress, 1839–1915* (Columbia: University of South Carolina Press, 1995).
Francis Augustin O'Reilly, *The Fredericksburg Campaign: Winter War on the Rappahannock* (Baton Rouge: Louisiana State University Press, 2002).
George C. Rable, *Civil Wars: Women and the Crisis of Southern Nationalism* (Urbana: University of Illinois Press, 1989).
George C. Rable, *Fredericksburg! Fredericksburg!* (Chapel Hill: University of North Carolina Press, 2001).
George C. Rable, *God's Almost Chosen Peoples: A Religious History of the American Civil War* (Chapel Hill: University of North Carolina Press, 2010).
Jonathan D. Sarna and Adam Mendelsohn, eds., *Jews and the Civil War: A Reader* (New York: New York University Press, 2010).

Mark S. Schantz, *Awaiting the Heavenly Country: The Civil War and America's Culture of Death* (Ithaca: Cornell University Press, 2008).

Barnet Schecter, *The Devil's Own Work: The Civil War Draft Riots and the Fight to Reconstruct America* (New York: Walker & Company, 2005).

Stephen W. Sears, *Chancellorsville* (New York: Houghton Mifflin, 1996).

Stephen W. Sears, *Gettysburg* (New York: Mariner, 2003).

Lonnie R. Speer, *Portals to Hell: Military Prisons of the Civil War* (Mechanicsburg: Stackpole Books, 1997).

Daniel E. Sutherland, *A Savage Conflict: The Decisive Role of Guerrillas in the American Civil War* (Chapel Hill: UNC Press, 2009).

Noah Andre Trudeau, *Like Men of War: Black Troops in the Civil War, 1862–1865* (Boston, MA: Little Brown & Co., 1998).

Gregory J.W. Urwin, ed., *Black Flag Over Dixie: Racial Atrocities and Reprisals in the Civil War* (Carbondale: Southern Illinois University Press, 2004).

Andrew Ward, *The Slaves' War: The Civil War in the Words of Former Slaves* (New York: Houghton Mifflin, 2008).

Jeffrey D. Wert, *General James Longstreet: The Confederacy's Most Controversial Soldier: A Biography* (New York: Simon & Schuster, 1993).

Dennis K. Wilson, *Justice under Pressure: The St. Albans Raid and its Aftermath* (Lanham: University Press of America, 1992).

WAR ON THE HOME FRONT

Topics Covered in this Chapter:

- Newspapers and Journalism During the War
- Art and Music During the War
- Internal Divisions Within the Confederacy
- Business and War in the North and South

8

Introduction

As newspapers spread word of the fighting at Gettysburg in the summer of 1863, northerners and southerners anxiously awaited the outcome. After the Confederate defeat, Lee offered to resign his command of the Army of Northern Virginia. President Jefferson Davis rejected the offer and Lee's army began to regain strength during the late summer, reiterating in the minds of many northerners the missed opportunity to crush Lee's weakened army after Gettysburg. Events quieted down momentarily in the East, but fighting in Tennessee, Arkansas, Missouri, the Indian Territory, South Carolina, and Kansas continued unabated.

By the fall of 1863 war was deeply woven into American culture, and music, art, and literature reflected the trauma of death and destruction. Although the Union victory at Gettysburg would prove significant over time, few recognized the importance of the battle and there seemed to be little evidence that either side was ready even to consider giving up. Confederates hoped that with each passing month northern citizens were growing war-weary and would soon conclude that continued fighting was too costly. The draft riots in July 1863 had given credence to such hopes, but the Emancipation Proclamation and success at Gettysburg boosted northern morale even as Lincoln's Democratic critics remained steadfast in their attacks on the president. At the same time, President Davis and the Confederate government knew that the longer the war lasted the more southern disadvantages in men and resources were laid bare. Davis, too, was attacked by political enemies within the Confederacy, and historians argue that internal fractures significantly hindered the South's ability to win the war.

Newspapers and Journalism During the War

Although colonial towns and villages had published newspapers and magazines as early as the 1600s, periodicals changed dramatically over the course of the mid-nineteenth century, and by the Civil War journalism had emerged as a well-established profession. Known for their political partisanship, the papers of the early 1800s were often edited by politicians rather than by writers or intellectuals. Joseph Dennie's *Port Folio* was an important pro-Federalist magazine in the early 1800s, and Duff Green edited the *United States Telegraph* in the 1820s and 1830s as a mouthpiece for Andrew Jackson and his Democratic Party friends. Throughout the antebellum era, American towns often published two newspapers, each supporting the main rival political parties. Even avowedly non-partisan periodicals such as Hezekiah Niles's *Weekly Register*, which was published in Baltimore between 1811 and 1836, often staked out bold and strident positions on issues from the Bank of the United States to pistol dueling. Still, for all their advocating for political parties and causes, antebellum newspapers, editors, and journalists began to make significant strides toward establishing professional standards in journalism. Press clubs were formed by the Civil War, and journalists began calling themselves "reporters," reflecting the newly emerging notion that articles should be presented in an objective fashion.

Much as modern newspapers do today, periodicals published during the war also offered political commentary even as they reported on battlefield events. In the North, newspapers such as Horace Greeley's *New York Tribune* strongly supported the Republican Party's prosecution of the war and pressured Union commanders to take a tough line against the Confederacy. James Gordon Bennett, Sr.'s *New York Herald* was more critical of the Republican Party and often supported Democratic policies. Both papers had broad popular appeal, with Bennett's paper boasting nearly 80,000 subscribers in the 1860s. Part of the growth in northern periodicals came from advances in printing technology; steam-powered presses facilitated the publishing of cheap periodicals, while improvements in the postal system vastly expanded the readership of monthly and quarterly magazines. *Harper's Monthly Magazine*, *Atlantic Monthly*, and *Godey's* were shipped to subscribers throughout the nation, including the South. Except for the four war years, when fighting disrupted the shipment of northern periodicals to the South, southerners avidly read magazines and newspapers published in New York, Boston, and Philadelphia. Editors improved the attractiveness of their periodicals by including engravings of famous statesmen and authors as well as scenes of faraway lands.

The *Atlantic Monthly* began publication in Boston just before the war, and the magazine published eyewitness accounts of battles mingled among its various poems and short stories. In 1862 it offered readers the first printing of Julia Ward Howe's "Battle Hymn of the Republic," and the magazine attracted subscribers by publishing work by Harriet Beecher Stowe, Ralph Waldo Emerson, and other popular northern writers. The magazine offered news of the war as well. In 1861 writer and soldier Theodore Winthrop offered an account of his New York Seventh Regiment as it left the city for battle:

> **It was worth a life, that march. Only one who passed, as we did, through that tempest of cheers, two miles long, can know the terrible enthusiasm of the occasion. I could hardly hear the rattle of our own gun-carriages, and only once or twice the music of our band came to me muffled and quelled by the uproar. We knew now, if we had not before divined it, that our great city was with us as one man, utterly united in the great cause we were marching to sustain. This grand fact I learned by two senses. If hundreds of thousands roared it into my ears, thousands slapped it into my back. My fellow-citizens smote me on the knapsack, as I went by at the gun-rope, and encouraged me each in his own dialect. Bully for you! alternated with benedictions, in the proportion of two bullies to one blessing.**

In reading such vivid accounts, men and women at home could experience the war vicariously.

The *Atlantic Monthly* was just one of dozens of magazines to which northerners could subscribe, but perhaps the most important were *Harper's Monthly Magazine* and *Harper's Weekly*. Published by the famous New York firm Harper and Brothers, the magazines were among the most popular periodicals in the country. Before the war disrupted the postal service, thousands of southerners actively subscribed to northern magazines. During the war *Harper's Weekly* became a vital news source for readers, with the rich and detailed illustrations helping to bring battles and generals to life, while *Harper's Monthly* published prose and poetry by the most respected and popular authors.

African American newspapers such as *The Christian Recorder* and *Frederick Douglass's Paper* were published during the war, helping to keep the cause of emancipation alive in the press. *The Recorder*, published in association with the African Methodist Episcopal Church, remained dedicated to promoting abolition even while it published religious and other news. Like the periodicals published for white audiences, the black press did not pretend to be non-partisan or objective.

Despite substantial obstacles, including frequent paper scarcity, southerners also published newspapers and magazines in the midst of the Civil War. Throughout the 1860s nearly 200 quarterly, monthly, and weekly journals were begun in the South. One problem for Confederate publishers was the diminishing supply of paper. By 1865, as one scholar has found, at least thirteen periodicals were printed on discarded wallpaper.[1] For editors, attracting high-quality contributions and capable printers proved as troublesome as obtaining usable paper. As one Virginia publisher complained during the war as he closed down his paper,

> **the proprietor has been reluctantly compelled to this decision in consequence of the lack of paper, ink, editors and printers . . . He furthermore begs to state that in consequence of the editor, the compositors and the printers having gone off to war, the devil only is left in the office.[2]**

Considering the obstacles before them, from the scarcity of paper to the absence of contributors, Confederate newspapers and magazines were surprisingly resilient. Many journals reported on the events of the war, defended slavery and states' rights in support of the Confederate cause, or published poems—particularly by women—to celebrate fallen soldiers and to trumpet the glory of the fight against Yankee tyranny. The *Southern Monthly*, published in Memphis in 1861 and 1862, lasted only a few issues but provided a forum for wartime literature. As they had before the war, magazines such as the *Southern Monthly* advocated a distinctly southern literature that was free from the taint of northern sentiments. Although not directed specifically at a female audience, journals such as the *Southern Monthly* eagerly published works

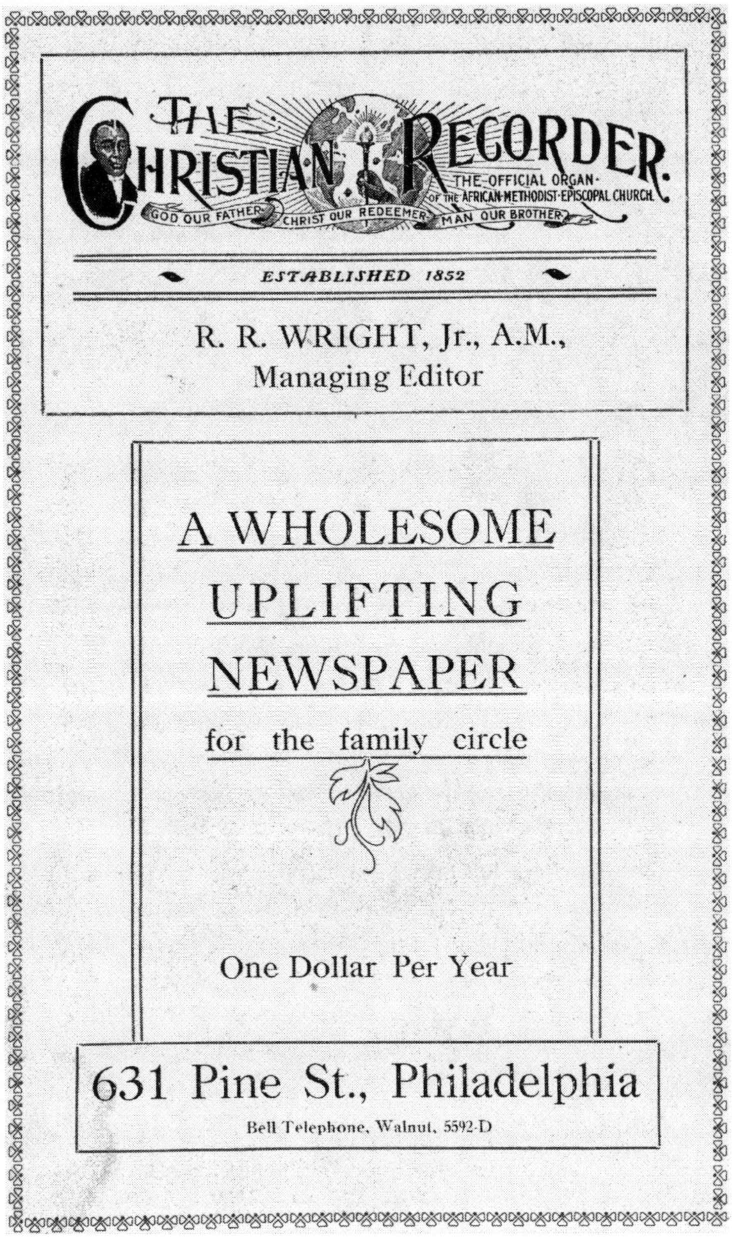

FIGURE 8.1 *Cover of* The Christian Recorder. *The Philadelphia colored directory, 1910: a handbook of the religious, social, political, professional, business and other activities of the Negroes of Philadelphia. Courtesy of the New York Public Library, b15335517*

by southern women. Similarly, *Southern Punch*, a Richmond weekly published between 1863 and 1865, reminded readers of the need for humor in the midst of war. The *Southern Illustrated News*, the *Magnolia*, and the *Illustrated Mercury* were other magazines that filled an important need for readers and authors on the home front. The first of these, the *Southern Illustrated News*, published in Richmond from 1862 to 1865, was a particularly important periodical for southerners.

While the *Southern Illustrated News* often published news from the battlefields, *The Southern Field and Fireside* bravely tried to maintain the traditional magazine content of short fiction, poetry, and serialized novels by leading women writers such as Sue Petigru Bowen, Mary Edwards Bryan, Annie R. Blount, Eliza Cook, Mary Bayard Clarke, Laura Lincoln, and Julia Pleasants Creswell. Important southern male writers, including Paul Hamilton Hayne and John R. Thompson, contributed to the weekly paper as well. While the magazine was generally focused on literature, child-rearing, agriculture, and domestic life, it occasionally offered views on the military and the political course of the war.

Similarly, *The Magnolia*, published in the Confederate capital from 1862 to 1865, targeted a female readership. The title page of the weekly journal featured a picture of a female writer busy at her desk. While avoiding politics, the paper published reports of the latest battles as well as news of Confederate government activities. Mixed in with such reports were short stories, serialized novels, poems, and letters to the editor, Charles Baillie. By 1863, the paper's title page featured a picture of "a more warlike woman with a helmet surrounded by globe, easel, writings, and books." A new feature was added, entitled "Notes on the War," bringing women subscribers updated information on the progress of Confederate forces. The magazine ceased publication in April 1865, shortly before Lee surrendered to Grant, enduring until the lack of supplies rendered continuation of the paper impossible. Despite its eventual demise, the paper demonstrated the determination of northern and southern journalists and editors to contribute to the war effort.

Perhaps most significantly, newspapers and magazines helped to stir patriotic feelings and a sense of duty among their readers. Religious magazines such as *The Southern Presbyterian Review* and *The Catholic Mirror* supplemented religious articles with news of the battlefield and military strategy. Articles on battlefield successes raised the hopes of readers on the home front, and tales of soldiers' bravery heartened families back home. Confederate and Union periodicals also related stories about women's wartime efforts, from forming sewing clubs to nursing soldiers back to health. Newspapers and magazines eagerly published patriotic poems by northern and southern women. In the South, as historian Elizabeth Varon has demonstrated, periodicals helped shape notions of Confederate womanhood, in which women could contribute to the southern cause while remaining true to appropriate female spheres. Readers of newspapers and magazines clung to stories of women's self-sacrifice in sending their husbands and sons into battle.

Art and Music During the War

Periodicals on both sides of the war featured political cartoons, an art form that had become popular well before the Civil War. Antebellum political rivals had lampooned each other with cartoons in newspapers, including the famous depictions of Lincoln during the 1860 presidential campaign as an ape with large ears and long arms, a caricature that continued in southern papers during the war. One of the most important Civil War cartoonists, German-born Thomas Nast, was famous for caricatures, such as his 1862 "Peace," which lampooned northerners who wanted to make peace with the Confederacy, as well as for his important battlefield renderings. Nast's cartoons appeared in *Harper's Weekly* during and after the war, and he earned a wide audience for his work in the late 1800s, when he first began drawing symbols to represent the political parties: the elephant for the Republican Party and the donkey for the Democrats.

FIGURE 8.2 *"The halt"—a scene in the Georgia campaign. Painting by Thomas Nast. Library of Congress, Prints and Photographs Division, LC-USZ62-98261*

"THE HALT"—A SCENE IN THE GEORGIA CAMPAIGN.

Literate Americans were exposed to art mostly through illustrations that appeared in popular magazines such as *Harper's Weekly* or *Godey's*. Wood-cut illustrations of famous politicians, far-off lands, or the latest fashions became fixtures of American newspapers and magazines during the antebellum period, and wartime publications such as the *Southern Illustrated News* and *Harper's Weekly* continued the tradition of including steel-engraved or wood-cut illustrations alongside stories and poems. Although poorly paid, illustrators were sent along with marches and onto the battlefields to record camp and battle scenes. Since they worked for private newspapers and received no official government imprimatur, the illustrators were sometimes barely tolerated by generals and soldiers. Bostonian Winslow Homer was one of the most important artists who helped sketch camp life and battles for northern periodicals, but he also created elaborate paintings that captured the experience of war. Engravings such as *The War for the Union* (1862) and paintings such as *Sharpshooter on Picket Duty* (1862) and *Prisoners from the Front* (1866) earned Homer fame and respect. Due to the work of these talented artists, Americans at home could visualize the toils of their husbands and fathers on the battlefronts.

While wood-cut and steel-engraved illustrations brought the war to life, photography changed the way Americans experienced war. By the late 1830s, the daguerreotype, an early form of photography that used a complex chemical process to record a black and white image on a mirror-like surface, initiated the art form. Many antebellum politicians, including Henry Clay, Daniel Webster, and Abraham Lincoln, had their pictures taken in this way. During the Civil War, New Yorker Mathew Brady and his associates, especially Alexander Gardner, George Barnard, and Timothy O'Sullivan, refined the art of photography. They amended the cumbersome daguerreotype process using the albumen print, liberating photographers from their studios to capture images of battlefields. Brady and his associates recorded some of our most memorable pictures of dead soldiers on the field, and brought for the first time realistic images of the costs of war back home to Americans. Brady and his photographers began taking pictures as early as the First Battle of Bull Run. Often bodies were moved and staged for effect, and photographers like Brady knew that staged pictures would garner more attention and more money. Brady opened a remarkable exhibition in New York in October 1862 entitled "The Dead of Antietam," the first time ordinary

THE ARMY OF THE POTOMAC—A SHARP-SHOOTER ON PICKET DUTY.—[FROM A PAINTING BY W. HOMER, ESQ.]

FIGURE 8.3 *The army of the Potomac: a sharp-shooter on picket duty. Courtesy of the New York Public Library, 1231531*

noncombatants witnessed such gruesome wartime deaths. To this day, Brady's battlefield photographs remain one of the most valuable records of the Civil War experience.

The Confederacy did not have the benefit of traveling photographers and studios, so there are few known pictures of the battlefield taken by southerners. However, every major town and city could boast of studios, so soldiers often had their portraits taken before leaving home. Many ambrotypes and tintypes, kinds of photographs popular in the 1860s, exist and they can tell us much about soldiers' uniforms and accessories. Wartime photos of Jefferson Davis and many Confederate generals were reprinted throughout the South.

Music was integral to the American Civil War experience, both at home and on the battlefield. On the home front popular songs, especially marches, waltzes, and polkas, helped to stir patriotic fervor on both sides. Songs glorified generals, regiments, and battles, and helped to bring newspaper stories of bravery and courage to life. Widely printed sheet music, with covers elaborately decorated, allowed women as well as men to share in the battle experience. Pieces for the piano, such as "General Bragg's Grand March," meant that young women could participate in the formation of a Confederate identity. Parades in northern and southern towns were often led by large bands playing songs such as "Battle Hymn of the Republic" or "The Southrons' Chaunt of Defiance."

On the battlefield and in the military camps music was similarly ever present. As southern poet John Esten Cooke wrote in his poem "The Band in the Pines," music could be evocative and even painful:

Oh, band in the pine-wood, cease!
Cease with your splendid call;
The living are brave and noble,
But the dead were bravest of all!
They throng to the martial summons,
To the loud triumphant strain;
And the dear, bright eyes of long dead friends
Come to the heart again.
They come with the ringing bugle,
And the deep drum's mellow roar,
Till the soul is faint with longing
For the hands we clasp no more.
Oh, band in the pine-wood, cease,
Or the heart will melt in tears
For the gallant eyes and the smiling lips
And the voices of old years.

Buglers helped keep order in the camps, rousing the troops in the morning and continuing to sound signals throughout the day when needed. Many regiments had their own bands, which often numbered a dozen or more musicians, playing a range of drums and horns, especially saxhorns—a kind of bugle. More than a hundred bands served the Confederacy and four times that many played for Union troops. On the march, soldiers were also accompanied by drummers, usually boys of thirteen or fourteen years old who were too young to fight. Many black musicians also formed bands for the Union, serving the cause of freedom without treading on northern racist fears of black troops.

Internal Divisions Within the Confederacy

Wartime photographs of Confederate leaders such as President Davis and Thomas "Stonewall" Jackson depicted resolute and determined politicians and generals, but such images belied deep divisions within the Confederate government. As historians William Freehling, Jon Wakelyn, and others have pointed out, the South during the Civil War was split along a number of geographical and ideological lines. Such divisions are not surprising given the fact that the region was never monolithic. Under the pressures of war, even though political leaders knew that internal schisms would weaken the Confederate cause, such profound divisions within the South could not be contained.

Among the most vocal politicians to question the Confederate government's prosecution of the war was Georgia's governor Joseph Emerson Brown. Born in 1821, Brown was the state's most popular politician, having won the governorship in 1857 and holding the post throughout the war. Brown's frustration with Davis and the Confederate government came from the Georgian's distrust of central authority, a problem that the Confederacy faced on a broad scale. After all, secessionists like Brown advocated leaving the Union because they resented centralized power; in the late 1850s southern fire-eaters denounced the federal government for trampling on states' rights. Since the days of the Nullification Crisis in the late 1820s and early 1830s, southern politicians railed against federal power and elevated the sovereignty of individual states. Yet the necessities of war required a centralized bureaucracy to guide the conduct of war and marshal resources and men. The Confederate government was caught in a paradox: the war began as a campaign for states' rights, but to fight the war effectively, Davis and his government needed broad federal authority. For Brown, ideological consistency demanded that he resist broad federal power. When the government instituted the controversial draft in April 1862, Brown responded angrily and for the rest of the war he was a painful thorn in Davis's side. In an 1862 letter to a fellow Georgian, Confederate Vice President Alexander Stephens, Brown complained that:

It seems military men are assuming the whole powers of government to themselves and setting at defiance constitutions, laws, state rights, state sovereignty, and every other principle of civil liberty, and that our people engrossed in the struggle with the enemy are disposed to submit to these bold usurpations tending to military despotism without murmur, much less resistance . . . I fear we have much more to apprehend from military despotism than from subjugation by the enemy.

After being reelected the following year, Brown continued to challenge Davis and his administration openly. He protested the Confederate government's attempts to impress slaves into military service and resisted Davis's periodic attempts to impose martial law in the state, all of which generated angry exchanges of letters between Brown and the administration.

Brown was hardly the only southern politician to tussle with Davis and the Confederate government. Henry S. Foote was born in Virginia, but spent much of the antebellum era crisscrossing the South, serving as senator and governor of Mississippi and finally settling in Tennessee by the outbreak of the war. He soon won election to the Confederate House of Representatives and from this position he relentlessly attacked Davis, whom he had despised since his days in antebellum Mississippi politics. Regarded as a bit of a crank by many of his Confederate colleagues, Foote continued to attack the South's prosecution of the war and even tried to defect to the North in 1864.

The hardships that white southern citizens suffered during the war generated war-weariness and criticism of the Confederate government. For example, several poor and nearly illiterate citizens in rural North Carolina sent a petition to Governor Zebulon Vance in early 1863. Complaining of their inability to buy bread and corn on which to live, the North Carolinians protested to Vance that "If this is the way we common people is to be treated in the confederacy we hope that you & your friends [will] let us try to maniage & defend our own State & if it is in your power to Remedy the present evils do it speedily." Vance had his own bone to pick with Davis and the government; like Brown, Vance repeatedly questioned the Davis administration and attacked the Confederate government for trampling on states' rights. Vance spoke out against conscription and kept the state courts open during the war, observing legal precedents that the Davis administration thought should be abandoned. Known as the "War Governor of the South," Vance earned fame for his stubborn resistance to the Confederate central government.

Vance hailed from the Blue Ridge Mountains, a region known for its suspicion of proslavery secessionists. In fact, up and down the mountain range from northeast Alabama and northwest Georgia, and through the upcountry regions of the Carolinas, Tennessee, and Virginia, many plain folk had resisted secession and questioned the legitimacy of the Confederacy. Earlier in the war, in the fall of 1861, the mountainous counties of Virginia split off and formed the new state of West Virginia. As historian William

Link notes in his book *Roots of Secession*, Appalachian Virginia had long resented its eastern neighbors, and its proximity to Ohio and Pennsylvania aligned its interests more with free states than with the large slaveholders of the Virginia tidewater. Under the leadership of Republican Francis H. Pierpont, mountain Virginians met in Wheeling and set up a rebel government that was formally embraced by the Union as a new state in early 1863.

Historians have found other significant geographical divisions within the Civil War South. Led by Upcountry Unionists such as William G. Brownlow, eastern Tennessee was known as a bastion of anti-Confederate ideology. This region had little direct involvement or interest in slavery. Robert Tracy McKenzie has found that merely 10% of eastern Tennessee yeomen owned one or more slaves. In fact, Brownlow, a prominent preacher and newspaper editor before the war, led a convention early in the war that threatened to secede from the rest of the state. Although this effort did not result in a new state, like the creation of West Virginia by Appalachian Unionists, Brownlow continued to criticize abolitionists and secessionists alike. Like many Unionist southerners, Brownlow supported slavery but rejected secession. After he was imprisoned in December 1861, Brownlow wrote a letter to Confederate Secretary of War Judah P. Benjamin:

You authorized Genl. Crittenden to give me passports [to the Union lines], and an escort to send me into the old government, and he invited me here for that purpose. But a third rate county court lawyer, acting as your Confederate attorney, took me out of his hands and cast me into this prison. I am anxious to learn which is your highest authority, the Secretary of War, a Major General, or a dirty little drunken attorney, such as J.G. Ramsey is! You are reported to have said to a gentleman in Richmond, that I am a bad man, dangerous to the Confederacy, and that you desire me out of it. Just give me my passports, and I will do for your Confederacy, more than the Devil has ever done. I will quit the country!

Brownlow finally received his passports and lived behind Union lines, but he never ceased criticizing the Confederacy and after Tennessee fell into Union hands near the close of 1864 he resumed his newspaper career in Knoxville.

While the Confederacy suffered internally from attacks by Brown, Foote, Vance, and Brownlow, it was further hampered by class divisions that had sprung up in the antebellum era and continued unabated during the war. White laborers and yeomen farmers remained as convinced as ever by 1863 that the Confederacy was motivated primarily by a desire to protect the political and economic interests of the wealthy planters. Yet even with such internal divisions, the Confederacy was united on the question of white control and the defense of slavery. While class conflict often surfaced before, during, and after the war, white racism was powerful enough throughout the middle of the nineteenth century to thwart attempts to form lasting political alliances between poor whites and African Americans. Historian Mark V. Wetherington argues in his book *Plain Folk's Fight* that yeomen farmers in rural Georgia willingly embraced the Confederate cause because they wanted to prevent an influx of freedpeople into their communities. Such racist fears would endure into the late nineteenth century, when terrorist paramilitary groups such as the KKK, often guided by poor farmers, helped unite whites regardless of their wealth or status.

There is little doubt, however, that internal rifts within the Confederacy weakened the South's war effort. As the war dragged on into 1864 and 1865, cries for peace from southerners would grow louder. Peace candidates, such as North Carolina editor William Woods Holden, would run in 1864 elections on platforms to end the war. As historian William W. Freehling argues, "anti-Confederate Southerners piled on psychological, economic, and geographic burdens that ultimately helped flatten white Confederates' resiliency."[3] This was especially true in the final years of the war, as black southerners took advantage of the collapse of Confederate authority to flee from slavery and take up arms against the South.

Business and War in the North and South

The Western Theater of the war was the site of considerable speculating, blockade running, and profiteering. Northern businessmen were eager to make money during the war, and the chaos created by battlefield disruptions provided opportunities to generate considerable profits. Up and down the Mississippi River, northern speculators able to secure passes to travel behind enemy lines went into the South to purchase cotton. Because of the Union blockade, southern farmers had difficulty selling their cotton crops, and so accepted the money offered by northern speculators. This underhanded trade vexed the Lincoln Administration. In response to a speculator's request, Lincoln wrote a letter in June 1863 that suggested just how worried he and his cabinet were over the embarrassing speculative trade in the Mississippi River Valley. He was particularly worried about the diverted attention of soldiers and officers:

Few things are so troublesome to the government as the fierceness with which the profits of trading in cotton are sought. The temptation is so great that nearly everybody wishes to be in it . . . The officers of the army, in numerous instances, are believed to connive and share the profits, and thus the army itself is diverting from fighting the rebels to speculating in cotton . . . The matter deeply affects the Treasury and War Departments, and has been discussed again and again in the cabinet.

Despite its efforts, the administration failed to stem the speculative tide. To make matters worse, Democrats charged that war contracts were riddled with political corruption. General Grant believed that Jewish Americans were behind much of this illicit trading. In December 1862, Grant issued General Orders No. 11:

The Jews, as a class violating every regulation of trade established by the Treasury Department and also department orders, are hereby expelled from the Department [of the Tennessee] within twenty-four hours from the receipt of this order.

Post commanders will see to it that all of this class of people be furnished passes and required to leave, and any one returning after such notification will be arrested and held in confinement until an opportunity occurs of sending them out as prisoners, unless furnished with permit from headquarters.

No passes will be given these people to visit headquarters for the purpose of making personal application of trade permits.

Jews across the North reacted angrily to attacks on their character, and within a few weeks Lincoln retracted the order. The cotton trade continued to leak through Union lines and the Union blockade throughout the war.

The war required the creation of a vast and powerful economic machine, and as Democrats were quick to point out, many businessmen profited from the illicit dealings. At first railroad companies transporting goods and soldiers to the lines tried to charge outrageous fees to the Union government. Laws passed in early 1862 essentially permitted the government take-over of the railroads during the war, but the government could not prevent profiteering altogether. As historian Mark Wilson has shown, the United States government spent almost two billion dollars (in 1860 terms) during the war, an amount unprecedented not only in American history to that point, but also in world history. By the end of the war, the Union economy had produced or supplied soldiers with "roughly 1 billion rounds of small arms ammunition, 1 million horses and mules, 1.5 million barrels of pork and 100 million pounds of coffee, 6 million woolen blankets, and 10 million pairs of trousers."[4] Such massive production fundamentally and permanently altered the American economy, as industries geared up for the wartime emergency.

Distribution of the supplies was a monumental undertaking, requiring extensive logistical planning and execution. The distribution was headed at the federal level by the quartermaster general in the Army Quartermaster's Department, an organization with a long history stretching back to the early 1800s. The quartermaster general was responsible for coordinating and purchasing military supplies, except for food, which was handled by the Commissary General of Subsistence. Clothing was a major responsibility that the quartermaster general tried to meet through contracts with domestic and European suppliers, but even under the competent leadership of quartermaster general Montgomery Meigs, the office often came up short. Ill-fitting and poorly made shoes in particular were a common complaint among soldiers. The generals had to contend with price-gouging by merchants and manufacturers who hoped to reap rich profits from war contracts. The quartermaster general oversaw the field quartermasters, who in turn oversaw the regimental quartermasters, in an organized and generally efficient system that significantly aided the Union cause.

One Union quartermaster, William G. Le Duc of Minnesota, managed to navigate the complicated bureaucracy of military commanders. He was a conscientious manager of funds and resources, and busily handled affairs in the field. In his diary, he recounted a typical day as quartermaster in November 1863, when he was also charged with establishing a supply depot:

I am out soon after daylight, write up what letters and dispatches have come, get breakfast, mount a horse, and am not much in my tent until night. First I go to the steamboat landing to see if they are pushing forward the stores; next to the railroad station, to see what goods have arrived . . . Next to the sawmills, to note the lumber on hand; next to the shipyard, to note progress on the steamboat, and hurry the work if possible.[5]

Le Duc was obviously responsible for many different tasks, and was respected by his superiors.

The Confederacy established a similar quartermaster system, but sent supplies throughout the region via a depot system that funneled resources to the field. Although they could boast of an abundance of cotton, wool was scarce. Confederates turned to foreign suppliers for wool, shoes, and other finished products no longer available from the North. Production and distribution weakened as the war progressed and more territory, including key depots, fell into Union hands. An inefficient rail system, including tracks with different gauges, significantly hindered Confederate attempts to transport men and supplies to the lines. Confederate quartermasters such as Abraham C. Myers tried valiantly to work around these disadvantages, while the Union Quartermaster Department could effectively exploit the Union's superior production capacity.

The Confederate states could boast of their own manufacturers, though they were smaller in number than those in the North. One of the important producers of Confederate ordnance and iron was the Tredegar Iron Works in Richmond, a manufacturer whose significance was magnified during the war. As historian Charles B. Dew found in his study of Tredegar, sales at the company increased from just over one million dollars in 1861 to more than nine million dollars in 1864.[6] Employing white and slave laborers, Tredegar was vital to the Confederacy's war effort until a fire destroyed the factory later in the war.

Despite the production at Tredegar and other southern manufacturers, the Confederacy and its citizens suffered greatly from a scarcity of resources and the disruption of trade. Before the war, the South became one of the richest regions in the world because of its valuable cotton crop and the slaves who picked it. During the 1850s, southern towns and cities invested much of this profit in internal improvements such as canals and railroads, in cultural institutions such as schools and libraries, and in new banks. The war caused some of these achievements to accelerate, and others to come to a screeching halt. The Union blockade severely hampered southern planters' ability to sell cotton, and as demands for food increased during the war, cotton production suffered. As historian Harold D. Woodman points out, however, during the war cotton production continued, though it dropped from 4.5 million bales in 1861 to just 300,000 in 1864. As a consequence, cotton prices per pound rose dramatically during the war, raising the level of temptation to make a profit. Planters who sold their crop to speculators in the North and West were harshly criticized by the southern press, but such criticism could not stem the steady flow of cotton into northern hands.

During the war, even basic necessities such as food and clothing were increasingly scarce, especially in the Confederate states. As the Union army and navy tightened their grip on internal and external trade, and as southern railroads, ports, and rivers fell into Union hands, southerners had a hard time securing salt, cloth, paper, coffee, and other basic goods. In the years before refrigeration, salt was used to preserve meat and was also used to cure leather. One of the most important southern salt-producing

FIGURE 8.4 *Tredegar Iron Works. Historic American Engineering Record (Library of Congress)*

BAKERY
NEMESIS & C
GRAND REAPING.
SOUTHERN WOMEN FEELING THE EFFECTS OF REBELLION, AND CREATING BREAD RIOTS.

FIGURE 8.5 *Richmond Bread Riot. Library of Congress, LC-USZ62-42028*

regions lay in Virginia, and by the end of 1864 that region had fallen under Union control. Floridians worked hard to boil sea water to obtain salt, perhaps that state's most significant role in the Confederacy. Salt was so vital to the Confederate war effort that Alabama's state government passed laws to encourage its production. Water from deep wells was boiled in large furnaces manned by dozens of men. At the beginning of the war, a bushel of salt might earn $2 or $3 in gold, but by the last months of the war a bushel could reach $7 or more, reflecting the inflation running rampant in the South. Coffee became especially scarce and expensive during the war. While about $3 could purchase a pound of coffee before the war, by the end of the conflict consumers had to come up with perhaps twenty times that sum in order to buy the same amount, a price out of reach of all but the most wealthy planters. As a result most southerners on the home front either went without or brewed their own concoctions, which might or might not resemble real coffee in taste and color.

Southerners on the home front did not take the suffering lying down. Consumers became frustrated and frightened when the price of even basic foods such as bread rose dramatically. In the first years of the war the cost of wheat had increased 300% while the price of items such as milk and butter rose 400%. In 1863 a series of riots broke out in Virginia, North Carolina, and Georgia. Hundreds of women in Richmond shattered shop windows to loot bread and other food as well as shoes and clothing. Some of the rioters were brought to trial and newspapers carried details of the proceedings. As the *Richmond Examiner* editorialized unsympathetically in 1863:

The reader will find in the report of evidence in the Police Court, the true account of a so-called riot in the streets of Richmond. A handful of prostitutes, professional thieves, Irish and Yankee hags, gallows-birds from all lands but our own, congregated in Richmond, with a woman huckster at their head, who buys veal at the toll gate for a hundred and sells the same for two hundred and fifty in the morning market, undertook the other day to put into private practice the principles of the Commissary Department. Swearing that they would have goods "at Government prices" they broke open half a dozen shoe stores, hat stores, and tobacco houses, and robbed them of everything but bread, which was just the thing they wanted least. Under the demagogue's delusion that they might be "poor people," "starving people," and the like, an institution of charity made a distribution of rice and flour to all who would ask for it. Considering the circumstances, it was a vile, cowardly, and pernicious act; but the manner in which it was received exhibits the character of this mob. Miscreants

were seen to dash the rice and flour into the muddy streets, where the traces still remain, with the remark that "if that was what they were going to give, they might go to h_l." It is greatly to be regretted that this most villainous affair was not punished on the spot. Instead of shooting every wretch engaged at once, the authorities contented themselves with the ordinary arrest, and hence the appearance of the matter in the police report of the morning.

Neither the newspapers nor the Confederate leadership sympathized with the rioters, accusing them of using the wartime privation as an excuse to cause trouble. Such attitudes, though, neglected the real and substantial suffering southerners—especially the poor—faced as goods became increasingly scarce and expensive.

So as 1863 came to a close and armies began setting up their winter headquarters, southerners were already beginning to feel the ill effects of the long war in the price and availability of everyday necessities. Inconvenience was one thing; the dramatic suffering and the numbers of dead after Gettysburg were nothing short of shocking. As the war dragged on into 1864, southerners on the home front would really experience privation when Union soldiers under William Tecumseh Sherman would embark on their March to the Sea.

Please visit the companion website www.routledge.com/cw/wells for additional study aids including chapter overviews, interactive quizzes, and more.

Discussion Questions

- What role did music and art play during the war? How might we compare art and music with other forms of creative expression, especially literature?
- Why weren't southern newspapers such as the *Richmond Examiner* more sympathetic to the riots in the South?
- How do you think the internal turmoil within the Confederacy affected the war effort?
- Historians often claim that the South has never been a monolithic region. How does the history of the region under the Confederacy confirm or contradict this view?

- Businessmen in the North and South felt that they had a right to profit from the war. Do you think this view is justified? Why or why not?
- Who were the leading artists and musicians during the war?
- If you wanted to study Civil War-era political campaigns, what types of sources might you seek? Where could you find these sources?

Notes

1 Ray Morris Atchison, "Southern Literary Magazines, 1865–1887" (Ph.D. dissertation, Duke University, 1956), 16.

2 Quoted in Frank Luther Mott, *American Journalism: A History of Newspapers in the United States* (New York: Macmillan Co., 1941), 363 and in Atchison, "Southern Literary Magazines," 15.

3 William W. Freehling, *The South vs. The South: How Anti-Confederate Southerners Shaped the Course of the Civil War* (New York: Oxford University Press, 2001), xiii.

4 Mark R. Wilson, *The Business of Civil War: Military Mobilization and the State, 1861–1865* (Baltimore: Johns Hopkins University Press, 2006), 1.

5 William G. Le Duc, *This Business of War: Recollections of a Civil War Quartermaster* (St. Paul: Minnesota Historical Society Press, 1963), 107.

6 Charles B. Dew, *Ironmaker to the Confederacy: Joseph R. Anderson and the Tredegar Iron Works* (New Haven, CT: Yale University Press, 1966), 271.

Further Reading

William A. Blair, *With Malice toward Some: Treason and Loyalty in the Civil War Era* (Chapel Hill: University of North Carolina Press, 2014).

Joseph Howard Brooks, *Joseph E. Brown of Georgia* (Baton Rouge: Louisiana State University Press, 1977).

Richard S. Brownlee, *Gray Ghosts of the Confederacy: Guerrilla Warfare in the West, 1861–1865* (Baton Rouge: Louisiana State University Press, 1984).

Victoria E. Bynum, *The Long Shadow of the Civil War: Southern Dissent and its Legacies* (Chapel Hill: University of North Carolina Press, 2010).

Albert Castel, *Civil War Kansas: Reaping the Whirlwind* (Lawrence: University of Kansas Press, 1997).

Peter Cozzens, *The Shipwreck of Their Hopes: The Battles for Chattanooga* (Urbana: University of Illinois Press, 1994).

Charles B. Dew, *Ironmaker to the Confederacy: Joseph R. Anderson and the Tredegar Iron Works* (New Haven: Yale University Press, 1966).

Michael Fellman, *Inside War: The Guerrilla Conflict in Missouri during the American Civil War* (New York: Oxford University Press, 1989).
William W. Freehling, *The South vs. The South: How Anti-Confederate Southerners Shaped the Course of the Civil War* (New York: Oxford University Press, 2001).
Thomas Goodrich, *Black Flag: Guerrilla Warfare on the Western Border, 1861–1865* (Bloomington: Indiana University Press, 1995).
Charles D. Grear, ed., *The Fate of Texas: The Civil War and the Lone Star State* (Fayetteville: University of Arkansas Press, 2008).
Bruce C. Kelley, *Bugle Resounding: Music and Musicians of the Civil War Era* (Columbia: University of Missouri Press, 2004).
William G. Le Duc, *This Business of War: Recollections of a Civil War Quartermaster* (St. Paul: Minnesota Historical Society Press, 1963).
J.G. Lewin, *Lines of Contention: Political Cartoons of the Civil War* (New York: Harper, 2007).
William A. Link, *Roots of Secession: Slavery and Politics in Antebellum Virginia* (Chapel Hill: University of North Carolina Press, 2003).
Robert R. Mackey, *The Uncivil War: Irregular Warfare in the Upper South, 1861–1865* (Norman: University of Oklahoma Press, 2004).
Stephanie McCurry, *Confederate Reckoning: Power and Politics in the Civil War South* (Cambridge, MA: Harvard University Press, 2010).
Robert Tracy McKenzie, *One South or Many? Plantation Belt and Upcountry in Civil War-Era Tennessee* (Cambridge: Cambridge University Press, 1994).
Gordon B. McKinney, *Zeb Vance: North Carolina's Civil War Governor and Gilded Age Political Leader* (Chapel Hill: University of North Carolina Press, 2004).
James M. McPherson, *Embattled Rebel: Jefferson Davis as Commander in Chief* (New York: Penguin Press, 2014).
Joe A. Mobley, *War Governor of the South: North Carolina's Zeb Vance in the Confederacy* (Gainesville: University Press of Florida, 2005).
Bruce Nichols, *Guerrilla Warfare in Civil War Missouri* (Jefferson: McFarland & Co. Inc., 2006).
David Sachsman et al., *Words at War: The Civil War and American Journalism* (Purdue, IN: Purdue University Press, 2008).
Yael A. Sternhell, *Routes of War: The World of Movement in the Confederate South* (Cambridge, MA: Harvard University Press, 2012).
Elizabeth Varon, *We Mean to be Counted: White Women and Politics in Antebellum Virginia* (Chapel Hill: University of North Carolina Press, 1998).
Jon L. Wakelyn, *Confederates Against the Confederacy: Essays on Leadership and Loyalty* (Westport: Praeger, 2002).
Mark V. Wetherington, *Plain Folk's Fight: The Civil War and Reconstruction in Piney Woods Georgia* (Chapel Hill: University of North Carolina Press, 2009).

Mark R. Wilson, *The Business of Civil War: Military Mobilization and the State, 1861–1865* (Baltimore: Johns Hopkins University Press, 2006).

Peter H. Wood, *Near Andersonville: Winslow Homer's Civil War* (Cambridge, MA: Harvard University Press, 2010).

Harold D. Woodman, *King Cotton and His Retainers: Financing and Marketing the Cotton Crop of the South, 1800–1925* (Lexington: University of Kentucky Press, 1068).

Steven E. Woodworth, *Six Armies in Tennessee: The Chickamauga and Chattanooga Campaigns* (Lincoln: University of Nebraska Press, 1998).

Steven E. Woodworth, *Nothing but Victory: The Army of the Tennessee, 1861–1865* (New York: Alfred A. Knopf, 2005).

THE UNION GRINDS TOWARD VICTORY

Topics Covered in this Chapter:

- Fighting in the Western Theater in Late 1863
- The Battlefield in Early 1864
- Politics and the 1864 Presidential Campaign
- Mobile Bay and the Fall of Atlanta
- Sherman's March to the Sea

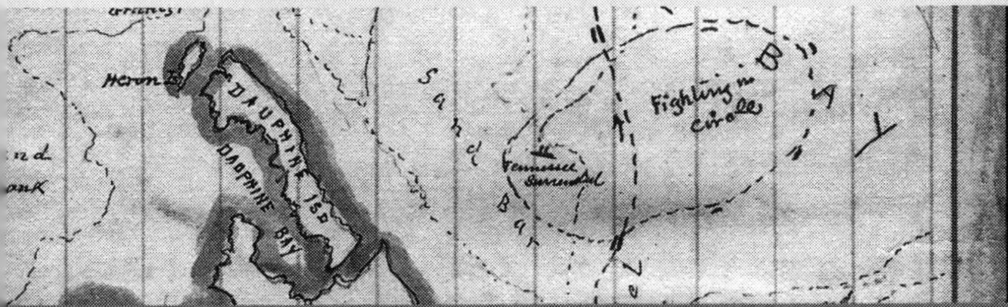

9

Introduction

Despite Union military successes in 1863, the North was far from forcing a southern surrender as 1864 began. In fact, some of the most savage and deadly fighting occurred in and around Virginia in the first half of 1864. Battles at Cold Harbor, Petersburg, and other sites offered proof to war-weary Americans that the war would continue indefinitely. Only following the fall of Atlanta and Union General William T. Sherman's devastating "March to the Sea" in the fall of 1864, Sheridan's victories in the Shenandoah Valley, and Farragut's closing of Mobile Bay did Confederate defeat appear on the horizon. After Sherman's March the war would continue into the early months of 1865, but by then the South was all but vanquished.

The stalemated battlefield situation in the first half of 1864, combined with northerners' fatigue over the long war, worried Lincoln and his administration. The president feared defeat in the November election, as resurgent Democrats nominated Union General George B. McClellan as their candidate. By late summer, the president was sure he was headed for defeat. Yet the northern electorate remained firmly behind Lincoln, and in the end he was the one claiming victory.

Fighting in the Western Theater in Late 1863

While Confederate politics were riddled with divisions, the southern military was similarly beset by personal animosity and command schisms. Some of the worst divisions within the Confederate military could be found in General Braxton Bragg's command, and the hatred and mistrust he seemed to inspire in his subordinates played a role in two important battles in the West in the latter months of 1863: the Battle of Chickamauga in Georgia in September, and the Battle of Chattanooga in Tennessee in late November.

Born in North Carolina, Bragg served in the Mexican–American War and fought at the Battle of Buena Vista, but his command style earned him many enemies even among his own soldiers and officers. The rank and file sometimes blamed Bragg for their lack of organization and resources, and Bragg was similarly disparaged within the Confederate army. As Edward Porter Alexander later recalled:

Unlike the armies in Va., which had never considered themselves defeated, our Western army had never gained a decided victory. Naturally, therefore, Lee enjoyed both the affection and confidence of his men, while there was an absence of much sentiment toward Bragg . . . Neither in armament, equipment, or organization was the Western army in even nearly as good shape as the Army of Northern Virginia. About one-third of the infantry was still armed only with the smooth-bore musket, caliber .69. Only a few batteries of the artillery were formed into battalions, and their ammunition was all of inferior quality.

Alexander clearly did not place all of the blame for the eventual failure of the Army of Tennessee on Bragg's shoulders, but at the same time he acknowledged the soldiers' general lack of devotion to their general.

When the Civil War broke out, Bragg was living in Louisiana and helped to lead the state militia. He saw action at Shiloh and in battles in Kentucky and his experience led to an appointment as commander of the Army of the Tennessee. Yet Bragg's tendency to engender distrust surfaced in northern Georgia in September 1863, when subordinates, including Leonidas Polk and D.H. Hill, refused to follow orders and attack Union troops under William Rosecrans's command. Rosecrans, fresh from a victory in the Tullahoma or

Middle Tennessee Campaign, had driven Bragg to the southeastern corner of Tennessee, captured the Tennessee town of Chattanooga, and was making his way south to attack Bragg's army. But the subordinates' delays allowed Rosecrans to gather resources and men, so that when Bragg attacked the Union forces he faced a strong enemy comprising the XIV, XX, and XXI Corps of the Army of the Cumberland, a total of about 60,000 men. Reinforcements under Lee gave Bragg a slight numerical supremacy. In a costly battle fought on September 19–20, 1863, Bragg and his Army of the Tennessee defeated Rosecrans's Army of the Cumberland, arguably the most significant Confederate victory in the West. Yet,

FIGURE 9.1 *General Braxton Bragg. Library of Congress, Prints and Photographs Division, LC-USZC4-7984*

Bragg was not able to destroy Rosecrans's Army of the Cumberland, which was allowed to turn back to Tennessee.

While Rosecrans retreated back to Chattanooga, Bragg seized the positive momentum of his battlefield victory to seek vengeance on his rivals within the military. He succeeded in removing Polk and Hill from their commands, but as a consequence his soldiers petitioned to have him replaced. Nathan Bedford Forrest had urged Bragg to pursue Rosecrans all the way to Chattanooga, but Bragg had stubbornly refused. After yet another confrontation, Forrest is supposed to have said to Bragg: "I have stood your meanness as long as I intend to. You have played the part of a damned scoundrel, and are a coward, and if you were any part of a man I would slap your jaws and force you to resent it . . . If you ever again try to interfere with me or cross my path, it will be at the peril of your life." Forrest himself had trouble getting along with others in the Confederate army, underscoring the personal hostilities that hampered the southern war effort.

Bragg eventually laid siege to Chattanooga, but weeks after his victory at Chickamauga. The battle for control of Chattanooga took

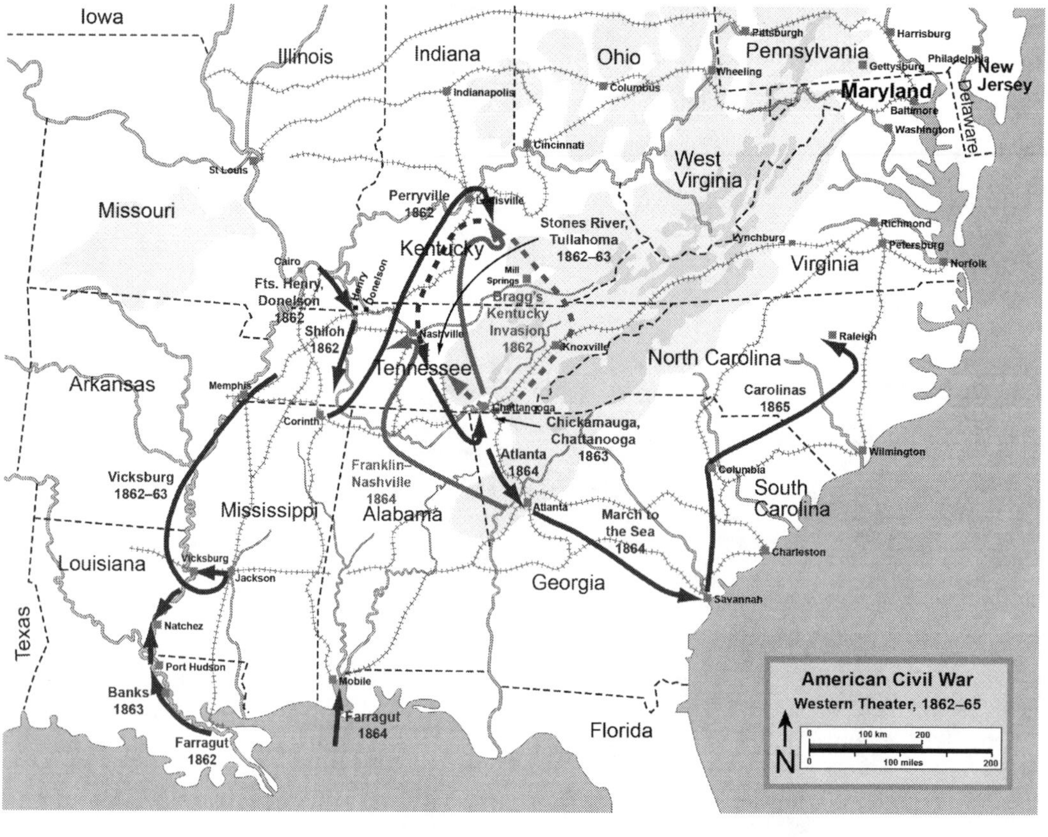

MAP 9.1 *American Civil War, Western Theater, 1862–1865. Black lines represent Union movements, while gray lines indicate Confederate movements. Map by Hal Jespersen, www.posix.com/CW*

place at the end of November 1863, and the Confederate defeat there would be as stunning as the southern victory had been just weeks before at Chickamauga. As Union private Arthur van Lisle lay wounded, he recalled about the battle:

> **All is turmoil and confusion. Artillery in our rear is firing over our heads into the enemy beyond . . . But our ranks are growing thin; our losses are frightful . . . It is becoming evident that the "Johnnies" are too many for us . . . Backward and forward surge the contending lines; and now—oh, my God!—the enemy comes with a wild rush and that ominous, terrifying rebel yell. They are passing over me, stumbling over our dead and wounded, falling among us, passing on. We are left behind, and the moans and groans of Union and Confederate wounded mingle in the smoke-stifling air, while many a poor fellow's agony is ended by stray shots which strike in our midst. Can I survive this awful anguish? Must I die here, to be laid in an unknown grave by the hands of the enemy? How long must I endure this torture of mind and body?[1]**

In the ensuing battle, General Ulysses S. Grant and the Union army captured Confederate positions at Lookout Mountain and Missionary Ridge, and nearly succeeded in completely decimating Bragg's army. Union casualties were fewer than 6,000 men, while Confederate losses numbered nearly 7,000. A major Confederate field army had been badly damaged, and recriminations began. Bragg blamed one of his officers for being drunk during the battle. So detrimental was the defeat that President Davis eventually replaced Bragg with Joseph E. Johnston. Perhaps most significantly, the Union victory made Chattanooga a springboard for an advance on Atlanta, permitting General William Tecumseh Sherman to open a campaign in spring 1864 to break the back of the Confederacy.

While Rosecrans was moving his army toward the clash with Bragg, further to the West bloody battles included deadly guerrilla warfare. As historians Daniel E. Sutherland and Robert R. Mackey have argued, guerrilla and irregular warfare played central roles in the war's outcome. While guerrilla warfare took place in the Eastern Theater, particularly by John Singleton Mosby's Confederates in northern Virginia, much of the war's guerrilla tactics took place in Missouri and northern Arkansas. In the mid-1850s, Missouri had sent "border ruffians" into Kansas to tilt elections in favor of proslavery interests, so the state had a long history of loosely organized raiders. During the Civil War, William Quantrill and his pro-South "bushwhackers" terrorized Union soldiers and their sympathizers. Often these guerrilla bands were little more than officially sanctioned gangs who looted stores, killed civilians, and burned towns. One of the most notorious actions by guerrilla bands during the war took place in the summer of 1863 in Lawrence, Kansas.

Born in Ohio and employed as a teacher, Quantrill became virulently pro-South in the 1850s and settled in Kansas on the eve of the war. He and his bushwhackers viewed Lawrence as a hotbed of abolitionist and pro-Union sentiment, as well as the home of the Unionist Jayhawkers. The Jayhawkers formed to combat pro-South guerrillas, and they proved a formidable enemy for Quantrill. To punish Lawrence and its Jayhawkers, Quantrill and hundreds of his bushwhackers descended upon the town on August 21, 1863. In the early morning mêlée, the bushwhackers murdered nearly 200 men and boys in what became known as the Lawrence Massacre, leaving the Kansas town looted and on fire. Union infantry and cavalry pursued Quantrill relentlessly until he was ambushed while conducting raids in Kentucky in the spring of 1865; but Quantrill, his raiders, and other guerrilla fighters such as William T. Anderson had achieved their objectives in the last years of the war by drawing resources and attention from Union leaders.

By the end of 1863, Lincoln and the Union army could point to important victories: repelling Lee's invasion of Pennsylvania at Gettysburg in July, taking control of the Mississippi River at Vicksburg in the same month, seizing Little Rock and Fort Smith, Arkansas in September, and defeating Bragg's Army of the Tennessee at the end of November. The war, however, was far from over. Confederates could also point to significant victories during the year, and southern political leaders hoped that as the war continued, northern citizens would grow weary of the fighting. The New York City draft riots in July had given Confederates some hope that northerners would tire of the war. Battles in early 1864 would buoy Confederate hopes momentarily and spur Lincoln's political opponents to step up their criticism of the president. Lincoln was so distraught that, by the summer of 1864, he was convinced that he was going to lose the presidential election later that fall.

The Battlefield in Early 1864

By January 1864 the opposing armies had generally settled into their winter quarters. Lee's southern army and Meade's Union forces were both headquartered in northern Virginia, as was Jeb Stuart's cavalry. Union forces numbered above 850,000 men, while Confederates could count more than 450,000.[2] Lincoln, worried that terms were coming up for veterans who would be returning home, called for another 500,000 troops to be drafted, and soon the age for draftees would be broadened to include recruits as young as seventeen and as old as fifty. War-weary northerners treated the news with something less than enthusiasm, and took the call for half a million new troops as evidence that Lincoln had no idea of when the war might end.

African Americans began to worry that white northerners were losing their resolve and that Lincoln was losing the confidence of the voters. "Africano" wrote a letter to the *Weekly Anglo-African* newspaper in 1864 urging northerners to remain committed to the war effort and expressing fear that Lincoln would lose his bid for reelection in the fall. This prospect filled "Africano" with dread, and he argued that Lincoln's defeat would mean:

> **The slave trade, not withstanding the solemn compact of the civilized world, will again be inaugurated regardless even of the principles of international law, and negroes will be at as high a demand as before the cannons of rebeldom belched their destructive missiles on the ramparts of Sumter. Forbid it, Muse! Forbid it, Heaven!**

Like many northern African Americans, "Africano" tried to bolster waning northern commitment to the war. In the early months of 1864 their fears appeared justified, as heavy battle losses sparked a political resurgence among those calling for peace. Democrats grew optimistic that Union battlefield reversals would increase their chances for political gains in the fall elections.

Until May, relatively few battles of note broke out in the East. A few minor battles rattled residents in Western North Carolina, northern Florida, and Mississippi. Florida, which had entered the Union in 1845 and then seceded in early 1861 to join the Confederacy, witnessed fighting at the Battle of Olustee in February, where Confederates staved off a Federalist attack. But in the same month a Confederate attempt to recapture New Bern in eastern North Carolina failed, and Union General Sherman marched on and destroyed Meridian in eastern Mississippi. On February 17 the CSS *Hunley*, a bold experiment that was essentially a primitive submarine, successfully attacked a Union ship in Charleston harbor. The sub sank soon after the incident and its sailors died, but the *Hunley* represented one more remarkable technological invention to emerge from the war.

As spring approached, northerners increasingly pinned their hopes on General Grant, who quickly became an idol among those who believed he could bring a rapid end to the war. Grant did indeed have a strategy for pressing the Confederacy's will to

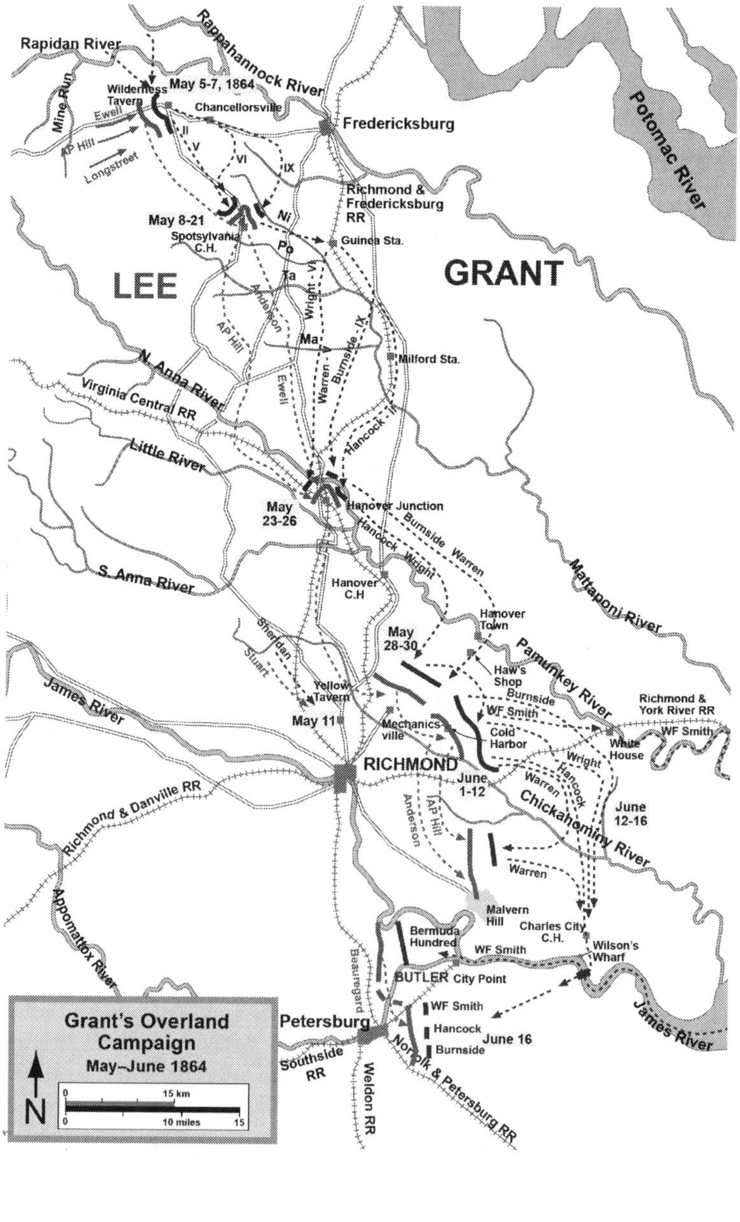

MAP 9.2 *Map of the East, 1864. Drawn by Hal Jespersen in Adobe Illustrator CS5. Wikimedia Commons*

fight, including a multi-pronged attack that would drive Union forces deep into the South to break the region's morale. Grant was rewarded for his successes in the West by being named commander in chief of the armies of the United States as Lt. General; the last person to hold that title was George Washington. The honor bestowed upon Grant offered further testimony to the tremendous faith that northerners placed in the man from Galena, Illinois.

While northerners rallied behind Grant, white southerners still suffered from internal division and dissent. Georgia's Joseph E. Brown and North Carolina's Zebulon Vance continued to challenge President Davis's wartime measures and to assert the authority of individual states. To make matters worse, deserter camps mushroomed throughout the South; Jones County, Mississippi residents continued to proclaim their loyalty to the Union; and dissident groups such as eastern North Carolina's "Heroes of America" sought an immediate cessation of hostilities. White southerners continued to revere Lee, but the Confederacy was no doubt weakened by internal disputes, deserters, and dissenters.

While Union and Confederate forces in the East prepared for the springtime battles sure to come, large-scale fighting erupted in the southwest. From March 10 to May 22, Union troops under Major General Nathaniel P. Banks engaged in the Red River Campaign. The Red River, which runs diagonally across northern Louisiana, saw numerous battles as Banks's 30,000-strong Army of the Gulf sought to capture Shreveport, Louisiana and possibly east Texas, as well as to gain control over the important southern port of Mobile, Alabama. Leading the opposing army was Confederate General Richard Taylor. Banks had more than double the number of troops under Taylor, but the Confederate general proved the better tactician. At the Battle of Mansfield in early April, Union forces were routed, and at the subsequent Battle of Pleasant Hill northern troops fared only modestly better, forcing Banks to retreat. For his ignominious defeat, Banks would be relieved of command, and the dejected general soon returned to Massachusetts politics. Union forces had little to show for their losses in the Red River Campaign.

In early May, the fighting dramatically escalated in Virginia, as Lee prepared for an expected assault on Richmond by Grant and his generals. Grant's Virginia Overland Campaign was part of his overarching plan to press the North's advantage in men and resources. The Union army was now committed to a war of attrition, in which the South would be worn down by the North's superior manpower and productive capacity. Lincoln, Grant, and their advisors knew that the Confederacy could not draft many more men. The pool of available Confederate soldiers was shrinking monthly, and in this new war of attrition, the Union could exploit its much larger pool of potential fighting men. The Confederacy's broadening of the age parameters for service offered further proof that the South did not have enough soldiers in uniform.

With such advantages in mind, on May 4, 1864 Grant crossed the Rapidan River, the major tributary of the Rappahannock River in the central part of northern Virginia. As Lee had expected, Grant was coming for Richmond, and neither side had any illusions about the deadliness of the combat. But the intense optimism caused by Grant's new role as Lt. General boosted morale among the Army of the Potomac. A Pennsylvania chaplain recorded the Union's crossing of the Rapidan River on May 4:

> **The dawn was clear, warm, and beautiful. As the almost countless encampments were broken up—[with] bands in all directions playing lively airs, banners waving, regiments, brigades, and divisions falling into line . . . the scene, even to eyes long familiar with military displays, was one of unusual grandeur.[3]**

The battles fought over the next several weeks saw some of the most intense fighting of the entire war. From June 1864 to the following spring, a series of battles erupted during the Richmond–Petersburg Campaign. Known as the Siege of Petersburg, the battles in and around the Confederate capital and the nearby town of Petersburg, Virginia involved deadly trench warfare in which General Grant tried repeatedly to take the railroad supply road between the two cities, a goal achieved in April 1865 that helped to end the war. During the campaign at the end of July 1864, Union forces blew up a mine, creating a large hole in which trapped soldiers became easy targets. Called the Battle of the Crater, the fighting resulted in heavy Union losses, especially among black soldiers.

Northern Virginia was already heavily battle-scarred by the time fighting resumed in the spring of 1864. Soldiers kept coming upon the remains of soldiers who had died during the first years of the war. As one Union soldier marched with Grant deeper into Virginia, memories of the fallen were all around. As he recalled:

FIGURE 9.2 *Map of the siege of Petersburg. Buyenlarge/Getty Images*

We reached Chancellorsville and bivouacked near the blackened ruins of the Old Chancellor House. Weather-stained remnants of clothing, rusty gun-barrels and bayonets, tarnished brasses and equipments, with bleaching bones and grinning skulls, marked this memorable field. In the cavity of one of these skulls was a nest with the three speckled eggs of a field bird. In yet another was a wasp nest. Life in embryo in the skull of death![4]

Other soldiers reported similarly macabre stories of these ghostly reminders of past battles. It is no wonder that soldiers took these solemn experiences with them long after the war ended and struggled with the memories of death and dying.

During Grant's Overland Campaign, his soldiers would add greatly to the ghostly remnants already on the ground. The first major combat took place in the wilderness near Spotsylvania, Virginia between May 5 and May 7. The Battle of the Wilderness took place in densely forested northern Virginia by design. Lee, with only about 60,000 soldiers, was greatly outmanned by Grant's force of more than 100,000, an advantage that could be diminished by the close combat on terrain that would negate Grant's ability to maneuver or commit all his troops simultaneously. Grant's superiority of artillery would be mostly nullified by the forest cover. Although Lee knew that such close combat would be especially deadly, the Confederate general felt he had little choice but to force Grant to engage him in the thick woods. For the same reason, Grant was reluctant to engage Lee in the wilderness. Lee, however, pressed the issue by sending forward Lt. General Richard Ewell's Second Corps and Lt. General A.P. Hill's Third Corps. Grant responded by sending Major General Gouverneur K. Warren's V Corps and Major General Winfield Scott Hancock's II Corps. Lee was able to strike the Union forces hard and cause nearly 18,000 casualties, but the Confederacy also suffered considerable losses, casualties that Lee and the Confederacy could ill afford. The battle proved inconclusive despite Grant's heavy losses, as on May 8, Grant simply sidestepped the Confederate army and continued moving southward. Rather than retreat in the face of stinging losses, as McClellan and other Union generals had done, Grant buoyed the morale of his troops by continuing the push into Confederate territory.

Lee pursued Grant and the two armies met again at the Battle of Spotsylvania, where they fought intensely between May 8 and May 21. In the early days of the battle Grant sought to exploit a weakness in Lee's line, but over the next several days Lee inflicted heavy casualties on Grant in fighting so intense that it flattened the landscape. After suffering significant losses, Grant once again maneuvered around Lee's forces and continued the Union march into Virginia. Fighting would prove even more deadly in the weeks ahead as the Union army continued its advance toward Richmond. Even veteran soldiers were overwhelmed by the loss of life. As Virginia's Marion Epperly wrote to his wife near the end of May:

Dear Mary, I can tell you it was a serious time to see so many of our dear boys fall to the ground and be cut to pieces by bombshells, and minnie balls. . . There is missing out of this Regt. 250 men killed wounded and missing . . . some of them is taken prisoners and I can't tell what has become of the rest.[5]

The Battle of Cold Harbor in early June 1864 marked the final days of Grant's costly Overland Campaign. The two armies were on familiar ground since they had fought on the same land during the Battle of Gaines' Mill during the Seven Days Battles back in 1862. The land was only ten miles from the Confederate capital in Richmond, so Lee was determined to hold firm to his ground. Bolstered by reinforcements from other divisions, Lee's army reached nearly 60,000 men, many of whom were veterans of intense combat. They constructed substantial fortifications and were firmly entrenched. Despite this fact, Grant attempted several assaults on the line during the first two weeks of June and was repelled with extensive losses. On June 3, Grant lost more than 6,000 men in just one hour in one of the ill-fated attacks on Lee's line.[6] Lee successfully defended Richmond in what was to be the last major victory for the Army of Northern Virginia. Grant had suffered more than 50,000 casualties during the Overland Campaign, but Lee also lost more than 30,000 of his men. Lee suffered more as a proportion of his overall army, but Grant, once greeted in the North as a savior, was now harshly criticized for his ill-fated assaults on Lee's forces and the dramatic losses the Union incurred. Lincoln, dismayed by the results and by the negative reaction in the northern press, feared he would lose reelection.

Politics and the 1864 Presidential Campaign

Even during war, politics continues, and Democrats and Republicans battled with ferocity throughout the 1860s. In the modern era, relatively few Americans bother to vote, and few devote much attention, time, or energy to partisan politics. Yet, as historian Mark E. Neely, Jr. has argued, mid-nineteenth century Americans enthusiastically engaged in politics. Citizens voted in percentages that put the twenty-first century to shame, and campaigns sparked popular rallies, massive parades, and cries for battle. Partisans displayed political buttons, posters, banners, and all kinds of campaign paraphernalia. Torch-light lamps with candidates' pictures could be found in night parades, and campaigns set up their own newspapers to promote candidates during the election cycle.

As Neely has also shown, however, the hyper-partisan political culture of Civil War America meant that newspapers and campaigns could distort the truth about battlefield successes. Republicans charged their opposition with treason; Democrats returned the verbal fire with claims that Lincoln pursued the war with a tyrannical obsession with power. The partisan press ratcheted up the rhetoric and demonstrated how precarious democracy can be during a time of civil war. Vitriol and mud-slinging often ruled the day, and newspapers in particular broadcast the extremist views of the political opposition.

Lincoln's opponents who wanted to negotiate a settlement with the Confederacy were known as Peace Democrats, and they criticized the president's prosecution of the war tirelessly. As historian Jennifer L. Weber has argued, Ohio was the key battleground as the 1863 fall elections for Congress and governorships approached. Lincoln and the Republicans were in a particularly bad position, as dissatisfaction with the administration ran high after the draft riots in July and after the Union's embarrassing defeat at Chickamauga in September. Lincoln could also point to successes at Gettysburg and Chattanooga, but these victories were not followed up by Union pursuits of the enemy. In Ohio, Lincoln's nemesis Clement Vallandigham, exiled to Canada, was running for governor as a Peace Democrat. Foreshadowing racist appeals that the party would employ to great effect in the later nineteenth and early twentieth centuries, the Peace Democrats claimed that whites were fighting and dying for the benefit of African Americans. This claim resonated with many northern whites, especially after Lincoln issued the Emancipation Proclamation. As Weber argues convincingly, Vallandigham and the Ohio Peace Democrats tried to paint the election as a referendum on abolitionism. They characterized the Republicans as radical antislavery activists who were willing to sacrifice countless white lives to end bondage. Lincoln's suspension of *habeas corpus* and his widely publicized placing of limits on First Amendment freedoms such as press and speech were also fodder for Democratic campaign speeches. Democrats claimed that the president had trampled upon basic Constitutional doctrines, and they mistakenly believed that Union soldiers were on their side.

In campaign speeches, Republicans in Ohio and elsewhere in the West and North charged the Peace Democrats with treason. Slapping their opposition with the label of "traitor" proved effective, especially among soldiers who resented the Peace Democrats' claim that the war should be abandoned. The results of the 1863 election show that such tactics worked, as Vallandigham and Peace Democrats throughout the Union went down to defeat, often in landslide proportions. The Democrats were not completely decimated, and in some pockets they won important victories,

FIGURE 9.3 *Presidential campaign, 1864. Candidates for President and Vice-President of United States. Election, Tuesday, November 8, 1864. Library of Congress, LC-DIG-pga-05844*

but the elections of November 1863 demonstrated clearly that Union voters were not ready to make peace with the South, and that Democrats were vulnerable to accusations of disloyalty. But by the summer of 1864, a resurgent Democratic Party would cause Lincoln and the Republicans to fear for the results of the forthcoming presidential election.

Presidential campaigns during wartime create alliances and coalitions that would not be observed during peacetime elections. The 1864 presidential election, in which Lincoln ran for a second four-year term, was certainly unusual. He earnestly sought the re-nomination of the Republican Party and his supporters waged a vigorous campaign despite numerous obstacles. Chief among these obstacles was the internal division within the Republican Party. Although Lincoln's loudest critics came from northern Democrats who wanted to negotiate immediate peace with the Confederacy, the president also faced considerable criticism within his party. Radical Republicans such as Massachusetts Senators Charles Sumner and Henry Wilson wanted Lincoln to take bolder stands on racial equality and the end of slavery. Such Republicans denounced those in their own party and within the Democratic Party who wanted to make peace with the South with or without slavery. For Sumner, Wilson, and like-minded Republicans, the rebels needed to be dealt with harshly, and they fiercely opposed any peace agreement that allowed slavery to survive in the South. Dissatisfied with what they saw as Lincoln's overly conciliatory policies regarding racial equality and slavery in the Border States, the Radical Republicans met at the end of May in Ohio to nominate John C. Fremont as their presidential candidate, the same man who had been the Republican Party's first nominee for president in 1856. Running against any compromise with slavery or the South, the new wing of the Republican Party called itself the Radical Democracy Party. Although a minority even in the North, the new party could seriously harm Lincoln's chances for reelection by siphoning off votes from the president's campaign.

Lincoln also confronted challenges from the Peace Democrats, some of whom wanted to end the war immediately with slavery intact in the South and some of whom took a more moderate approach. Thomas Seymour of Connecticut joined Clement Vallandigham in advocating an immediate end to the war, even if it meant that slavery remained entrenched in the South. These Copperheads, as they were known, had significant support in many northern and midwestern communities. At the same time, more moderate Peace Democrats such as New York's Horatio

Seymour wanted a negotiated end to the hostilities. The Democrats settled on Union General George B. McClellan, who supported the war effort but opposed Lincoln's leadership of the Union, as their candidate. The party's platform, written by conservative Peace Democrats such as Vallandigham, called for an end to the fighting. The Democratic platform charged that during the war "the Constitution itself has been disregarded in every part, and public liberty and private right alike trodden down." This claim was a reference to the Lincoln Administration's limitations on *habeas corpus* and freedom of speech. But the platform was so critical of the president and so strident in its call for peace that even McClellan himself did not support it entirely.

While the Peace Democrats met and formulated their platform, the War Democrats joined with Lincoln and his supporters. During wartime, the party in power often joins with the party out of power to form a united front. Lincoln joined with War Democrats to establish a new, temporary coalition known as the National Union Party that brought together the president's supporters and those Democrats who wanted to continue the war until the victory over the South was won. In early June the National Union Party met in Baltimore and despite minor opposition nominated Lincoln for a second term. Lincoln's new running mate, replacing lackluster Vice President Hannibal Hamlin, was Andrew Johnson of Tennessee. A War Democrat, Johnson was born in North Carolina but made his political career in Tennessee. Johnson supported the Union and opposed secession, and was the only senator from a seceding state not to resign his position. He supported Lincoln's prosecution of the war and was rewarded for his loyalty by being nominated as the vice presidential candidate for the National Union Party.

Peace Democrats were pleased with the Republicans' internal split, which they saw as their best chance of unseating the president. However, the Republican schism did not last through the entire campaign. Realizing that the platform of the Peace Democrats would leave slavery intact, Radical Republican nominee Fremont decided to withdraw his candidacy in September. He understood that by running a more radical campaign to compete against Lincoln, he might be handing the election to the Peace Democrats, a burden too heavy to bear for the staunchly antislavery Fremont.

During the summer and early fall of 1864, the campaign waged on in both the press and in the halls of Congress. Peace Democrats vilified Lincoln and Grant, while Radical Republicans argued that the president had been too timid in dealing with the slave power. For his part, Lincoln was grateful to be re-nominated. On June 9, he wrote to the National Union Party that he welcomed the confidence placed in him and agreed that "it was not best to swap horses when crossing streams." Although Lincoln had numerous critics, his campaign could fall back on the argument that it was better to maintain stability and consistency in keeping both the Republicans and the president in power. All eagerly awaited the election on November 8, with no side confident of victory.

Mobile Bay and the Fall of Atlanta

The summer and fall of 1864 were difficult months for the Confederacy and by the end of the year it appeared that southern defeat was inevitable. Part of Grant's war of attrition was to stage a multi-pronged attack deep into southern territory. Naval tactics continued to play an important part in the Union's overall strategy, and Rear Admiral David Farragut was charged with attacking Mobile Bay in Alabama. Farragut had deep roots in the South; his mother was born in North Carolina and Farragut himself was born in 1801 near Knoxville. But he was a stout Unionist and made no effort to hide his belief that secession was treason. He was a fleet commander from 1862 onward, and by the summer of 1864 he was entrusted with the important task of securing Mobile Bay and its environs for the Union. In August 1864 Farragut had reached the bay, which was defended by Confederate forts as well as a dangerous minefield. Farragut is supposed to have said "damn the torpedoes—full speed ahead!" At the Battle of Mobile on August 5 and at subsequent battles at nearby Fort Gaines and Fort Morgan, the Union forces won important victories and captured the Confederate ironclad CSS *Tennessee*. The port city of Mobile was isolated for the rest of the war, unable to send supplies into the southern interior.[7]

Another important piece of Grant's plan was to continue Sherman's penetration into the Deep South. After storming through eastern Tennessee and northwestern Georgia, Union Major General Sherman set his sights on Atlanta. In the Atlanta Campaign, Sherman fought a series of important battles against Confederate forces under John Bell Hood, who had replaced Joseph E. Johnston as head of the Army of Tennessee in July. Sherman had some of his most trusted officers, including George H. Thomas, James B. McPherson, John Schofield, and Oliver O. Howard, guiding a

FIGURE 9.4 *Capture of Mobile, Alabama. Library of Congress, Geography and Map Division*

combined force of about 100,000 soldiers. During the Atlanta Campaign, Hood counted on William J. Hardee, Leonidas Polk, and Joseph Wheeler to guide a powerful but comparatively smaller force of more than 50,000. At the battles of Rocky Face Ridge, Resaca, New Hope Church, Pickett's Mill, Kennesaw Mountain, and Peachtree Creek, Union forces made substantial progress and closed in on Atlanta. The city was an important railroad and manufacturing hub, and was the last major industrial center in the Deep South still producing items for the Confederacy. After the numerous battles between May and July, Sherman and his men pushed like a dagger in a downward thrust from northern Georgia to the outskirts of Atlanta. Southerners on the home front knew the importance of the Fall of Atlanta to their hopes for a Confederate victory. As Georgia's *Macon Daily Telegraph* argued in July 1864:

There are some who, in their patriotism and desire to keep up the spirits of our people, affect to look upon the fall of Atlanta as a matter of small consequence now

that there appears a chance of its capture by the enemy. Many of our papers, too, have begun to prepare the mind of the people for its downfall, by asserting that even if the enemy should eventually succeed in capturing the city, it would make no material difference to the cause of the South, but would be a barren conquest of the enemy.

We would . . . moderate the assertion, by saying that the fall of Atlanta would not be a mortal blow to our cause, but it would be a severe one, and a blow that would be felt throughout the Confederacy, and from which we could only recover by timely and energetic action. If we but look at the position of Atlanta—its strategic situation as the grand centre of the Confederate States, we easily discover that its capture and retention would secure to the enemy a base of operations of far greater superiority than Nashville or Chattanooga are, or could ever be.

The Battle of Atlanta on July 22, 1864 and the subsequent siege of the city were important turning points in the war and aided in President Lincoln's reelection. The Union's Army of the Tennessee, led by Major General James B. McPherson, who would be killed during the fighting, attacked Confederate forces trying to defend the city. For several days the fighting settled into a siege in which Sherman's army attempted to force Atlanta's surrender. After cutting off supply lines that fed the city, Sherman finally accepted Atlanta's surrender on September 2. Sherman forced the evacuation of the city. Then his troops burned almost all of the developing city's buildings, leaving only a few hundred behind. As Union soldier Lysander Wheeler remarked in a letter to his family:

I went to Atlanta last Friday to view the remains of the Gate City [Atlanta]. Gate to Purgatory I should judge by the looks. Most every building is marked either with bombshells or bullets there and some families yet remaining. It is the most poverty stricken place I have yet been in . . . It, and every other southern city deserve nothing better than a general destruction from Yankees. We could see where their slave pens and auction sales had been. The more I see of this miserable country the more I think these rebels deserve to be severely dealt

with, for the high sin they have been guilty of committing in buying and selling their betters. God will bring this country out of thicket yet.[8]

The scenes of destruction described by Wheeler became the backdrop for Margaret Mitchell's 1936 novel *Gone with the Wind*. As Sherman reported to Lincoln, "Atlanta is ours, and fairly won." Georgians might have disagreed with Sherman whether in fact the city was "fairly won," but the victory was a total one. After recuperating in Atlanta for several weeks, Sherman then set upon his next target: to slice through Georgia and South Carolina and try to bring the South to its knees.

Sherman's March to the Sea

Sherman's army carved a destructive path through Georgia so devastating that it has become known as the "March to the Sea." After leaving Atlanta on November 15, 1864, Sherman's army continued to move through Georgia until it captured Savannah at the end of December. Sherman and his soldiers cut a path about sixty miles wide and not only fought off military challenges from

FIGURE 9.5 *Sherman's March to the Sea. Library of Congress, Geography and Map Division*

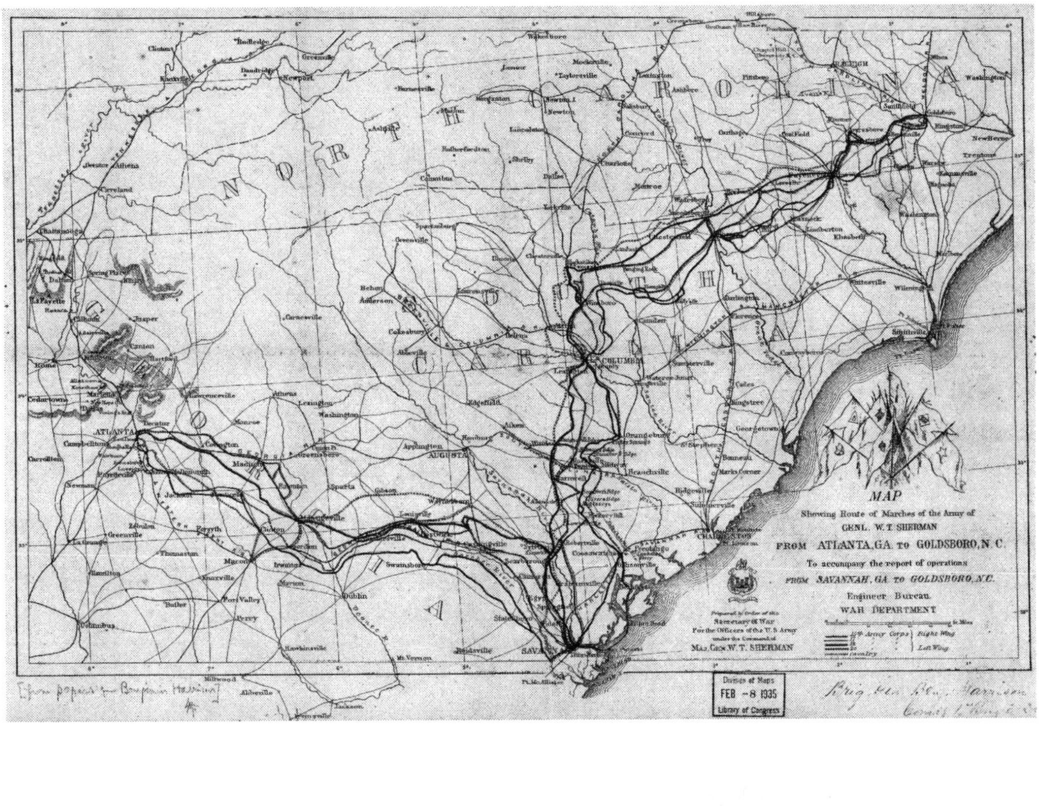

the Confederates, but also destroyed farms, buildings, and towns, his troops looting the possessions of ordinary citizens along the way. Sherman has often been faulted by later generations (especially by white southerners) for the wanton destruction his army inflicted on non-combatants. From Sherman's perspective, white southerners were rebels and deserved harsh treatment. He determined that on the campaign his soldiers would "forage liberally on the country." Sherman gave orders for soldiers to stay out of southerners' homes and not to loot except what vegetables and meat were needed to survive. Alas, the soldiers failed to follow this order and many took silver, money, and valuable artifacts from southern homes. The Union soldiers destroyed railroad tracks, heating and bending the rail ties around trees in a defiant act that became known as "Sherman's neckties." Sherman authorized

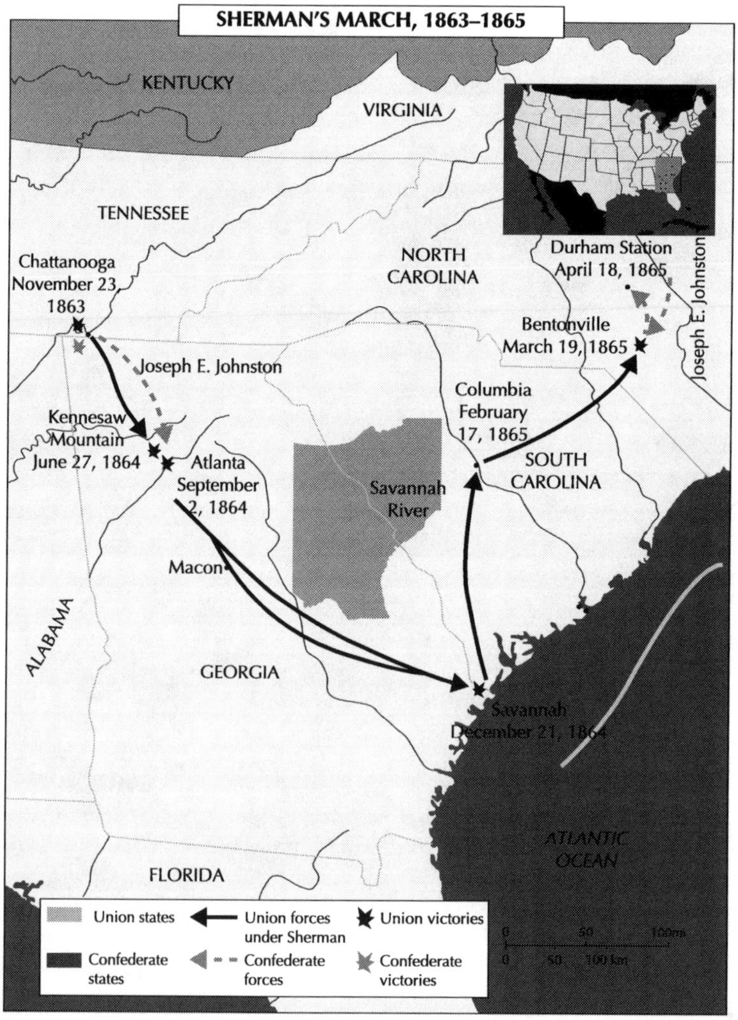

MAP 9.3 *Map of Sherman's March*

his men to "appropriate freely" any "horses, mules, wagons, &c., belonging to the inhabitants," but he recommended that when possible these goods should be taken from the rich rather than the poor. Again, such rules were not always followed. As Illinois soldier James Connolly penned in his diary while in Georgia during the march:

> **Our men are foraging on the country with the greatest liberality. Foraging parties start out in the morning; they go where they please, seize wagons, mules, horses and harnesses; make the negroes of the plantation hitch up, load the wagons with sweet potatoes, flour, meal, hogs, sheep, chickens, turkeys, barrels of molasses, and in fact everything good to eat . . . Our men are living as well as they could at home and are in excellent health.[9]**

The same could hardly be said of the southern common folk, who were suffering greatly from spiraling inflation that rendered Confederate money virtually worthless and from a lack of food and supplies. In the end, however, Sherman's March had the desired effect: the destruction broke the back of the Deep South and eventually forced the Confederacy to surrender.

The march itself was about 300 miles, and by mid-December Sherman had edged closer to Savannah. Hardee and his well-fortified army of more than 10,000 men opposed the Yankee soldiers. But Sherman soon received additional heavy artillery from the navy, and on December 17, poised to lay siege to Savannah, he sent a message to Hardee demanding the city's surrender. Hardee fled with his men, leaving Savannah Mayor Richard D. Arnold to surrender the city to Sherman. The Union Major General accepted the surrender, occupied the city, and sent a telegram to President Lincoln: "I beg to present you as a Christmas gift the City of Savannah, with one hundred and fifty guns and plenty of ammunition, also about twenty-five thousand bales of cotton." A grateful Lincoln willingly accepted the "gift" and knew that the recent success of Sherman's March to the Sea not only made Union victory in the war far more likely, but also significantly improved the president's chances of reelection.

Sherman continued to strike at the heart of the South by moving from Savannah to Charleston and then through central South Carolina to the state capital at Columbia. The widespread destruction continued, perhaps even more intensely since the Yankees recognized South Carolina as the instigator of secession.

It was easy to blame the state for the war, and easier still to take out the frustration of years of war on the state's inhabitants. William Gilmore Simms, the Old South's most important and prolific novelist, despaired at the destruction and looting of his personal library as well as of South Carolina's historic towns. Writing of Columbia's ruin, Simms lamented that:

It has pleased God, in that Providence which is so inscrutable to man, to visit our beautiful city with the most cruel fate which can ever befall states or cities. He has permitted an invading army to penetrate our country almost without impediment; to rob and ravage our dwellings, and to commit three-fourths of our city to the flames . . . Humiliation spreads her ashes over our homes and garments, and the universal wreck exhibits only one common aspect of despair.[10]

Simms's complaints, like those of thousands of other white southerners, fell on deaf ears, for Sherman and the Union army believed that the rebels brought the war on themselves. Historian Lisa Tendrich Frank has argued that the actions of Union soldiers during the march blended the battlefront and home front because soldiers often entered the homes of white elite women to look for food and other goods. There is no doubt, as historian Anne Sarah Rubin has demonstrated, that Sherman's March remained a painful memory for generations of white southerners.

Union successes in Mobile Bay and in Georgia and South Carolina helped to secure the presidential election for Lincoln. First, the president had the overwhelming support of Union soldiers—by some counts more than 70% of soldiers voted for Lincoln. Engaged in the fighting, most soldiers wanted to continue the war until victory was achieved. Union soldier Dolphus Damuth expressed his strong opinions about the election in an October 1864 letter home to his family:

You wanted to know what I thought of McClellan. I like *him* well enough, but the party that nominated him and the platform that he stands on I despise and we can't expect any more of him than the men who nominated him and support him. Do you suppose you can make a soldier believe that an armistice would be right? . . . I intend to say that any man that votes against [Lincoln] and for McClellan votes against his country and right and favors rebels and treason.[11]

Many other soldiers felt that a vote for McClellan and the Democrats was a vote for surrender to the slave power. Newspaper editorials conducted their own battles to win the minds of voters, and both parties held rallies, parades, and speeches to support their candidates.

The results of the election proved Damuth's point that his fellow soldiers supported Lincoln, but the president did not win reelection unchallenged. In fact, McClellan received 1.8 million votes (45%) from war-weary Americans, while Lincoln earned 2.2 million votes (55%). However, the vote in the Electoral College—212 votes for Lincoln and only 21 for McClellan—was a landslide, and the Democratic ticket was only able to win New Jersey (McClellan's home state), Kentucky, and Delaware. Although Lincoln won the large states of New York and Pennsylvania by less than 4%, he captured all of New England, the Midwest, and the Far West. Union soldiers reveled in the victory, and Lincoln, gratified by the reaffirmation of the voters' confidence, prepared to deliver his Second Inaugural Address the following March.

Please visit the companion website www.routledge.com/cw/wells for additional study aids including chapter overviews, interactive quizzes, and more.

Discussion Questions

- Why did Lincoln believe in late summer 1864 that he would likely lose his bid for reelection?
- What was Lee's strategy for winning the war as 1864 opened? What was Grant's strategy for victory when he took command of the Union forces?
- Why were African Americans concerned about the course of the war in 1864?
- How important to the Union's eventual victory was the fall of Atlanta?
- Sherman argued that the necessities of war justified the destructive "March to the Sea" in November and December 1864. White southerners argued that the march damaged their homes and property unnecessarily. Which side do you agree with? Why?
- Political elections during wartime are often different from those of peacetime. What advantages and disadvantages did

Lincoln and his Democratic challenger McClellan have as they headed into election day in 1864?

- Watch the movie version of *Gone with the Wind*. In what ways might the story be made more historically accurate? How does the movie depict African Americans? How does it portray white southern men and women?

Notes

1 Lisle quoted in Richard Wheeler, *Voices of the Civil War* (New York: Thomas Y. Crowell Co., 1976), 354–355.

2 Mark Swanson, *Atlas of the Civil War Month by Month* (Athens: University of Georgia Press, 2004), 80.

3 Reverend A.M. Stewart quoted in Richard Wheeler, *Voices of the Civil War* (New York: Thomas Y. Crowell Company, 1976), 380.

4 Union soldier Warren Goss quoted in ibid., 381.

5 Robert E. Bonner, *The Soldier's Pen: Firsthand Impressions of the Civil War* (New York: Hill & Wang, 2006), 96.

6 Swanson, *Atlas of the Civil War*, 90.

7 Ibid., 94.

8 Wheeler quoted in Bonner, *The Soldier's Pen*, 107–108.

9 Connolly quoted in Christopher J. Olsen, ed., *The American Civil War: A Hands-on History* (New York: Hill & Wang, 2006), 217.

10 Simms quoted in ibid., 218.

11 Damuth quoted in Bonner, *The Soldier's Pen*, 144.

Further Reading

Albert Castel, *Decision in the West: The Atlanta Campaign of 1864* (Lawrence: University Press of Kansas, 1992).

Tom Chaffin, *The* H.L. Hunley: *The Secret Hope of the Confederacy* (New York: Hill & Wang, 2008).

Charles Bracelen Flood, *1864: Lincoln at the Gates of History* (New York: Simon & Schuster, 2009).

Michael J. Forsyth, *The Red River Campaign of 1864 and the Loss by the Confederacy of the Civil War* (Jefferson: McFarland, 2010).

Lisa Tendrich Frank, *The Civilian War: Confederate Women and Union Soldiers during Sherman's March* (Baton Rouge: Louisiana State University Press, 2015).

Ernest B. Furgurson, *Not War but Murder: Cold Harbor 1864* (New York: Knopf, 2000).

Gary W. Gallagher, ed., *The Wilderness Campaign* (Chapel Hill: University of North Carolina Press, 1997).

Gary W. Gallagher, ed., *The Spotsylvania Campaign* (Chapel Hill: University of North Carolina Press, 1998).

James G. Hollandsworth, Jr., *Pretense of Glory: The Life of General Nathaniel P. Banks* (Baton Rouge: Louisiana State University Press, 1998).

Gary Dillard Joiner, *Through the Howling Wilderness: The 1864 Red River Campaign and Union Failure in the West* (Knoxville: University of Tennessee Press, 2006).

Ari Kelman, *A Misplaced Massacre: Struggling over the Memory of Sand Creek* (Cambridge, MA: Harvard University Press, 2013).

James Lee McDonough and James Pickett Jones, *War so Terrible: Sherman and Atlanta* (New York: W.W. Norton & Co., 1987).

Mark E. Neely, Jr. *The Union Divided: Party Conflict in the Civil War North* (Cambridge, MA: Harvard University Press, 2002).

Mark E. Neely, Jr. *The Boundaries of American Political Culture in the Civil War Era* (Chapel Hill: University of North Carolina Press, 2005).

Megan Kate Nelson, *Ruin Nation: Destruction and the American Civil War* (Athens: University of Georgia Press, 2012).

Gordon C. Rhea, *The Battle of the Wilderness* (Baton Rouge: Louisiana State University Press, 1994).

Gordon C. Rhea, *The Battles for Spotsylvania Court House and the Road to Yellow Tavern* (Baton Rouge: Louisiana State University Press, 1994).

Gordon C. Rhea, *Cold Harbor: Grant and Lee* (Baton Rouge: Louisiana State University Press, 2002).

Anne Sarah Rubin, *Through the Heart of Dixie: Sherman's March and American Memory* (Chapel Hill: University of North Carolina Press, 2014).

John C. Waugh, *Reelecting Lincoln: The Battle for the 1864 Presidency* (New York: Crown, 1998).

Jennifer L. Weber, *Copperheads: The Rise and Fall of Lincoln's Opponents in the North* (New York: Oxford University Press, 2006).

UNION VICTORY AND AFRICAN AMERICAN FREEDOM

Topics Covered in this Chapter:

- The Battlefield in Early 1865 and Lincoln's Second Inaugural Address
- The Assassination of President Lincoln
- Capture of Jefferson Davis
- Emancipation!

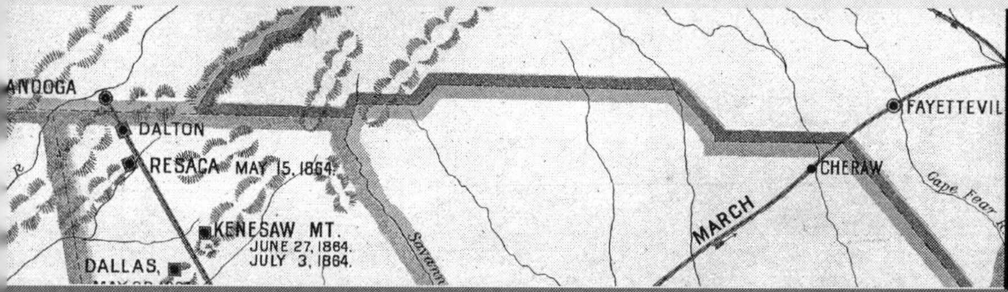

10

Introduction

As 1865 opened, the Confederacy was in dire straits. Weakening troop morale, a growing sense among southern citizens that defeat was inevitable, the running away of tens of thousands of slaves, and the terrifying Union war machine all sapped the southern will to fight. By late January, Confederate troops numbered fewer than 450,000 while Union forces continued to build toward one million soldiers. Sherman's devastating march through georgia would continue through the Carolinas. The last remaining key southern ports would soon fall to the Union Navy.

Yet some potent Confederate forces remained, including Lee's army, and Grant knew that the Virginia general, who was given command of all Confederate forces on January 31, would not surrender easily. Lincoln delivered his inspirational Second Inaugural Address on March 4, and the newly reelected president promised a firm but conciliatory approach to reunification. Lincoln, who had already laid down his basic proposal for reconstructing the Union in 1863 with the Ten Percent Plan, which would have readmitted former Confederate states when 10% of the states' residents took the oath of allegiance to the Union, began to look in earnest for the end of the war and the abolition of slavery even as Lee's army limped on. Finally cornered, Lee surrendered on April 9, 1865 at Appomattox, effectively ending the fighting.

In addition to the end of large-scale battles, the spring of 1865 would also witness the end of slavery in America. The Thirteenth Amendment to the United States Constitution abolished slavery and ensured that human bondage would no longer divide North from South. Although slavery ended as a result of the war, race continued to be a central concern in the nation. Freedpeople would face segregation and racism nearly everywhere they went in post-Civil War America.

Lincoln would not get to see the full outcome of his successful prosecution of the war. Assassinated in Washington shortly after Lee's surrender, Lincoln would only be permitted a brief glimpse of the reunion. As the battlefield quieted, new controversies erupted over how to end slavery and how to bring the rebellious South back into the Union. In the period known as Reconstruction, whites and blacks, northerners and southerners, and politicians and voters would battle over the shape of the new nation.

The Battlefield in Early 1865 and Lincoln's Second Inaugural Address

Early in 1865, southern morale was so weakened that powerful Confederate leaders began seeking terms for peace. White southerners suffered from the debilitating effects of the war in numerous ways. Most obvious was the tens of thousands of families struck by the losses of fathers, brothers, sons, and husbands. Since the draft age was widened to those between the ages of seventeen and fifty, deaths spread across not one but many generations, from young men in their teens to those in their fifties. Aside from the dramatic loss of life, southerners also faced rapidly spiraling inflation that rendered Confederate currency nearly worthless. At the start of the war, many white southern families had converted their gold and other valuables into Confederate dollars to show their support for the southern war effort. Now with each passing month, the money was worth less and less, so that by 1865 not even southerners themselves valued Confederate currency. The South's ability to import goods suffered from the closing of ports by the Union navy and the destruction of railroad lines and public buildings, and Sherman's success in the Deep South meant that the internal movement of goods and routine patterns of trade were significantly disrupted. The Confederacy desperately sought relief, even in the form of peace with the Yankees.

By February 1865, President Jefferson Davis advocated a policy shift that would have been unimaginable earlier in the war: the recruiting and arming of black soldiers to fight for the Confederacy. Historian Bruce Levine has found that during the early months of 1864 Major General Patrick Cleburne had argued that the Confederacy should identify and train for combat a small group of able slaves. Although the Confederate leadership was not prepared to follow Cleburne's recommendation at the time, by early 1865 Davis and his military advisors, including Lee, had agreed on the need to consider arming slaves. The policy shift came too late in the war to have any appreciable effect on the Confederacy's chances for victory. If anything, the proposal to arm enslaved men to fight for the Confederacy, unthinkable in 1861 or 1862, showed the South's desperation.

In early February, President Lincoln and Secretary of State Seward agreed to meet Confederate leaders to discuss peace. Representing the South was Vice President Alexander Stephens, Virginia Senator Robert M.T. Hunter, and other officials who hoped to negotiate a peace that might keep slavery or some semblance of the Confederacy intact. Lincoln, however, was not prepared to discuss any terms except the complete surrender of the Confederacy. Somewhat reluctantly, Lincoln agreed to meet on February 3 aboard the steamboat *River Queen* near Newport News, Virginia. In what would become known as the Hampton Roads Conference, the Confederates had offered an outlandish plan to reunite the country by joining forces to attack French forces in Mexico. Even more troubling was that Stephens and Hunter had no real authority to authorize the surrender of the Confederate armies. The meeting lasted for four hours and concluded with no results. Lincoln proved willing to begin to talk peace, but the wild plan to attack Mexico was not what the president had in mind. He was determined that the Union forces would continue to press the South for an unconditional surrender. The fighting would continue.

While Union and Confederate forces in Virginia, exhausted from winter trench warfare, re-formed into battle-ready troops in the early months of 1865, the Carolinas bore the brunt of Sherman's angry army as it carved a path through the heart of South Carolina and then turned north and east into North Carolina. As the first state to secede, South Carolina was blamed for inciting the rebellion in the first place, and Union soldiers were eager to lay waste to the Palmetto State. Even Sherman knew that he would be hard pressed to keep his soldiers from burning and looting as they marched northwest from Charleston to the capitol at Columbia. Writing to General Henry W. Halleck before leaving Savannah, Sherman underscored his soldiers' anger toward South Carolina. To his surprise, Sherman even encountered anger toward the state from other southerners:

The truth is, the whole army is burning with an insatiable desire to wreak vengeance upon South Carolina. I almost tremble at her fate, but feel that she deserves all that seems in store for her. Many . . . a person in Georgia asked me why we did not go for South Carolina; and, when I answered that we were en route for that State, the invariable reply was "well, if you will make those people feel the utmost severities of war, we will pardon you for your desolation of Georgia."

As Sherman's letter makes clear, divisions within the South, present since the beginning of the war, were felt even more acutely as the Confederacy began to collapse. Considerable controversy emerged over the burning of Columbia, with some in the Union press accusing white southerners of torching the city and laying the blame on Sherman's forces. Probably some important buildings were in fact set alight by Confederate sympathizers who did not want resources to fall into Union hands; this was a common practice throughout the South. But undoubtedly Sherman's soldiers also contributed mightily to the South Carolina capital's devastation.

After Columbia fell, Sherman's army left South Carolina and marched into North Carolina. Confederate President Davis brought Joseph E. Johnston back into command to thwart the Union advances through the Tarheel State. At the Battle of Bentonville on March 19, 1865 Johnston struck hard at part of Sherman's army but ultimately had to retreat to Raleigh and then Greensboro. Confederates refused to give up even though overall morale was waning. As rebel Charles Hutson wrote his father in March, "The enemy is determined to subjugate us . . . We have only to buckle on the armor of war & to bring this struggle to a final issue—to determine to live free or die."[1]

In the meantime, action heated up in Virginia, the site of so many battles and the resting place of so many dead soldiers. By March 1865 Virginia's towns and countryside were scarred by four years of bitter fighting. After hunkering down in trenches during the winter near Richmond, Lee decided that Union military pressure necessitated a move to the southwest. Grant's Appomattox

Campaign at the end of March and early April continued to press Lee at the Battle of Five Forks on April 1 and the Third Battle of Petersburg the following day. Lee abandoned Richmond and Petersburg, hoping to reach Confederate forces in North Carolina, but Grant would not permit the Confederate General to get away. Instead, Grant strengthened his forces with cavalry under Major General Philip Sheridan to spearhead the pursuit, with the infantry of VI Corps supporting the effort. Following battles at Lewis's Farm, White Oak Road, Dinwiddie Court House, and Sutherland's Station, Grant had Lee on the run until the two armies met at the Battle of Sayler's Creek on April 6. There Lee suffered considerable losses but still attempted to continue his retreat. The 24th and all-black 25th Corps joined the 5th Corps in relieving Sheridan's cavalry, which held Lee in place during the night of April 8–9.

Union cavalry led by George Armstrong Custer cut Lee off and seized trainloads of Confederate supplies in fighting around Appomattox Station in the evening of April 8. The fighting the following day was more of a skirmish. At the Battle of Appomattox Court House on April 9, Lee struggled to get to supplies from Lynchburg, Virginia but was met by the Union V Corps. Lee was cornered, and he surrendered in the early afternoon on that day to General Grant. As Lee remarked "There is nothing left for me to do but to go see General Grant and I would rather die a thousand deaths." Lee sent word to Grant that he was prepared to surrender and Grant responded by letting Lee choose the location of the meeting. A Confederate aide selected the home of Wilmer McLean, a sturdy house built before the war. Ironically, McLean had moved from his previous home near Manassas to avoid further fighting.

To his credit, Grant did not gloat during the surrender. At first the two veterans of the Mexican–American War, who had not seen each other for many years, talked of old times, but soon they turned to the business at hand. Lee offered his unconditional surrender, and Grant accepted and allowed rebel officers and soldiers to return home under parole. Grant could have been more vindictive but as he later wrote, he "did not want to exult over their downfall" and on April 10, 1865 generously allowed Lee to address his army in a formal ceremony disbanding his troops. As Lee noted in the address:

After four years of arduous service marked by unsurpassed courage and fortitude, the Army of Northern Virginia has been compelled to yield to

overwhelming numbers and resources. I need not tell the survivors of so many hard fought battles, who have remained steadfast to the last, that I have consented to the result from no distrust of them. But feeling that valor and devotion could accomplish nothing that could compensate for the loss that must have attended the continuance of the contest, I have determined to avoid the useless sacrifice of those whose past services have endeared them to their countrymen.

Mercifully for Virginia and for soldiers on both sides, the battles in that state came to an end. As many had predicted, once rebellious white southerners learned of Lee's surrender, other officers across the region waved the white flag as well. Skirmishes cropped up in the southwest in May and June 1865 but these were minor and had no effect on the outcome of the war. Once Lee surrendered, all sides knew, the Civil War was effectively over.

The scene of Lee's worn soldiers surrendering their weapons imprinted upon the memories of all who were present. Union General Joshua Chamberlain wrote of the ceremony as he witnessed it firsthand:

Before us in proud humiliation stood the embodiment of manhood: men whom neither toils and sufferings, nor the fact of death, nor disaster, nor hopelessness could bend from their resolve; standing before us now thin, worn, and famished, but erect, and with eyes looking level into ours, waking memories that bound us together as no other bond.

Chamberlain's point that there was a unique bond between white soldiers of both sides for all that they had been through was a theme carried into the early twentieth century, as the remaining Confederate and Union veterans gathered together periodically to remember the war.

According to legend, Lee was so impressed with Grant's generosity during the surrender that he did not permit friends to denounce the Union General. Grant's graciousness toward Lee reflected the sentiments expressed in President Lincoln's Second Inaugural Address on March 4. Regarded as one of the most important speeches in American history, Lincoln remarked that although both sides had tried to avoid war, the division between free labor and slavery was too great. The war, Lincoln argued, was divine judgment for the sin of slavery. At the same time the president claimed that he would seek the Confederacy's surrender "with malice toward none; with charity for all." This pacifying theme was directed in large part toward white Confederates.

Although Sherman's March would live in infamy in the minds of white southerners, the Union army offered many examples of leniency and mercy as the war ended. When Lee surrendered at Appomattox, Union forces under Joshua Chamberlain saluted the defeated southern troops, with "honor answering honor." And when Confederate General Joseph E. Johnston surrendered the Army of Tennessee to Sherman in mid-April 1865, Sherman offered more than a week's worth of rations to the tired and hungry Confederate soldiers, a generous token that earned Sherman the respect of Johnston and his troops.

African Americans celebrated Lee's surrender and spilled out into the streets of southern towns to celebrate the Union victory. They appreciated the significance of Grant's triumph and knew that the defeat of the Confederacy meant the end of slavery. After Grant reached Richmond in early April, securing the Confederate capital for the Union, President Lincoln traveled through the city to mark the occasion. African Americans relished the chance to celebrate the conquest and to see the president in person. J.J. Hill, a black Union soldier, recalled the scene:

> **What a spectacle! I never witnessed such rejoicing in all my life. As the President passed along the street the colored people waved their handkerchiefs, hats and bonnets, and expressed their gratitude by shouting repeatedly, "Thank God for his goodness; we have seen his salvation." . . . All could see the President, he was so tall. One woman standing in a doorway as he passed along shouted. "Bless the Lamb—Bless the Lamb." Another one threw her bonnet in the air, screaming with all her might, "Thank you, Master Lincoln." A white woman came to a window but turned away, as if it were a disgusting sight.[2]**

Hill and the other African Americans celebrating that day hoped that the Union capture of the Confederate capital would soon mean the end of the war and the dreamed-of end to bondage in

FIGURE 10.1 *Last letter written by General Lee before his surrender. Getty Images*

America. Their hopes and aspirations for freedom were bound up in their deep-seated faith in President Lincoln.

Lincoln's Second Inaugural Address confirmed the suspicions held among many African Americans that the president had undergone a transformation during his first term in office. The pre-presidential Lincoln, while clearly opposed to slavery and far more devoted to African American freedom than most Americans, was hardly a radical. As historian Eric Foner has pointed out, for many years Lincoln advocated colonization—the return of black Americans to Africa—as the best solution to the nation's race problem. And as he announced in speeches both before and after his election in 1860, Lincoln was more determined to end the southern rebellion than he was devoted to the total destruction of slavery. In fact, Lincoln reminded white southerners in 1861 that he would not touch slavery where it already existed; like other Republicans, Lincoln was merely opposed to its spread to the southwestern territories. This approach to slavery positioned Lincoln firmly in the mainstream of the Republican Party, but Lincoln's claim that he would not intrude on slavery in the South was too conservative for black activists such as Frederick Douglass. For much of the early years of Lincoln's presidency, Douglass had remained a tepid supporter at best. Although Lincoln extended a hand to Douglass by inviting the African American abolitionist to the White House, a move that should not be dismissed because it was symbolically important, Douglass withheld his enthusiasm for Lincoln's policies. In Douglass's eyes, Lincoln was simply too conservative, too slow in his push to limit slavery, and too moderate in his calls for the end of the Confederate rebellion with or without slavery intact.

Although the Emancipation Proclamation earned Lincoln greater respect among black abolitionists such as Douglass, African Americans pressured the president to go further and faster in denouncing slavery. In the later years of the war, abolitionists sensed a shift in Lincoln's stance on slavery, and many believed that he would push for the end of bondage as a condition of reunion with the North. Lincoln's support for a constitutional amendment to abolish slavery offered further proof of his shifting ideology and by early 1865 the president had placed himself clearly on the side of total abolition. After years of uneasiness in their relationship, the bond between Douglass and Lincoln was firm as the president delivered his Second Inaugural Address. The president even expressed support for black suffrage. Unfortunately for Douglass and other African Americans, they would lose their advocate when an assassin's bullet killed Lincoln in April 1865, just as Unionists were celebrating Lee's surrender at Appomattox.

The Assassination of President Lincoln

A festive mood marked many northern cities when Lee's surrender became common knowledge. Newspapers in northern and midwestern cities such as Boston, Philadelphia, Milwaukee, Detroit, and New York held parades and rallies commemorating the end of the war, and small towns from New England to California reveled in the successful conclusion of the fighting. Union and Confederate soldiers began returning home to families and communities, even as the memories of those loved ones lost in four years of conflict remained vivid. The losses were substantial: more than 700,000 soldiers died from disease or in battle since the firing of shots at Fort Sumter in April 1861. Tens of thousands more were physically maimed from wounds or the amputation of limbs. The trauma of the war would last for decades and the ripple effects of the battles would play out in politics, culture, and society well into the twentieth century.

In mid-April 1865, however, with news of Lee's surrender still fresh, Americans were in the mood to rejoice at the end of the war. The nation's capital erupted with enthusiastic and festive parades, and the president himself was not above a little relaxation. On April 14, 1865 the president and his wife Mary Todd Lincoln attended a play at Ford's Theater in Washington, just a few blocks from the White House and the Capitol Building. One of the actors prominently and regularly featured at the theater was John Wilkes Booth, a Confederate sympathizer determined to kill the president.

Booth's hatred for Lincoln and abolitionism was well known among his family and friends, so much so that they often avoided visiting him, lest they fall prey to one of Booth's anti-Lincoln diatribes. By 1865, Booth was one of America's best-known and popular actors. Born in 1838 in Maryland, Booth hailed from British parents who had immigrated to America in 1821. While still a teenager, Booth began acting in Shakespearean plays throughout the eastern United States and by the Civil War his performances were very much in demand, though his support for secession and the Confederacy did not sit well with northern audiences. In fact, Booth was arrested in St. Louis in 1863 and fined for making pro-Confederate statements.

The arrest only spurred Booth on more, and the following year in 1864 he began devising a plot to kidnap the president. Booth gathered money and conspirators, including David Herold, Lewis Powell, George Atzerodt, and several other Confederate sympathizers. After Lincoln's reelection in November 1864, Booth's plan to kidnap the president evolved into a more fiendish plan to kill Lincoln and several members of the cabinet. When Booth heard that the president would attend the play at Ford's Theater, a venue Booth knew well, he acted quickly to put his murderous plan into action. Powell was supposed to assassinate Secretary of State Seward, while Atzerodt was responsible for killing Vice President Johnson. Although his ultimate motives are unclear, Booth may have hoped that by killing Lincoln, Johnson, and Seward he would destabilize the Union and open the door for a Confederate resurrection. Booth was saddened and angered by Lee's surrender and he may have expected to revive the South's flagging fortunes with the group assassination.

Booth carried out his part of the plan with determination and drama. At about 10 o'clock on the night of April 14, as the president, his wife, and guests watched the performance of *Our American Cousin*, Booth slipped into the president's box and fired a .44 caliber Derringer at the back of his head. Lincoln would survive until the next morning but his wounds were fatal. Meanwhile, Powell managed to stab Seward, but the cabinet secretary would eventually recover from the devastating wounds. Luckily for Johnson, Atzerodt lost his nerve and could not carry out his part of the plot. After Booth shot the president, the actor leapt onto the stage, shouting "*Sic semper tyrannis*!" (Latin for "thus always to tyrants"). Historians dispute whether Booth broke his leg as he jumped onto the stage or when he fell from his horse after fleeing the theater.

The injured Booth managed to escape Washington and hide out in Maryland and Virginia, receiving help for his broken leg from Dr. Samuel Mudd. While forces scoured the countryside for Booth, the nation mourned the assassination. Ultimately Booth

FIGURE 10.2 *John Wilkes Booth. Library of Congress, LC-DIG-npcc-27147*

would be cornered and killed on April 26, and several of his conspirators, including a boarding-house owner named Mary Surratt, were executed by hanging on July 7 for their roles in the plot. Dr. Mudd and others suspected in aiding Booth were sentenced to life in prison off the coast of Florida. Yet the hangings and prison sentences could not soothe the nation's grief.

An outpouring of sadness at the assassination engulfed the country, historian Martha Hodes and other scholars have found, and mourners lined the streets of Washington to view the casket of the dead president. Tens of thousands of people would pay homage to the slain president as his body was transported by train to its final resting place in Springfield, Illinois. Vice President Johnson, a Tennessee Democrat, was now officially the commander in chief, but he would have considerable trouble earning the respect and affection of the country, and his years as president would be marked by hostile relationships with members of Congress.

Americans reacted with anger and sorrow at the news of Lincoln's assassination, and much of their grief was expressed through literature. Walt Whitman, Herman Melville, and other important authors and poets gave voice to the shock and despondency Americans felt. Writing in April 1865 shortly after Lincoln's death, novelist and poet Lydia Maria Child noted that "the assassination of our good president shocked and distressed me." White southerners did not express the same level of dismay as many northerners, but even many former rebels saw the president's murder as a horrific act. The nation's African Americans saw Lincoln's death as a tragedy for them especially. The freedpeople in the South worried that they had lost perhaps their most powerful advocate.

All of the fury and melancholy after Lincoln's assassination culminated in important poems by leading authors. Whitman, for example, expressed his sadness in "O Captain! My Captain!" One of the most famous poems written during the war years, Whitman's classic verse was popular at the time:

O Captain! my Captain! our fearful trip is done;
The ship has weathered every rack, the prize we sought is won;
The port is near, the bells I hear, the people all exulting,
While follow eyes the steady keel, the vessel grim and daring:
But O heart! heart! heart!

O the bleeding drops of red,
Where on the deck my Captain lies,
Fallen cold and dead.

O Captain! my Captain! rise up and hear the bells;
Rise up—for you the flag is flung—for you the bugle trills;
For you bouquets and ribboned wreaths—for you the shores a-crowding;
For you they call, the swaying mass, their eager faces turning;
Here Captain! dear father!
This arm beneath your head;
It is some dream that on the deck,
You've fallen cold and dead.

My Captain does not answer, his lips are pale and still;
My father does not feel my arm, he has no pulse nor will;
The ship is anchored safe and sound, its voyage closed and done;
From fearful trip, the victor ship, comes in with object won;
Exult, O shores, and ring, O bells!
But I, with mournful tread,
Walk the deck my Captain lies,
Fallen cold and dead.

For Whitman, Lincoln was the captain of a ship on a "fearful trip," a reference to the war itself. Whitman credits the dead president with having brought the "ship," or the nation, into harbor "safe and sound." Whitman, like many Americans, honored Lincoln for having guided the country over four years of horrific suffering and loss.

Capture of Jefferson Davis

By the time Lee surrendered to Grant, President Davis and the Confederate cabinet knew that they would have to flee Richmond and find a new capital. Although many white southerners, including leading Confederate politicians, believed that defeat was inevitable, Davis and his closest advisors were determined to carry on the war, perhaps by shifting the remaining southern forces to the West. At first, Davis established a new Confederate capital in Danville, near the border with North Carolina. Davis then fled to Charlotte, North Carolina. There he wrote to his wife Varina and revealed his concerns for the future:

I think my judgment is undisturbed by any pride of opinion or of place, I have prayed to our heavenly Father to give me wisdom and fortitude equal to the demands of the position in which Providence has placed me. I have sacrificed so much for the cause of the Confederacy that I can measure my ability to make any further sacrifice required, and am assured there is but one to which I am not equal, my Wife and my Children. How are they to be saved from degradation or want is now my care.

Union troops were in hot pursuit of Davis, in part because many northerners suspected the Confederate president's involvement in the plot to assassinate Lincoln. Although Davis appears to have had no part in Lincoln's murder, he was chased throughout the Deep South by Union forces.

The fall of Richmond was a harsh blow to Confederate hopes, but in exile Davis tried to keep up southern morale. In what would be his last proclamation as president, Davis tried to assuage southern fears that the fall of the Confederate capital spelled imminent defeat of the South. To the people of Virginia, Davis announced that:

Animated by the confidence in your spirit and fortitude, which never yet has failed me, I announce to you, fellow-countrymen, that it is my purpose to maintain your cause with my whole heart and soul; that I will never consent to abandon to the enemy one foot of the soil of any one of the States of the Confederacy; that Virginia, noble State, whose ancient renown has been eclipsed by her still more glorious recent history, whose bosom has been bared to receive the main shock of this war, whose sons and daughters have exhibited heroism so sublime as to render her illustrious in all times to come—that Virginia, with the help of her people, and by the blessing of Providence, shall be held and defended, and no peace ever be made with the infamous invaders of her homes by the sacrifice of

any of her rights or territory. If by stress of numbers we should ever be compelled to a temporary withdrawal from her limits, or those of any other border State, again and again will we return, until the baffled and exhausted enemy shall abandon in despair his endless and impossible task of making slaves of a people resolved to be free.

Davis, in exile with his cabinet, his wife Varina, and their children, was captured in Georgia on May 10, 1865 by the First Wisconsin and Fourth Michigan cavalry. In the process of fleeing the Union horsemen, Davis threw on his wife's cloak, leading to later claims that Davis had fled in women's clothing. Designed to ridicule the Confederate former president, reports of a cross-dressing Davis delighted northerners and culminated in a popular song entitled "Jeff in Petticoats." Magazines such as *Harper's Weekly* poked fun at Davis and published cartoons of him fully dressed from head to toe in feminine attire.

FIGURE 10.3 *Jefferson Davis's attempted escape in woman's clothes with a knife in his hand. Library of Congress, Rare Book and Special Collections Division, Alfred Whital Stern Collection of Lincolniana*

Davis was imprisoned for two years at Fort Monroe in Virginia and later his wife Varina joined him at the fort. The former Confederate president was reduced to the humbling status of prisoner while Republican and Democratic politicians debated his fate. While some thought the humility of defeat was punishment enough, others (including many Radical Republicans) wanted to charge Davis with treason and for a time it looked as if a trial would be held. But Davis was ultimately released and pardoned under a general amnesty granted by President Johnson on Christmas Day 1868. Davis wrote a history of the rise and fall of the Confederate government after the war and took his belief in the legitimacy of secession and the righteousness of the Confederate cause to his grave in 1889.

Emancipation!

African Americans throughout the South were keenly aware of Davis's imprisonment and the fall of the Confederate government. Although the vast majority of enslaved people were illiterate and could not read the latest newspaper reports of the war, they nonetheless had their own ways of disseminating information. The "grape vine," or the oral transmission of stories, passed information from black community to black community, from large cities to small villages. Celebrations of the war's end, coupled with expectations that Confederate defeat would mean the abolition of slavery, erupted in African American communities and on plantations throughout the South in the spring and early summer of 1865.

One of the most remarkable celebrations to end slavery occurred in Texas in June 1865. On June 18, Union General Gordon Granger captured Galveston and Texas came completely under federal control. The following day, Granger issued General Order No. 3:

The people of Texas are informed that, in accordance with a proclamation from the Executive of the United States, all slaves are free. This involves an absolute equality of personal rights and rights of property between former masters and slaves, and the connection heretofore existing between them becomes that between employer and hired labor. The freedmen

are advised to remain quietly at their present homes and work for wages. They are informed that they will not be allowed to collect at military posts and that they will not be supported in idleness either there or elsewhere.

Conflating "June" and "nineteenth," African Americans began an annual "Juneteenth" celebration marking the end of slavery in America, celebrations that still take place each year around the country.

African American hope that the end of the war would also mean the end of slavery came to fruition in the form of the Thirteenth Amendment to the United States Constitution. Throughout the course of the war, northern Republicans discussed the possibility of a Constitutional Amendment to make slavery illegal. That the war might end slavery even as it ended the southern rebellion was a possibility that arose in part from necessity. As we have seen, Union military leaders struggled with the problem of fugitive slaves who had fled southern plantations to find safety and security behind Union lines. During the war Union officers had experimented with ways to confront the challenge of feeding, sheltering, and protecting runaway slaves. For most of the war, Lincoln kept tight control over such experiments, fearing that if the Union moved too quickly or too boldly to free the slaves then Border States such as Maryland, Missouri, and Kentucky might join the Confederacy. The Emancipation Proclamation had placed Lincoln and the Union clearly on the side of freedom, but the document applied only to the rebellious states, not to the Border States. By 1865, however, Republican fears that slave states on the border might leave the Union had lessened considerably. Freed from such worries, Union officers and the Lincoln administration renewed experiments in black freedom and soon proposed a new amendment to the Constitution that would outlaw slavery forever.

As historian Michael Vorenberg has argued, by 1864 Radical Republicans in the Senate were determined to codify abolition in the Constitution. In part, Vorenberg found, Republican attitudes on the need to abolish slavery were influenced by the Emancipation Proclamation, an important document that did not seem to go far enough to complement the impending Union victory. One early sponsor of legislation to outlaw slavery, Missouri Senator John Henderson, proposed a new law in January 1864 and in April of that year the Senate passed a bill that would change the nation's founding blueprint for government. The debate in the House of Representatives was more contentious, but the prospects for a new amendment outlawing slavery improved when Lincoln insisted that it become part of the Republican Party Platform in 1864. Lincoln and his supporters pressed hard for the amendment and in January 1865 the House of Representatives passed it as well. Under the process laid out in Article V of the Constitution, proposed amendments once passed by Congress then had to be ratified by three-quarters of the state legislatures, a mark achieved by December 1865.

Along with ending the southern rebellion, the Thirteenth Amendment was one of the most important outcomes of the Civil War. The Constitution ratified in 1787 was clearly a proslavery document; it not only counted slaves as three-fifths of a white person for purposes of representation but also promised southern

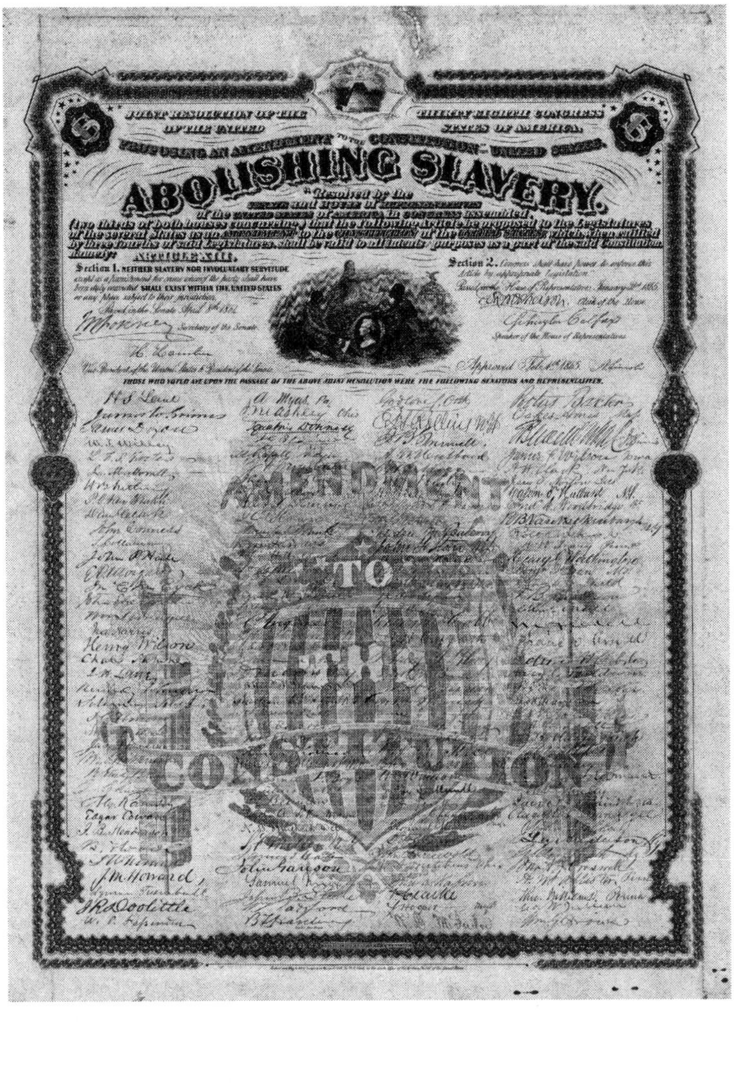

FIGURE 10.4 *13th Amendment abolishing slavery. Library of Congress, Rare Book and Special Collections Division, Alfred Whital Stern Collection of Lincolniana*

slaveholders that any runaways who made it to freedom and were caught would be returned to bondage. The Thirteenth Amendment made all of the other clauses and sections protecting slavery moot. Slavery was abolished as a fundamental underpinning of America. Freedom was redefined to include African Americans, and southern states had to ratify the amendment before they could be readmitted into the Union.

Yet, as crucial as the Thirteenth Amendment was to African Americans, the question of to what extent key rights such as suffrage would be extended to the freedmen remained unresolved at the end of 1865. Throughout American history, leaders had believed that suffrage could only be exercised properly by citizens who were independent. Since freedpeople had little or no immediate prospects for economic independence, even many Republicans worried that the franchise would be lost on African Americans.

Radical Republicans such as Massachusetts Senator Charles Sumner believed that economic independence required black ownership of land, but there were few precedents Sumner could point to. One of the Union experiments with the new status of southern African Americans came as a result of General Sherman's devastating march through the Deep South. In mid-January, Sherman issued Special Field Order No. 15, which dedicated a 400,000-acre swathe of coastal land in northeast Florida and southeast Georgia to freedmen, known as "Sherman's Reservation."[3] Plots of land were distributed in forty-acre allotments so that the freedpeople could become independent of white control. Unfortunately for the freedpeople, the redistribution of land was short-lived; new President Johnson rescinded the order. But the experiment showed that at least some in the Union believed that only by taking land from wealthy white plantation owners and subdividing it among the former slaves could black freedom be secured. Given the fact that the vast majority of southern African Americans could not read or write, had few personal possessions, did not own land to farm, and lacked even the most basic implements for farming, it is no surprise that many Republicans seriously considered redistributing land to the former slaves.

Talk of redistributing land to the freedpeople continued throughout 1865 and the early years of Reconstruction. The phrase "forty acres and a mule" reflected the common belief that these were the basic requirements for a prosperous farm. Alas, the debates over whether to redistribute land would soon die down without a permanent grant. The decision not to redistribute land

and wealth to newly freed African Americans would prove one of the cruelest legacies of postwar Reconstruction.

The end of slavery would transform the South, though it would take decades for the long-term effects of emancipation and the reconstruction of the southern economy to play out. Historian John Majewski has argued that white southerners had envisioned an economically independent Confederacy that would promote industry alongside agriculture. The reality of the war dashed these dreams. No longer would the region rely so heavily on cotton. The running away of slave property during and after the war, and the widespread destruction southern cities and towns suffered during various campaigns, would decimate the region's infrastructure and economy. A gradual recovery of the southern economy and society began in the 1870s and picked up steam in the 1880s. But considering the advances made in southern urbanization and industrialization in the 1840s and 1850s, the war set the region back several decades. Suffering from the humiliation of defeat, the destruction of their dreams for a new independent southern nation, and waylaid by an economy in tatters, white southerners returned to old appeals to racism and violence. There were many white southerners, especially those who joined the region's new Republican Party, who spoke out against racial violence perpetrated by groups such as the Ku Klux Klan. But many other white southerners either participated in or turned a blind eye to the new reign of terror that beset African Americans after the end of slavery.

Please visit the companion website www.routledge.com/cw/wells for additional study aids including chapter overviews, interactive quizzes, and more.

COMPANION @ WEBSITE

Discussion Questions

- What were the key obstacles still standing in the way of Union victory as 1865 began?
- How did the Thirteenth Amendment forever change the meaning of freedom in America?
- What issues regarding black freedom were left unresolved even after slavery was abolished?
- After years of fighting, Lee and Grant seem to have been cordial, almost friendly to each other at Appomattox. What accounts for this mutual respect? Is there something about the

nature of war that accounts for the behavior of Union and Confederate officers and soldiers after Lee's surrender?

- The possibility of taking land and wealth from one group and giving to another, less economically advantaged group has always been troubling for Americans. What were the arguments for and against the redistribution of land to African Americans after the Civil War? In what ways would black freedom have looked different if the proposals for "forty acres and a mule" had been fulfilled?
- Radical Republicans were critical of the way in which Grant, Chamberlain, and other leaders handled Lee's surrender at Appomattox. Why were Republicans upset?
- Conduct basic research into the Union and Confederate economies during the war. What caused Confederate currency to become worthless by the end of the war? What is inflation and how does it affect an economy?
- It is widely known that most African Americans in the South were illiterate and so they left behind relatively few written sources indicating their reaction to emancipation. What sources might historians use therefore to understand the freedpeople's reaction to emancipation?

Notes

1 Hutson quoted in Robert E. Bonner, *The Soldier's Pen: Firsthand Impressions of the Civil War* (New York: Hill & Wang, 2006), 183.

2 Hill quoted in Richard Wheeler, *Voices of the Civil War* (New York: Thomas Y. Crowell Co., 1976), 456–457.

3 Mark Swanson, *Atlas of the Civil War Month by Month* (Athens: University of Georgia Press, 2004), 104.

Further Reading

Terry Alford, *Fortune's Fool: The Life of John Wilkes Booth* (New York: Oxford University Press, 2015).

Michael B. Ballard, *A Long Shadow: Jefferson Davis and the Final Days of the Confederacy* (Jackson: University Press of Mississippi, 1986).

Robin Blackburn, *The American Crucible: Slavery, Emancipation and Human Rights* (New York: Verso, 2010).

Dennis K. Boman, *Lincoln and Citizens' Rights in Civil War Missouri* (Baton Rouge: Louisiana State University Press, 2010).

William J. Cooper, *Jefferson Davis, American* (New York: Knopf, 2000).

William C. Davis, *An Honorable Defeat: The Last Days of the Confederate Government* (New York: Houghton Mifflin, 2001).
Seymour Drescher, *Abolition: A History of Slavery and Antislavery* (Cambridge: Cambridge University Press, 2009).
Daniel A. Farber, *Lincoln's Constitution* (Chicago,: University of Chicago Press, 2003).
Eric Foner, *The Fiery Trial: Abraham Lincoln and American Slavery* (New York: W.W. Norton & Co., 2010).
Daniel L. Fountain, *Slavery, Civil War, and Salvation: African American Slaves and Christianity, 1830–1870* (Baton Rouge: Louisiana State University Press, 2010).
Joseph Glatthaar, *General Lee's Army: From Victory to Collapse* (New York: Free Press, 2008).
A. Wilson Greene, *The Final Battles of the Petersburg Campaign: Breaking the Backbone of the Rebellion* (Knoxville: University of Tennessee Press, 2008).
Janette Thomas Greenwood, *First Fruits of Freedom: The Migration of Former Slaves and Their Search for Equality in Worcester, Massachusetts, 1862–1900* (Chapel Hill: University of North Carolina Press, 2010).
Martha Hodes, *Mourning Lincoln* (New Haven: Yale University Press, 2015).
Harold Holzer, ed., *Lincoln and Freedom: Slavery, Emancipation, and the Thirteenth Amendment* (Carbondale: Southern Illinois University Press, 2007).
Michael W. Kauffman, *American Brutus: John Wilkes Booth and the Lincoln Conspiracies* (New York: Random House, 2004).
Kate Clifford Larson, *The Assassin's Accomplice: Mary Surratt and the Plot to Kill Abraham Lincoln* (New York: Basic Books, 2008).
Bruce Levine, *Confederate Emancipation: Southern Plans to Free and Arm Slaves during the Civil War* (New York: Oxford University Press, 2006).
Bruce Levine, *The Fall of the House of Dixie: The Civil War and the Social Revolution That Transformed the South* (New York: Random House, 2013).
John Majewski, *Modernizing a Slave Economy: The Economic Vision of the Confederate Nation* (Chapel Hill: University of North Carolina Press, 2009).
William Marvel, *Lee's Last Retreat: The Flight to Appomattox* (Chapel Hill: University of North Carolina Press, 2002).
Kate Masur, *An Example for All the Land: Emancipation and the Struggle over Equality in Washington, D.C.* (Chapel Hill: University of North Carolina Press, 2010).
James McPherson, *Battle Cry of Freedom: The Civil War Era* (New York: Oxford University Press, 1988).
Alexander Mendoza, *Confederate Struggle for Command: General James Longstreet* (College Station: Texas A&M University Press, 2008).

Clarence L. Mohr, *On the Threshold of Freedom: Masters and Slaves in Civil War Georgia* (Athens: University of Georgia Press, 1986).

Edward Steers, Jr., *Blood on the Moon: The Assassination of Abraham Lincoln* (Lexington: University Press of Kentucky, 2001).

James L. Swanson, *Manhunt: The 12-Day Chase for Lincoln's Killer* (New York: William Morrow, 2006).

James L. Swanson, *Bloody Crimes: The Chase for Jefferson Davis and the Death Pageant for Lincoln's Corpse* (New York: William Morrow, 2010).

Hans Louis Trefousse, *Thaddeus Stevens: Nineteenth Century Egalitarian* (Chapel Hill: University of North Carolina Press, 1997).

Noah Andre Trudeau, *Out of the Storm: The End of the Civil War, April–June 1865* (Boston: Little Brown & Co., 1994).

Alexander Tsesis, *The Thirteenth Amendment and American Freedom: A Legal History* (New York: New York University Press, 2004).

Alexander Tsesis, *The Promises of Liberty: The History and Contemporary Relevance of the Thirteenth Amendment* (New York: Columbia University Press, 2010).

Elizabeth R. Varon, *Appomattox: Victory, Defeat, and Freedom at the End of the Civil War* (New York: Oxford University Press, 2013).

Michael Vorenberg, *Final Freedom: The Civil War, the Abolition of Slavery, and the Thirteenth Amendment* (Cambridge: Cambridge University Press, 2001).

Jay Winik, *April 1865: The Month that Saved America* (New York: HarperCollins, 2001).

Joshua Zeitz, *Lincoln's Boys: John Hay, John Nicolay, and the War for Lincoln's Image* (New York: Viking, 2014).

RECONSTRUCTION BEGINS

Topics Covered in this Chapter:

- African Americans and the Freedmen's Bureau After the War
- Andrew Johnson and Presidential Reconstruction
- Politics and Elections
- Congressional Reconstruction, 1866–1872
- Johnson's Impeachment
- White Southern Retrenchment

11

Introduction

The end of the Civil War settled key questions that had been vexing the nation since its inception. Slavery, an American institution since the earliest days of Virginia's Jamestown colony, would no longer be permitted. Although the effects of bondage would last for generations, and though the end of slavery did not mean the end of racism or the establishment of racial equality in either the North or the South, the Thirteenth Amendment to the Constitution ensured that slavery could no longer haunt the Republic. Yet the end of the war also meant that four million freedpeople now needed protection, food, shelter, education, and work. Much of Reconstruction, the period between 1865 and 1877, would be devoted to assessing and trying to meet the needs of the newly freed African Americans. The Freedmen's Bureau, the American Missionary Association, and thousands of northern "carpetbaggers" (a derisive term southern whites used for northerners who moved to the South) worked hard to provide for the freedpeople. Formerly enslaved men and women also worked tirelessly to take action themselves. Thousands of African Americans across the South joined mutual aid societies, established schools, and formed organizations of all kinds to ease the transition to freedom.

But the need was great, and so was white southern resentment at northern interference in their region, although many white southerners saw the end of the war as the chance to remake the South. Thousands of white southerners joined the Republican Party and tried to work toward a New South without slavery; and for a time it appeared that southern Republicans, both white and black, might indeed be able to put the region on a different path, one that was not free of racism or social injustice but perhaps a New South that would move in the direction of a more progressive economy and society. It was not to be. Just as congressional Republicans determined to remake the South, so too did white southern political leaders dig in their heels to keep the region under white control. So while the war ended long-standing debates about the legitimacy of slavery, profound questions and issues remained: What role would the millions of former slaves play in a reconstructed Union? Would blacks and whites be able to live and work peacefully in the same nation? How much would racism undermine the progress of freedpeople? Would the former slaves be able to vote and enjoy the full civil rights of white citizens?

The end of the Civil War also settled the issue of secession. No longer could southerners claim with any credibility the right to withdraw from the Union, though reactionary southerners would continue to make such claims well into the twentieth century. At the end of the war, all the former Confederate states had to rescind their secession ordinances to be readmitted into the Union. Still, the debate over state power versus federal authority did not calm down after the war; in fact, the corridors of power in Washington struggled not only with how much authority the federal government should exercise in protecting the civil rights of former slaves, but Washington itself was deeply divided between the president and Congress. Although the Fourteenth Amendment provided a definition of citizenship that embraced African Americans, the controversy over state and federal government powers persisted into the late nineteenth century and continued to occupy the nation throughout the twentieth century.

So Reconstruction was a crucial period in the nation's history because of the new questions that arose after the war. Slavery and secession were dead forever. But the shape the newly reestablished Union would take was far from settled by 1877. Americans fought over competing and even contradictory visions of the nation's future.

At the outset of Reconstruction, though, few knew what to expect. The nation had ventured deep into unchartered territory. Since the Founding Fathers had not anticipated secession, there was no clear plan for rebuilding the Union. How exactly does a country so horrifically divided for four long and deadly years reconstitute itself? Should Congress or the president play the leading role in formulating policy? Would former Confederates be permitted to rejoin the United States? If so, what limitations if any should be placed on their rights? Should they be punished for rebelling against the Union? What should be done to help the former slaves find work and shelter? Who would protect them against vengeful whites? Throughout the years after the war the nation wrestled with these weighty questions.

African Americans and the Freedmen's Bureau After the War

Throughout the war enslaved people ran away from their masters in the hope of finding freedom and protection behind Union lines. As we have seen, Union leaders reacted to fleeing slaves with a range of policies, from treating them as fugitives from justice to welcoming runaways as newly emancipated. With the end of the fighting, however, their status as free men and women was settled. In late 1865 and throughout 1866 the central concern became how to provide basic necessities for the former slaves.

The Bureau of Refugees, Freedmen, and Abandoned Lands, known as the Freedmen's Bureau, was authorized by President Lincoln in March 1865 to help provide housing, food, education, and advice on work contracts formed with former masters. Initially Lincoln intended the agency to last for one year, and in early 1866 President Johnson tried to end the bureau, but with the help of Republicans in Congress the Freedmen's Bureau endured until 1872. Although the bureau failed to provide freedpeople with the one thing they needed most—land and a means to farm for themselves —the agency succeeded in educating tens of thousands of former slaves. In fact, the South today still bears the marks of the bureau in the form of predominantly black institutions of higher education (HBCUs) that dot the region, including Johnson C. Smith University in Charlotte, North Carolina and Fisk University in Nashville, Tennessee.

Part of the Department of War, the Freedmen's Bureau was headed by Union General Oliver O. Howard, a career army officer born in Maine. After graduating from the U.S. Military Academy in 1854, Howard, an avid Christian, considered joining the ministry. But with the beginning of the Civil War Howard decided to help put down the southern rebellion and saw considerable action during the fighting, including the amputation of his right arm in the summer of 1862.

For a time, Howard's leadership came under significant criticism. At the Battle of Chancellorsville in May 1863, Stonewall Jackson's forces heavily damaged Howard's XI Corps. At the Battle of Gettysburg in July of the same year, Howard's XI Corps once again fared poorly in the face of attacks by Confederate Lt. General Richard S. Ewell. Howard's forces, sent to the Western Theater of the war after Gettysburg, acquitted themselves much better for the duration of the fighting, and even fought alongside Sherman in the March to the Sea. The "Christian General," as Howard became

308
HARPER'S WEEKLY.
[May 19, 1866.
A.R.W.
"MUSTERED OUT" COLORED VOLUNTEERS AT LITTLE ROCK, ARKANSAS.

FIGURE 11.1 *"Mustered out" volunteers at Little Rock, Arkansas / A.R.W. Library of Congress, LC-USZ62-138382*

known, ended the war with his reputation intact, a standing that led to his appointment as commissioner of the Freedmen's Bureau in May 1865.

Union leaders recognized the bureau's importance in helping former slaves make the transition to freedom. After the war, African Americans roamed the South in search of work, shelter, and lost loved ones. For decades under slavery, families were split by sale and by masters moving to lands in the southwestern states. Spouses, children, parents, and siblings desperately sought the whereabouts of family members. Some walked or boarded trains; others with the help of Freedmen's Bureau agents wrote letters to ascertain the status of loved ones. Historian Heather Andrea Williams discovered that the heart-rending search for family members after the Civil War gave lie to the masters' claims that they were the paternalistic heads of black families. In fact, the search for separated family members testified to the strong family ties of the formerly enslaved.

In addition to helping freedpeople find loved ones, the bureau tried to enforce fair contracts between African Americans and white farmers. As Leon Litwack, Eric Foner, Jacqueline Jones, Tera Hunter, and other scholars of Reconstruction have pointed out, one of the key questions immediately after the war was how the devastated southern economy would adapt to emancipation. Former slave owners would no doubt seek to take full advantage of the freedpeople's illiteracy and inexperience in formulating free labor contracts. Some white farmers did make honest attempts to reemploy former slaves on legitimate terms; others tried to reestablish slavery under a new name. Freedmen's Bureau agents provided legal advice and even brought cases of injustice to courts. Other agents, motivated by racism, appeared less kind, and were as determined to force former slaves into agricultural work as were southern whites. But on the whole the bureau helped thousands of former bondspeople obtain fairer labor contracts.

The bureau provided other help as well. Agents distributed millions of food rations and established medical clinics. The most significant achievement of the agency, however, came in education. As we have seen, teaching enslaved African Americans to read and write was illegal in many southern states before and during the war. The monumental task of educating the freedpeople, beginning with providing basic literacy, began under the bureau's leadership. Along with the American Missionary Association and thousands of northerners who came South to teach the former slaves, the Freedmen's Bureau helped raise the literacy rate of African Americans from less than 10% at the end of the war to a majority by 1900. More than a thousand schools for freedmen had been established by the 1870s, and former slaves flocked to them. Young children sat alongside elderly blacks and together they learned to read and write for the first time. The Freedmen's Bureau even wrote its own textbook to be used in its schools. Congress chipped in with millions of dollars to fund teachers' pay, new buildings, and school supplies.

As important as the Freedmen's Bureau was to educating the former slaves, African Americans did not by any means rely solely on governmental help. On the contrary, ex-slaves quickly established a rich and lively culture in which they could build the community, religious, and family bonds officially denied them under slavery. Associations and organizations of all kinds, from fraternal and mutual aid societies to church congregations, flourished. As historian Bettye Collier-Thomas has argued, the African Methodist Episcopal (AME) and African Methodist Episcopal Zion churches would prove powerful community and religious institutions, as well as springboards for generations of black leaders, including women. These African American associations were central to easing the transition from slavery to freedom. In mutual aid and farmers' groups, black families pooled their resources to buy seed and farming equipment. Lodges and fraternal organizations helped families pay for food in tough times, helped defray the costs of funerals, and aided widows and their children. They established schools by the hundreds to educate the new generation of freedpeople, and provided legal defense for those accused of crimes. And they provided a sense of unity and community in the face of economic and social turmoil.

The Union Leagues, funded in large part by Radical Republican leaders in Congress, were among the most important new groups in the postwar era. As historian Steven Hahn argues in his important work *A Nation under Our Feet*, African Americans in rural areas engaged in politics, often through organizations such as the Union League. Started in 1862, the league promoted loyalty to the Union and Lincoln's policies (hence the fact that they were also called Loyalty Leagues). African Americans joined the Union League in significant numbers after the Civil War and helped to spread support for Republican policies in the South. In fact, as Michael W. Fitzgerald found in his valuable study of the Union Leagues of the Deep South, members often met in secret for fear of reprisals from white Democrats. In addition to providing African Americans with a vital political forum, the leagues also fought for economic and social justice; in states such as Alabama and Mississippi, Fitzgerald shows, Union Leagues used labor strikes and boycotts to thwart white planter domination of black farmers. Part political forum, part agrarian uprising, the Union League movement helped the freedpeople negotiate the new economic and social relations of the South.[1]

Black workers also formed unions to help secure better wages and working conditions. Historian Tera Hunter proved in *To 'Joy My Freedom* that African Americans in Reconstruction-era Atlanta joined workers' unions to combat white racism. Former slaves flocked to southern towns and cities, where men found work as carpenters, bricklayers, masons, and similar jobs and where women engaged in domestic service as washerwomen, nurses, maids, and cooks. Cities also provided venues for a range of leisure activities, from dancing and singing to sports. Urban former slaves, however, could not escape racist attempts to control them. Despite the promise of freedom, African Americans would find the postwar South a violent and often unwelcoming place. And they knew that they could not rely on President Andrew Johnson for protection or aid.

Andrew Johnson and Presidential Reconstruction

For most of 1865 and the first part of 1866, President Andrew Johnson guided national policies regarding Reconstruction. Johnson was something of a puzzle for American voters. Born in North Carolina in 1808 to a poor family, Johnson escaped from an apprenticeship at a young age and made his way to Tennessee, where he became a tailor. He gradually climbed the rungs of the political ladder, from the state legislature to governor and then to the U.S. Senate as a Democrat. For much of his life, Johnson expressed disdain for the rich and powerful, sentiments that led him to denounce calls for secession before the Civil War. Johnson was so suspicious of elite whites that he remained loyal to the Union even after Tennessee seceded in 1861, the only prominent white southern federal office holder to remain convinced throughout the war that secession was treason. In response to claims that he favored African Americans, Johnson is supposed to have replied, "damn the negroes; I am fighting those traitorous aristocrats, their masters."

Lincoln rewarded Johnson for his loyalty to the Union by placing him on the ticket as a vice presidential candidate in 1864 even though Johnson was well known to run in Democratic circles. Per the Constitution, Johnson assumed the presidency upon Lincoln's assassination (Johnson had no vice president while he served as chief executive from 1865 to 1869). Although in wartime it is common for presidents to reach out to members of the opposing party, Republicans were suspicious of Johnson the day he assumed office. His Reconstruction policies infuriated Republicans, leading to a rift that culminated in Johnson's impeachment.

While Lincoln had recommended a conciliatory approach to a defeated and humiliated South, Johnson's policies in the eyes of Republicans let white southerners off the hook too easily. At first, Johnson stipulated that former Confederates merely had to take an oath of allegiance to the United States to regain citizenship; wealthier and more prominent Confederate military and political leaders would have to apply to the president directly for a pardon. Former rebellious states had to ratify the Thirteenth Amendment ending slavery, but Johnson allowed these states to hold elections at the end of 1865, races that many former rebels and Confederates won. Republicans, especially radical leaders such as Charles Sumner of Massachusetts, recoiled at the thought of governing side-by-side with the same leaders that had led the nation into four years of war.

Radical Republicans fumed that Johnson was permitting the South to reestablish systems of racial control that Union soldiers had fought to dismantle. In the months after the war ended, southern states had begun replacing slave codes with black codes. These new laws limited the rights of former slaves, established systems of segregation that would become the hallmark of the new Jim Crow South, and sought ways to control black freedom to work and live. Black codes placed unemployed ex-slaves into an apprentice system, provided penalties for vagrancy, and circumscribed blacks' freedom to travel. As the 1866 Penal Code of Alabama stated:

SEC. 2. Be it further enacted, That the following persons are vagrants in addition to those already declared to be vagrants by law, or that may be hereafter be so declared by law; a stubborn or refractory servant; a laborer or servant who loiters away his time, or refuses to comply with any contract for a term of service without just cause; any such person may be sent to the house of correction in the county in which such offense is committed; and for want of such house of correction the common jail of the county may be used for that purpose.

SEC. 3. Be it further enacted, That when a vagrant is found, any justice of the peace of the county, must upon complain made upon oath, or on his own knowledge, issue his warrant to the sheriff or any constable of the county, to bring such a person to him; and if, upon examination and hearing of testimony, it appears to the justice, that such person is a vagrant, he shall assess a fine of fifty dollars and costs against such vagrant; and in default of payment, he must commit such vagrant to the house of correction . . .

SEC. 4. Be it further enacted, That if any apprentice shall leave the employment of his or her master or mistress without his or her consent, said master or mistress may pursue and recapture said apprentice and bring him or her before any justice of the peace of the county, whose duty it shall be to remand said apprentice to the service of his or her master or mistress; and in the event of a refusal on the part of said

apprentice so to return, the said justice shall commit said apprentice to the jail of said county on failure to give bond until the next term of the probate court, and it shall be the duty of said court, at the first term thereafter, to investigate said case, and if the court shall be of opinion that said apprentice left the employment of his or her master or mistress without good case, to order him or her to receive such punishment as may be provided by the vagrant laws which may be then in force in this State, until he or she shall agree to return to his or her master or Mistress.

The black codes and the southern elections in late 1865 convinced Radical Republicans in Congress that white southerners had little intention of remaking the racial politics of the region. The rise of white resistance to even the most benign Reconstruction policies convinced congressional Republicans even more strongly that they would have to wrest control of Reconstruction from President Johnson and from the white former Confederates once again holding political office throughout the South.

Politics and Elections

The congressional elections in 1866 provided the venue for Radical Republicans to make their case to the northern electorate that Johnson was too lenient on the South. Democrats charged that Republicans were overreaching. The Civil Rights Act of 1866, Democrats claimed, was just one outcome of Republican ideals. Illinois Republican Senator Lyman Trumbull was an early sponsor of the bill. By 1866, Trumbull had already built a reputation for advocating measures to aid the former slaves. He helped draft the Thirteenth Amendment and became a leader in the Republican caucus in Congress, leadership that brought him into conflict with President Johnson. In an April 1866 speech before the Senate, Trumbull criticized the president for threatening to veto civil rights bills passed by Congress. If we cannot secure the civil rights of ex-slaves, Trumbull argued, then emancipation would be nothing more than "a cheat and a delusion." Trumbull's criticisms of the president, along with angry words from other Republicans, made clear that the relationship between Congress and the executive branch was deteriorating badly with each passing month.

Despite President Johnson's opposition, the Civil Rights Bill was passed by Congress in April 1866, the first time Congress had overridden a presidential veto on a major piece of legislation. The law overruled the Supreme Court decision in the Dred Scott case, which in 1857 had claimed that African Americans could not be citizens under the Constitution. The Civil Rights Act of 1866 left no doubt that the freedpeople were American citizens:

That all persons born in the United States and not subject to any foreign power, excluding Indians not taxed, are hereby declared to be citizens of the United States; and such citizens, of every race and color, without regard to any previous condition of slavery or involuntary servitude, except as a punishment for crime whereof the party shall have been duly convicted, shall have the same right, in every State and Territory in the United States, to make and enforce contracts, to sue, be parties, and give evidence, to inherit, purchase, lease, sell, hold, and convey real and personal property, and to full and equal benefit of all laws and proceedings for the security of person and property, as is enjoyed by white citizens, and shall be subject to like punishment, pains, and penalties, and to none other, any law, statute, ordinance, regulation, or custom, to the contrary notwithstanding.

Worried that a future Supreme Court decision might overturn the law, Republicans pushed for a new Constitutional Amendment to ensure that the federal government recognized black citizenship, and all the rights that citizenship included. The Fourteenth Amendment would prove vitally important to all Americans, but especially to the former slaves.

The most significant features of the new amendment, adopted in July 1868, were the Citizenship Clause, the Due Process Clause, and the Equal Protection Clause. The three clauses soon fell under legal debate and led to numerous Supreme Court cases heard over the coming decades. The citizenship clause was eventually interpreted to mean that all persons (excluding Native Americans) born in the United States were citizens. Again, this clause directly countered the Supreme Court's ruling in the Dred Scott case, which had stipulated that blacks could not be considered citizens under the law. The Due Process Clause, intended to protect former slaves and their property rights, was instead employed to protect corporations from government regulation. In cases such as *Lochner v. New York* (1905) and *Adkins v. Children's Hospital* (1923) judges used the Due Process Clause to thwart laws designed to help workers. Similarly, the Equal Protection Clause had been put forth to defend the rights of African Americans, but in the late nineteenth and early twentieth centuries, conservative judges used the clause to impart their own particular ideological interpretations on society. The Supreme Court's infamous *Plessy v. Ferguson* (1896) ruling, which established the "separate but equal" doctrine, became the legal basis for racial segregation. While courts in the late 1800s and early 1900s would distort the original intent of the Fourteenth Amendment, Democrats charged that protection for black civil liberties would lead to an unnatural social equality between the races.

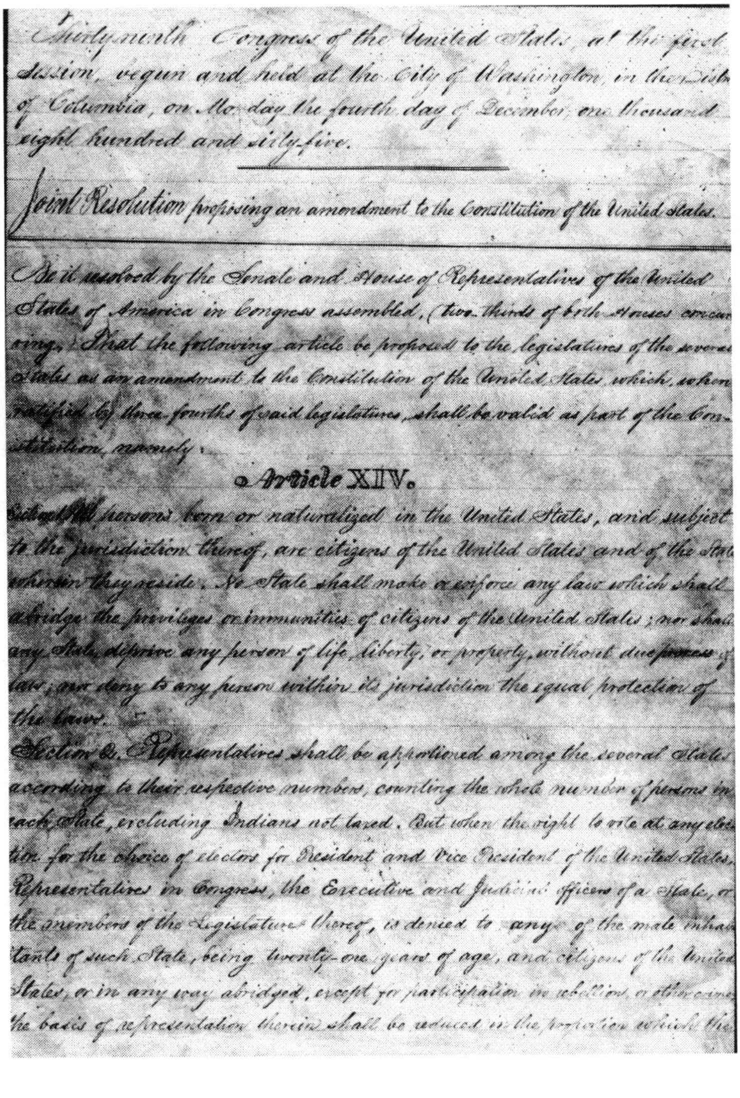
Thirty-ninth Congress of the United States, at the first session, begun and held at the City of Washington, in the District of Columbia, on Monday the fourth day of December, one thousand eight hundred and sixty-five.

Joint Resolution proposing an amendment to the Constitution of the United States.

Be it resolved by the Senate and House of Representatives of the United States of America in Congress assembled, (two thirds of both Houses concurring,) That the following article be proposed to the legislatures of the several States as an amendment to the Constitution of the United States, which, when ratified by three fourths of said legislatures, shall be valid as part of the Constitution, namely:

Article XIV.

Section 1. All persons born or naturalized in the United States, and subject to the jurisdiction thereof, are citizens of the United States and of the State wherein they reside. No State shall make or enforce any law which shall abridge the privileges or immunities of citizens of the United States; nor shall any State deprive any person of life, liberty, or property, without due process of law; nor deny to any person within its jurisdiction the equal protection of the laws.

Section 2. Representatives shall be apportioned among the several States according to their respective numbers, counting the whole number of persons in each State, excluding Indians not taxed. But when the right to vote at any election for the choice of electors for President and Vice President of the United States, Representatives in Congress, the Executive and Judicial officers of a State, or the members of the Legislature thereof, is denied to any of the male inhabitants of such State, being twenty-one years of age, and citizens of the United States, or in any way abridged, except for participation in rebellion, or other crime, the basis of representation therein shall be reduced in the proportion which the

FIGURE 11.2 *Draft of the 14th Amendment to the United States' Constitution. Getty Images*

Democratic candidates for office spoke out against miscegenation, or the biological mixing of the races, to heighten white fears of black sexuality. Democrats made special appeals to working- and lower-class whites, targeting ethnic groups such as the Irish and Germans, to convince them that racial equality would mean blacks competing with whites for jobs. In some cases the appeals failed; Germans in St. Louis and other cities tended to side with the Republicans. But in local and national elections Democratic candidates rarely missed an opportunity to argue that Republican rule meant the social and political equality of the races.

Republicans shot back with equal venom against Democratic claims. Republican Thaddeus Stevens, weary of Democratic charges against his party, grew angry at President Johnson and the Democrats. On the house floor, Stevens declared:

What is negro equality, about which so much is said by knaves, and some of which is believed by men who are not fools? It means, as understood by honest Republicans, just this much, and no more: every man, no matter what his race or color; every earthly being who has an immortal soul, has an equal right to justice, honesty, and fair play with every other man; and the law should secure him those rights.

As Stevens's comments show, much of the debate over Reconstruction focused on the rights of the freedmen and freedwomen. Perhaps most importantly in the eyes of Radical Republicans, the former slaves needed the right to vote.

The issue of black suffrage divided the nation. Democrats and their adherents, including President Johnson, declared that providing blacks with the right to vote drew the South closer to "negro equality" and white subordination. Moderate Republicans worried that supporting black suffrage would leave them open to Democratic attacks of favoring African Americans at the expense of whites. Radical Republicans argued that without granting suffrage to ex-slaves, emancipation would hold little meaning; using the ballot box southern whites would quickly reestablish racial control.

African Americans knew the importance of the right to vote, and they argued vigorously for suffrage. In South Carolina, for example, African Americans gathered soon after the war ended to make their wishes known. In a memorial to Congress, black South

Carolinians thanked the Freedmen's Bureau for its aid, called for a system of public education, and asked for government protection. But as these formerly enslaved knew, the fruits of liberty required suffrage. As their memorial argued:

> **We ask that equal suffrage be conferred upon us, in common with the white men of this state . . . because "all free governments derive their just powers from the consent of the governed"; and we are largely in the majority in this State, bearing for a long period the burden of onerous taxation, without a just representation. We ask for equal suffrage as a protection for the hostility evoked by our known faithfulness to our country and flag under all circumstances.**

Suffrage was central to the claims of African Americans and Radical Republicans, but the issue was so controversial that protection for the right to vote would have to wait until the Fifteenth Amendment was ratified several years later.

Democrats and Republicans battled intensely during the congressional campaigns of the summer and fall of 1866. President Johnson, officially unaffiliated with either party but clearly favoring the Democrats, traveled throughout the country in a speaking tour known as the "Swing Around the Circle." Although Johnson was known as a solid debater, he was constantly heckled during his speeches by audience members. He broke from his speeches to answer the hecklers, and in general his remarks in favor of a quick reuniting of the nation did not go over well. Although the president had been viewed as a southern moderate, which was why Lincoln ran with him on the 1864 ticket, Johnson's position on racial segregation had hardened in the 1860s. By 1866 Johnson worried like other Democrats that whites were losing the racial control they had long enjoyed. He railed against proponents of racial equality and spoke out strongly against black suffrage.

Despite Johnson's persistence, the Republicans had a significant advantage: most of the former Confederate states were prohibited from voting, while events before the fall elections convinced many voters that the white South remained staunchly opposed to change. A series of riots across the South in May and June laid bare the racial tensions of the postwar South, and urban areas experienced some of the worst manifestations of these tensions. While enslaved and even free African Americans had worked and lived in southern cities before the war, in the years following the war's conclusion, African Americans, looking for work and protection from rural paramilitary groups such as the Klan, moved to cities in large numbers. The unsettled economy and the new social relations meant that southern cities were primed for explosion. And explode they did. In early May, Memphis, a city that saw its black population increase from a few thousand in 1860 to about 20,000 just five years later, erupted in a race riot. Tensions ran high between the city's overwhelmingly white Irish police force and African Americans—especially black Union Army soldiers. After three days of fighting, prompted at first by an attempt by the police to arrest former black soldiers, nearly fifty people were killed, forty-six of them African American. A few months later, at the end of July, New Orleans experienced a similar but bloodier riot in which almost 250 people were killed. White and black Republicans, angry that white Democrats remained stubbornly committed to harsh racial policies, met in a convention at Mechanics' Hall. A large mob of angry whites confronted the conventioneers and in the ensuing mêlée many of the Republicans were killed.

Race riots such as those in Memphis, Nashville, New Orleans, and other cities indicated to many northern voters that the postwar South remained unreconstructed. Calling for more stringent measures to control racism and violence, the Radical Republicans stood to gain in the fall elections. And when the results of the 1866 congressional elections came in, the Republicans had won in a landslide, more than the two-thirds majority needed to override a presidential veto. The Republicans captured more than 77% of the seats in the House of Representatives (173 seats), while the Democrats held just 21% (43 seats).

The Radical Republicans were clearly in the driver's seat now, and they would move quickly to remake completely national Reconstruction policies. The radical faction of the party had a history of pushing for social justice before and during the war. In the 1850s party radicals had advocated the immediate end to slavery and during the war the same activists pushed Lincoln in the direction of racial equality and total victory against the Confederacy. When northern politicians had called for ending the war and making peace with the South, the Radical Republicans had stood firm for unconditional surrender. When Lincoln promoted more lenient policies toward a defeated South, such as his Ten Percent Plan, which he proposed in December 1863 and would have readmitted former Confederate states when 10% of the voting population took an oath of allegiance to the United

States, the radicals rallied around more stringent measures such as the Wade–Davis Bill. The latter bill, passed in Congress in July 1864 but vetoed by President Lincoln, would have allowed former Confederate states back into the United States only when a majority (as opposed to merely 10%) of the voting population pledged their allegiance to the Union. In addition, voters had to swear that they had not supported the Confederacy, a stipulation that became known as "the ironclad oath." Lincoln, not wishing to be bound by any specific plan for reconstituting the Union, never signed the bill. Although the Wade–Davis Bill failed, it signaled that many Republicans wanted a tougher line against the South.

Now that the war was over and the 1866 elections had swung heavily in their favor, the radicals were ready to take a central role in Reconstruction, led by Charles Sumner in the Senate and Thaddeus Stevens in the House. Hated in the South and a hero among Radical Republicans, Sumner could point to a long history

FIGURE 11.3A *Charles Sumner. Library of Congress, IC-DIG-pga-00048*

FIGURE 11.3B *Thaddeus Stevens. Library of Congress, LC-DIG-pga-04115*

of advocacy on behalf of African Americans. As a senator from Massachusetts, he spoke out vigorously against the Fugitive Slave Act of 1850 and his repeated denunciations of slavery led to a beating on the Senate floor in 1856. Egotistical and a merciless debater, Sumner did not always have the respect or affection of his Senate colleagues, but few Americans in the mid-nineteenth century fought as hard for the principles enshrined in the Declaration of Independence. In one Senate debate during Reconstruction, Sumner even advocated the desegregation of public spaces:

The Senator makes a mistake which has been made for a generation in this Chamber, confounding what belongs to society with what belongs to rights. There is no question of society. The Senator may choose his associates as he pleases. They may be white or black,

or between the two. That is simply a social question, and nobody would interfere with it. The taste which the Senator announces he will have free liberty to exercise, selecting always his companions; but when it comes to rights, there the Senator must obey the law and I insist that by the law of the land all persons without distinction of color shall be equal in rights. Show me, therefore, a legal institution, anything created or regulated by law, and I show you what must be opened equally to all without distinction of color. Notoriously, the hotel is a legal institution, originally established by the common law, subject to minute provisions and regulations; notoriously, public conveyances are common carriers subject to a law of their own; notoriously, schools are public institutions created and maintained by law; and now I simply insist that in any of these institutions there shall be no exclusion on account of color.

Sumner was ahead of many of his radical Republican colleagues in making such claims, but in general his fellow radicals agreed that equality, especially the right to vote, should be enjoyed regardless of race.

While Sumner rallied the radicals in the Senate, Pennsylvania's Thaddeus Stevens was a powerful radical voice in the House. Although Stevens died in 1868 and so did not live to see the end of Reconstruction, he nonetheless played an important role in formulating policies after his party's gains in the 1866 elections. Soon after the elections, as North Carolina Republican William W. Holden later recalled, Stevens revealed the early stages of his new plan for reconstructing the South, that:

It would be best for the South to remain ten years longer under military rule, and that during this time we would have territorial governors, with territorial legislatures, and the government at Washington would pay our general expenses as territories, and educate our children, white and colored both.[2]

Stevens's plan would culminate in the high watermark for Congressional Reconstruction: the Military Reconstruction Acts of 1867.

Congressional Reconstruction, 1866–1872

Radical Republicans were determined to use their dramatic gains in the 1866 elections to overhaul Reconstruction. Johnson was stripped of most of his power to shape policy; he would veto more than twenty bills passed by Congress and the Republicans overrode his veto almost every time. Much to the dismay of the white South, activists such as Sumner and Stevens were now formulating policies regarding the readmission of rebellious states into the Union, the treatment of former slaves, and the status of former Confederates. Known as "Radical Reconstruction" or "Congressional Reconstruction," the period between 1866 and the early 1870s placed new burdens on the white South.

One of the first acts of the Republican-dominated Congress in 1867 was to fulfill Thaddeus Stevens's call to send military forces back into southern communities to enforce black civil rights. The Military Reconstruction Acts in many ways marked the high point of Radical Republican attempts to remake the South. Congress divided the former Confederate states (except Tennessee, which had already been readmitted into the Union) into five districts, each with a general acting as provisional governor to oversee the protection of black civil rights. About 20,000 troops were sent to these military districts and, between March 1867 and March 1868, Congress refined the acts to provide paths for readmission into the Union. Under the authority of the U.S. Army, the former rebellious states had to rewrite their constitutions and permit people of color to vote. Along with these stipulations, many ex-Confederates were prohibited from voting. Under military reconstruction African Americans voted and held office in unprecedented numbers.

Protecting the right of African Americans to vote became a central concern for Radical Republicans in the late 1860s, as white supremacist groups tried to intimidate former slaves and prevent them from voting. First proposed in Congress in February 1869 and then ratified by the required three-quarters of the states in early 1870, the Fifteenth Amendment was brief but important:

Section 1. The right of citizens of the United States to vote shall not be denied or abridged by the United States or by any State on account of race, color, or previous condition of servitude.

Section 2. The Congress shall have power to enforce this article by appropriate legislation.

The amendment did not grant universal suffrage. States still retained the power to place requirements on voting. In the late nineteenth and early twentieth centuries, southern states would use this loophole to limit the ability of African Americans and even many whites to vote. The poll tax required voters to pay a fee, which many poor black and white southerners were unable or unwilling to pay. Other states passed literacy tests that excluded blacks and whites who could not read or write, while state and local governments devised other tests to ensure only middle- and upper-class whites could vote. By the turn of the twentieth century tens of thousands of lower-class blacks and whites had been disfranchised throughout the South.

Despite the limitations of the Fifteenth Amendment, it was a significant addition to the Constitution. Together with the Thirteenth and Fourteenth Amendments, the Fifteenth helped to enshrine in the Constitution many of the basic principles of freedom and citizenship. Congress wanted to incorporate the three Reconstruction Amendments into that founding document to prevent future Supreme Court decisions from overturning emancipation and black civil rights. Alas, court decisions in the late 1800s would in fact limit the effect of the Fourteenth and Fifteenth Amendments by exempting states from their provisions. During the Civil Rights Movement of the 1950s and 1960s, however, the Reconstruction Amendments would be reinvigorated to buttress support for black rights. Black and white Republicans during and after Reconstruction would fight against southern white attempts to roll back civil rights gains and use political and legal means to protect the power of emancipation.

The revolutionary nature of Reconstruction under radical Republican rule can be seen most clearly in the election of hundreds of former slaves to local, state, and national office in the late 1860s and the 1870s. Since very few African Americans lived in northern states, almost all of the new black politicians came from the South. Joined with white Republicans, new black leaders such as Hiram Revels of Mississippi (the first black U.S. senator), Blanche K. Bruce, also of Mississippi and the first black senator elected to a full term, and South Carolina's Joseph Rainey (the first black member of the house) participated directly in shaping Reconstruction policy.

Born free in North Carolina in 1827, Revels became a barber and then traveled to Indiana, Ohio, and Illinois for college. During the Civil War he served in the Chaplain Corps, building upon his early experience in the ministry. After the war, Revels moved with

FIGURE 11.4A *Hiram Revels. Library of Congress, LC-DIG-cwpbh-00554*

his large family to preach in Natchez, Mississippi. Natchez had been known for its wealthy, large plantations and ironically the same town became the basis for Revels's political ascendance. He attracted notice for his oratorical and leadership skills in the Mississippi state legislature (voters did not directly elect U.S. senators until the passage of the Seventeenth Amendment to the Constitution in 1916; before that date senators were chosen by state legislators). Revels was overwhelmingly selected to serve out the term of Albert Gallatin Brown, who had resigned when Mississippi seceded in 1861. Revels, who occupied the office from February 1870 to March 1871, thus became the first black member of Congress, a feat made possible only because of the disfranchisement of white former Confederates and the protection of black voting rights under the Military Acts. In his brief time as senator, Revels spoke in favor of racial integration, including the integration of public schools in Washington, D.C., supported black workers in their attempts to secure jobs, and backed funding for railroad construction.

Although he was the first African American to serve in Congress, Revels was not the last. In fact, Blanche K. Bruce, elected as a Republican senator from Mississippi in 1875, served an entire six-year term. Born to an enslaved mother in Virginia in 1841, Bruce

FIGURE 11.4B *Hon. Blanche Kelso Bruce of Mississippi. Library of Congress, LC-DIG-cwpbh-05070*

was freed by his master (who was also his father) and attended Oberlin College. During the war Bruce helped organize a school for African Americans in Missouri. After the war he moved to Mississippi and became a prominent landowner, which would be the basis for his rise to political power under Republican rule. In 1879, in what must have seemed to many white southerners as a complete overturning of the social and political order, Bruce, a former slave, presided over the Senate. Bruce even attracted a handful of votes for the vice presidential nomination at the 1880 Republican convention. Although he failed to secure that nomination, Bruce later became a U.S. Treasury official and thus the first African American to have his signature printed on American currency.

Bruce had a remarkable career, but black politicians served throughout the Reconstruction-era South. South Carolina witnessed the election of dozens of black politicians. Republican Joseph Rainey served throughout the 1870s as a U.S. Representative from that state's 1st District, the first African American to serve in the House. Although both his parents were slaves, Rainey himself grew up free and joined the family barber business. During the war Rainey and his wife fled to Bermuda, but in 1866 they returned to South Carolina. Almost immediately Rainey took advantage of

FIGURE 11.4C *Joseph Rainey. Library of Congress, LC-DIG-cwpbh-00664*

the unusual political situation to run for office; in 1868 he helped to draft the state's new constitution. He would win four elections as a member of the U.S. House in the 1870s and in 1874 served as speaker pro tempore.

Other African American politicians won office in South Carolina, the home of states' rights ideology and secession. Richard H. Cain, a minister in the AME Church, served in the state Senate and then two terms as a member of the U.S. House in the 1870s. He was born free in Virginia but grew up in the Midwest. His church work brought him to Charleston after the war, where he quickly used his ministry as a launching point for a role in Republican politics. Similarly, Robert Smalls, a former slave who earned fame for commandeering a Confederate ship and sailing from Charleston harbor to freedom in the North, served South Carolina in the U.S. House for three terms in the 1870s and 1880s. Smalls worked for a system of free public education and became a tireless advocate for the Republican Party. "Every colored man who has a vote to cast," Smalls once said, "would cast that vote for the regular Republican Party and thus bury the Democratic Party so deep that there will not be seen even a bubble coming from the spot where the burial took place." Not surprisingly, African Americans such as Smalls saw the Republicans as the party that pushed for and won emancipation. As Thomas Holt, Philip Dray, and other historians have shown, African American politicians played a central role in Reconstruction. Blanche Bruce, Josiah T. Walls, John Willis Menard, and hundreds of other black Republicans changed the nature of southern politics for a brief time after the end of the Civil War. Unfortunately the large numbers of black politicians and their prominence in southern politics would also lead white southerners to step up efforts to reestablish white control as Washington became embroiled in an unprecedented political battle.

Johnson's Impeachment

By early 1868, the heated rhetoric between Republicans, especially the radicals in Congress, and President Johnson had reached new levels of mutual disdain. Yet the issues at stake were much more important than the mutual hatred between the president and Congress. Reconstruction was a battle between the branches of the government for control and influence. The executive and legislative branches each saw themselves as the proper authority over Reconstruction policy, and the struggle for preeminence erupted in the first hearings for impeaching the president in the nation's history. As president, Johnson had clearly aligned himself with the Democrats and supported a quick restoration of the Union, positions that drew the executive branch into direct conflict with the Republican-dominated Congress.

In February and March 1868, congressional Republicans charged Johnson with violating the Tenure of Office Act, a law Congress passed the previous year in direct defiance of executive authority. The act required the president to secure congressional approval when he wanted to dismiss a member of his cabinet. Knowing Johnson would consider this an affront to executive power, Republicans waited for the president to defy the law. When Johnson dismissed Secretary of War Edwin Stanton, he had taken the bait. In early 1868, both houses of Congress voted to begin the impeachment process. Article Two of the Constitution provides for the impeachment of the president if "high crimes and misdemeanors" are found. "Impeachment" does not mean removal from office; rather the term applies to the process, as laid down in the Constitution, for holding hearings on the president's conduct. Republicans charged Johnson with eleven articles of impeachment, but the primary charge was that he had violated a law passed by Congress. On the impeachment committee sat some of the most vocal Republicans, including Thaddeus Stevens, Benjamin F.

Butler, and John A. Logan. From March to May, with Supreme Court Chief Justice Salmon P. Chase presiding, Congress debated the claims that Johnson's violation of the Tenure of Office Act was an impeachable offense.

Johnson barely escaped conviction during the trial. The Constitution stipulates that a guilty verdict requires a two-thirds majority. In the final tallies, thirty-five senators voted guilty and nineteen not guilty. The Radical Republicans stood one vote short of conviction. Several Republicans, including Kansas senator Edmund G. Ross, thought the proceedings were politically motivated and joined the Democrats in voting for acquittal. Johnson had mounted a vigorous defense of executive power and Republicans failed in their efforts to oust the president.

The nation remained transfixed throughout the proceedings and tickets to watch the trial were sought after by capital residents and by people who had traveled to Washington for the event. Newspapers carried blow-by-blow accounts of the trial and the presentation of the evidence. Although the Republicans failed to remove the president, they succeeded in demonstrating to Johnson the extent of their power. Johnson would not be a candidate during the presidential campaign of 1868.

Leading the Republican ticket in 1868 was none other than the Union war hero Ulysses S. Grant. The Democratic candidate, Horatio Seymour, a former New York governor, had little chance of victory. Republicans "waved the bloody shirt," as they would do for many future campaigns, to remind voters that the southern secessionists were members of the Democratic Party and that during the war the Copperheads (northern Democrats) were obstacles to Union victory. Grant won the election of 1868 handily, garnering 214 electoral votes while Seymour managed only eighty. The popular vote was closer (53% to 47%) but the victory was clear enough to provide Grant considerable momentum heading into his first term. Ultimately Grant would squander much of that momentum, as his administration became embroiled in major scandals. In the meantime, white southerners would take advantage of a distracted President Grant to dig in their heels on racial equality.

White Southern Retrenchment

White southerners were not uniformly opposed to creating a new South generally free from the reactionary racial policies of slavery. In fact, for the first time the Republican Party made significant gains throughout the South. North Carolina's William W. Holden and South Carolina's James L. Orr were just two prominent white southerners who embraced the Republican Party during Reconstruction. Perhaps the most visible southern Republican was former Confederate General James Longstreet. A South Carolina native, Longstreet fought closely with Lee at Gettysburg and other battles, and after the war he became an insurance and railroad executive in New Orleans. Longstreet's business interests and his friendship with President Grant led the former Confederate officer into the Republican Party to the shock and dismay of his southern friends.

The tradition of southern dissent that was seen before and during the war, though always a minority of the white population, remained visible during the first years of Reconstruction. As historian James Alex Baggett and other scholars have pointed out, scalawags, a term conservative whites angrily used for southern dissenters, spoke out for racial reconciliation throughout the Reconstruction period. Such dissenters, many of them

FIGURE 11.5 *Lt. General Jas. Longstreet. Library of Congress, LC-DIG-ppmsca-38007*

middle-class professionals and businessmen, wanted the region to move beyond its legacy of ultra-conservatism and racial violence.

The Republican Party established newspapers and networks in the region, and held rallies and parades to drum up support. Many white Republicans were elected to office in the former Confederate states, leading some historians to argue that in the years immediately after the war a window opened briefly, an opportunity to change the South's entrenched racism and conservatism and to channel the region's energy toward a new and different future, a future that would embrace the end of slavery, cultural modernization, and economic diversification. Prominent spokesmen for a new economy that would reduce the region's dependence on the cotton crop, expand manufacturing enterprises, and fund railroad construction and other projects rang out in journals such as the New Orleans monthly magazine *De Bow's Review*. Before the war began, southern middle-class merchants and professionals called for a regional program of economic and cultural modernization. Now many of those same middle-class activists saw an opportunity to realize their prewar agenda and many joined the Republican Party as the means to accomplish that agenda.

Despite such optimism for a new dawn in the South, the dark clouds of racism and reactionary politics once again obscured any visions of a reformed region. Many southern whites refused to accept the new social order, in which African Americans would be free from white control. As an essayist in one southern magazine wrote:

It is absurd to say that two races so dissimilar as the whites and blacks, when their numbers are equal, can live in peace where they enjoy equal political privileges, where they sit on the same juries, serve in the same legislature and hold similar offices. It is an impossibility. One race or the other must be subordinate. So it has always been and so it will always be. Does any one believe that the white people of Massachusetts or any Northern State would give the negroes the same political rights with the whites if they were equal or nearly equal in numbers? Where there are only a few negroes it makes but little difference, for then the white race will be the dominant and governing race. But it is not so in the Gulf States. If the negroes enjoy equal political privileges with the whites, one race or the other must leave the country.[3]

Whites in both urban and rural areas complained that the former slaves acted arrogantly and refused to work. They moaned about the haughtiness of black women who refused to wash dishes as they were told and of black men who demanded unreasonable wages. And whites especially resented the notion that blacks would be able to participate on equal political footing with whites. Almost all of the former slaves joined the Republican Party, understandably viewing the organization as the party of emancipation. Much to the dismay of conservative whites, black Republicans became active in local southern politics.

Secret paramilitary organizations such as the Ku Klux Klan rose quickly and powerfully after the war to combat the perceived threat from black political activism and assertiveness. In Pulaski, Tennessee in late December 1865, a handful of former Confederate soldiers formed the KKK, choosing its name by combining the Greek word for circle, *kyklos*, and the word "clan." The KKK was not the only such group formed to intimidate blacks and white Republicans; the Knights of the White Camellia formed in 1867 and the Southern Cross appeared in 1865. Other white supremacist organizations mushroomed in the 1870s, including the White League and the Red Shirts. The KKK, however, was the most powerful.

The KKK operated within a decentralized structure. Individual chapters of the KKK functioned independently, but all members dedicated themselves to ensuring white rule by threatening freedpeoples and harassing Republican Party activists. Formulated by former Confederate General George Gordon, the KKK's organizing principles were to root out anyone working toward racial equality in the South. One of the early leaders of the Klan, former Confederate General Nathan Forrest, became the "Grand Wizard."

Under the leadership of local members the KKK embarked on a program of violence, terrorizing rural and urban blacks and anyone promoting black civil rights, especially the right to vote. Between the late 1860s and the early 1870s, the Klan was responsible for hundreds of murders and thousands of assaults throughout the South. Lynching became a common occurrence in states such as Mississippi, where the Klan operated with the help of state and local white officials. In fact, many white governmental officials were themselves active members of the Klan. Riding with hoods drawn during the night, the Klan could carry out its violent plans with little fear of reprisals until the federal government stepped in to squelch the Klan with the Force Act in 1870 and the Ku Klux Klan Act in 1871.

FIGURE 11.6 *Watertown, N.Y. division of the Ku Klux Klan with skull and bones arranged on the floor in front of them (1870). Courtesy of the Library of Congress Prints and Photographs Division*

As the presidential election of 1872 approached, Republicans had good reason to expect a victory. Many white southerners remained staunchly unreconstructed and continued to employ violence to intimidate blacks. Magazines such as *Harper's Weekly* published engravings of lynchings and KKK meetings, and stories about white racism filled many newspaper columns. Radical Republicans read about these same horrors and pushed for new laws to combat the KKK and similar terrorist groups. The Force Act of 1870 and the Civil Rights Act of 1871 were designed to protect civil rights by allowing people of color the right to sue for damages. For now voting was protected by federal instead of state law. Although historians debate their effectiveness in stemming racial violence, the laws made clear that Congress would not ignore the outrageous abuses inflicted by the KKK.

Republican leaders pointed to the surge in racial violence and the proliferation of terrorist groups such as the KKK as proof that the federal government needed to take a harder line when dealing with former Confederates. Republican politicians kept the racial violence in the news by holding hearings in which witnesses testified to the lawlessness of the New South. Even white southern Republicans publicly chastised the KKK, and newspapers across the country printed stories, pictures, and cartoons highlighting southern racial violence.

Democrats charged that the stories were embellished for Republican political gain, and they denied that the KKK and other paramilitary white supremacist organizations were running rampant in the South as the Republicans claimed. Postwar Democrats did not hide the fact that they were a "white man's party." In elections throughout the country Democrats tended to prey on public fears of black rule, threatening that once in power Republicans would enforce racial equality and integration.

Please visit the companion website www.routledge.com/cw/wells for additional study aids including chapter overviews, interactive quizzes, and more.

Discussion Questions

- Who were some of the leading African American politicians during Reconstruction and what policies did they advocate?
- How would you characterize President Andrew Johnson's Reconstruction policies?
- How did southern whites respond to the Reconstruction policies of the federal government?
- Why did African Americans vote overwhelmingly for the Republican Party in the years following the Civil War?
- Why was President Andrew Johnson impeached? What does his impeachment say about the divisions not just between Democrats and Republicans but also between executive and legislative power?
- In your judgment, was the Freedmen's Bureau a success or a failure? Use evidence to support your claim.
- Why did Presidential Reconstruction give way to Congressional Reconstruction?
- Visit the Library of Congress website and read the black codes that southern states enacted following the Civil War. In what ways did these laws resemble the slave codes of the pre-Civil War era? Were Republicans correct in claiming that the black codes were little more than an attempt to reestablish white racial control?

Notes

1 Michael W. Fitzgerald, *The Union League Movement in the Deep South: Politics and Agricultural Change During Reconstruction* (Baton Rouge, 1989), 6.
2 William Woods Holden, *Memoirs of W.W. Holden* (Durham, 1911), 85.
3 "Designs of Radicalism," *De Bow's Review* 4 (December 1867), 536.

Further Reading

James D. Anderson, *The Education of Blacks in the South, 1860–1935* (Chapel Hill: University of North Carolina Press, 1988).

James Alex Baggett, *The Scalawags: Southern Dissenters in the Civil War and Reconstruction* (Baton Rouge: Louisiana State University Press, 2003).

Peter W. Bardaglio, *Reconstructing the Household: Families, Sex, and the Law in the Nineteenth-Century South* (Chapel Hill: University of North Carolina Press, 1995).

Andrew Billingsley, *Yearning to Breathe Free: Robert Smalls of South Carolina and His Families* (Columbia: University of South Carolina Press, 2007).

Thomas J. Brown, ed., *Reconstructions: New Perspectives on Postbellum America* (New York: Oxford University Press, 2006).

Stephen Budiansky, *The Bloody Shirt: Terror after the Civil War* (New York: Viking, 2008).

Ronald E. Butchart, *Northern Schools, Southern Blacks, and Reconstruction: Freedmen's Education, 1862–1875* (Westport: Greenwood Press, 1980).

John Carpenter, *Sword and Olive Branch: Oliver Otis Howard* (New York: Fordham University Press, 1999).

Dan T. Carter, *When the War Was Over: The Failure of Self-Reconstruction in the South, 1865–1867* (Baton Rouge: Louisiana State University Press, 1985).

Paul A. Cimbala, *Under the Guardianship of the Nation: The Freedmen's Bureau and the Reconstruction of Georgia* (Athens: University of Georgia Press, 1997).

Patricia C. Click, *Time Full of Trial: The Roanoke Island Freedmen's Colony, 1862–1867* (Chapel Hill: University of North Carolina Press, 2001).

Barry Crouch, *The Freedmen's Bureau and Black Texans* (Austin: University of Texas Press, 1992).

Gregory P. Downs, *After Appomattox: Military Occupation and the Ends of War* (Cambridge, MA: Harvard University Press, 2015).

James Downs, *Sick from Freedom: African-American Illness and Suffering during the Civil War and Reconstruction* (New York: Oxford University Press, 2012).

Philip Dray, *Capitol Men: The Epic Story of Reconstruction Through the Lives of the First Black Congressmen* (Boston: Houghton Mifflin Co., 2008).

Laura F. Edwards, *Gendered Strife and Confusion: The Political Culture of Reconstruction* (Urbana: University of Illinois Press, 1997).

Carole Emberton, *Beyond Redemption: Race, Violence, and the American South after the Civil War* (Chicago: University of Chicago Press, 2013).

Garret Epps, *Democracy Reborn: The Fourteenth Amendment and the Fight for Equal Rights in Post-Civil War America* (New York: Henry Holt & Co., 2006).

Mary Farmer-Kaiser, *Freedwomen and the Freedmen's Bureau: Race, Gender, and Public Policy in the Age of Emancipation* (New York: Fordham University Press, 2010).

Randy Finley, *From Slavery to Uncertain Freedom: The Freedmen's Bureau in Arkansas, 1865–1869* (Fayetteville: University of Arkansas Press, 1996).

Michael W. Fitzgerald, *The Union League Movement in the Deep South: Politics and Agricultural Change During Reconstruction* (Baton Rouge: Louisiana State University Press, 1989).

Michael W. Fitzgerald, *Splendid Failure: Postwar Reconstruction in the American South* (Chicago: Ivan R. Dee, 2007).

John Hope Franklin, *Reconstruction after the Civil War* (Chicago: University of Chicago Press, 1961).

Thavolia Glymph, *Out of the House of Bondage: The Transformation of the Plantation Household* (Cambridge: Cambridge University Press, 2008).

Steven Hahn, *A Nation under Our Feet: Black Political Struggles in the Rural South from Slavery to the Great Migration* (Cambridge, MA: Harvard University Press, 2003).

James G. Hollandsworth, *An Absolute Massacre: The New Orleans Race Riot of July 20, 1866* (Baton Rouge: Louisiana State University Press, 2001).

Thomas Holt, *Black over White: Negro Political Leadership in South Carolina during Reconstruction* (Urbana: University of Illinois Press, 1977).

Tera W. Hunter, *To 'Joy My Freedom: Southern Black Women's Lives and Labors after the Civil War* (Cambridge, MA: Harvard University Press, 1997).

Jack Hurst, *Nathan Bedford Forrest: A Biography* (New York: Knopf, 1993).

Caroline E. Janney, *Remembering the Civil War: Reunion and the Limits of Reconciliation* (Chapel Hill: University of North Carolina Press, 2013).

Jacqueline Jones, *Soldiers of Light and Love: Northern Teachers and Georgia Blacks, 1865–1873* (Chapel Hill: University of North Carolina Press, 1980).

Jacqueline Jones, *Labor of Love, Labor of Sorrow: Black Women, Work, and the Family from Slavery to the Present* (New York: Basic Books, 1985).

Leon Litwack, *Been in the Storm so Long: The Aftermath of Slavery* (New York: Knopf, 1979).

Gretchen Long, *Doctoring Freedom: The Politics of African American Medical Care in Slavery and Emancipation* (Chapel Hill: University of North Carolina Press, 2012).

William S. McFeely, *Yankee Stepfather: General O.O. Howard and the Freedmen* (New Haven: Yale University Press, 1968).

Robert C. Morris, *Reading, 'Riting, and Reconstruction: The Education of Freedmen in the South, 1861–1870* (Chicago: University of Chicago Press, 1981).

Amy Feely Morsman, *The Big House after Slavery: Virginia Plantation Families and Their Postbellum Domestic Experiment* (Charlottesville: University of Virginia Press, 2010).

Michael Perman, *Reunion Without Compromise: The South and Reconstruction: 1865–1868* (Cambridge: Cambridge University Press, 1973).

Howard N. Rabinowitz, *Southern Black Leaders of the Reconstruction Era* (Urbana: University of Illinois Press, 1982).

George C. Rable, *But There Was No Peace: The Role of Violence in the Politics of Reconstruction* (Athens: University of Georgia Press, 1984).

Heather Cox Richardson, *The Death of Reconstruction: Race, Labor, and Politics in the Post-Civil War North, 1865–1901* (Cambridge, MA: Harvard University Press, 2001).

Heather Cox Richardson, *West from Appomattox: The Reconstruction of America after the Civil War* (New Haven: Yale University Press, 2007).

Joe M. Richardson, *Christian Reconstruction: The American Missionary Association and Southern Blacks, 1861–1890* (Athens: University of Georgia Press, 1986).

William L. Richter, *Overreached on all Sides: The Freedmen's Bureau Administrators in Texas, 1865–1868* (College Station: Texas A&M Press, 1991).

Hannah Rosen, *Terror in the Heart of Freedom: Citizenship, Sexual Violence, and the Meaning of Race in the Postemancipation South* (Chapel Hill: University of North Carolina Press, 2009).

Julie Saville, *The Work of Reconstruction: From Slave to Wage Laborer in South Carolina 1860–1870* (Cambridge: Cambridge University Press, 1994).

Leslie A. Schwalm, *A Hard Fight for We: Women's Transition from Slavery to Freedom in South Carolina* (Urbana: University of Illinois Press, 1997).

Leslie A. Schwalm, *Emancipation's Diaspora: Race and Reconstruction in the Upper Midwest* (Chapel Hill: University of North Carolina Press, 2009).

Rebecca J. Scott, *Degrees of Freedom: Louisiana and Cuba after Slavery* (Cambridge, MA: Harvard University Press, 2005).

Brooks D. Simpson, *Let Us Have Peace: Ulysses S. Grant and the Politics of War and Reconstruction, 1861–1868* (Chapel Hill: University of North Carolina Press, 1991).

Mark Wahlgren Summers, *A Dangerous Stir: Fear, Paranoia, and the Making of Reconstruction* (Chapel Hill: University of North Carolina Press, 2009).

Elizabeth Lee Thompson, *The Reconstruction of Southern Debtors: Bankruptcy after the Civil War* (Athens: University of Georgia Press, 2004).

Michael Wayne, *The Reshaping of Plantation Society: The Natchez District, 1860–1880* (Baton Rouge: Louisiana State University Press, 1983).

Heather Andrea Williams, *Self-Taught: African American Education in Slavery and Freedom* (Chapel Hill: University of North Carolina Press, 2005).

Heather Andrea Williams, *Help Me to Find My People: The African American Search for Family Lost in Slavery* (Chapel Hill: University of North Carolina Press, 2012).

Joel Williamson, *After Slavery: The Negro in South Carolina during Reconstruction, 1861–1877* (Chapel Hill: University of North Carolina Press, 1965).

COLLAPSE OF RECONSTRUCTION

Topics Covered in this Chapter:

- Republican Party Politics
- Economic Panic in 1873
- Redemption and White Supremacy
- The "Compromise" of 1877 and the End of Reconstruction
- The Legacy of Reconstruction
- Labor and Capital Battle in 1877

12

Introduction

Reconstruction began to wane by 1873 and then ended altogether in 1877. A severe economic depression erupted in 1873, crippling the nation's economy and diverting attention and resources away from the racial politics of the South. A new wave of labor strife struck northern and midwestern cities, and political power in Washington pivoted from helping the freedmen to defending the rights of employers to control their workers. Public and private armies would be redeployed from the New South to cities such as Chicago, Pittsburgh, and New York. Even Radical Republicans concluded that the most potent challenge facing the nation was not southern white supremacists but labor unions trying to organize for better wages and working conditions.

Equally important to the end of Reconstruction was the growing sense that the federal government had done much for the former slaves, from the Freedmen's Bureau to the Reconstruction Amendments. Voters became fatigued with the notion of further aid for the freedpeople, and decided that with the right to vote African Americans could chart their own course without federal aid. Unfortunately, given southern white legal, political, and economic power, the ex-slaves stood little chance once the last federal troops began leaving the South in 1877. By the 1890s, whites had firmly established Jim Crow laws that left no doubt as to which race controlled the South.

As Reconstruction collapsed, white southerners, most of them Democrats, regained political control of southern states, a process they called "Redemption." In just a little over a decade, between 1865 and 1877, the nation underwent three phases: Presidential Reconstruction, Congressional or Radical Reconstruction, and Redemption. Those were years of turmoil but also years of remarkable progress for African Americans. With the completion of Redemption in 1877, however, the South's course for the next century would be clearly charted: one-party Democratic control in politics, the triumph of white demagogues who preyed on fears of "racial amalgamation," the subjugation of African Americans into low-paying jobs, the constant threat of lynching or other racial violence, and segregation in nearly every phase of public and private life.

Republican Party Politics

During the period between 1866 and 1871, Radical Republicans had hefted the full weight of the federal government and its armed forces behind reconstructing the South. The Reconstruction Amendments, the Freedmen's Bureau, the Military Reconstruction Acts, and laws to quash racial violence aided the freedpeople in practical and symbolic ways. Violence against blacks had quieted, although it lay just beneath the surface of southern society. Ex-slaves voted by the thousands, helping to elect a cadre of black politicians at the local, state, and national level. Former white Confederates were disfranchised and largely prevented from undertaking the worst expressions of racial control. Black literacy rates rose, as generations of former slaves learned in schools established by missionaries and the Freedmen's Bureau. Southern Republicans for the first time appeared as a viable political power to compete with southern Democrats. The southern economy, though devastated beyond imagination by the war, received infusions of investments from northern capitalists. While the South faced real and mammoth problems, from seething white hostility at federal intervention to a wrecked economy and the loss of millions of dollars invested in slaves, the brief period known as Radical or Congressional Reconstruction had made substantial progress in creating a New South.

Yet, by 1877 Reconstruction was over and by 1900 new barriers between the races had been firmly established. By the late

1800s, black codes segregated the Jim Crow South, lynchings of African Americans reached unprecedented heights, poor blacks were jailed for small offenses and sent off to toil in convict leasing systems, southern Democratic politicians routinely and unabashedly proclaimed the superiority of the white race, and tens of thousands of African Americans had become entrapped in sharecropping and other unfair farming contracts. How could the early promise of Radical Reconstruction have collapsed so quickly and so completely?

As historian Heather Cox Richardson has argued in her important book *The Death of Reconstruction*, the explanation lay partly in the growing economic concerns facing the nation, and partly in the divisions within the Republican Party. As we will see, an economic panic in 1873 generated fear that the economy had to be the nation's number one concern. While some Republicans grew worried over the state of the economy, others continued to maintain the federal government's leading role in reconstructing the South. Not all Republicans, it should be remembered, supported the Radicals' plans for black suffrage and racial equality. Many of these northern, midwestern, and western Republicans had shunned abolitionism before and during the Civil War, and they now recoiled at Radical plans to persist in using military force in pursuit of racial justice. Existing divisions within the party over Reconstruction policies were sharpened in Grant's first administration.

When President Grant took the oath of office for his first inaugural in March 1869, black and white Republicans cheered. African Americans hung portraits of Grant alongside their engravings of Lincoln, and their trust seemed to have been repaid, as hundreds of black politicians won office under Republican rule. While the southern economy faced dire straits after the war, the economy of the former Union states prospered. Entrepreneurs secured millions of dollars in private and public funds to build textile mills and other manufacturing enterprises. Chinese, Irish, and black laborers laid railroad tracks in unprecedented numbers. In less than ten years between the end of the war and 1873, more than 35,000 miles of track were laid. Banks, corporations, and oil companies mushroomed throughout the West and North. John D. Rockefeller's Standard Oil, founded in 1870, could boast of a near monopoly of the refinement and transportation of oil. Large tracts of public land were virtually handed to wealthy capitalists to build railroads. Land grants, financial kickbacks, bribes, and "donations" ensured that politicians would do the bidding of the rich and powerful.

Rampant corruption soon infected Grant's administration. In August 1869, Jay Gould and Jim Fisk tried to corner the gold market with the help of Grant's brother-in-law Abel Corbin. Together the three connived, without Grant's knowledge, to drive up gold and silver prices and to increase railroad shipping. Chaos in the markets erupted on September 24, 1869, known as Black Friday, in which the value of gold plummeted. President Grant discovered the plot, but not before much damage had been inflicted on the economy and on voters' confidence in his leadership. Yet the gold crisis was just the beginning. In 1872 the Credit Mobilier scandal enriched corrupt congressmen in an elaborate system of insider trading. An outraged public faulted Republican politicians and Grant took his share of the blame for the continuing corruption of Washington, a trend that endured into Grant's second term as president.

As the 1872 presidential campaign approached, Republicans, including Grant, had lost much support. But the Democrats were in a poor position to challenge Grant in the election. The Democratic Party, vulnerable to charges of treason and the "waving of the bloody shirt" for its prewar support of secession and its wartime opposition to Lincoln and total Union victory, would win only two presidential elections between 1864 and 1912. Despite a presidency weakened by scandals, Grant had little to fear from the Democratic Party. When some Republicans split from their party, however, and formed the Liberal Republican Party, the Radical Republicans grew concerned. Much to Grant's dismay, the Liberal Republicans joined with the Democrats to attempt to defeat the president's campaign for a second term.

The scandals of Grant's first term greatly alarmed many Republicans. Calling for lower tariffs, clean and efficient government, and distrustful of radical calls for black suffrage, Liberal Republicans formulated a "reform" platform and threw their weight behind the Democrat nominee for president, Horace Greeley of New York. Something of a political opportunist and a long-time editor of the influential *New York Tribune*, Greeley promised an honest government led by the elite. In addition, Liberal Republicans trumpeted the value of local self-government, a euphemism for white rule in the South. In the fourth plank of its platform, Liberal Republicans declared that:

Local self-government, with impartial suffrage, will guard the rights of all citizens more securely than

any centralized power. The public welfare requires the supremacy of the civil over the military authority, and freedom of person under the protection of the habeas corpus. We demand for the individual the largest liberty consistent with public order; for the State, self-government, and for the nation a return to the methods of peace and the constitutional limitations of power.

In part, Liberal Republicans had concluded that gullible voters had been manipulated by savvy politicians and their attempts at reform sought to break down what they perceived to be a centralization of federal power during and after the war. Although Liberal Republicans and Democrats united behind Greeley's candidacy, Grant easily won a second term in a landslide. Grant

FIGURE 12.1A *Horace Greeley. Library of Congress, LC-DIG-cwpbh-00704*

FIGURE 12.1B *A campaign poster of the election of 1872. MPI/Stringer/Getty Images*

won 386 electoral votes to Greeley's 66, and Grant captured more than 55% of the popular vote while Greeley managed less than 44%.

Grant handily won another term in 1872, but the scandals continued. In 1875 his Secretary of War William Belknap, caught in a bribery scandal over trade with Native American tribes in the West, was forced to resign. Corruption disgraced Grant's years as president, leading later historians to judge his presidential leadership harshly, but there is little evidence that Grant himself was dishonest. Rather it appears Grant was guilty of surrounding himself with crooked and untrustworthy advisors.

Economic Panic in 1873

While malfeasance marred Grant's second term between 1873 and 1877, the nation's attention soon became absorbed in a deep and dramatic financial crisis. The Panic of 1873 was the worst the nation had ever seen and lasted until 1879, with ripple effects that lasted even longer. Although the economic depression began in Europe, the United States shared in the blame. Rampant investment speculation, the overbuilding of railroad tracks, the move to the gold standard in 1873, and the lack of government regulation or oversight contributed to the depth of the crisis.

By the summer of 1873, keen observers might have sensed a looming financial panic. The Coinage Act of 1873 moved the federal government to a system of currency based only on gold, an attempt to stabilize the economy in the tumultuous postwar period, which lowered demand for silver and also its value. But the rapid expansion of the railroad industry in the years following the war and the extension of credit to finance the industry were perhaps the primary causes of the panic. The large banking firm Jay Cooke & Company declared bankruptcy in September 1873, and this led almost immediately to the shuttering of other banking and railroad businesses. Financial leaders became so alarmed

FIGURE 12.2A *The severe financial crisis of 1873. Kean Collection/Getty Images*

FIGURE 12.2B *The severe financial crisis of 1873. Hutton Archive/Stringer/Getty Images*

that they closed the New York Stock Exchange for more than a week. The panic was not mere hysteria; unemployment reached nearly 15%, a quarter of the country's railroad companies declared bankruptcy, and thousands of businesses failed across the nation.

The panic hit African Americans especially hard. Thousands of them had deposited money in the Freedmen's Savings and Trust Company, which went bankrupt during the panic. The federal government offered no protection for depositors and many black southerners suffered a cruel economic blow just as they were saving hard-earned money.

Farmers in the South and West also suffered from the economic dislocation of the 1870s. In fact, as historian Matthew Hild and others have found, the 1870s gave birth to a new wave of political activism among laborers and farmers known as the Populist Movement. Beginning with organizations such as the Grange and the Agricultural Wheel, farmers rose up to protest the high cost of transporting goods via the railroads, high interest rates, and the

FIGURE 12.3A *The seal of the Knights of Labor. The Granger Collection, NYC—All rights reserved*

FIGURE 12.3B *American Labor leader John Mitchell. Library of Congress, LC-DIG-ggbain-00946*

gold standard. Small farmers in Texas, Arkansas, South Carolina, and other states banded together in cooperative efforts to purchase grain elevators, pool transportation costs, and share farm implements. Low cotton prices and the high cost of farming had put tens of thousands of small farmers in an economic bind and their angry objections to usurious banks and railroad monopolies helped shape policies to end unfair business practices.

Farmers' organizations were joined in the 1870s and 1880s by new unions formed by workers in the South and West. One of the most important early unions was the Knights of Labor, led by Terence Powderly. Their demands seem tame today; one of their main objectives was to enact an eight-hour workday. But in the 1870s and 1880s, unions such as the Knights had to contend with charges that labor organizations too strongly resembled socialism. The Knights flatly rejected the tenets of socialism, but that did not stop corporate leaders and politicians leveling accusations that collective bargaining smacked of European "isms." Despite considerable opposition from the elite, the Knights succeeded for a time in drawing support from the working class. By 1880 the Knights had more than 25,000 members and at its height in the mid-1880s more than half a million American laborers counted themselves among the Knights. Blamed in large part for the Haymarket Riot in Chicago in 1886, the Knights quickly lost popularity and gave way to other unions in the early twentieth century.

Many unions and farmers' associations called for blacks and whites—especially in the South—to come together to fight economic injustice. In fact, groups throughout the southern states put aside racial differences to battle against entrenched wealth and power. In Virginia in the 1870s, the Readjuster Party became perhaps the most successful of the biracial coalitions to emerge in the wake of the Civil War. Historian Jane Dailey points out that the Readjusters, led by former Confederate General William Mahone, earned their name because they supported reducing or "readjusting" the state's substantial debt, which had been deepened by the late antebellum push for internal improvements. In the late 1870s, Mahone and like-minded Readjusters put together a platform that joined the interests of white Republicans, black voters, and disaffected Democrats. To their advocacy of reducing the state's debt, the Readjusters added support for repealing the poll tax, which had prevented many poor black and white Virginians from voting, and for an improved public education system. In the 1880s the party won the governor's office and Mahone himself became a United States senator.

As white farmers and laborers suffered from low crop prices and high debt in the postwar period, so too did African Americans confront significant financial difficulties. Even with the help of the Freedmen's Bureau, black farmers, the vast majority of whom could not read or write, were tricked into signing unfair contracts with white landowners. The fact that no sustained program of land redistribution took root during Reconstruction meant that landless ex-slaves were forced into unfair agreements. Sharecropping and tenant farming emerged in the late nineteenth century as the only means by which former slaves could make a living as farmers. Under tenant farming, a landowner grants temporary use of a small plot of land to a farmer who might own tools and livestock. A sharecropper usually rents all the necessary items for farming, from seed to tools, from a landowner and then pays that owner with a portion of the harvest. Both systems emerged out of the complex social and economic negotiations between black farm laborers and white planters. While many black farming families understandably considered sharecropping and tenant farming improvements over servitude, both systems exploited the freedpeople's lack of education and land.

At the same time, black laborers endured low wages, dishonest employers, and harsh working conditions. Unless they were artisans who might maintain some control over their economic situation by virtue of their skills as carpenters or masons, black workers faced racial discrimination in all phases of employment. As a result, black farmers and unskilled laborers had every incentive to join with whites in biracial organizations such as the Readjusters.

Biracial coalitions held out the promise of overturning entrenched power and wealth, but the use of racism to divide lower-class whites and blacks proved too entrenched itself to be overcome. As we have seen, white Democrats in the postwar period became remarkably effective at trumpeting the dangers of black suffrage and racial equality. Southern Democratic candidates for state, local, and national offices harped on the notion that Republicans and former slaves couldn't wait to overthrow the "white man's democracy" and establish "negro rule." Even Virginia's Readjusters could maintain political power only until the early 1880s, and by 1900 the farmer–labor coalitions had begun to wane amid bogus charges of socialism and in the face of overwhelming state and corporate power. Perhaps most daunting was the inability of biracial groups to vault the hurdle of racism, so effectively exploited by demagogic political leaders. Even as farmer–labor organizations sought to gain a foothold in the 1870s, white southerners were fighting mightily to retake political control of the region from Radical Republicans. In the final phase of Reconstruction, the period known as Redemption, southern Democrats managed to reassert one-party rule and white control so completely that the "Solid South" would remain solid for a hundred years.

Redemption and White Supremacy

Racial violence and shifts in federal Reconstruction policies led to the Redemption of the South. In May 1872, Congress passed the Amnesty Act, which restored voting rights to tens of thousands of former white Confederates. Although a few hundred southern political and military leaders remained disfranchised, most of the rank-and-file Confederates could vote once again, and with the shrill cries of "negro rule" echoing throughout the South, these former Confederates were not disposed to vote with the Republicans. As historian Michael Perman argues in his study of southern politics in the 1870s, *The Road to Redemption*, both the Democrats and Republicans were internally divided, as factions within each party competed for dominance. What is clear, however, is that politics and violence went hand-in-hand in the postwar South. In particular, the brutality against white and black Republicans contributed significantly to Redemption.

In the 1870s, southern towns and cities were wracked by a series of violent riots and racially charged clashes that made it clear that the South was far from reconstructed. Historian James Hogue has examined many of these riots and found them filled with racial hatred and violence. The Colfax Massacre, for example, erupted in April 1873 in Louisiana and led to the death of dozens of former slaves. A contested local election sparked the unrest, and whites blamed black Republicans for the disputed results. According to reports, many freedmen who surrendered were killed nonetheless. Newspaper accounts across the country expressed outrage at the murders, and U.S. Attorney J.R. Beckwith brought charges against several men under the Enforcement Act. The failed prosecutions only encouraged similar deadly uprisings throughout the South.

The Hamburg Massacre in 1876 demonstrated the simmering tensions throughout the South and led to the redemption of South Carolina. The fight began over a controversy on a public road and soon spread from the small town of Hamburg to white outrage throughout the state, resulting in several deaths.

The well-publicized mass murders in places such as Colfax, Louisiana and Hamburg, South Carolina masked hundreds of smaller, little-known lynchings throughout the Reconstruction South. African Americans, especially men, did not know when a minor transgression might cause a white mob to form and stage a lynching. In the Jim Crow South, a strict code of behavior governed the relationship between whites and blacks, but minor incidents often flared into widespread unrest. If they were domestic servants, blacks were supposed to enter white homes through the back door. Hotels, inns, restaurants, theaters, and other public venues marked off separate areas for blacks or excluded them altogether. African Americans were expected to step off into streets to let whites pass and avert their eyes. Whites commonly referred to blacks not by their first names but with demeaning terms such as "boy." "Disrespecting" a white person, with seemingly innocuous words or even staring, could lead to racial brutality.

Many lynchings were reported in newspapers but many more were accomplished without the knowledge of federal authorities.

As Fitzhugh Brundage and other historians have made clear, lynchings were often public events designed to scare other African Americans into compliance with the region's racial code. Often lynchings entailed castration or other mutilation; blacks were sometimes burned alive. A national outcry against these illegal practices emerged under the moral leadership of black activists such as Ida B. Wells, whose anti-lynching campaign brought much-needed light to how commonplace lynchings became in states such as Mississippi in the late nineteenth century. Lynchings often occurred under the leadership of the KKK or other white paramilitary organizations.

In the 1870s the KKK remained a threat to carpetbaggers, scalawags and to African Americans. But the KKK was soon joined by other terrorist factions, some with regional appeal and some whose reach extended only over a county or group of counties. Organized in Louisiana in 1874, the White League joined with the Democratic Party to redeem that state. Unlike the secretive KKK, the White League welcomed public attention and the press, but was no less deadly. In fact, members of the league killed white Republicans, including elected officials, in the Coushatta Massacre in Louisiana. With little fear of federal retribution, the White League and the Democrats regained control of Louisiana's state government in 1876.

Another white supremacist organization, the Red Shirts, started harassing Republicans in Mississippi in 1875 and quickly spread to other southern states. Like the White League, the Red Shirts threatened black and white Republicans in the open, with no fear of punishment. Red Shirts infiltrated Republican rallies and speeches, terrorized voters at the polls, and published tracts stating plainly that any attempts to establish "negro rule" would be met with death. Active especially in Mississippi and the Carolinas, the Red Shirts remained vigorous in the region into the twentieth century.

If African Americans escaped violence and intimidation perpetrated by white supremacist groups, they might still fall victim to the convict leasing system. Black codes and Jim Crow laws passed by state and local governments established a range of new offenses for which blacks could be prosecuted. Laws restricting freedom of movement, loosely constructed laws against vagrancy, and a host of broadly interpreted rules governing black behavior made it easy for southern whites to reassert racial control in the wake of the Civil War.

While outlawing slavery, the Thirteenth Amendment contained a loophole that permitted those convicted of crimes to be pressed into labor. As Mary Ellen Curtin, Douglas Blackmon, and other scholars have shown, thousands of African Americans were arrested for petty and vaguely defined "crimes." Once arrested and swiftly convicted in a legal system that prohibited blacks from serving on juries until the mid-twentieth century, African Americans might be hired out to any number of labor camps common in the South. Convicts labored in digging trenches, building roads and railroads, cutting lumber, making turpentine and rope, and farming land under the auspices of paying their debt to society. As David M. Oshinsky argues in *Worse than Slavery*, African Americans toiled—many until they died of abuse, hunger, or thirst—in prisons and labor camps such as Mississippi's notorious Parchman Farm.

By the end of Reconstruction, convict leasing had become a central feature of the South's political economy and legal system, and a way to keep former slaves firmly under white control. Redemption in the South was not just the political retaking of state governments; as whites reestablished Democratic rule in the former Confederate states, they also avidly sought to recreate familiar patterns of racial hierarchy that had remained in place since the early 1600s. While slavery ended with the Thirteenth Amendment, southern whites found other ways to maintain their social, economic, and cultural power.

Even as whites "redeemed" the South, Radical Republicans were putting together the final pieces of legislation to remake the South under Reconstruction. Under the leadership of Senator Charles Sumner and Congressman Benjamin Butler, the Civil Rights Act of 1875 made racial discrimination illegal in public accommodations such as hotels, theaters, and public transportation. It was a bold law, intended to enforce social equality among the races, and conservatives reacted with fury.

White southerners railed against the law for attempting to govern individual private behavior between the races, and to their delight the Supreme Court would declare the law unconstitutional in the 1883 Civil Rights Cases. Congress, the court decided, had no authority to regulate personal behavior; the Fourteenth Amendment protections against racial discrimination applied only to governments and not to the private acts of individuals. Because of the court's decision, African Americans would have to wait nearly a century for protection against racial discrimination in public accommodations. The Civil Rights Act of 1964 would finally begin to accomplish what the law passed in 1875 intended: racial equality in inns, transportation, and other public venues.

Although struck down by the Supreme Court, the Civil Rights Act of 1875 symbolized the desire of Radical Republicans not just to provide political equality between whites and blacks, but also their earnest yearning for a fundamentally new southern society:

Where as it is essential to just government we recognize the equality of all men before the law, and hold that it is the duty of government in its dealings with the people to mete out equal and exact justice to all, of whatever nativity, race, color, or persuasion, religious or political; and it being the appropriate object of legislation to enact great fundamental principles into law: Therefore,

Sec. 1. Be it enacted by the Senate and House of Representatives of the United States of America in Congress assembled, That all persons within the jurisdiction of the United States shall be entitled to the full and equal enjoyment of the accommodations, advantages, facilities, and privileges of inns, public conveyances on land or water, theaters, and other places of public amusement; subject only to the conditions and limitations established by law, and applicable alike to citizens of every race and color, regardless of any previous condition of servitude.

Sec. 2. That any person who shall violate the foregoing section by denying to any citizen, except for reasons by law applicable to citizens of every race and color, and regardless of any previous condition of servitude, the full enjoyment of any of the accommodations, advantages, facilities, or privileges in said section enumerated, or by aiding or inciting such denial, shall, for every offence, forfeit and pay the sum of five hundred dollars to the person aggrieved thereby, to be recovered in an action of debt, with full costs; and shall also, for every such offense, be deemed guilty of a misdemeanor, and, upon conviction thereof, shall be fined not less than five hundred nor more than one thousand dollars, or shall be imprisoned not less than thirty days nor more than one year: Provided, that all persons may elect to sue for the State under their rights at common law and by State statutes; and having so elected to proceed in the one mode or the other, their right to proceed in the other jurisdiction shall be barred.

But this proviso shall not apply to criminal proceedings, either under this act or the criminal law of any State: And provided further, That a judgment for the penalty in favor of the party aggrieved, or a judgment upon an indictment, shall be a bar to either prosecution respectively.

Sec. 4. That no citizen possessing all other qualification which are or may be prescribed by law shall be disqualified for service as grand or petit juror in any court of the United States, or of any State, on account of race, color, or previous condition of servitude; and any officer or other person charged with any duty in the selection or summoning of jurors who shall exclude or fail to summon any citizen for the cause aforesaid shall, on conviction thereof, be deemed guilty of a misdemeanor, and be fined not more than five thousand dollars.

Despite the last efforts of Radical Republicans to change the South's racial injustice, one by one the former Confederate states shifted from Republican rule under the protection of the federal government to white southern Democratic control. By July 1870, all eleven rebellious states had been readmitted to representation in Congress. All had ratified the Thirteenth and Fourteenth Amendments, white former soldiers were once again allowed to vote, and federal government support for military control of the South had already reached its pinnacle. As a result, by January 1876 all the former Confederate states except for Florida, South Carolina, and Louisiana had been redeemed. Federal troops still enforced Reconstruction policies in those three states as the 1876 presidential campaign opened, but not for long.

The "Compromise" of 1877 and the End of Reconstruction

With Grant determined to uphold George Washington's precedent in serving just two terms, the Republican nomination was up for grabs in 1876. Several candidates vied for the nomination, including popular Maine Representative James G. Blaine and Ohio Governor Rutherford B. Hayes. The early ballots revealed that Blaine was in the lead, but not all party leaders were convinced that he was the best candidate to lead the party. After several years of scandals under the Grant Administration and after the economic problems experienced in the Panic of 1873 and its aftermath, the Republican Party was by no means guaranteed victory in the 1876 election. After several more ballots, party leaders settled on Hayes, a former Union officer and prominent Ohio politician. After embarking on a law career in Cincinnati, Hayes had served briefly as a member of the U.S. House of Representatives and then as governor.

At their convention in St. Louis, the first major party convention held west of the Mississippi River, the Democrats nominated New York Governor Samuel J. Tilden. A politician who made his reputation by supporting New York business interests and by fighting the corruption at Tammany Hall, Tilden appeared the perfect candidate to clean up the corruption that seemed to plague Washington. Democrats nominated Tilden enthusiastically, believing that victory was within the party's grasp after getting trounced in recent presidential elections.

The presidential election of 1876 would prove to be one of the most controversial in American history, matched perhaps only by the disputed election in 2000. One problem that emerged as the 1876 election returns came in was the persistent and widespread charges of voting fraud in the Deep South. Republicans produced evidence suggesting that ballots were designed to confuse former slaves. Other party officials offered credible evidence that white Democrats and paramilitary groups had intimidated black voters and scalawags to keep them from casting ballots for Republican candidates. After the disputed votes were reconfigured, Tilden had still won the popular vote by about 250,000 ballots. The number that really mattered, though, was the vote in the Electoral College, and to everyone's surprise and frustration the electoral vote was tied. The election of 1876 had sparked a constitutional crisis.

To decide how to proceed, Congress created a fifteen-member commission to settle the dispute. Comprising members of the House, Senate, and the Supreme Court, the commission met to consider the legitimacy of votes cast in the South. Although no firm evidence exists to prove the claims, it became clear that Republican and Democratic members of the commission had struck what critics would later deride as the "Corrupt Bargain." In the so-called Compromise of 1877, the commission's recalculation of South Carolina's votes gave the election to the Republican candidate Hayes. In return, angry detractors claimed, the Republicans agreed to remove the final troops from Florida, South Carolina, and Louisiana, the only former Confederate states that remained under

FIGURE 12.4 *Samuel L. Tilden and Thomas A. Hendricks on the presidential campaign poster in the election of 1876. Library of Congress, LC-USZC2-2484*

federal control. As a result of this unwritten compromise, Democrats had surrendered the White House in exchange for the end of Reconstruction. Florida and Louisiana fell into Democratic hands in January 1877 and South Carolina in April. Redemption was complete.

The Legacy of Reconstruction

Ever since the 1870s, historians have debated the achievements and failures of Reconstruction. Eric Foner, whose important book *Reconstruction* remains the leading study in the field, argues that the legacy of the period is complicated and nuanced. On the one hand, Reconstruction led to the end of slavery, the three Reconstruction Amendments, the election of hundreds of African Americans to national, state, and local offices, and bold commitments to the civil rights of former slaves. The Freedmen's Bureau had educated thousands of blacks and had distributed millions of dollars in aid to the freedpeople.

On the other hand, Redemption left former slaves, most of them illiterate and unfamiliar with the nature of labor contracts, at the mercy of southern whites. African Americans themselves knew all too well what the future likely held now that white northerners were backing away from Reconstruction. Black Americans never relied solely on the support of sympathetic whites; as we have seen, African Americans formed political, cultural, religious, and social associations of all kinds to promote independence and press for the fullest meaning of freedom in the new nation. Yet, as we have also seen, by the 1870s, white supremacist groups such as the KKK, the Red Shirts, and the White League intimidated blacks and their white sympathizers with little fear of punishment. Freedmen formed black militias to combat the violence, but they could only do so much. As blacks feared, the end of Radical Reconstruction and its military protection meant that lynchings became a common feature of life in the South into the twentieth century. Because no land was distributed to the former slaves, tenant farming and sharecropping became a customary way of life for generations of blacks. Convict leasing trapped blacks accused of petty offenses in a nefarious web of harsh labor. The Corrupt Bargain seemed to sacrifice the future of former slaves for the Republicans' claims to the White House.

In the late nineteenth century many white historians, especially those from the South, depicted Reconstruction as a period of unjust and corrupt rule by Republicans that inflicted unfair policies on white southerners. The Dunning School of historians, led by Columbia University professor William A. Dunning, argued in a series of books that Reconstruction was dominated by dishonest, fanatical, and power-hungry politicians who overturned the traditional and legitimate racial hierarchy in favor of negro rule.

The Dunning School's claims did not go unchallenged. The important and influential black scholar W.E.B. Du Bois took on the Dunning School with his study *Black Reconstruction*, published in the early 1900s. Born in western Massachusetts in 1868, Du Bois became one of the most important black intellectuals for many decades until he died in 1963. Du Bois argued that black Republicans aided the former slaves significantly and advocated racial justice in the face of white violence. Later scholars, including Litwack and Foner, would help rescue black and white Republicans and the legacy of Reconstruction from the claims leveled by Dunning and his adherents. Although historians disagree about much regarding the period known as Reconstruction, generally they agree that while reforms did much to challenge white rule, the true tragedy of Reconstruction was not that it went too far, but rather that it accomplished too little in its attempts to remake the South.

Labor and Capital Battle in 1877

As Redemption and the Compromise of 1877 ended Reconstruction, Americans—especially those in the northeast and upper Midwest—turned their attention to the economy. In the wake of the 1873 panic, workers and their employers faced a mutual hostility unprecedented in its depth and breadth. While skilled workers had formed unions and associations for their mutual benefit in the decades before the Civil War, the 1870s witnessed the beginning of prolonged labor strife. America's workforce, of course, suffered terribly in the aftermath of the 1873 economic depression. Meager benefits and wages were cut even further as businesses struggled to stay afloat. Workers responded by forming unions and staging strikes at levels unprecedented in the nation's history. Before the Civil War, the young Republican Party had asserted that labor and capital were allies, and that they shared common interests in growth and economic development. As industrialization and urbanization picked up steam, especially in the postwar North, that Republican Party ideology was in danger of caving in on itself. Labor unions and wealthy capitalists began to see their interests as conflicting, not shared.

What became known as the Great Railroad Strikes of 1877 began in July. The Baltimore & Ohio Railroad cut wages for its labor force a second time; workers responded angrily, and violence erupted in West Virginia, Pennsylvania, Illinois, and Maryland. Strikers tried to block the B&O Railroad from transporting goods and West Virginia's governor responded by calling in state and then federal troops to put down the strike. But violence then flared in Maryland and Pennsylvania as once again the state and federal governments sided with the corporations and tried to quell the strikes. Often soldiers refused to fight against workers, many of whom they knew personally. But the persistent attempts by political and business leaders to end the collective action led to brutality in Pittsburg, Philadelphia, Chicago, and smaller towns in Pennsylvania and Illinois. The strikes lasted for several weeks during July and August 1873 and began to subside only when the president sent federal troops into cities and towns in sufficient numbers to overcome the desperate workers.

Just as race emerged as a central concern of Reconstruction, so too did the question of whether capital and labor could come to an accommodation. In fact, the financial panic of 1873 led many political leaders to turn their attention away from the racial problems that lingered in the South. Even many Radical Republicans concluded that they had accomplished all they could for the former slaves, and they pointed to the Fifteenth Amendment and the protection of the right to vote as the lasting legacy of Reconstruction. As the 1870s closed, northerners' fears began to focus increasingly on their own economic, political, and social future—not the South's. The financial crisis and the struggle between workers and their employers, politicians declared, now demanded the nation's full attention.

COMPANION @ WEBSITE

Please visit the companion website www.routledge.com/cw/wells for additional study aids including chapter overviews, interactive quizzes, and more.

Discussion Questions

- What were the three phases of Reconstruction? What distinct characteristics did each phase possess?
- How did southern whites reassert racial supremacy after the Civil War? How did the black codes compare to the slave codes?
- How was the legal system complicit in reestablishing white supremacy during Reconstruction?
- Discuss the divisions within the Republican Party in the 1870s and 1880s. Who were the Radical Republicans? How did they differ from the Liberal and regular Republicans?
- In your judgment, what were the key factors that led to Redemption and the end of Reconstruction? Be sure to use detailed evidence to support your argument.

- Assess the legacy of Reconstruction. In what ways did Reconstruction policies help to bring racial justice to the South? In what ways did these policies come up short?
- How has historians' understanding of and appreciation for Reconstruction changed since the late nineteenth century?
- Some historians have argued that while the North won the Civil War, the South won the battle over Reconstruction. Explain your view and defend your argument using detailed supporting evidence.
- Although no firm or formal evidence proves that a corrupt bargain was struck in 1877, historians generally agree that some sort of informal compromise was crafted to give the Republicans the White House and to end military rule in Florida, Louisiana, and South Carolina. What grounds if any exist to support these claims?

Further Reading

Ed Ayers, *Vengeance & Justice: Crime and Punishment in the 19th-Century South* (New York: Oxford University Press, 1984).

Ed Ayers, *The Promise of the New South: Life After Reconstruction* (New York: Oxford University Press, 1992).

Bruce E. Baker, *What Reconstruction Meant: Historical Memory in the American South* (Charlottesville: University of Virginia Press, 2007).

Deborah Beckel, *Radical Reform: Interracial Politics in Post-Emancipation North Carolina* (Charlottesville: University of Virginia Press, 2010).

Ira Berlin, *The Long Emancipation: The Demise of Slavery in the United States* (Cambridge, MA: Harvard University Press, 2015).

Douglas A. Blackmon, *Slavery by Another Name: The Re-Enslavement of Black Americans from the Civil War to World War II* (New York: Doubleday, 2008).

David Blight, *Race and Reunion: The Civil War in American Memory* (Cambridge, MA: Harvard University Press, 2001).

W. Fitzhugh Brundage, *Lynching in the New South: Georgia and Virginia, 1880–1930* (Urbana: University of Illinois Press, 1993).

W. Fitzhugh Brundage, *Under Sentence of Death: Lynching in the South* (Chapel Hill: University of North Carolina Press, 1997).

Jane Turner Censer, *The Reconstruction of White Southern Womanhood, 1865–1895* (Baton Rouge: Louisiana State University Press, 2003).

Mary Ellen Curtin, *Black Prisoners and Their World, Alabama, 1865–1900* (Charlottesville: University of Virginia Press, 2000).

Jane E. Dailey, *Before Jim Crow: The Politics of Race in Postemancipation Virginia* (Chapel Hill: University of North Carolina Press, 2000).

Don H. Doyle, *New Men, New Cities, New South: Atlanta, Nashville, Charleston, Mobile, 1860–1910* (Chapel Hill: University of North Carolina Press, 1990).

Edmund L. Drago, *Hurrah for Hampton! Black Red Shirts in South Carolina during Reconstruction* (Fayetteville: University of Arkansas Press, 1999).

Mark Elliott, *Color-Blind Justice: Albion Tourgee and the Quest for Racial Equality from the Civil War to Plessy v. Ferguson* (New York: Oxford University Press, 2006).

Leon Fink, *Workingmen's Democracy: The Knights of Labor and American Politics* (Urbana: University of Illinois Press, 1983).

Gilbert C. Fite, *Cotton Fields No More: Southern Agriculture 1865–1980* (Lexington: University of Kentucky Press, 1984).

Joseph Gerteis, *Class and the Color Line: Interracial Class Coalition in the Knights of Labor and the Populist Movement* (Durham: Duke University Press, 2007).

William Gillette, *Retreat from Reconstruction: 1869–1879* (Baton Rouge: Louisiana State University Press, 1980).

Allen C. Guelzo, *Fateful Lightning: A New History of the Civil War and Reconstruction* (New York: Oxford University Press, 2012).

Grace Elizabeth Hale, *Making Whiteness: The Culture of Segregation in the South, 1890–1940* (New York: Pantheon, 1998).

Matthew Hild, *Greenbackers, Knights of Labor, and Populists: Farmer–Labor Insurgency in the Late-nineteenth-century South* (Athens: University of Georgia Press, 2007).

James Keith Hogue, *Uncivil War: Five New Orleans Street Battles and the Rise and Fall of Radical Reconstruction* (Baton Rouge: Louisiana State University Press, 2006).

Michael F. Holt, *By One Vote: The Disputed Presidential Election of 1876* (Lawrence: University Press of Kansas, 2008).

Stephen Kantrowitz, *Ben Tillman and the Reconstruction of White Supremacy* (Chapel Hill: University of North Carolina Press, 2000).

LeeAnna Keith, *The Colfax Massacre: The Untold Story of Black Power, White Terror, and the Death of Reconstruction* (New York: Oxford University Press, 2008).

Charles Lane, *The Day Freedom Died: The Colfax Massacre, the Supreme Court, and the Betrayal of Reconstruction* (New York: Holt, 2009).

William R. Leach, *Land of Desire: Merchants, Power, and the Rise of a New American Culture* (New York: Pantheon, 1993).

Nicholas Lemann, *Redemption: The Last Battle of the Civil War* (New York: Farrar, Straus & Giroux, 2006).

Leon F. Litwack, *Been in the Storm So Long: The Aftermath of Slavery* (New York: Knopf, 1979).

M. John Lubetkin, *Jay Cooke's Gamble: The Northern Pacific Railroad, The Sioux, and the Panic of 1873* (Norman: University of Oklahoma Press, 2006).

Roy Morris, *Fraud of the Century: Rutherford B. Hayes, Samuel Tilden, and the Stolen Election of 1876* (New York: Simon & Schuster, 2003).
Justin Nystrom, *New Orleans after the Civil War: Race, Politics, and a New Birth of Freedom* (Baltimore: Johns Hopkins University Press, 2010).
Susan Eva O'Donovan, *Becoming Free in the Cotton South* (Cambridge, MA: Harvard University Press, 2007).
David M. Oshinsky, *Worse than Slavery: Parchman Farm and the Ordeal of Jim Crow Justice* (New York: Free Press, 1996).
Michael Perman, *The Road to Redemption: Southern Politics, 1869–1879* (Chapel Hill: University of North Carolina Press, 1984).
Howard N. Rabinowitz, *Race Relations in the Urban South, 1865–1890* (New York: Oxford University Press, 1978).
William H. Rehnquist, *Centennial Crisis: The Disputed Election of 1876* (New York: Knopf, 2004).
Heather Cox Richardson, *The Death of Reconstruction: Race, Labor, and Politics in the Post-Civil War North, 1865–1901* (Cambridge, MA: Harvard University Press, 2001).
Brooks D. Simpson, *The Reconstruction Presidents* (Lawrence: University Press of Kansas, 1998).
Andrew L. Slap, *The Doom of Reconstruction: The Liberal Republicans in the Civil War Era* (New York: Fordham University Press, 2006).
Andrew L. Slap, ed., *Reconstructing Appalachia: The Civil War's Aftermath* (Lexington: University of Kentucky Press, 2010).
Diane Miller Sommerville, *Rape and Race in the Nineteenth-Century South* (Chapel Hill: University of North Carolina Press, 2003).
Mark Wahlgren Summers, *The Press Gang: Newspapers and Politics, 1865–1878* (Chapel Hill: University of North Carolina Press, 1994).
Robert E. Weir, *Beyond Labor's Veil: The Culture of the Knights of Labor* (College Station: Penn State University Press, 1996).
Elmus Wicker, *Banking Panics of the Gilded Age* (Cambridge: Cambridge University Press, 2000).
C. Vann Woodward, *Reunion and Reaction: The Compromise of 1877 and the End of Reconstruction* (Boston: Little Brown & Co., 1951).
C. Vann Woodward, *The Strange Career of Jim Crow* (New York: Oxford University Press, 1955).
Richard Zuczek, *State of Rebellion* (Columbia: University of South Carolina Press, 1996).

AMERICA IN THE LATE NINETEENTH CENTURY

Topics Covered in this Chapter:

- The Rise of a New South
- Race and Class in the 1880s and 1890s
- Gilded Age Politics
- Literature, Culture, and Society
- Memorializing and Remembering the Civil War

13

Introduction

In 1901, President Theodore Roosevelt invited one of the nation's leading black educators and spokesmen, Booker T. Washington, to the White House. Years before, in the midst of the Civil War, President Lincoln hosted prominent antislavery activist Frederick Douglass on Pennsylvania Avenue. Now, nearly four decades later, a Republican president once again paid homage to the party's civil rights history by welcoming Washington to a meeting over tea. African Americans hailed the meeting as evidence that they figured prominently not just in the Republican Party's constituency, but also in the political debates over the nation's future. Colorful buttons were made to commemorate the meeting between Washington and Roosevelt, with the word "Equality" featured prominently on the table between the drawings of the two men. Given the recent struggles over slavery, war, and emancipation, the symbolically important encounter seemed worth celebrating and remembering. After the meeting, however, many newspapers across the country blasted the president for meeting with Washington.

The meeting between the president and the nation's most visible black leader masked deep and intractable problems of race and class that still wracked the country at the turn of the twentieth century. As historian

Laura F. Edwards reminds us in her study of the post-Civil War era, the issues that consumed Reconstruction continued to shape the nation into the 1900s. By the late 1800s, positive signs of progress could be discerned if one looked hard enough: a new middle class of African American professionals and businessmen had emerged to play prominent roles in economy and society; labor unions, some of whom welcomed black workers, rose up to battle for social justice; a new Populist Party had emerged in 1892 to challenge the two-party stranglehold on the American electoral system; women organized to promote female suffrage and gender equality; and public schools were beginning to spread throughout the South to educate new generations of black and white students. On balance, however, it quickly became clear that deep and abiding problems still beset the nation, particularly its black citizens.

In the late 1800s, conservatives in the South had reestablished white dominance using both legal and extra-legal means. White supremacist groups such as the KKK revived, aided by the Democrats' one-party rule. In part to escape the racial violence and economic despair of the rural South, African Americans flocked to New South cities such as Nashville, Atlanta, and Charlotte, a migration that fundamentally reshaped the region's urban landscape. In southern cities, though, blacks found all-too familiar patterns of racist demagoguery and attempts to keep them in low-paying jobs. White political campaigns often turned on which candidate could most effectively argue against "negro rule." A new generation of white demagogic politicians such as James K. Vardaman and Ben Tillman set precedents for racist rhetoric that would continue into the late twentieth century. The U.S. Supreme Court limited the power of the Fourteenth Amendment to promote racial equality, and the American economy continued to be dominated by a stunningly wealthy class of elite businessmen who could count on corrupted politicians to enact laws to their liking. The Gilded Age, as humorist Mark Twain called the era for its veneer of gold masking profound inequality and maldistribution of wealth, was an unfortunate time to be a white or black laborer.

Yet all was not dark. For farsighted Americans, the horizons of the twentieth century promised greater racial and gender equality. Sparked by tireless activism, the Nineteenth Amendment in 1920 granted the suffrage to women. And the Civil Rights Movement of the 1950s and 1960s, led by the ideological descendants of Frederick Douglass and Ida B. Wells, finally began to settle some of the key issues vexing the nation since 1865. In what is sometimes referred to as "the Second Reconstruction," the Civil Rights Movement of the mid-twentieth century witnessed a commitment to racial equality not seen since the 1870s.

The Rise of a New South

The end of the Civil War brought the end of slavery and therefore a new economic and social system to the southern states. Millions of dollars invested in slaves disappeared, land claims were thrown into chaos by the war, and cities and regional infrastructure were devastated. Many white southerners, while they bemoaned the end of slavery and the old ways, saw the end of slavery as an opportunity to embark on a new departure, as the late historian C. Vann Woodward phrased it. Pro-growth businessmen and their champions, such as James D.B. DeBow, editor of an influential financial magazine, pushed the defeated South to diversify its economy and invest in banks, railroads, and industries. As we have seen, before the Civil War a new southern middle class had emerged to promote an agenda of economic and cultural modernization. These southerners made considerable progress in the 1850s in encouraging southern state legislatures to spend heavily on new railroads and other internal improvements. With the war over, these same middle-class southerners renewed their calls for a new path. The region should no longer depend on cotton but should instead devote equal energy to other crops; railroads, banks, and cities needed to be reconstructed; public school systems should be developed to educate southern children; southern entrepreneurs should invest in textile mills, lumber production, and other industries. Just as they had before the war, the southern middle class promoted enterprise, thrift, energy, and work.

Among the most vocal leaders of the New South was Atlanta's Henry W. Grady. Born in Georgia in 1850, Grady became a journalist after the war. As editor and part owner of the *Atlanta Constitution*, Grady helped build that paper into a leading southern daily before his death in 1889. Known as an excellent speaker, Grady used his visible role in the newspaper business and his oratorical skills to articulate the demands of the pro-business New South. In one of his most famous speeches, delivered in New York in 1886, Grady declared that:

We fought hard enough to know that we were whipped, and in perfect frankness accept as final the arbitrament of the sword to which we had appealed. The South found her jewel in the toad's head of defeat. The shackles that had held her in narrow limitations fell forever when the shackles of the negro slave were broken. Under the

old régime the negroes were slaves to the South; the South was a slave to the system. The old plantation, with its simple police regulations and feudal habit, was the only type possible under slavery. Thus was gathered in the hands of a splendid and chivalric oligarchy the substance that should have been diffused among the people—as the rich blood, under certain artificial conditions, is gathered at the heart, filling that with affluent rapture, but leaving the body chill and colorless.

The Old South rested everything on slavery and agriculture, unconscious that these could neither give nor maintain healthy growth. The New South presents a perfect democracy, the oligarchs leading in the popular movement: a social system compact and closely knitted, less splendid on the surface, but stronger at the core; a hundred farms for every plantation, fifty homes for every palace; and a diversified industry that meets the complex need of this complex age.

The New South is enamored of her new work. Her soul is stirred with the breath of a new life. The light of a grander day is falling fair on her face. She is thrilling with the consciousness of growing power and prosperity. As she stands upright, full statured and equal among the people of the earth, breathing the keen air and looking out upon the expanded horizon, she understands that her emancipation came because through the inscrutable wisdom of God her honest purpose was crossed, and her brave armies were beaten.

In his famous "New South" speech, Grady paid homage to the Old South while acknowledging that the region now faced different challenges. Such challenges could be overcome, Grady believed, by utilizing the untapped resources of the South. The lack of powerful labor unions, the vast timber that comprised southern forests, and the rise of urban areas were just some of the southern resources waiting to be incorporated into the New South's economy. Grady wanted northern investors to bring their capital to this New South. Grady, however, was no believer in racial equality. As Grady and like-minded white southerners pushed the economy in new directions, they did not include equality for African Americans in their plans. Even though the southern economy would grow dramatically in the 1880s, and the white southern middle class would continue to champion cultural and economic progress, suffrage and other rights for formerly enslaved people did not figure into their plans for a New South. In fact, while important gains were won under Radical Reconstruction, former slaves must have felt as if precious little had changed as Reconstruction came to a close in 1877.

Race and Class in the 1880s and 1890s

The end of Reconstruction was a difficult time for African Americans. Seemingly abandoned by the strong federal military protection that had permitted the election of hundreds of black Republicans to office, African Americans saw their gains quickly evaporate. White Democrats quickly overturned previous black electoral gains and took over positions at nearly every level of government. African American farmers, now trapped in debt as sharecroppers or tenant farmers, faced intimidation by paramilitary groups for small offenses against the racial order.

African Americans debated vigorously their response to the end of Reconstruction and to the challenges of segregation. Booker T. Washington, the former slave who became an important African American leader, argued that African Americans had to acknowledge the social reality of the late nineteenth-century America and the white power structure. Specifically, Washington thought that black Americans should focus on self-improvement, hard work, and education, and that gains would be made gradually over time. In his famous "Atlanta Address" in 1895, Washington

FIGURE 13.1 *The Atlanta Conference, N.A.A.C.P. Courtesy of the New York Public Library, 1168433*

asserted that since blacks lacked economic and political power, direct confrontation over civil rights would lead to disaster. Other African American leaders, notably W.E.B. Du Bois, the first African American to earn a PhD at Harvard University, criticized Washington's approach as the "Atlanta Compromise." Du Bois and like-minded activists would go on to found the National Association for the Advancement of Colored People (NAACP) in 1909 to push for more rapid and radical change.

Southern cities promised new opportunities for economic independence. Although much of the urban South was destroyed during the war, and cities such as Columbia and Atlanta lay in ruins, northern and southern entrepreneurs joined forces in the 1880s and 1890s to rebuild them. African Americans actively helped to shape the urban areas of the New South. As the late historian Howard N. Rabinowitz found in his study *Race Relations in the Urban South*, about 15% of southern African Americans resided in urban areas by 1890. While that number appears small, it represented a dramatic increase over previous levels. Nashville's black population, just 23% of the city's overall population in 1860, rose to 39% in 1890. Atlanta's black population rose from 20% in 1860 to 43% in 1890. Montgomery and Raleigh had black majority populations by 1890.[1] Since comparatively few African Americans lived in northern cities, southern African Americans made up more than two-thirds of the nation's black urban dwellers.

As Rabinowitz, Robert C. Kenzer, Tera Hunter, Leslie Brown, and many other historians have shown, the urban South was a complex place for African Americans. On the positive side, a new black middle class had emerged after the war. Black men owned and operated barbershops, funeral parlors, restaurants, and dry goods stores. Black newspaper editors such as George Allen Mebane promoted black businesses and associations formed to encourage African American entrepreneurs. In Durham, North Carolina, as historian Leslie Brown shows, black teachers and nurses gained middle-class respectability, and these African Americans often criticized the behavior and lifestyles of lower-class blacks, creating class tensions within the black community. A few African Americans became doctors, lawyers, dentists, and business executives.

While a new class of professional and commercial African Americans emerged in the late 1800s, and skilled carpenters and masons could reach a kind of middling status within the black community, the vast majority of black southerners remained in low-paying jobs. Tera Hunter's study of Atlanta found that black women most commonly became washerwomen, child nurses, cooks, and maids. When necessary, washerwomen and other domestics joined together in strikes to fight for better wages and treatment, or to oppose the influx of cheaper Chinese laborers.

Despite their roles as domestic servants, these women formed vibrant communities. Leisure activities, from dancing to clubs and sports, enriched the lives of black Atlantans. A new, more complicated black society was emerging in the postwar urban South, in which a small black elite sought leadership of a growing black middle class and a much larger mass of African American laborers.

Segregation marked life in southern cities. Separate restaurants, hotels, railcars, shops, schools, and virtually all other private and public venues were separated by race. While lower-class blacks and whites might find more opportunities to mingle during work or after-hours drinking and gambling, for the most part southern society demanded segregation.

While the races had long been separated in the South, race relations in the late nineteenth century were undergirded by a new legal doctrine. The South's increasingly complicated racial make-up, a consequence of generations of forced and consensual sex between blacks and whites, required finer and finer definitions of "black" and "white." Of course, the reality was that southerners of all shades of skin color proliferated in rural and urban areas. In part to simplify the complicated nature of race, southern state legislatures defined as "black" anyone with one-eighth or more African blood. In 1890 Louisiana passed such a law designating a so-called "octoroon" as black. Despite the attempts to define race in precise terms, the laws proved difficult to enforce.

Homer Plessy, a Louisianan with one-eighth African American blood, set in motion one of the most important Supreme Court cases in American history. In June 1892, Plessy boarded a train car in New Orleans that had been designated as "whites only," flouting Jim Crow laws mandating segregation. Born in New Orleans during the Civil War, Plessy was personally familiar with the region's segregation laws but he refused to abide by the racial mandates. Supported by the local Committee of Citizens, a group of educated New Orleans African Americans, Plessy planned to challenge the state's segregation laws. When he refused to board the railcar designated for blacks, Plessy was arrested, setting the legal wheels in motion.

The case eventually made it to the Supreme Court, which handed down its decision in a 7–1 vote in *Plessy v. Ferguson*

FIGURE 13.2 *Man going in "colored" entrance of movie house on Saturday afternoon, Belzoni, Mississippi Delta, Mississippi. Library of Congress, LC-USF33-030577-M2*

(1896). Writing the majority opinion for the court, Justice Henry Billings Brown approved a doctrine that would become known as "separate but equal." As long as separate accommodations were available, such as a black railcar in addition to a white one, segregation did not violate Fourteenth Amendment rights. The problem, of course, was that the accommodations were almost never equal between blacks and whites, a fact finally recognized by the Supreme Court in 1954, when the *Brown v. Board of Education* decision declared that "separate but equal" public schools were inherently unequal. Other court cases eroded the gains of Reconstruction. In *Williams v. Mississippi* (1898) the Supreme Court decided that state literacy tests and poll taxes for voter registration did not amount to illegal racial discrimination because the laws excluded poor and illiterate whites as well. While technically true—the state laws did in fact disfranchise thousands of whites as well as blacks—the court ignored the fact that such laws were designed to keep large numbers of former slaves from voting.

Segregation was not just the way of life in the South. As blacks who traveled north quickly discovered, racism was rampant in northern cities such as Boston, Philadelphia, and Chicago. Jim Crow laws had migrated north as well. When African Americans began moving to the North and Midwest in large numbers in the early 1900s to take advantage of job prospects in the auto industry and other manufacturing industries, they were met by fierce hostility. Race riots broke out throughout the early 1900s, culminating in a series of bloody conflicts in 1919 in Chicago and other cities.

Gilded Age Politics

While the nation continued to be vexed by racial violence in the late 1800s, the problem of political corruption continued to plague Washington. In the eyes of American workers, wealthy businessmen had distorted the political system and democracy itself by fostering an alliance with political leaders of both parties. Democrats and Republicans often paid lip service to the need for reform, and Republicans in Congress managed to enact a few legislative provisions to institute civil service examinations and reduce the number of political appointments. But the alliance between big business and the government was so powerful and pervasive that many Americans in the laboring class began to support socialism, communism, and other movements that promised a more equitable distribution of wealth and power.

Workingmen's political parties sprang up in the northeast and Midwest in the 1870s and 1880s, just as southern and western farmers were forming farmers' associations such as the Farmers' Alliance, the Grange, and the Agricultural Wheel. The workers' parties pushed for fundamental changes to American capitalism, including greater government regulation of the free market to ensure better wages, shorter workdays, an end to child labor, and safer working conditions. Many of these organizations wrote manifestos and other documents to lay down their principles. The Workingmen's Party of Illinois, for example, published a new socialist "Declaration of Independence" in 1876 that was based on the American Declaration but which included new protections for workers. In their new declaration, the workers argued that:

The present system has enabled capitalists to make laws in their own interests to the injury and oppression of the workers. It has made the name Democracy, for which our forefathers fought and died, a mockery and a shadow, by giving to property a [dis]proportionate amount of representation and control over legislation. It has enabled capitalists, through their control over

> **legislation, to secure government aid, in land grants and money loans, to selfish railroad corporations, who, by monopolizing the means of transportation are enabled to swindle both the producer and the consumer . . . In every stage of these oppressions we have petitioned for justice in the most reasonable and humble terms; we have asked in the name of humanity, for the sake of our starving wives and children and our own manhood, only a fair allowance of life's necessities . . . We have elected officials to represent us in legislative bodies, hoping for partial alleviation of our sufferings, but the power of capital has invariably corrupted them, and our efforts have been fruitless.[2]**

As the workingmen's declaration shows, American socialists appealed to native sentiments and even patriotism in calling for the regulation of capitalism and its political partners. Neither were the Illinois socialist workers alone; tens of thousands of laborers in many different industries joined the socialists, communists, and other organizations that promised to combat the combined power of the financial and political elite. The influence of American socialists would wax and wane until the Great Depression of the 1930s convinced many that capitalism had failed. During the 1930s, American socialists experienced some of their largest gains in membership since the 1870s and 1880s.

The anger of American workers posed a problem for both Democrats and Republicans in the late 1800s. Since neither party seemed to union organizers to be responsive, workers began to form third parties. The most powerful of these third parties was the Populist Party, also known as the People's Party, which for a brief period in the 1890s managed to win considerable support. A coalition of farmers and laborers, the Populist Party won dozens of state and local offices in the Midwest and South, and even captured a few federal offices. In 1892 the party formulated the Omaha Platform, which called for a progressive income tax, an end to national banks, an eight-hour workday, and government ownership of important industries such as the railroads and the telegraph system. Since the railroads and telegraphs were necessary for the public good, the populists argued, those industries should be run by the government in the public's interest rather than for private profit.

The Omaha Platform and its socialist ideas were not fringe elements of American politics. In the 1892 presidential election the Populist Party nominee, James B. Weaver, won over one million votes as well as electoral votes in Kansas, Colorado, Idaho, North Dakota, and Nevada. And many of the planks in the Omaha Platform, including the graduated income tax and the direct election of senators, would later be incorporated into constitutional amendments. The party supported the Democratic Party nominee in 1896, Nebraska's William Jennings Bryan, who won over farmers with his famous "Cross of Gold" speech. Like the populists, Bryan supported bimetallism, or using both gold and silver in the backing of American currency, making it easier for farmers to pay off debts. By 1900, the People's Party had waned, and the Democratic Party absorbed many of its core ideas.

Women played an active role in the Populist Movement, reflecting women's vocal participation in the nation's political culture. Women were especially active in the Farmers' Alliance; Southern women such as Bessie A. Dwyer of Texas wrote editorials

FIGURE 13.3 *Harrison and Reid, and the people. Library of Congress, LC-USZ62-85438*

FIGURE 13.4 *Suffragists marching. Library of Congress, LC-B201-3643-12*

for magazines and newspapers associated with the Farmers' Alliance. Although historians often date the beginning of the women's rights movement to the 1848 meeting at Seneca Falls, New York, after the war the push for gender equality gained thousands of followers. Elizabeth Cady Stanton, Carrie Nation, Susan B. Anthony, and other activists advocated female suffrage and greater opportunities for women in traditionally male professions. Even before the war, teaching, nursing, and domestic service had shifted to roles for women. But beginning in the 1870s, women called for the opening up of professional careers in law, medicine, and even government. Until the late twentieth century, considerable tension existed between white and black women in the fight for racial and gender equality. Many white leaders of the women's movement excluded black women, who had to battle racial and gender discrimination simultaneously.

Not until the late twentieth century would women enter the workforce in large numbers, but in the late 1800s black and white women rose to prominence as novelists and editors. In the South, women such as Augusta Jane Evans became popular authors with novels including *Beulah*, *St. Elmo*, and *Inez*. Black women writers earned fame in the postwar era as well. Anna Julia Cooper, born to an enslaved mother in North Carolina just before the Civil War, published *A Voice from the South* in the 1890s and was one of the first African American women to earn a doctoral degree. Black and white women also continued to play leading roles in the newspaper and magazine business. Eliza Nicholson owned and edited the important New Orleans daily newspaper *Picayune*

FIGURE 13.5 *Anna Julia Cooper. Courtesy of the New York Public Library, 1252571*

in the late 1880s. After the war white women formed press associations and in the late 1800s the Colored Press Association was an important organization for black journalists and editors.

The press associations reflected a broader movement in the late nineteenth century in which black and white women formed clubs and organizations of all kinds. The Women's Christian Temperance Union tried to ban alcohol consumption, believing that drunkenness led to domestic abuse, gambling, and poverty. Other groups promoted religious faiths, education, and healthy living habits. Women figured prominently in the Red Cross and in efforts to promote sanitation in urban areas. The club movement proved to be important for expanding women's political influence and convincing many Americans that women deserved suffrage. Thanks to persistent activists such as Stanton and Anthony, women secured the right to vote when the Nineteenth Amendment became a part of the Constitution.

Literature, Culture, and Society

In the immediate aftermath of the war, literary and artistic Americans were in no mood to remember the suffering and death of the previous four years. Walt Whitman's "Drum-Taps" and Herman Melville's *Battle-Pieces; and Aspects of the War* were among the few poems to memorialize the war. In *Battle-Pieces*, Melville collected poems that invoked the horror of the war, such as "The Apparition":

Convulsions came; and, where the field
Long slept in pastoral green,
A goblin-mountain was upheaved
(Sure the scared sense was all deceived),
Marl-glen and slag-ravine.
The unreserve of Ill was there,
The clinkers in her last retreat;
But, ere the eye could take it in,
Or mind could comprehension win,
It sunk!—and at our feet.
So, then, Solidity's a crust—
The core of fire below;
All may go well for many a year,
But who can think without a fear
Of horrors that happen so?

Despite its eloquence, *Battle-Pieces* sold only a few hundred copies by the 1870s, reflecting Americans' weariness with death and the war.

Southern writers also recalled the war and its suffering in poetry and prose published right after the war. Henry Timrod, the "Poet Laureate of the Confederacy," published a famous poem in 1867 to memorialize fallen Confederate soldiers. In "Ode: Sung on the Occasion of Decorating the Graves of the Confederate Dead at Magnolia Cemetery" Timrod helped Charlestonians consecrate a cemetery:

Sleep sweetly in your humble graves,
Sleep, martyrs of a fallen cause;
Though yet no marble column craves
The pilgrim here to pause
In seeds of laurel in the earth
The blossom of your fame is blown,

And somewhere, waiting for its birth,
The shaft is in the stone!
Meanwhile, behalf the tardy years
Which kept in trust your storied tombs,
Behold! your sisters bring their tears,
And these memorial blooms
Small tributes! but your shades will smile
More proudly on these wreaths to-day,
Than when some cannon-moulded pile
Shall overlook this bay.
Stoop, angels, hither from the skies!
There is no holier spot of ground
Than where defeated valour lies,
By mourning beauty crowned.

Confederate and Union cemeteries, many of them built on the battlefields or on the grounds of former prisons, were hallowed grounds for families who had lost loved ones. At the site of Andersonville prison in Georgia, northern states erected monuments to memorialize the thousands of Union prisoners who died there.

While monuments would begin to spring up in cemeteries, town squares, and in Civil War battlefields in the late 1800s, writers and artists turned to realism to confront the postwar landscape. In short, American realism was an attempt to portray a subject in a manner most faithful to its true state. Realistic depictions of nature, urban streetscapes, or people occupied artists, while novelists and short-story writers sought fiction that reflected real-life situations and characters.

Painters and photographers sought to depict society in ways faithful to real life. Mathew Brady's wartime photography had brought the stark realism of war's brutality to Americans, and in the late 1800s realism became a central feature of American culture. Before World War I painters such as Winslow Homer, Thomas Eakins, Mary Cassatt, John Singer Sargent, and others tried to paint realistic depictions of American life. Photographic exhibitions by realist artists such as Alfred Stieglitz earned respect in the art world and were attended by an enthusiastic public.

Mark Twain, Henry James, and William Dean Howells, three of the most important writers in American realism in the late nineteenth century, shaped the country's literary culture after the Civil War. Born in Missouri in 1835, Samuel Clemens wrote under the pseudonym Mark Twain and published *The Adventures of*

Tom Sawyer (1876) and *The Adventures of Huckleberry Finn* (1884). In short stories such as "The Man that Corrupted Hadleyburg," which appeared in *Harper's Monthly* magazine in 1899, and "The Million Pound Banknote," Twain satirized the American pursuit of wealth. Money and materialism had corrupted American society in Twain's eyes and his criticism of the nation's obsession with becoming rich can be seen clearly in *The Gilded Age: A Tale of Today* (1873), a work of fiction whose title has ever since served as a shorthand for the materialism and corruption of late nineteenth-century America.

Like Twain, Howells was a Midwesterner who employed humor and satire to highlight the American infatuation with monetary gain. Born in Ohio in 1837, Howells moved to New York and became an important editor, novelist, and short-story writer in the post-Civil War period. The most prominent literary critic after the war, Howells edited the *Atlantic Monthly* and published novels including *The Rise of Silas Lapham* (1885). In this novel, Silas Lapham pursues wealth and notoriety in the paint industry. Lapham's values are repeatedly tested in the moral tale, reflecting the real-life tensions between America's love of wealth and its values that Howells believed lay at the center of the nation's contemporary experience.

Just as important as Twain and Howells to realism was Henry James, an American-born writer who was so disgusted by the materialism rampant in his native country that he lived most of his later life in England. In the short story "The Jolly Corner," published in 1908, the character Spencer Brydon confronts differences between life in American and Europe. Brydon concludes that he was indeed better off in Europe, having avoided the corrupting influence of business and politics in America.

While Twain, Howells, and James lent their literary talents to American fiction, other writers used journalism to explore the poverty and desperation of urban life in late nineteenth- and early twentieth-century America. Jacob Riis, Theodore Dreiser, Upton Sinclair, Frank Norris, and other writers earned fame as literary culture shifted from realism to naturalism, in which man is at the mercy of larger forces beyond his control. These writers exploded the myths perpetuated in American culture—found in the Horatio Alger tales—that all one needed to become rich and successful was hard work. In his novel *Sister Carrie* (1900), Dreiser used fiction to argue that one's lot in life was determined more by luck and birth rather than by hard work.

FIGURE 13.6A *Thomas Eakins. All Fenn/Time Life Pictures/Getty Images*

FIGURE 13.6B *Thomas Eakins swimming in his own painting, "The Swimming Hole." A. Y. Owen/Getty Images*

FIGURE 13.6C *Mary Cassatt. The Granger Collection, NYC—All rights reserved*

FIGURE 13.6D *Mary Cassatt's "Françoise with a Black Dog." Buyenlarge/Getty Images*

Memorializing and Remembering the Civil War

Perhaps the most notable trend in American literature in the late 1800s and early 1900s was the romanticizing of the Old South. Long before Margaret Mitchell's *Gone with the Wind* appeared in 1936, white Americans in all regions of the country celebrated the old plantation and the southern cavalier. White northerners began to embrace the Old South almost as much as white southerners themselves. Novels and stories depicting the supposedly simple farming culture of the slave South, often using black dialect that later generations would criticize as racist, sold thousands of copies throughout the country. Joel Chandler Harris was a native Georgian whose Uncle Remus stories, originally published in *The Atlanta Constitution* newspaper where Harris worked, became wildly popular in all regions of the country. Harris published the stories, as he put it, to "preserve in permanent shape those curious mementoes of a period that will no doubt be sadly misrepresented by historians of the future." Just a few decades after the war ended, Americans were fully aware that future generations would find the war and its legacy to be highly contested.

Other writers such as Walter Hines Page and Owen Wister popularized the notion that the old southern cavalier was a central figure in the evolution of American culture. Wister's 1902 novel *The Virginian: A Horseman of the Plains* linked the southern cavalier to the virtuous and independent western cowboy, while Page edited numerous newspapers in the North and South and helped to keep the memory of the antebellum South alive in the minds of readers.

While it is difficult to explain why so many white northerners embraced the Lost Cause ideology and read so avidly about tales of the Old South, part of the explanation no doubt has a lot to do with what was happening in American society more broadly at the time. America's economy was fraught with struggles between capital and labor; the western frontier was rapidly disappearing as an untamed wilderness; the increasing industrialization and urbanization of America generated romantic longing for the nation's agricultural past; and an influx of immigrants from eastern and southern Europe reshaped the ethnic make-up of the country. All of these factors likely contributed to Americans' attempts to reconnect with what they wanted to remember as a simpler past.

As African American intellectuals such as W.E.B. Du Bois pointed out, however, the way white northerners and southerners chose to remember the Civil War and Reconstruction had profound, negative effects for blacks. Writers such as Thomas Dixon glorified the KKK and criticized Radical Reconstruction, sentiments reflected in the racist early silent film by D.W. Griffith *The Birth of a Nation* (1915). Based on Dixon's 1905 novel *The Clansman, The Birth of a Nation* depicted the KKK as American heroes in protecting the white South from black invaders.

Films helped commemorate a particular view of the Civil War and Reconstruction, but so too did periodicals. Magazines, which had been central to American culture well before the war, also helped to keep Americans' interest in the Civil War and its legacy alive. In the North popular monthlies including *Harper's* and *Century* published stories of battles and wartime heroism, even before the war was over. In an essay entitled "Heroic Deeds of Heroic Men," author John S.C. Abbott thrilled readers of *Harper's* with tales such as the following:

> **In our last number we left the heroic patriot army in its disastrous march from the Chickahominy to the James, toiling through the mire and forest of White Oak Swamp. During the long hours of the night of Sunday, the 29th of June, the rear-guard toiled slowly along through the swamp roads, over which the army they had rescued had gone before them. The iron Sumner, chafing and rebelling against the order to fall back, and scarcely consoled by the thought of his salvation from the Army of the Potomac, carried his men, his guns, and his flags safely through to the other side of the morass.**

This dramatic recounting of fighting in Virginia was repeated in popular periodicals throughout the late nineteenth and twentieth centuries and reminded succeeding generations of the sacrifices Union soldiers had rendered.

Of course, white southerners also published their recollections of the war in popular magazines. *Confederate Veteran* was a monthly published in Nashville between 1893 and 1932. Each issue was packed with testaments to the Lost Cause, information on veterans' groups, and the latest efforts to erect statues or monuments. One issue in 1895 provided notice of a veterans' reunion meeting in Houston, black and white pictures of battlefields, obituaries of veterans who had recently passed, and embellished tales such as "How a Virginia Girl Saved Lee's Army." Like their northern counterparts, southern magazines often related dramatic tales of wartime bravery, similar to this story from the pages of the *Confederate Veteran*:

Miss Claudine Rhett, wrote from Columbia, S.C, October 30th: Last Sunday night, we had a large gathering of Survivors, and citizens, at the First Baptist Church of this city, where the convention which passed the ordinance of Secession first met, to listen to the annual sermon preached to Camp Hampton, by the Rev. S.P.H. Elwell, their chaplain, himself a one-armed Confederate soldier.

This discourse was eloquent, manly, and true to the principles of "the right of self-government." His text was from Samuel, 2d book, 27th verse: "How are the mighty fallen and the weapons of war perished." Gen'l M. C. Butler commands Camp Hampton.

During a pause in one of the engagements fought in Virginia, Col. M.C. Butler, of Hampton's Cavalry, and Major Farley, the famous scout, were sitting quietly on horseback talking together, when suddenly a ball struck Col. Butler above the ankle, passed through his horse, killing it, proceeded to crush Major Farley's leg, and killed his horse also.

Some of the soldiers rushed quickly forward, and disengaged the fallen officers from their dead horses, but it was found that both of these gentlemen would have to suffer the amputation of a limb. Surgeons were sent for, and they were laid in the shade of a big tree near by.

When the surgeon, Dr. B.W. Taylor, arrived to perform the double operation, he first approached Col. Butler, the ranking officer, and said to him, "Colonel, I have very little chloroform, but I will share it equally between you and the Major."

"No," replied Col. Butler, "keep it all for Farley, who is worse off than I am. I can bear the pain without it."

The ordeal was accordingly endured, without the aid of this alleviating adjunct of surgery, and the generous hero happily survived the operation!

While Americans explored the meaning of the Civil War and its legacy in novels, short stories, popular magazines, and films, they also formed associations whose purpose was to memorialize the war. White southerners formed veterans' and memorial groups, some of which endure today. In the decades following the end of the Civil War, white southerners invoked the Lost Cause, the notion that the Old South symbolized values of tradition, heritage, independence, states' rights, and honor that were worth preserving. In southern popular culture, especially in novels and short stories, the Lost Cause narrative no doubt helped white southerners deal with the humiliation of defeat. The narrative usually included claims that antebellum southern society was morally superior to the North's, that secession had been a just attempt to assert southern independence against an overreaching federal government, and that the simpler agricultural life of the prewar years trumped the turmoil of increasingly crowded, dirty, and dangerous northern cities.

The Lost Cause ideology found expression in organizations founded to keep the Confederacy alive in memory. The Sons of Confederate Veterans and the United Daughters of the Confederacy were formed in the late nineteenth century to preserve Confederate history and keep veterans' causes alive. Founded in Richmond in 1896, following on the heels of the United Confederate Veterans establishment in 1889, the SCV has been instrumental over the last century and a half in promoting the Lost Cause.

Women, too, played active roles in shaping public memory of the war. Caroline Janney has shown that Ladies' Memorial Associations were vital and popular. Such groups reburied Confederate dead in southern cemeteries after the war, held parades, and published newsletters and magazines. The UDC, founded in 1894, is open to women related to Confederate veterans. Like the SCV, the UDC remains active today and boasts of local chapters throughout the South.

Like their northern counterparts, the SCV and the UDC became embroiled in politics, and Civil War remembrance is still emotionally charged even in the present day. Historian David Blight has argued that the construction of public memory among white Americans emphasized the reunification of North and South, consciously leaving African Americans out of this process. Periodically tempers flare between white and black southerners over the meaning of the war and its legacy. Thousands of statues, plaques, buildings, and other ways to memorialize the war have been erected in the 150 years since the war ended, and many of these remain controversial. Public buildings on college campuses and in town squares throughout the South bear the names of Confederate veterans, some of whom later joined the KKK or other white supremacist groups. Anger erupted in the late 1900s and early 2000s over whether the Confederate flag is a symbol of southern racism or an honorable emblem of southern heritage. Groups such as the UDC and SCV have attracted the ire of African Americans and many historians for down-playing the racist and proslavery ideology of the Confederacy.

Union veterans' groups, such as the Grand Army of the Republic, an organization founded in Illinois, subsided in popularity in the 1870s but then grew in membership in the 1880s and 1890s. Ultimately involving nearly half a million veterans, the GAR had state and local arms that promoted fellowship among former Union soldiers. Yet the GAR quickly became more than a fraternal veterans' group. During and after Reconstruction the GAR worked closely with the Republican Party and helped to shape national policy toward reconciliation with the South. Many members of the GAR advocated aid for the former slaves and some supported black suffrage, and African Americans even formed local chapters of the GAR themselves. The GAR held parades in local communities, gathered for annual encampments, and rallied support for Republican policies and veterans' causes, until it dissolved in the mid-twentieth century.

The SCV, UDC, GAR, and other associations helped keep the memory of the war alive with a wide range of memorials, from battlefield cemeteries to monuments and statues. The "mystic chords of memory," as Lincoln so eloquently put it in his first inaugural address, were preserved in the postwar era in marble, stone, and metal. An elaborate system of cemeteries had been established to bury the dead on both sides of the war, and most of the graves were individually marked. Northern and southern veterans' groups also raised money to build monuments and statues at the cemeteries. At Gettysburg by the late 1800s, hundreds of such memorials had been constructed.[3]

A series of cycloramas, huge and dramatic paintings depicting Civil War battles, drew national attention and thousands of visitors in the late 1800s and early 1900s. Painted during the 1880s, the cycloramas brought battles to life before films had been invented. The Atlanta Cyclorama, completed by the American Panorama Company, depicts the Battle of Atlanta and can still be viewed today. The Battle of Gettysburg cycloramas were shown in Chicago and other cities. One of the surviving examples, which opened in Chicago in 1883, shows Pickett's Charge in large, colorful panels.

So even before the turn of the nineteenth century, Americans had already begun elaborate efforts to remember the war. The meaning of the war and its aftermath would shape generations of Americans. In every way possible, from art to performances to music to print, Americans North and South struggled with the legacy of the Civil War and Reconstruction, a struggle that continues today, 150 years later.

* * *

As we witnessed during the recent commemorations of the 150th anniversary of the Civil War, the battles, people, and ideas of the mid-nineteenth century are still very much part of our national dialogue. Reenactors periodically gather to replay important Civil War battles. Popular novels such as Michael Shaara's *Killer Angels* (1974) and Charles Frazier's *Cold Mountain* (1997), as well as Hollywood films such as *Glory* (1989) and *Gettysburg* (1993), continue to attract large readership and audiences. Ken Burns's remarkable documentary series *The Civil War* appeared on PBS in 1990 to critical and popular acclaim, sparking a renewed interest in the war and its important legacy.

During future commemorations of the Civil War, perhaps the most important task is to be honest, forthright, and truthful in the telling of the past. The job of historians is not to glorify the past or its actors, but rather to depict as accurately as possible what really happened. Granted this is not as easy as it sounds, since all of us carry biases with us to our understanding of the past. Historians acknowledge the difficulty of being objective even as they strive to present truthful accounts of earlier times. As emotionally powerful as the Civil War, slavery, and Reconstruction still are today, it remains vitally important that we not deify leaders such as Lee or Lincoln, nor gloss over the motives behind secession. Confronting our past truthfully requires bravery and fortitude, virtues readily seen in the lives and actions of nineteenth-century black and white Americans themselves.

COMPANION @ WEBSITE

Please visit the companion website www.routledge.com/cw/wells for additional study aids including chapter overviews, interactive quizzes, and more.

Discussion Questions

- What challenges did America's working class face in the late 1800s?
- Why has the late nineteenth century been called the Gilded Age? What does this phrase suggest about the values of the period?
- What role did the middle class play in late nineteenth-century America?
- In what ways does the Civil War still resonate in American culture today?

- Do you think the Civil War is more often remembered today in the North or South? Why?
- What Civil War monuments or memorials have you seen? What images or events do they portray?
- How different was the New South from the Old South?
- What principles did men such as Henry W. Grady incorporate into the New South ideology?
- African Americans generally regard the Confederate flag as a racist emblem, while some white southern groups emphasize the flag's historical significance. Who do you think is correct and why?
- Research recent battles over Civil War remembrance in American culture. What motivates Americans black and white to debate the meaning of the war even today?
- What have been the most controversial attempts to memorialize the Civil War in recent years?

Notes

1 Howard N. Rabinowitz, *Race Relations in the Urban South, 1865–1890* (Athens: University of Georgia Press, 1978), xxi, 19.
2 Quoted in Philip S. Foner, *We, the Other People: Alternative Declarations of Independence by Labor Groups, Farmers, Woman's Rights Advocates, Socialists, and Blacks, 1829–1975* (Urbana: University of Illinois Press, 1976), 101–102.
3 Thomas J. Brown, *The Public Art of Civil War Commemoration: A Brief History with Documents* (Boston, MA: Bedford/St. Martin's Press, 2004), 17.

Further Reading

Michelle Alexander, *The New Jim Crow: Mass Incarceration in the Age of Colorblindness* (New York: New Press, 2010).
Bruce E. Baker, *What Reconstruction Meant: Historical Memory in the American South* (Charlottesville: University of Virginia Press, 2007).
David W. Blight, *Race and Reunion: The Civil War in American Memory* (Cambridge, MA: Harvard University Press, 2001).
David W. Blight, *Beyond the Battlefield: Race, Memory, and the American Civil War* (Amherst: University of Massachusetts Press, 2002).
Leslie Brown, *Upbuilding Black Durham: Gender, Class, and Black Community Development in the Jim Crow South* (Chapel Hill: University of North Carolina Press, 2008).
W. Fitzhugh Brundage, *The Southern Past: A Clash of Race and Memory* (Cambridge, MA: Harvard University Press, 2005).

Jane Turner Censer, *The Reconstruction of White Southern Womanhood, 1865–1895* (Baton Rouge: Louisiana State University Press, 2003).

Karen L. Cox, *Dixie's Daughters: The United Daughters of the Confederacy and the Preservation of Confederate Culture* (Gainesville: University Press of Florida, 2003).

William C. Davis, *The Cause Lost: Myths and Realities of the Confederacy* (Lawrence: University Press of Kansas, 1996).

Thomas A. Desjardin, *These Honored Dead: How the Story of Gettysburg Shaped American Memory* (Cambridge, MA: Da Capo Press, 2003).

Laura F. Edwards, *Gendered Strife and Confusion: The Political Culture of Reconstruction* (Urbana: University of Illinois Press, 1997).

Douglas R. Egerton, *The Wars of Reconstruction: The Brief, Violent History of America's Most Progressive Era* (New York: Bloomsbury Press, 2014).

Alice Fahs and Joan Waugh, eds., *The Memory of the Civil War in American Culture* (Chapel Hill: University of North Carolina Press, 2003).

Gaines M. Foster, *Ghosts of the Confederacy: Defeat, the Lost Cause and the Emergence of the New South, 1865–1913* (New York: Oxford University Press, 1987).

Joe B. Fulton, *The Reconstruction of Mark Twain: How a Confederate Bushwhacker Became the Lincoln of Our Literature* (Baton Rouge: Louisiana State University Press, 2011).

Gary W. Gallagher, *The Myth of the Lost Cause and Civil War History* (Bloomington: Indiana University Press, 2000).

Gary W. Gallagher, *Causes Won, Lost, and Forgotten: How Hollywood and Popular Art Shape What We Know about the Civil War* (Chapel Hill: University of North Carolina Press, 2008).

Paul M. Gaston, *The New South Creed: A Study in Southern Mythmaking* (New York: Random House, 1970).

Thavolia Glymph, *Out of the House of Bondage: The Transformation of the Plantation Household* (Cambridge, UK: Cambridge University Press, 2008).

David R. Goldfield, *Still Fighting the Civil War: The American South and Southern History* (Baton Rouge: Louisiana State University Press, 2002).

James Oliver Horton and Lois E. Horton, eds, *Slavery and Public History: The Tough Stuff of American Memory* (New York: New Press, 2006).

Tony Horwitz, *Confederates in the Attic: Dispatches from the Unfinished Civil War* (New York: Pantheon, 1998).

Caroline E. Janney, *Burying the Dead but Not the Past: Ladies' Memorial Associations and the Lost Cause* (Chapel Hill: University of North Carolina Press, 2007).

Robert C. Kenzer, *Enterprising Southerners: Black Economic Success in North Carolina, 1865–1915* (Charlottesville: University of Virginia Press, 1997).

A. J. Langguth, *After Lincoln: How the North Won the Civil War and Lost the Peace* (New York: Simon & Schuster, 2014).

Edward Linenthal, *Sacred Ground: Americans and their Battlefields* (Urbana: University of Illinois Press, 1991).

Anne E. Marshall, *Creating a Confederate Kentucky: The Lost Cause and Civil War Memory in a Border State* (Chapel Hill: University of North Carolina Press, 2010).

Stuart McConnell, *Glorious Contentment: The Grand Army of the Republic, 1865–1900* (Chapel Hill: University of North Carolina Press, 1992).

James M. McPherson, *Drawn with the Sword: Reflections on the American Civil War* (New York: Oxford University Press, 1996).

W. Scott Poole, *Never Surrender: Confederate Memory and Conservatism in the South Carolina Upcountry* (Athens: University of Georgia Press, 2004).

Howard N. Rabinowitz, *Race Relations in the Urban South, 1865–1890* (Athens: University of Georgia Press, 1978).

Roy Rosenzweig and David Thelen, *The Presence of the Past* (New York: Columbia University Press, 1998).

Kirk Savage, *Standing Soldiers, Kneeling Slaves* (Princeton: Princeton University Press, 1997).

Rebecca Sharpless, *Cooking in Other Women's Kitchens: Domestic Workers in the South, 1860–1960* (Chapel Hill: University of North Carolina Press, 2010).

Nina Silber, *The Romance of Reunion: Northerners and the South, 1865–1900* (Chapel Hill: University of North Carolina Press, 1993).

Timothy B. Smith, *This Great Battlefield of Shiloh: History, Memory, and the Establishment of a Civil War National Military Park* (Knoxville: University of Tennessee Press, 2004).

Mark Wahlgren Summers, *The Ordeal of the Reunion: A New History of Reconstruction* (Chapel Hill: University of North Carolina Press, 2014).

Joan Waugh and Gary W. Gallagher, eds., *Wars within a War: Controversy and Conflict over the American Civil War* (Chapel Hill: University of North Carolina Press, 2009).

Charles Reagan Wilson, *Baptized in Blood: The Religion of the Lost Cause, 1865–1920* (Athens: University of Georgia Press, 1983).

Index